HELPING YOUNG CHILDREN GROW

"I Never Knew Parents Did So Much"

HELPING YOUNG CHILDREN GROW

"I Never Knew Parents Did So Much"

ERNA FURMAN

INTERNATIONAL UNIVERSITIES PRESS, INC.

Madison   Connecticut

Library of Congress Cataloging in Publication Data

Furman, Erna.
  Helping young children grow.

  Bibliography: p.
  Includes index.
  1. Child development.   I. Title.
HQ767.9.F87   1987   649'.1   87-3196
ISBN 0-8236-2322-X

Second Printing, 1988

Manufactured in the United States of America

Contents

Contents

Introduction: How We Learn About Child Development

We learn most things either by taking in previously unknown facts or by marshaling what we already know within ourselves and thinking it through in such a way as to reach a new level of understanding. With both methods, the relationship with the teacher and his influence as a model play an important role. With the first way of learning, the teacher presents new facts; with the second way, he or she assists us in developing our own thinking—the Socratic method. In dialogues, Socrates's pupils struggled to formulate their ideas and he, as teacher, questioned their evidence, reasoning, and conclusions to help them note their mistakes and refine their understanding. The special enjoyment and sense of inner conviction we derive from this form of learning has not been lost through the millenia. Most of us can recall some experience with it and know how good it feels. One high school senior, participating in one of our child development courses, put it this way: "What I learned today was especially meaningful because I knew it for the first time, and yet it had been with me all along and been part of my daily experience without me realizing it."

In practice we usually combine both methods of learning. However well we utilize, and are helped to utilize, the knowledge that already lies within us, we still need to add new facts from without. However eager we are to take in new facts, to make them truly our own, we still need to fit them in with what we already know, so that new and old knowledge become a coherent whole and can serve us as a base for further understanding and mastery. With some subjects, such as reading, history, and mathematics, we primarily tend to acquire new facts because, at least initially, we know little or nothing about them. Even in these fields, however, effective learning increasingly depends on our ability to use and develop what we know, to integrate new facts into our existing inner framework, and to build on it. Other subjects, and child development is among them, can never be learned simply by taking in new facts. One reason for this is that we are not novices. All of us have, through our own experiences, accumulated a body of knowledge in this field. Another reason is that this subject calls not only upon our intellect, but also involves our feelings, attitudes, and values. These have, in individual ways, molded our intellectual perception and understanding of child development in the past, and they continue to exercise a special influence on any additional learning we undertake.

In learning about child development, therefore, it is very necessary to draw on our available knowledge and to use it to develop and formulate our own better understanding. It is just as necessary to add new facts in a manner and at a pace which allow us to integrate them effectively.

This is not always easy. Insofar as the new facts are in accord with what we already think, feel, and know, we assimilate them readily. They are not totally foreign and may merely extend or deepen our prior knowledge. But when the new facts run counter to our own ideas, when they seem quite strange, and may even be felt as a threat, we cannot fit them into our own framework. How do our minds cope with this hurdle?

One way is to bury, or set aside, in ourselves all that we know, feel, and think, and to take in eagerly all the new knowledge that is available. We pile the newly presented facts on top of our previous experience without making the necessary inner confrontations and connections. But the new knowledge never truly becomes a part of ourselves. It remains isolated in our minds, fails to advance our real understanding, and cannot be applied to solving problems. We tend to forget it after a while, or set it aside as useless, and we look for a "newer," different body of knowledge, or we make do without. Gradually the old buried experience resurfaces and takes over the void. Most of us can recall taking a class in which we crammed in long lectures and whole bookfuls of new facts, but since we could never integrate them into our own life experience, we can now recover only meaningless relics or muddled dicta. Such has been the fate of many an erudite course or book on child development.

Another way is to reject the new, uncongenial facts outright in favor of our own knowledge. Freud said that education, government, and psychoanalysis—and we may add child development—comprise the most difficult professions because so many people consider themselves experts on the basis of their limited personal experience. All of us have indeed been educated and governed, and have experienced inner stress and turmoil. Most of us have also educated others, governed their lives to some extent, and helped them with their troubles, as parents, relatives, baby-sitters, friends, or even in one or another professional capacity. Regardless of whether we fared well or poorly, these experiences have been such an intimate part of our lives for as long as we can remember that we are apt to view them as a qualifying certificate. Sometimes we even believe that people are naturally endowed with expertise in these fields. Many a young mother and father have been too ashamed to admit their panicky helplessness in figuring out what their baby was crying for, or how to comfort him, because they thought that all other parents knew naturally the right thing to do. After all, "anybody knows what to do with a little kid," and therefore does not need to consider unsettling new knowledge. When we face newly presented facts about child development with this frame of mind, we can only reject them.

Is it possible to overcome these tendencies in ourselves and to make learning about child development more productive? There is a way, but it is hard, its pace is slow, and its extent depends on the individual makeup of the learner's personality. It consists of using the Socratic method of thinking through and formulating what we know within ourselves, and of then adding new facts selectively, at times when we have pinpointed gaps in our knowledge and seek more information. As we contrast old and new facts and ideas, we may decide to revise some old knowledge, or we may find some of the new unacceptable but can at least consider them thoughtfully. An active learning process gets under way. With the help of the newly marshaled and more clearly understood old knowledge we sample and test the new knowledge. Some of it is gradually and effectively linked and interwoven with what we already know, some is set aside, perhaps to remain unacceptable, perhaps to be mastered and integrated later. Sometimes this process of learning proceeds so smoothly and quietly that we hardly know we are learning at all. ("Why, I knew this all along.") Sometimes it leads to joyful moments of insight: "Ah, of course, so that's what it is!" And at other times it frustrates and angers us as we grapple with an unfamiliar idea, doubt or attack it. The process does not end when the lesson ends, or even when the course ends. We keep mulling things over and reexamining them in the light of later experiences. The idea has become our own thing.

We have found this way of learning child development to be the most successful, although it is time-consuming, arduous for both student and teacher, and not without some limitations. Several of us, at the Cleveland Center for Research in Child Development, have used this method since the early fifties with hundreds of professionals in the fields of health and education as well as with parents. Since 1976 it has been used with many more hundreds of senior high school students. However, all this work of teaching and learning, first without and later with the help of this book, has involved personal contact between teachers and students, has utilized live and lively discussions between them, and has been facilitated by their close working relationship, as described in the accompanying *Teacher's Guide.*

Can a writer and reader work together in a similar fashion? I trust we can. This volume tries to approximate the same way of teaching, to reach out to you, the interested reader, and to engage your active participation. Your task is not an easy one. It is indeed much more difficult than that of the learner in the classroom. How you go about it and to what extent you use the material, is up to you. My good wishes accompany you in your endeavor, and I offer a few suggestions: Before you begin to read a chapter, take time to think about the topic yourself. What do you think and feel about it? Can you relate your ideas to specific situations you have observed or experienced? Do these situations confirm your opinions or are they at odds with them in some instances? What might be the reasons? Perhaps you can figure them out and resolve any discrepancies to your own satisfaction. Perhaps you have even increased your understanding and, like one of my past students, can say, "When you are first asked to figure out your own answers you sort of feel you can't do that and you don't know what to think or say. But once you give it a go, it's really so easy and it all comes so naturally, like finding the pieces of a puzzle and suddenly it all fits. It's fun." Perhaps your puzzle pieces did not fit together and you are left annoyed, with bits and pieces of ideas that don't match. In either case, your efforts will pay off. They may help you to consider and evaluate the written text. Maybe its thoughts and examples will fit in with what you know, maybe they will look at the topic from a different angle, maybe they will seem strange and offer no solutions. Before you decide to accept or reject them, test them out. Observe closely children you know in your work or home, and children you don't know but encounter by chance in the street, supermarket, bus, at the movies, wherever. See whether your observations shed more light on the topic. If you feel sufficiently comfortable with some of the approaches described in the book, try them out and see how they work. You may not feel happy with your effort or with the results, but you will at least gain more food for thought.

When you have worked through a topic, ask yourself what you remember of it, how it related to your experiences with children, what seemed important to you, and what more you would like to know about it.

Regardless of whether you could use all, some, or none of what the book offered, your own mental work will have helped you to see the issues more clearly, to marshal your own thinking and experience, and to pinpoint areas of uncertainty. Perhaps the discussion of the next, or later topics will prove helpful, when themes reappear in new contexts or when new ideas illuminate previously presented ones. Your own thinking, like the chapters, weave to and fro and make connections. Although the various aspects of child development are arranged in a sequence which facilitates learning, do not hesitate to skip around, to read later chapters, or parts of chapters, first. You may, in this way, want to link an earlier topic with a later one, or you may just be interested in another aspect. In class discussions topics are often interwoven and aspects are taken up "out of order," in keeping with the students's observations, questions, and thoughts. It is your book, use it in the way which you feel best suits your interests.

Obviously, this book is not intended to impose on you or to convince you. It is neither a big meal you should swallow whole, nor an authoritarian dictum you should bow to and believe. Understanding how children develop and mature is a lifelong quest to get to know and appreciate our fellow humans and a part of ourselves. Let us proceed with respect and good will.

PART I

RELATIONSHIPS

1
Different Kinds of
Relationships

If someone were to ask us about our experiences with children, we would be likely to think of the different capacities in which we interacted with children, as a baby-sitter, nursery school teacher, children's librarian, camp counselor, tutor, grade school teacher, pediatrician, pediatric nurse. We may have worked in a day care center, played with children in the neighborhood, had younger brothers, sisters, nieces, or nephews; we may be a mother or father. We may think that these experiences taught us a lot, or a little, about a particular child, about children in general, about children in a certain age group. We may feel that our experiences were enjoyable or frustrating, that we did a good job and handled our charges well, or that we failed. And we may think of the children as good or bad, smart or foolish, obedient or obstreperous. And if we were asked what kind of relationship we had with these children, we are apt to describe it as good or bad; good if we liked the child and he or she seemed to like us and conformed to our demands, and bad if we didn't get along, got angry at one another, and couldn't get him or her to do as we wished. We rarely think of our relationships with children in terms of different types of relationships with specific functions and goals.

In the adult world we are implicitly aware of these differences. We distinguish a boyfriend–girl friend relationship, a husband–wife relationship, a friendship, a teacher–student relationship, a doctor–patient relationship, a relationship among co-workers, or one between employer and employee, a

3

relationship with neighbors, relationships with different relatives, and many more. Sometimes we welcome it when our
tie with a person encompasses two or more types of relationship, for example when a neighbor also becomes a friend. At
other times we resent it when our partner in a particular
relationship attempts to change its nature; for example, when
a neighbor starts to act like he were our parent, doctor, or
lover. Although we expect some relationships to remain the
same, with others we take it for granted that they will change.
Our relationships with our parents, children, even with husband or wife, are bound to change to meet the partners'
different needs in different phases of life or under special
circumstances, such as during periods of illness or special
stress. We consider these relationships especially solid and
adequate when they can adapt in this way; for example, when
a couple can grow old together, or when one of them can nurse
and "mother" the other through a long sickness. We also
know how hard such a change can be and how often relationships fail because we cannot accept or bring about a change
in their functions and goals; for example, when parents cannot accept their children's growing up and continue to relate
to them as dependants.

We usually maintain many different relationships. In
each of them our partner shares our understanding of it and
joins us in its fulfillment by contributing his part. What
exactly his or her part is depends of course on the type of
relationship, and sometimes on what the partners mutually
agree upon, or on the custom of the society they live in.
Whereas husband-wife relationships exist all over the world,
there are considerable cultural and individual differences in
what marital partners expect from their relationship, what
each needs to contribute toward its maintenance, and to what
extent their contributions are the same or different and complement one another. The relationship is satisfactory to
the extent that both parties participate in achieving
shared expectations.

In our relationships with children we often do not think
along similar lines. We may not be so clear about the nature
and functions of our own role with a child; for example, when
we baby-sit we may relate to the child as a peer–playmate, but

we may fail to think of ourselves as parent-substitutes. We may play or watch TV with them, but may not remind them to keep safety rules or take charge of their getting to bed on time. We usually are even less clear about the child's understanding of his or her relationship with us; for example, we may not wonder, or try to find out, whether the five-year-old who comes to our activity class expects us to act like his teacher, or baby-sitter, or parent, and even if he does expect us to be his teacher, does he already understand what a teacher-pupil relationship is all about? Does he perhaps just expect us to teach him but not himself to engage in learning? Does he know that a "good" relationship with a teacher shows in a lot of working and learning? When we are confused about our own role, we are apt to confuse the child. When he or she misunderstands what kind of relationship is appropriate, it will show in inappropriate expectations and behavior. How irritated, frustrated, and unhappy we get with one another when we expect a child to learn what we teach, but he expects us to care for him and demands that we give him candies instead of lessons, or that we accompany him to the bathroom! Yet it does not mean that we are bad teachers or that he is spoiled or naughty. It simply means that there was a misunderstanding about the kind of relationship each expected to develop.

There is, of course, a good reason why we tend to mix our relationships with children and why they so often misunderstand or fail to contribute their part to the kind of relationship we have in mind in a given situation. Children do not necessarily know what different kinds of relationships are about or how they need to participate in them.

What kind of relationship do children know? When and how do they get to know the other relationships?

Some people assume that children know only one kind of relationship, namely that of being taken care of and of having their needs and wants gratified. The child's only contribution to that relationship is to make his demands known and to feel satisfied when they are met. When we attempt to relate to children in this way, we try to gain their love by giving them what we think they want or by allowing them to do as they wish, and we expect them to dislike us when we cross them, let them wait, or make demands on them. We may even feel that we do not matter to them as people in our own right, that they would like anybody who gratifies them, and, when they become dissatisfied, would turn away and seek out another person who would be "nicer" to them in their terms. Although many of us know that such an attitude is a bit exaggerated, that there is more to a child's love than getting what he wants, there is a kernel of truth in this assumption about children's relationships. Children, and young children especially, are indeed very helpless, needy, and dependent, and their survival and well-being hinges on adequate care by others. The primitive bond between the caring, need-fulfilling person and the cared–for, needy one is very basic. It is one part of the parent–child relationship, but it is not the whole story.

We all know that even very young children are not simply satisfied when their needs are fulfilled. When a mother hands over to us the care of her ten-month-old baby, we often find that he does not let us feed him and put him to sleep peacefully. On the contrary, he may altogether forego having his needs gratified by a stranger and may scream or fuss until his mother returns. It seems his mother is more important to him than his food or sleep! A year or so later, when this baby has grown into a toddler, we may meet him and his mother at the grocery store. Instead of sitting con- tentedly in the seat of the shopping cart and munching his cookies, he is bent on grabbing items off the shelves, poking and tearing packages, demanding to hold things that are apt to spill, and running off into the far aisle. Nor is he necessar- ily unhappy. The glint in his eyes, the excited screech as he speeds up to escape his mom's pursuit, as well as his skill in finding just those things to do which are contrary to mother's wishes, suggest that he is out for a good fight and tease—his way of having time with Mom. But in another year or so he will be a preschooler and enjoy very different relation- ships. In his nursery school he will like his teacher, may even like to play cooperatively with other boys and girls, and will be happy to meet his old neighbor who lets him help in the garden. With his mom and dad as well as in all these other new relationships, he will spend much time and effort on showing off and impressing those he loves: "Look at me!"; "See what I can do!" Nothing will please him more than to be admired by them: "My, how strong you are!"; "How big you are!"; "You really look handsome in your new suit." In fact, having a relationship at that age seems to mean the equivalent of a mutual admiration society.

By the time the child gets old enough to be in public school his relationships have changed again. He is ready for a working relationship with his teacher, is eager to learn to read and do arithmetic, shares his teacher with twenty peers, and easily waits several hours for his mother and for his lunch. In the afternoon he may want to play with a friend. On Sunday he enjoys cleaning the car with his dad. He may even join an athletic group and meet with peers and coach in a weekly swim or baseball game. Obviously, this young schoolboy has come a long way and already maintains many different kinds of relationships. Even his relationship with his mother has changed once again. He may like to talk things over with her. He may help her with chores and may make her a present for her birthday. No doubt he still needs and wants her to cook and care for him, but is that not also true of us grown-ups? Don't we look for a measure of need satisfaction in our relationships: a wife who prepares a good meal, a husband who provides money for our wants, a boss who offers pleasant working conditions, a secretary who brings us a cup of coffee?

When we look at relationships in this way we may say that some of the most primitive, early aspects of relationships, those of need satisfaction, diminish in degree as we grow but are never altogether given up. At the same time, the more advanced aspects of relationships—our emotional investment in the other person as a person, rather than as a fulfiller of needs, and our ability to maintain different kinds of relationships with different persons—start quite early and develop gradually during childhood.

When we live with a baby from the time he is born and have a chance to follow his developing relationships day in day out, until he grows up, we see changes almost every day. We see how new ways of relating make their occasional little beginnings, gradually become more frequent, and eventually overtake an earlier kind of relationship, much as a big wave rolls in over the top of its forerunner. But we also see earlier types of relating resurface at times. Some forward moving changes come so fast and strong, we can hardly keep up with observing them. At other times there appears to be a lull or return to older patterns. Each child's development has its own unique intricate interplay of forward running waves and backwash. In addition to their personal ways of developing relationships, all children share an overall progressive sequence of maturational waves. Since the characteristics of each of these waves is most pronounced when it reaches its crest, we often describe them in that form. For the sake of simplicity, we then set aside the many individual variations and focus on what is most typical and what all have in common.

As children's relationships reach one maturational crest after another, they undergo great changes. The differences between successive phases are sometimes much bigger than we realize. For this reason, we can never speak of children as one group of people. At best we can view and compare children at several points in their growth—as babies, toddlers, nursery schoolers, schoolchildren, as preadolescents and adolescents, keeping in mind also that all babies are not alike, all toddlers are not alike, and so on. Each is a unique individual, each encounters different experiences in life, and each copes with them in his or her own way.

We can now begin to answer some of our earlier questions. What kind of relationship do children know? At each stepping stone in their mental growth, children know and maintain the kind of relationship that belongs to that step or phase. Children gradually get to know about different kinds of relationships with different people day by day, year by year, phase by phase. While each child develops in his own way at his own pace, all children's relationships share certain phase-appropriate similarities and characteristics.

Let us now think about the third question we posed: How do children develop these different relationships? When we speak of maturation and successive steps shared by all, we imply an inherent potential, an internal timetable and path that indicate when and in which direction we move along. Yet

we all know that children's relationships do not grow automatically, nor do they always reach "the end of the line" to
maturity. Some schoolchildren are very appropriate in their
relationships with teachers, others are "babies" and expect
parental care instead of lessons from their teachers. Even
some adults may continue infantile, dependent relationships,
or may enjoy fighting and teasing their loved ones as little
toddlers do, or showing off to them, like preschoolers. Individual experiences during a person's mental growth account
for most of these differences and variations. With relationships particularly, it stands to reason that nurture plays a big
part, along with nature. After all, relationships are always a
two-way street, one person inteacting with another and each
affecting the other. We will trace in some detail how relationships develop and change. At the start of this venture, let us
keep in mind that each step in growth depends on what
preceded it. Just as a house cannot have a second floor without a first one, and a tree cannot sprout a crown without a
trunk, so more advanced and varied relationships have to
rest on the foundation of earlier ones.

What is the earliest relationship? And how does it come
about?

2
The First Relationship—
Mother and Baby

When we think of children under five years old, we recognize very quickly that, however much they may like us and others, their most important relationships are with their parents. And when we are with the youngest ones, the babies and toddlers, there is little doubt in our minds that their first and most intimate bond is with their mothers, or mothering persons. We know something of that relationship because the words of the spiritual, *Sometimes I Feel Like a Motherless Child* touch a chord in most of us. Even as adults, often or rarely, we have times when we long for someone to accept us as we are and to care for us unconditionally, to comfort us, to protect us from turmoil inside ourselves and from dangers outside, to be with us when we are lonely or to share a good time, to know what we need and to provide it, be it a meal, or a hug, or a kind word. It wouldn't do if just anyone tried to give us all this. We want it to be a person we know so well and who knows us so well that we can trust her to know what we want and to do her part just as we want it, a person with empathy and understanding who cares for nothing more than to care for us.

The young child's relationship with his mother indeed includes this kind of fulfillment of bodily and emotional needs, maintenance of security, protection against excessive stimulation from within and harm from without, gratification of wants and relief from discomforts. Above all, it includes the assurance that all these "services" will be provided consistently and lovingly, in tune with the child's personality and adapted to the situation at hand. To care in a

11

caring way is the hallmark of mothering. The child's first relationship is with the caring person, the one who mothers him or her. The child knows her, needs her, wants her, and loves her for it.

There is, however, a big difference between adults who longingly recall what this relationship is about and the young child who experiences it. Preschoolers and even toddlers at times welcome and indeed need their mothers' total and unconditional care, but most of the time they relate to their mothers in much more complex ways. Their ideas of loving and being loved include much more give and take, albeit in infantile forms such as admiring and being admired, or teasing and having a mental tug-of-war for power. Instead of enjoying mother's ministrations, they often much prefer to do for themselves—"Let me do it"; "I want to do it all by myself"—and they are quite often opposed to mother's ideas of what is good for them. We see, therefore, that at these developmental phases, the mother-child relationship has already adapted itself to the child's changing needs. The mother's role no longer focuses primarily on basic need fulfill-ment but now extends to helping the child to care for himself, to keep himself safe, to modify his wants and urges, and become a social member of the family with new skills.

Babyhood is the only time when the relationship with the mother consists almost exclusively of ongoing empathic ful-fillment of bodily and emotional needs. For the baby, this kind of relationship is neither a luxury nor an occasional treat, but a basic necessity. It assures his physical and men-tal survival. These are strong words. Do they mean that a baby could actually die without this kind of relationship? Yes, they mean just that.

Many people recognize that a baby needs to be fed, kept clean and dry, comforted when ill or in pain, perhaps even picked up and held or rocked at times, but they assume that anyone can perform these ministrations. This is not so. Unless the baby's bodily needs are met often enough by the same person in the same satisfying way so that he can get to know her and rely on his pleasurable interactions with her—that is, form a mutual bond, a relationship—the baby tends to become listless, fails to gain weight and develop, withdraws interest from his surroundings, and becomes prone to infections and diseases to which he succumbs by the end of his first year in some instances. Studies have shown that initially healthy babies die in institutions which provide flawless hygiene and balanced, nutritious feeds but offer no opportunity for establishing a relationship with a consistent caring person. This is not due to cruelty or ill-treatment on the part of the personnel, but inevitably stems from nurses working in shifts and having to care for so many babies that they can merely attend to their bodies (Spitz, 1945, 1946). We do not really know why babies do not live and prosper under adequate physical care. Loving, within an ongoing relationship, seems to be a necessary ingredient.

Winnicott (1940) said that there is no such thing as a baby, there is only a mother-and-baby. He meant not only that a baby is totally helpless on his own and would not survive many days without being cared for, but also that it requires mothering in the sense of consistent loving care. This alone makes need fulfillment a reliably pleasurable experience and gratifies the baby's many emotional needs— mother's companionship, her smiling, touching, looking at him, caressing, her voice and her smell, her stimulations, and her calming of him. This need-fulfilling relationship with the mother is essential for the baby's physical survival and for helping him to thrive in bodily terms. It also lays the foundation of his mind and personality. Through this relationship he gets to know and like himself, forming an idea of "I," and he gets to know and love his mother, forming an idea of "you." One hopes that the first relationship with mother will be "good enough"—again Winnicott's words—to assure that the pleasures he experiences with her will make him seek her and want her for her own sake, and will make him love himself so much that he will not want to come to harm. The love of mother as a person, not just as a fulfiller of needs, will pave the way for all of the child's future relationships, within the family and with outsiders, even as an adult, and will enable him to benefit from these relationships. The liking of himself will serve him to protect his own body and to safeguard his sense of well-being which is so essential to self-preservation in all of us throughout life. The importance of the first mother-child relationship is not limited to the baby's first year. It serves as the cornerstone of later personality growth.

HOW DOES A BABY FORM THIS FIRST RELATIONSHIP WITH HIS MOTHER?

Newborn babies do not know their mothers or themselves but they are endowed with a potential for relating to people and for developing a personality. The baby utilizes the pleasurable experiences of having his needs fulfilled as a means for establishing a concept of himself, of mother, and of their interaction. Initially the mother is probably indistinguishable from the self; for example, feeling hunger, pain, sucking and swallowing milk, being contained in holding arms, filling up inside, looking into mother's eyes, feeling satiated, all flow together and make up a unit of experience. Repeated over and over it becomes a memory, an image. It does not distinguish between parts of self and parts of mother. Even many months later we can observe one-year-olds sitting on mother's lap at times and handling her body as though it were their own. Along with such experiences of oneness come others which gradually show the child that parts of the experience are always there, others not; for example, the hunger and sucking are there but the milk, smiling eyes, and holding arms come and go. When the screaming baby calms down on hearing mother's approaching voice or step, it is a sign that he has made a beginning differentiation between self and mother. His own touching of himself and her handling of him when she changes his diaper or gives him a bath, alerts him to other parts of his body as well as to mother's separateness because touching oneself and being touched feel very different.

At best a baby's first-year concept of self includes only some parts of his body—the ones he sees and feels most often. It is a primitive, circumscribed bodily self. His concept of his mother is also limited. He does not know all of her body and even less about her as a personality, but he senses her moods very keenly. Above all he knows when he needs her. As soon as he feels a need he looks or calls for her and his gratification depends on her meeting his need at once, in the "right" way, in the way he expects it because he is used to it. Even we grown-ups sometimes grumble when we have to wait for a meal, when it is served differently from usual, or does not taste the way we like it. For the baby such delays and changes are sheer tragedy because the familiar constitutes his world and without it his world falls apart. If, however, he can trust that mother fulfills his needs consistently and in the right way his interest gradually shifts from his needs to the mother herself. Up to a point she becomes more important than the needs. When the infant has no bodily needs, mother is called for company, for playing little games, for laughing and cooing together. Sometimes babies love this new part of the relationship with mother so much that they don't want to go to sleep. Having mother with them is so much fun they may refuse to be fed or comforted by others because they miss her so much. In the second half of his first year, when a baby screams at mother's leaving, when he resists being fed by a stranger or cries at the mere sight of him, he is not spoiled. Rather, he has made the remarkable developmental step of knowing and loving his mother and of appreciating her importance in his life. It also implies that he has some idea of himself as separate from her.

The same pleasurable experiences which have enabled the baby to love his mother have also led to his liking his self. It feels good and he wants it to remain feeling good. He protests when he is hurt or uncomfortable or when he is in danger of losing mother, because she is essential to his sense of well-being. The baby who bangs the high chair, throws his toy, screams, or even bites mother's arm in angry protest, is not naughty. By directing his "attacks" against mother and things he shows that he has made the important developmental step of caring for himself and his well-being, and therefore directing his anger away from his own body. In addition to the physiological pain barrier, this loving investment of one's own body is crucial to self-preservation.

AND WHAT ABOUT THE MOTHER'S PART IN THIS RELATIONSHIP?

Under normal conditions, nature assures that the biological mother becomes her baby's consistent caring person, that she has the stamina to perform this arduous task, and derives satisfaction from it. During the many months while the baby lives inside his mother he is a part of herself, bodily and mentally. She knows him as a real separate person only from his movements and hiccups, and her hope or fears about him represent her own thoughts. Birth brings about a big step in perceiving the child as a person in his own right but, at the same time, he remains a part of the mother mentally, and when she holds her baby and nurses him their bodily unit is also restored. The only difference is that before birth the baby was an inside part of her, whereas after birth he is an outside part of her. This feeling of physical and emotional oneness is essential to the mother's own well-being and helps her in her mothering. In caring for him she cares for a part of herself. When she nurses her baby (let's remember that bottle feeding has become possible only very recently), she knows from the sensations in her breasts when the baby gets hungry. Usually her body even awakens her during the night at times when the baby is ready for a feed. The child's satiation coincides with her own relief and makes both of them feel relaxed and comfortable. Nursing becomes a joint pleasurable experience and assures the baby of mother's consistent closeness and care. And when some ill befalls her baby, the mother feels it much as though it had happened to herself. Her own well-being is restored only as he is helped to feel safe and well again. The biblical story of Solomon's judgment reminds us that this special mother–child bond has been recognized and understood through the ages.

Of course, getting to know a new baby, learning to recognize his different cries and signals, and looking after him round the clock is a very demanding job. Even the most devoted, healthy mothers get very tired and do not relish their mothering task all the time. But usually nature gives a mother enough strength and resilience to take full care of her baby, to extend herself to her other children as well, to keep house after a fashion, and even to function a bit as a wife.

However, being the biological mother is not a guarantee of good and enjoyable mothering. A host of factors may interfere with a mother's ability to care for her child effectively and she may find it difficult or impossible to utilize her natural advantages. Among these factors are ill-health in mother or baby, variations in the mother's psychological makeup, unhelpful advice or lack of support from relatives, doctors, or nurses, or external circumstances, such as financial concerns and worries about her other relationships. The capacity to mother is fostered by natural factors but it is not "instinctive." Some of it stems from a mother's own experiences of being mothered and of developing values of mothering from early models. Other aspects are closely linked to the many specific circumstances of the pregnancy, delivery, postnatal interactions with the baby, and concurrent experiences. Much of mothering has to be learned by being with the baby. In fact, a mother's care of her baby enables her to develop as a mother. If she is separated from her child or has little caring contact with him, maternal development is jeopardized, just as muscles atrophy when they are not sufficiently exercised.

DOES THE CARING PERSON HAVE TO BE THE MOTHER?

In theory anyone can be a good "mother," now that bottle feeding is possible, but the task is immeasurably harder than that of the natural mother. This becomes sadly evident when a mother dies or is permanently separated from her baby, and his care has to be assumed by others. Professional twenty-four-hour nursing care is not only extraordinarily expensive but impossible to arrange with one person, however kind he or she may be. A nurse or housekeeper works at most for ten to twelve hours daily and needs an occasional day off. As a result, two or more nurses need to be employed. Even family members—father, older siblings, or relatives—usually find the total continuous care of the baby too exhausting and need time off to rest, to attend to their other responsibilities and interests, and to take care of their own needs (Barnes, 1964). For them, as it is for the employed nurse, the ongoing, unremitting attention to the baby's needs represents much more giving than getting because they care for the baby as a separate loved one, not as a part of themselves. The baby's satisfaction does not coincide with their own as is true for the functioning natural mother much of the time.

Many adoptive mothers (Schechter, 1970; Menning, 1977; Blum, 1983), some grandmothers, nannies, foster mothers, and some fathers (Pruett, 1983) manage to overcome this handicap. Although the baby never was a part of their own body and cannot return to bodily oneness with them through breast-feeding, their strong wish to mother, as well as their willingness to work at it, may enable them, in time, to form a unit with the baby. Then they not only love him as a separate person but as a part of themselves. It is a remarkable and admirable human achievement.

Fortunately, situations of total substitute care do not arise as often as those of partial or temporary substitute care.

TO WHAT EXTENT IS IT POSSIBLE FOR ONE OR MORE PEOPLE TO SHARE THE CARE OF THE BABY WITH THE MOTHER?

This question may arise from necessity, such as the mother's illness or her need to earn to support her family. It may be posed for reasons of convenience or preference; for example, the mother's wish to rest more or devote herself to other interests. Some women's personalities allow them to mother effectively part-time, but if they have to spend all their time with their babies they experience difficulty. For them, part-time substitutes help to preserve the positive aspects of their mothering. The question of substitute care may, however, also be based on the belief that it is helpful to the baby to have more than one person care for him. Some people think that the mother's exclusive care makes a baby too dependent on her and that this accounts for his difficulty in accepting baby-sitters and tolerating separations. Some feel that the more sitters a baby has, the easier it is for him to accept changes. There are others who think that a baby needs more than one relationship and should not be deprived of enjoying other members of the family, acquaintances, or playmates. Some hold that the father in particular should have an equal share in the baby's care so that he will form a relationship with the child and not feel left out. And others yet claim that a mother's absorption with her baby is a cultural phenomenon that stems from the loss of the extended family and results in tying women to the home and depriving them of a full personal life.

Let us consider these concerns.

Many mothers would very much like to devote themselves fully to their babies' care. They suffer and miss their babies when they have to leave them for a part of the day. They fear that their babies suffer from their absence, and they feel bad about their inability to change the circumstances. Some mothers are not forced to go to work but still feel bad when they leave their babies for a few hours occasionally or regularly.

It helps to remind ourselves that babies do not need perfect mothering. They need good enough mothering. The important question is whether the mother's care enables her baby to establish and maintain a relationship with her. This does not depend solely on how much time she gives him, but on how she cares for the baby when she is with him, whether she keeps her child in mind even when she is not with him, and how she helps him to tolerate the periods without her. For example, such matters as what kind of sitter she chooses, how she instructs the sitter, how she arranges the transition of care to the sitter, whether the sitter is always the same person, whether the baby remains in familiar surroundings, are all significant. What constitutes good enough mothering depends on the combination of such factors as well as on the nature of the baby. Babies vary in their ability to utilize mothering. Their individual requirements also differ, and change from time to time, for example during periods of illness.

A mother can gauge by the child's physical and mental development whether her plan is working out well. It is a good sign when, toward the middle of his first year, the baby has built an adequate attachment to the mothering person, recognizes her, looks for her, and increasingly in the subsequent months, reacts to her leaving and to her absences. The empathic mother recognizes her baby's ways of reacting. It may be crying, restlessness, unusual alertness, refusal to sleep or withdrawal into sleep, distress on mother's return, changes in eating patterns, and many others. This contrasts with the common belief that all is well if "he doesn't mind and doesn't even notice." Such uncaring behavior may mean that the child is not taking the crucial developmental step from prime interest in need fulfillment to interest in the need fulfilling person. This step may fail to take place, may be delayed, or may be only partially achieved when the baby's early needs have not been fulfilled in a good enough manner or when the ministering person has not been consistently enough the same to meet the baby's confident expectation and deserve his loving investment. Multiple caretakers as well as inadequate care during the first year encourage the child to remain focused on his needs in an egocentric manner and, insofar as he considers the person, to care mainly about how he or she serves him rather than who and what kind of people they are.

The baby's dependence on the mother, at this stage, is a healthy development, as is his difficulty in separating from her and his wariness or protest when others take over his care. Valuing and loving a person does indeed bring with it the fear of losing her and the anger and pain of being separated, but it also goes hand in hand with those aspects of relationships which grow from it and which prove important later on in this and many other societies—loyalty, consideration, and a willingness to forego some of one's own gratifications for the sake of the loved ones. Those who welcome a baby's indiscriminate acceptance of anyone who fills his needs, foster a similar self-centeredness and lack of loyalty in the adult, for example, one who does not care who his spouse is as long as she satisfies his needs, or one who abandons his children when they are not satisfying. Of course, the one-year-old is not a grown-up person. A baby's age-appropriate attachment is only the first step on the long road toward mature relationships. Actually, the baby's relationship with his mother is far from considerate. He is demanding, uncompromising, does not hesitate to bite his loved one, and even when he puts food in mother's mouth he is not altruistic but merely enjoys doing to her what she has so often done to him. Nevertheless, without a first relationship with the caring person, the baby can never become a caring adult.

The development of this one-to-one relationship is not

necessarily jeopardized when a baby is held or handled by a sitter. Family members are often the best sitters. The child is used to seeing them, and they have a special investment in him. The extended family can indeed be very helpful as long as it is congenial and supportive.*

However, during the first few months, the baby does not appreciate the caretakers as people in their own right. He accepts their care as satisfactory to the extent that it approximates that of the main mothering person. When their way of meeting the baby's needs differs from hers it upsets him. At this stage, it is important that the baby's upsets not be so frequent and so severe as to interfere with his ability to get to know his mother and himself. He has as yet no capacity or want for varied relationships. He does not miss even his father, unless the father is his main mothering person.

DOES THAT MEAN FATHERS ARE LEFT OUT?
WHAT IS THEIR ROLE WITH THE BABY?

A man may wish that he could bear a child and may envy the special biological and psychological bond of the mother–child unit. But the fact that he cannot have this role does not make him redundant nor does he have to content himself with being a mother-substitute. Some fathers like baby-sitting and do it well, others don't. This is not their most important contribution, nor is it the only or even the best avenue toward a relationship with the infant. The father's special role with the baby is altogether different from that of the mother or principal caretaker (R. A. Furman, 1983).

*The frequent lack of an extended family in our society has led to some misconceptions about it. Prior to the perfection of bottle feeding, the mother had to nurse her baby, and as a result, could never leave him for long, regardless how many others were ready to take over. In preindustrial societies, where nursing on demand is customary and complementary foods are unavailable, the mother usually carries her child with her for many months wherever she goes and while she works. Also, while the extended family is always available, a mother cannot choose to accept or reject it. The closer the ties are with the extended family group, the more a society tends to regulate the role of each member and the ways in which they interact. The individual usually has little or no freedom of choice. Thus, for different reasons and in different ways, a mother's complaint about being tied down and not being able to realize her own personal potential during her child's babyhood, has been as applicable in the past and in other culture patterns as in our present society.

The father-child relationship develops along somewhat different lines from the mother-child relationship. While the baby is never an integral part of his body, mentally and emotionally, however, the infant is very much a part of him, and in this respect, his earliest, even prenatal relationship with the baby parallels the mother-child relationship. During the baby's first weeks and months, the father's role and gratification does not lie in his direct interaction with the baby but in his ability to relate to the mother-child unit as a whole. This enables him to feel with mother and baby, to protect and support them, and to be active on their behalf vis-à-vis the environment at the time of their greatest vulnerability. In this way the father's role in relation to the mother-child unit is akin to the mother's role with the infant: in caring for them he cares for himself. When the father is prevented from assuming this part, because of external circumstances or for reasons within his own personality, his development as a father is jeopardized, as happens with the mother when she is deprived of contact with her baby. But, beyond that, the father's special investment of the mother-child unit is essential to the mother who builds her relationship of devotion to the child with the help of his devotion to them. In this complex and mutually dependent interaction, each represents to the other both a loved person and a part of his or her self. This double investment, though different in mother and father, makes the parent-child relationship unique. In the first year, the mother functions as a part of the child and helps him build his initial self. In addition to his role of protecting and supporting the mother-child unit, the father, and others who are close to the infant, soon begin to meet the baby's developing interest in relationships with people other than the mothering person. At later points in the child's growth the father's role changes and both parents complement aspects of their son's or daughter's personality.

WHEN IS A BABY READY FOR ADDITIONAL RELATIONSHIPS?

When the baby's needs are no longer as urgent as they were initially, and when his relationship with his mother has progressed to the point where he loves her as a person, the infant begins to show interest in other people and derives pleasure and stimulation from their different human responses. As long as he feels assured of mother's presence and available care, the well-developed baby in the latter part of his first year welcomes familiar people's specific approaches. He enjoys special brief interactions with them and builds individual relationships unrelated to need fulfillment with the father, with older siblings, and with other familiar people. One boy had lost his father through death at eleven months of age. For many years he kept poignant memories of little games with his dad and of the special way his dad picked him up high for a hello hug. In this kind of early relationship the father is loved as a person in his own right. The perception of him—his different look, feel, sound, and smell—is appreciated and the interaction he offers enriches the little child's experiences.

Of course, this specific early father–child relationship exists only in addition to the need-fulfilling mother–child relationship. When a need arises in mother's presence, such as fatigue or a hurt, the baby usually quickly abandons his father, cries and reaches for his mother. When a need arises during mother's absence, the baby treats the father as a mother-substitute and he then pleases the child when he acts as much as possible like the mother. The additional new relationships seem brief but they are important developmental steps.

WHAT HAPPENS WHEN THE EARLY MOTHER–BABY RELATIONSHIP IS NOT SO IDEAL, WHEN STRESSES INTERFERE?

For many of us and for many who are close to us, life has indeed been far from ideal. When we think about the importance of the early mother–child relationship we often wonder how we, and those we know, weathered the hardship of early upheavals and what impact they have had on later development. Let us look at some of the interferences, gauge their effect on the baby, and consider different ways in which they may be dealt with.

WHAT HAPPENS WHEN EARLY MOTHERING
IS INADEQUATE, FOR EXAMPLE WHEN
A MOTHER DOES NOT REALLY WANT
HER BABY?

In the light of what we said earlier, a totally unwanted and uncared for child does not survive. The adequacy and inadequacy of mothering is difficult to rate on a scale. It has to be gauged by the baby's responses and development. If his care was poor, by average standards, but the infant is in fair physical and emotional health, he must have received a measure of loving care that was good enough. The infant probably managed to utilize its positives to best advantage. Sometimes a mother comes to love a child she was not ready for earlier and is then able to help her child catch up or make up. To some extent, and within certain individual time limits, infants can utilize a later opportunity, compensate for what they had missed, or modify earlier experiences (Provence and Lipton, 1962).

WHAT HAPPENS WHEN EARLY MOTHERING IS
INTERRUPTED TEMPORARILY THROUGH
SEPARATION, OR PERMANENTLY, FOR EXAMPLE
WHEN THE MOTHER DIES OR WHEN THE BABY
IS TAKEN FROM A FOSTER HOME AND PLACED
IN AN ADOPTIVE HOME?

When an infant has to cope with a separation or a complete change of mothering person, he undergoes a major stress. However, it is always better to have had some good mothering and lost it than never to have had it at all. Built-up reserves from good care and his own stamina may enable him to cope with the upheaval and, in time, to continue his development. The effects of separations and of changes in mothering person also depend very much on the timing and circumstances. For example, a gradual takeover of care by a familiar person who is able to recognize and soothe the child's upset reaction, differs greatly from a sudden shift to a stranger who is unable to understand and meet the baby's needs.

The younger the baby, the more his upset tends to show in bodily distress. The older baby's feeding and sleep patterns may also be interfered with for some time but he is likely to have an additional, more specific emotional response to the loss of the loved person. He may show fear, sadness, and anger. These are appropriate signs that he is acknowledging the difficult reality and attempting to master the situation. Indications of more severe distress are loss of appetite, loss of weight, physical ill-health, or prolonged periods of bodily discomfort, loss of interest in the surroundings, withdrawal, listlessness, apathy.

Although separations and changes in mothering person are indeed stressful events for a baby, he often manages to overcome them and to continue to develop with the help of his own strength and the loving care extended to him.

WHAT, IF ANY, ARE THE LASTING DAMAGES OF INADEQUACIES, INTERRUPTIONS, OR CHANGES IN MOTHERING?

Most people's early upsets and stresses, just like their good experiences, play a part in shaping their personalities and contribute to their individuality and uniqueness. Each has his quirks and idiosyncracies, each also has his weak spots which may not bother him much or which, like old scars, may be touched off only now and then under special circumstances when current experiences combine with old trouble spots. Early hurts and deficits are sometimes overshadowed by later development and compensated for with the help of subsequent achievements.

However, not all of us are so fortunate. In some cases early upheavals and deficits combine with stresses during the toddler and preschool stages; in others the unhappy experiences during babyhood actually impair the infant's development and leave lasting scars. Of these the most serious are an infant's inability to build or renew his beginning relationship with a loved one and to establish or reconstitute a sense of bodily well-being.

If a baby was never able to make the step from wanting need-fulfillment to relating to the need-fulfilling person for her own sake, or if the interruptions of such a relationship produced such a setback that the baby could not rebuild this kind of relationship, all his future capacity for relationships may be jeopardized. This not only deprives him of the pleasure of later relationships but also interferes with his personality development because it is formed with the help of later relationships. Studies have shown that inadequately formed and/or repeatedly interrupted relationships during the early years may result in psychopathic, criminal, and some forms of delinquent personalities (Bowlby, 1944, 1951; Friedlander, 1947; A. Freud, 1949a). This may contribute to major difficulties in maintaining adult close relationships and in functioning as a parent.

The second area of difficulty, the poor sense of bodily well-being, may affect a person's later ability to like and safeguard his body. This may contribute to bodily ills stemming from psychological causes, to accident proneness, or to suicidal tendencies. Whereas personality difficulties that result from later developmental interferences usually can be treated and helped, those aspects that are rooted in the earliest deficits tend to be unalterable (Fleming, 1974).

IS IT ALWAYS THE FAULT OF MOTHERING WHEN CHILDREN HAVE DIFFICULTIES?

The role of parenting is so important that all of a child's ills are often attributed to parental failure, but it is not always the mother's fault. Parents themselves feel so responsible for their children's development and welfare that they tend to accept the blame. Even in babyhood, however, when mothering is indeed of supreme importance, it is not the only important factor.

A baby's individual endowment and physical health play a crucial part. For example, an infant's congenital deficit, such as blindness, deafness, or a neurological problem, may interfere with his capacity to get to know and distinguish mother and self; or an anomaly of his mouth or digestive tract may render eating consistently unpleasurable; or an illness and necessary medical and surgical treatments may impose their own severe stresses. Hospitalization may, in addition, cause interruptions in mothering. There are also subtler difficulties in babies which may make them more vulnerable and less able to utilize mothering; for example, a very low tolerance for stimuli from within and without may cause ordinary noises or minor changes in routine to be experienced as very distressing and disruptive. To some extent, mothers can adapt themselves to the special needs of each child and their particularly empathic care may even compensate for the stresses caused by other factors. However, in some situations even the best mothering cannot provide a continuous and pleasurable enough milieu to foster the early developments.

The older the child, the more structured his own personality becomes, and the more he interacts with the wider community, the less can we look to mothering as the sole or primary cause of the child's difficulties. Even with careful and skilled professional investigation, it is sometimes hard to determine the part played by past or present mothering and the way it interacts with other old and recent experiences to produce specific psychological problems.

DOES IT MAKE A DIFFERENCE WHETHER A BABY IS NURSED OR BOTTLE-FED?

When a mother wants to nurse her baby, works at establishing breast-feeding (it usually takes a few weeks to accomplish), and comes to enjoy it, it is the easiest and most satisfying way for the mother to feed her baby and affords both of them a natural opportunity to be close and to get to know and love each other. However, when a mother is not comfortable with the idea of nursing, or when she is unable to breast-feed, she can use the bottle-feeding periods similarly as a way of relating with the baby. The important factor is that feeding be accompanied by loving care and personal interaction. Unfortunately, both nursing and bottle-feeding can be administered impersonally or without being in proper tune with the child's emotional needs.

DOES THE CHILD'S ORDER IN THE FAMILY
MAKE A DIFFERENCE TO HOW HE
IS MOTHERED?

Each child receives his own kind of mothering. With each child the mother has to invest herself anew and build a unique mother-child relationship. Its special nature does not depend on the numerical order of the child within the family but on other factors—the baby's looks and responses, the mother's physical and emotional health, the experiences associated with the child's birth, and other current and past circumstances. The mother's previous experiences with mothering will also play a part. They may prove helpful or make it more difficult.

IS EARLY MOTHERING DIFFERENT FOR
TWINS?

Each twin requires individual good enough mothering. His twinship is not a substitute for maternal care; on the contrary, it is more likely to be a measure of interference. The twins' simultaneous needs may make it harder for a mother to attend adequately to both children, especially if their smallness at birth requires more frequent feedings and special handling. Also, twins may be an additional source of unhelpful stimulation to one another; for example, a twin may be woken by the other's cry or by the noises that accompany the other's care. Some admirable mothers manage nevertheless to give each twin good enough individual mothering.

WHAT ABOUT CULTURAL DIFFERENCES IN
EARLY MOTHERING?

There are many individual and cultural variations in mothering. However, all need to provide good enough continuous loving care to assure a baby's physical survival and to lay the foundation for his mental development—a beginning concept of self and of the person(s) he seeks to fulfill his bodily and emotional needs. The extent to which these needs are satisfied or frustrated and the manner in which it is done, affect the ways in which the child's personality develops. And this is where individual, cultural, and racial differences in child rearing begin, in that they determine to a considerable extent the mothering person's choice of which needs she will gratify, when and how. For example, a mother's handling of the baby's sucking (breast, bottle, or own thumb) and his eating (self or spoon-feeding, soft or chewy foods) shapes not only his attitudes to feeding but many developing character qualities—dependence or independence, tendency to seek and enjoy new pleasures or to persist with the familiar, ability to substitute one gratification for another, or insistence on a certain form of satisfaction. At the time it may seem of little consequence whether he nurses a few more months or sucks his fingers or holds his bottle before sleeping, or whether, when, and how he gets to like new foods. However, in their own way, and little by little, these early variations in mother–child interaction become the building blocks of the child's personality with its own characteristics and values, and suited to adjust within his own family and community.

3

The Baby-Sitter

Baby-sitting is often regarded as an unskilled and unimportant job, and perhaps for that reason most of us have had some experience with it, at one time or another. If all seemed to go well, we considered ourselves good sitters. If, as happens more often, things did not go so well, we may have blamed the child's parents, or they may have blamed us, or, most likely, parents and sitter reproached the child for being naughty. Actually, baby-sitting, like parenting, is a difficult, skilled, and important job. The sitter takes the parent's place and is entrusted with the child's safety and welfare, at least temporarily and to some extent. Being responsible for someone's life and well-being is no minor task, especially when that somebody is unable to take care of himself.

As adults we are so used to functioning independently that it is difficult to empathize with the young child's predicament, except perhaps when we become very ill. Then we may find ourselves nearly as helpless and incompetent, and as dependent on others to make us safe and comfortable. In that situation most of us want to make quite sure that we can really trust our caretakers—doctor and nurse—to do right by us. We don't like it at all when "our" doctor or nurse leaves us in the care of substitutes we don't know so well or who may not know enough about us. We certainly would get very upset if we found that our physician, or his substitute, did not take the job of looking after us very seriously. Our feelings would become the more intense and urgent, the more we would be incapacitated and unable to care for our own needs. And imagine if, on top of all that, we could not talk and make ourselves understood! Just like a baby!

Baby-sitting, however, is not only important to our little charges. It is also important to us as sitters. Our role as parent-substitutes brings us into close contact with the most intimate parts of children's lives and affords us a unique opportunity to observe, study, and understand them. Let us therefore look closer and trace the course of the infant's dependence on need fulfillment and how this affects his developing relationships.

BABY-SITTING WITH BABIES

We know already that the consistent loving care by the mothering person paves the way for the baby to experience a sense of well-being and to get to know himself and the person he depends on for his comfort. As soon as the mother and her way of taking care are sufficiently remembered to feel familiar and to be expected (and this can happen within a few weeks or a couple of months), the baby also recognizes changes in person and care and reacts to them with varying degrees of distress, usually accompanied by behavioral changes. The baby-sitter may find it difficult to feed the baby, or to comfort his crying, or to calm him enough to help him go to sleep.

Within a few more months the infant comes to appreciate his mother as being so essential to his bodily and mental welfare that he may not feel safe unless he is fully assured of her availability. He may not even want to be held by a stranger when he can see mother, much less when she is not around. He has no way to understand that he will survive with the help of others or that mother will eventually return. Her leaving means the end of his world. It is not uncommon for babies to respond with rage and/or inconsolable distress and even to refuse need fulfillment when they are suddenly left with a stranger. And waking up to see a strange face often marks the beginning of weeks of sleep disturbance.

No doubt, some of us have also had the experience of "never having much trouble" with a baby. This usually happens when the baby has had a lot of opportunity to get to know us in his mother's presence, when she has fully acquainted us with her ways of taking care, and has perhaps gradually allowed us to do some things for him under her supervision, and when he has experienced our care only during brief maternal absences. Seeing us with mother then comes to mean something like, "Mom is going away but will come back, and this substitute is pretty okay." The process of getting acquainted and learning to trust the baby-sitter is especially prolonged and laborious during babyhood because there are as yet no words to explain matters and no abstract thinking with which to grasp them. Of course, with baby-sitters who are members of the family there is a built-in way of getting to know them in mother's presence which makes it much easier.

Although their dependence on the loved one is great, babies are not as helpless as it seems. From their third month on, they usually master the skill of sucking their own thumb or fingers and can utilize it to give themselves pleasure and comfort quite independently. It is a remarkable achievement in many ways and differs greatly from the random sucking that takes place in utero and postnatally when the hand happens to be near the mouth but cannot be actively brought to it or kept there. Active thumb sucking helps the baby to differentiate self from nonself, to get to know a new part of his body, to manipulate it at will. Moreover, the thumb is always available, in contrast to mother who may take a while to respond to the child's signals, and in contrast also to a pacifier which falls out and cannot be retrieved by the child himself. Although thumb sucking cannot still big hunger or relieve other really pressing needs, it goes quite a ways in alleviating little discomforts and tensions, both bodily and emotional. When we watch a baby waking up we can witness how a small need grows into a big one and to what extent sucking helps to ease it. We may first observe sucking movements, then active thumb or finger sucking for quite a while, and only eventually crying bursts out. Once babies can suck their thumb or fingers they can take care of some needs on their own, can wait a little for other needs to be met, and can more easily calm and comfort themselves before falling asleep. In short, they have taken a step toward independence. Some mothers, for that very reason, do not welcome thumb sucking. They link it in their minds with all the later ways in which children will want to do their own thing, will not need the parent, and therefore perhaps will be impervious to the parent's injunctions. Yet, in other ways, parents value a child's independence and a baby who sucks his thumb is a good bit easier to take care of, for mother and sitter.

In the latter part of the first year, infants often acquire another way of comforting themselves. This new way helps them particularly to deal with the longing for mother who is now seen as a separate person and who is not always close by. I am referring to the fact that babies create a *transitional object*. The term was coined by Winnicott (1953), elaborated by Stevenson (1954), and refers to the space between infant and mother, the transition between them. Characteristically, the transitional object is not a part of the child's or mother's body, but something that reminds a bit of each or represents a part of their interaction. Out of many possible objects in his environment, the baby chooses a certain one and invests it with a symbolic meaning. It is his first imaginative creation and, in this sense, is the forerunner of his later much more complex and sophisticated creativity. The transitional object may be a piece of soft blanket or its silky lining, a diaper, a soft small toy. There are many individual variations in its shape, texture, smell, or other quality that may feel essential about it to the infant. The baby's choice of materials, like his budding imagination, is limited. Even a pacifier or milk bottle can become a transitional object and may account for the fact that the child is unwilling to relinquish them for many months or even years. Many of us remember our own transitional object, that first treasured possession which mothers often help safeguard, sensing its importance. The transitional object does not make the child as self-sufficient as his own thumb because a "blankie" can fall out of reach or get lost, but it is easier to keep around than mother. Many a baby-sitter has been saved much trouble by the fact that the infant or young toddler could use his blanket or soft toy to ease the stress of being separated from his mother.

The older baby is also beginning to do some things for himself, particularly drinking from a cup and eating solid foods. This too makes him less directly dependent on mother and sitter.

The more "independent" a baby is and the more ways he has of comforting himself, the more he is ready to seek and enjoy the familiar baby-sitter as a person in his own right, not just as a mother-substitute. He may like a specific little hand game or song which the sitter introduces and which becomes an expected pleasurable interaction in their relationship. Games of the peek-a-boo variety often become favorites because their theme of predictable go away–come back, disappearance and reappearance, helps to master the presence and absence of the mother which preoccupies so much of the older baby's feeling and thinking.

BABY-SITTING FOR TODDLERS

We can observe further changes in the interaction between need fulfillment and the mother–child relationship when we baby-sit with toddlers (roughly between the ages of one-and-a-half to two-and-a-half years old).

Sandra, at twenty-two months, often visited her aunt's home with her mother and enjoyed playing with her teenage cousins who joked and frolicked with her and allowed her to play with many of their things to her heart's content. She was usually reluctant to leave, dawdled, and begged to stay on. One day her wish was granted. An overnight visit was planned. Sandra seemed to look forward to it, arrived proudly with her little bag of belongings and hardly bothered to bid her mother goodbye. All went well. Dinner was a bit hectic with Sandra messing and grabbing at foods, running to and from the table, and wetting herself although she usually kept herself clean. This was attributed to her being so busy and having extra fun, rather than as a sign of her missing her mother. It was only at the next period of need fulfillment, bedtime, that Sandra's longing for her mother overwhelmed her. When going to bed could no longer be put off, she began to cry for her mother and was so upset that the mother was called, came and took her home.

Marc, at twenty-three months, had met his baby-sitter several times in mother's presence. On the day when the sitter was to look after him she arrived in the afternoon. Marc had already been told that Mom and Dad would go out for the evening. He followed the grown-ups around listening on and off to mother telling the sitter about where things were and what their routines were like. After the parents were gone, Marc began to show the sitter around. He introduced her to his toys and books and told or indicated to her what she was to play with him. But he was not keen on doing what she asked of him and he would not allow her to do anything for him. He was intent on doing everything all by himself, even when he was not really up to it. He insisted on climbing into and out of his high chair, pouring his own milk from the pitcher, pulling the cookie box off the shelf, turning on his bathwater, putting on his pajamas (half way and backwards). With some activities, his independence was merely time-consuming, with others it led to messes and near disasters. Regardless, he adamantly refused help, resented interference, and persisted in his efforts while the sitter trailed and hovered near him attempting to keep him safe. When he finally dropped off to sleep, clutching his teddy with one arm and sucking his thumb with the other, the exhausted sitter had to tackle the extensive cleanup in the wake of Marc's independence.

John, aged two years, five months, had his grandparents as sitters for a day and night while his parents went out of town. He knew his grandparents quite well from periodic visits. He also was a clever thinker and talker, could understand his mom's explanation of and preparation for the separation, and could make his own needs known in words. All this helped him to have a rather good though subdued day with his sitters who entertained him appropriately. He refused to nap, ate a small dinner, and, in the evening, put off getting ready for bed. Although it was getting late and he was obviously tired, there was still always one more thing he wanted to do. His bunny which had been unattended during the earlier part of the day, was now being clutched tightly. When grandmother finally insisted on "bathtime now," he protested angrily and then wailed a heartrending, "I want my Mommy to wash me." Grandma compromised by washing him with a lick and a promise and allowed him to wash his bunny. This calmed him and he later announced that he had washed both bunny and himself! The next stressful time was lying down to sleep. Angry screams and tears were finally helped by grandma staying with him for a while, telling him that Mom and Dad loved him and would return in the morning, and by bunny being tucked in with him.

All three children were healthy, well-functioning toddlers. They could walk, understand, and use speech to a considerable extent, and were interested in things and people. Compared to the needy dependent baby they were quite self-sufficient. They could feed themselves, could get around and help themselves to some foods, could ask for what they wanted in words. They could get most of their clothes off and could help with getting some of them on. At times they could even use the toilet to keep clean and dry.

How did this relative independence affect their relationships? It certainly made for a marked change. The toddlers had much more wish, time, and energy for relationships with people other than the mother and they enjoyed interactions with friendly adults in her presence. Sandra had so much fun with her cousins that she repeatedly wanted to stay with them. It was only when these "additional" relationships assumed the role of mother-substitutes during the mother's absence, that the toddlers did not welcome the sitters' ministrations. At the peak times of bodily and emotional need they either preferred to forego need satisfaction (small dinners, refusal to be washed and go to bed), or they wanted to fill their own needs (especially Marc), or they angrily and helplessly called for their mothers. Marc and John could comfort themselves better with the help of thumb sucking and their soft toys. Sandra who had no means of self-comfort, became overwhelmed.

In the course of development, the need-fulfilling early bond with the mother is not transferred to the relationships with others, except under the stress of necessity or, occasionally, as a way to tease Mom ("Today I want grandma to tuck me in"). Normally, the early relationship with the mother is used to assist the child in learning to take care of himself. The more and better the child gradually achieves what we might call "being mother to himself," the more are his relationships with parent and others freed of basic need-fulfilling dependency. The parental role of caring for the child goes hand in hand with that of helping him to care for himself. This task begins with caring for one's own bodily needs. It ends in young adulthood when people take care of themselves in the fullest sense of the word, including earning their own living and looking after their health. Many young adults, usually quite independent at college or in their job, still call home when they get sick, before they call a doctor.

All along, the job of self-care, of mothering oneself, includes not only the gratification of needs but some of the giving of love that is part and parcel of the mother's early bodily care. As she encourages and appreciates the child's care of himself she invests that love in the process of her teaching and his learning and it becomes part of his liking to care for himself. Marc's insistence on doing everything for himself has many reasons. One of them is loving himself as mother would love him if she were there. A child may well enjoy the company of a familiar sitter and trust him to a considerable extent to fill many aspects of the parental role, but it is always more difficult for him to hand over the care of his body. The younger the child and the less he can do for himself, the harder it is to accept the sitter for need fulfillment. However, even much older children want nobody but their mom at times of illness, injury, or danger to their welfare. At these times once again they feel unable to care for their own bodies. This is also true in periods of mental stress, of misfortune, upset, or loneliness, when children and even adults, reexperience early feelings of helplessness and distress and long for the mother's loving care for which it is so difficult to substitute.

The children in our examples were neither ill nor threatened by special danger or misfortune. They only suffered the mental stress of separation. Even that was considerably lessened for them by their mothers' explanations and preparation, by their own understanding of when mother would return, and by their relationships with the familiar sitters. The sitter, and even more so, the toddler, would have had a much harder time if the child had not known the sitter, had been surprised by his mother's absence, and known nothing about her return, or if the child had become ill or injured. Such distress may have shown at the time in crying, in being very angry, uncooperative, or unapproachable, in reverting to babylike behavior, such as crawling and babbling, or in upsets around eating, toileting, and sleeping. Oftentimes toddlers appear to manage the stressful period well, but the disturbance manifests itself later and may then persist for a long time. Sitters cannot know of such aftermaths and even parents may miss the links between the stress of separation and the subsequent behavioral changes or disturbance. The individual variations of ensuing difficulties are too great to enumerate. Among the more common ones are fears, clinginess, or the opposite, namely, wandering off and getting "lost," interferences in sleeping, eating, and toilet training, and exacerbations of conflicts in the mother–child relationship.

The toddler's relationship with his mother is, in any case, much less harmonious than it was during babyhood. Sandra, Marc, and John showed some of the toddler's typical determination and contrariness, attempt to control the adult, the drive to do everything oneself and go off and explore, especially where one is not supposed to. Although some of their behaviors were exaggerated with the sitter, for example, Marc's "me-do-it," others would have been more noticeable with their mothers; for example, teasing, provoking, and mixing love and anger to such an extent that it would often be difficult for Mom to tell whether a hug was meant to be a caress or an attack. Some mothers describe this relationship by saying, "My child is so positive these days," and others call it, "so negative." We might say that, whereas the baby uses his mother to learn to recognize her and himself as different bodies, the toddler utilizes his relationship with his mother to establish her and himself as separate minds, and tests the limits of their boundaries. The toddler can better distance himself the more he can count on mother's availability, on her just being there. Wanting to care for himself, learning how to do it, and turning to things and people for new pleasures, all are a part of this healthy maturational step. But mother has to be there to be left and to be returned to at will. When mother is not there physically, or when she is emotionally unavailable for more than a few hours, the toddler's newly gained mental self is endangered and the threat of needs going unfulfilled again becomes paramount. Some toddlers may then react by reverting to extreme dependency, others may adopt a precocious defensive independence and distance themselves from the give and take of relationships, as if to say, "You don't need me, so I don't need you" and perhaps even, "I don't need anybody." The strange sitter has no way to help the child. The familiar and understanding sitter can assist him in mastering a stressful period.

Some people think that baby-sitting for the littlest ones is easy because their needs are so basic and their powers so limited. Actually baby-sitting with them is the most difficult because for them the stress of separation from the mother is so great, and they find it so hard to accept substitutes.

WHAT HAPPENS WHEN THERE IS A SEVERE INTERFERENCE IN THE TODDLER'S RELATIONSHIP WITH HIS MOTHER; FOR EXAMPLE, LONG OR REPEATED SEPARATIONS, PERMANENT INTERRUPTION, INADEQUATE MOTHERING, ILLNESS, AND HOSPITALIZATION?

In the case of all major stresses during the first year, a great deal depends on how they are handled, who takes the place of the mothering person, and whether several stresses coincide or follow one another in close sequence. The individual child's disposition and stamina also vary as well as the nature of his earlier development and subsequent experiences. The caring adults can always find more helpful ways of assisting a child in coping with stresses when they appreciate that his situation is very difficult. With appropriate help even the most severe upsets can be mastered or at least alleviated (E. Furman, 1984a).

Insofar as the toddler–mother relationship helps the child to differentiate his personality from hers, to achieve an appropriate balance between independence and dependence, and to learn to love mother in spite of some conflicts and disappointments, interferences in the mother–child relationship at that stage threaten these developments. This may manifest itself in personality disorders which make a person focus on himself and be unable to relate to or feel with others. In extreme cases it may lead to self-centered, impulse-ridden, psychopathic or delinquent behavior. Another pathology, almost opposite in form, may show in primitive dependence on loved ones, inadequacy in independent functioning, difficulty in being alone, and severe emotional reaction to loss and disappointment. In extreme cases it contributes to some forms of depression or mental prostration.

Among the more common milder consequences are persisting aspects of toddler characteristics in relationships; for example, an excess of mixed feelings, argumentativeness, hostility, possessiveness, and a need to control the loved one (E. Furman, 1981a).

However, severe interferences in the mother–toddler relationship may also affect other areas of the personality and its maturation. For example, the development of speech and its effective use for thinking and communication are linked primarily to the ongoing mother–toddler relationship and to the mother's enjoyment of talking with her child (Hall, 1982b).

ARE THUMB-SUCKING AND "BLANKET"-TYPE POSSESSIONS REALLY HELPFUL? DO THEY NOT DEVELOP INTO BAD HABITS AND "PROPS" THAT MAKE A CHILD LOOK BABYISH LATER, MAKE HIS TEETH GROW CROOKED, AND ARE UNHYGIENIC?

Many responses and behaviors which are healthy and appropriate at one developmental level may become inappropriate and indicative of difficulty at later stages. Normally, thumb sucking gives way to other forms of self-comfort as the child grows older and transitional objects tend to be replaced by dolls and toys which the child uses for imaginative and manipulative play. By the time he or she attends nursery school, thumb sucking and transitional objects are used occasionally or not at all. When early behavior persists, it is not because it was there in the first place but because something got in the way of its being replaced by a more advanced form; for example, thumb sucking in later phases may have lost its original function and come to represent the child's attempt at coping with different stresses and conflicts. When a person keeps on wearing the same dress, year in, year out, for all occasions, we would probably not think that this could have been avoided if she had never gotten that dress. We would rather wonder what her reasons are for not changing to a different dress.

BABY-SITTING WITH PRESCHOOLERS

Well-developed three-, four-, and five-year-olds are often most enjoyable to baby-sit with, provided they know and trust the sitter, understand where mother is, and can gauge the time of her return, and provided also that they are neither ill nor under special stress. Need fulfillment and relationships are by then much less intertwined and self and mother are much more clearly and stably conceived as separate persons in the preschooler's mind. Relationships with others are assuming a new importance as well, so that the sitter is not only a mother substitute but a potentially interesting person. With and from the sitter one can learn more about the world and he or she can also supply the ever welcome admiration for the child's "Look at me," "See what I have," and "See what I can do."

Four-year-old Jennifer first met her sitter-to-be on an afternoon outing to the ice cream parlor which her mother had arranged as a pleasant way to get acquainted. Jennifer had a chance to boast of all the things she had and could do and asked many questions of the sitter, including some personal ones about the sitter's clothes, jewelry, home, and family. On the day mother was to leave Jennifer for the evening, they all had several hours together in the home first. Jennifer participated in showing the sitter around and familiarizing her with all the rules and routines. Mother served Jennifer an early dinner. After the parents left there were games and stories and a long period of Jennifer dressing up like a big lady, saying goodbye to her dolls, and tucking them into the doll buggy. She was proudly independent in taking her bath and getting ready for bed and basked in the sun of the sitter's praise and admiration, but she could also ask for and accept help appropriately. Actual bedtime was a little harder. Jennifer's teddy "needed" two extra stories and there was a call for a drink after lights out. When the sitter reminded Jennifer of Mom's bedtime rule, Jennifer said that Mom could not really know because she was not home, so couldn't she stay up later. When this was refused, she asked wistfully whether it was time yet for Mom and Dad to return and then asked the sitter to be sure to remind them to kiss her as soon as they arrived. The sitter promised and Jennifer dropped off to sleep.

Although this is not an unusual baby-sitting experience, we all can no doubt recall others that were nowhere near as smooth. Unfortunately, children at that age often cannot yet tell us—sometimes do not even realize—what concerns them: "I miss my Mom"; "I am mad she left me"; "I am worried she won't come back"; "She likes going out with Dad better than staying home with me"; "She doesn't love me"; "I don't love her, she was mean today"; "I want to be grown up, I want to do what I please"; "I hate having a sitter instead of Mom." Instead of knowing and verbalizing their concerns, children may show them in fears, disobedience, crying over little things, or distracting themselves with excited fun and exaggerated activity, or resenting the sitter and making life miserable for her.

When the stress is minor, children's own means of coping are adequate; for example, Jennifer used dressing up and doll play to cope with her wish to go out like mother and to leave others rather than be left herself. She gained self-esteem from her independent dressing and bathing. She used the sitter for comfort at bedtime, and she asked in words about the parents' return and love for her. Some children can be helped when the sitter speaks with them of the parents, of their and the child's missing of one another, of how hard it can be to feel left out, and of how pleased they will all be to be together again.

When the stress is major, the child's means prove inadequate and thoughts and feelings get to be expressed in behavior that is not appropriate. Just how big the stress is depends not only on the actual circumstances of the specific baby-sitting period but includes all the many factors which have affected the child's life recently and in the past. When the stress becomes excessive, the young child's personality achievements crumble. Need-fulfilling periods are usually the first to suffer; for example, in day care centers, meals, naptimes, and end-of-the-long-day periods are chronically beset with difficulties. Next, the newly acquired interests in people and activities forfeit pleasurable investment. The children wander around listlessly, disregard or misuse toys, and, directly or indirectly, demand mothering care or fall back on their self-comforting habits.

BABY-SITTING WITH SCHOOL-AGE CHILDREN

Except in situations of illness or severe stress, children from about six to eleven years of age are truly masters of their daily bodily needs. In fact, this aspect of their lives is relatively so independent of the relationship with the mothering person that a meal prepared differently or one that includes new foods may be quite welcome. They also enjoy a variety of relationships, activities, and interests which are satisfying in themselves. These developmental changes give the sitter a chance to build individual specific relationships with the children which are mutually enjoyable. It is no longer necessary to be as much like mother as possible in many areas. In baby-sitting with children in this age group it is very evident that the role of the parent–child relationship has shifted. Almost imperceptibly over the years, need fulfillment and learning to take care of one's needs, getting to be a person in one's own right, and functioning independently have receded into the background. Instead, the parent–child relationship serves to help the child build and maintain inner controls over his wishes and feelings and assists him in conforming to rules that affect not only his safety but ways of living with others according to family and community expectations. The parent substitute is usually so busy with these aspects that he or she barely notices the absence of demands for need fulfillment and the diminished stress of missing mother. In some ways the current responsibilities may seem bigger: "You can't play soccer in the neighbor's yard"; "You can't bike down to the drugstore"; "No, your friend can't stay for dinner and sleep over." Obviously, these changes do not mean that parents are no longer necessary or that the relationship with them is less important. Schoolchildren need their parents and miss them, but in different ways. In order to understand them better we shall have to follow the changing course of the parent–child relationship and its effect on the child's personality growth.

Competent baby-sitters know intuitively that their relationship with the child has to approximate the age-appropriate role of the parents' relationship. With very young children this means being familiar and consistent with the mother's ways of fulfilling needs and being aware of the stress of separation. With older children the task includes establishing the kind of relationship that will enable them to accept the sitter as the representative of the family's rules of living. When sitters have the time and the know-how to build this kind of relationship, they are trusted and can work in harmony with the children's expectations of themselves. "Look, you and I know that your parents don't think it's right to go to the playground after dinner. I wouldn't be a good sitter if I let you go and you wouldn't feel good about it either in the end. So let's just have a game at home." When, however, the sitter is strange to the children, unfamiliar with their usual routines and standards, and unskilled at forming the right kind of relationship, he is apt to find himself in the midst of chaos—a situation similar to that of being an inexperienced elementary school substitute teacher who is suddenly put into the void left by the absence of the familiar class teacher.

AREN'T ALL CHILDREN, EVEN VERY YOUNG ONES, SOMETIMES GLAD TO BE AWAY FROM THEIR PARENTS?

When children are old and competent enough not to need a sitter they can genuinely enjoy being away from their parents. To some extent this also applies to school-aged children who enjoy varied relationships and activities, who like to practice and test their independence, and who have learned to combine appropriately the demands of their own conscience with the idea that, to a certain extent, different situations and groups operate on their own sets of rules and expectations. For example, it's okay to run around and yell in a neighborhood ball game but not at school or at the store. Also, it is always easier for children to leave their parents and know they are there to return to, than to be left by them.

With some older, and most younger children, however, the wish to get away from the parents and their rules may stem from different motives. With toddlers, as with Sandra in our earlier baby-sitting example, the wish to leave mother, to demonstrate how little one needs her, and to tease her even by turning lovingly to others, are part and parcel of the relationship with the mother. The child can enjoy it as long as he can be sure that he can return to her any time, and the reunion is as much a part of his toddler love and need as is the getting away.

Toddlers, and older youngsters even more so, also often want to leave mother as a way of paying her back for having been left by her. The more they have felt helpless, hurt, and angry by her real or imagined "disloyalty" in leaving them, the more they apparently relish their chance to turn away to supposedly "better" people and things. Instances of this kind of reaction can be observed in most nurseries or day care centers. There are usually one or more children who could barely wait for the end of the school day, but when mother finally comes to get them they keep her waiting. Under the pretext of having to play with just one more toy, dawdling over dressing, or talking to others, they manage to convey to mother just how frustrating it is to be left unnoticed while your loved one is busy. Most mothers become quite irritated, but some understand and say, "I guess it's been a long time. I missed you too" (E. Furman, 1984a).

At a later point, the same behavior can even represent a way of being like the parents. For example, Kevin's parents were usually thrilled to go out, ready to "have a ball." He gathered from their remarks that they left behind not only their children but also their usual ways of behaving. In time he, like they, felt it was a mark of being grown up to want to "get away from it all" and shed the restrictions of family life.

Whereas these and other factors may contribute to the children's not-so-genuine enjoyment of being without the parents, it is also true that children have many impulses which they have not yet learned to curb or modify and which cause more or less conflict in the parent–child relationship. When the children resent the parental rules and restrictions, they sometimes hope to indulge themselves without their supervision. They may want to eat different kinds or quantities of food, watch forbidden TV programs, play excited games or hit one another, in short, when the cat's away, the mice can play. The baby-sitter who allows the children this kind of fun may be welcomed at the time but may not have an opportunity to witness the less happy aftermath, when the children's own guilt or the parents' disapproval catches up with them. As one child put it, "It was short-run fun but long-run misery."

4

The Early Father-Child Relationship

In some societies the paternal and maternal roles and functions are clearly defined by custom and law, leaving little or no leeway for individual variations. In other societies, or at other times within the same society, the lines of responsibility are less rigidly drawn, allowing much room for familial and personal preference. In our Western post industrial culture patterns, earlier widely accepted models of parenting have undergone considerable change during this century. Related customs and laws are in a state of flux and many different ways of parenting are socially recognized and accepted. This has given groups, families, and individuals a new freedom of choice and opportunity to renovate the fabric of society. It has also burdened us with the need to make choices and to evaluate their effects.

Many of us have struggled to adapt to these societal changes and have attempted to meet our society's demand on us to come up with individual "rules" of parenting. Faced with this task we have felt a greater need than before to explore and understand human nature and the child's psychological requirements. Does a child need a mother and a father? Does each parent have specific roles to fulfill? What happens when mother and father reverse roles or share them equally? Some hope that a father's participation in the baby's earliest bodily care will make him a closer and more meaningful person to the child. Others feel that he will become less important when he ceases to be the family disciplinarian and wage earner. And others yet consider father redundant if mother can provide for her child, or mother redundant if father assumes the task of child care.

As we come to understand better some of the basic patterns and progressions of human mental growth and clarify for ourselves the facilitating roles of the environment, we may be able to answer some of these questions for ourselves to some extent. However, our answers will not provide us with ready prescriptions for bringing up children or for shaping societies. Since parenting is a complex psychological process, rather than a scientific endeavor, a mother's and father's knowledge of child development, however well versed they may be, is at best a helpful contributing factor. Its usefulness will depend on the way in which they integrate it into the other important determinants of their parenting: their individual personalities, past and present experiences, and actual interactions with each child—all within the context of their society.

With this in mind, let us consider our discussions of the child's changing needs and of his interactions with his parents and others as explorations of human growth, not as recipes for child rearing or as norms for an ideal society.

THE FATHER'S ROLE WITH HIS BABY

We have already touched on the development and nature of the father's role. We noted that through his relationship with the mother and their joint anticipation of the baby's birth he may invest his infant mentally as a part of himself already during the months of pregnancy. In that sense the beginning of his relationship with his child is similar to and yet different from that of the mother who includes the child as a bodily as well as a mental part of herself.

As we then followed the development of the mother–child relationship in babyhood, we focused on its close connection with the mother's ongoing care of the baby's bodily needs and the baby's pleasurable experience of being cared for, an interaction which enables the baby to get to know and like both himself and her. We mentioned that during these early months of the baby's life the most important aspects of the father's role are his devotion to the mother–baby unit, his protectiveness of them, and his support for and appreciation of the mother's care of the baby. This helps her to fulfill her task, to enjoy it, and to find it worthwhile. Caring for a baby absorbs a mother in an endless succession of little details, most of which may seem insignificant or even distasteful to adults who are not involved with babies: the way the infant nurses, the hours he sleeps, the times he seems to have a tummy ache, how and when to bathe him, the color and consistency of his bowel movements, whether the new diapers cause him a rash, whether he spits up when he is helped to burp, and many more. Usually, nobody but the father can share the mother's interest in these events, can listen to her accounts of the baby's activities, empathize with her concerns, and appreciate her efforts, because only he has a similar and shared loving investment in their child. However, just because infant care is so absorbing and so focused on primitive bodily concerns, the mother also needs the father's adult companionship. He talks with her about people and events outside the home, shares his thoughts about them, asks her for her views, and appreciates her contribution to their joint adult concerns. In doing so he enriches her life and helps her to regain an appropriate inner balance. When mothers cannot avail themselves of the father's mental support for their care of the baby and when he cannot fulfill their needs for adult companionship, it becomes very difficult for them to devote themselves to their babies. Some mothers then tend to become low in spirits, dissatisfied with themselves, and withdrawn or morose with their babies. Others take flight into activities and interests away from their babies. In either case, their mothering is impaired and their enjoyment of it diminished.

How about helping her with the care of the baby? A father may like to assist the mother by being the baby's occasional or regular baby-sitter. During the infant's first months this does not help him or the child to form a specific relationship. It also does not help the mother to enjoy mothering more, unless it happens in addition to not instead of the father's support and appreciation of her task. This is similar to other situations in our lives when we find ourselves con-

fronted with a new and demanding task. When someone we
care about takes an interest in our struggles, it helps us to
persevere, to master it, and to gain satisfaction from it. It
helps us much less in the long run when that person simply
takes over the job at times, either with the idea of relieving us
of an unpleasant chore or to show us how much better he can
do it.

We have also already discussed the fact that, in the latter
half of the first year, the well-developed infant begins to form
specific new relationships in addition to the now well-
established relationship with the mother. Fathers and
siblings are usually the first to whom the baby's interest
turns. They are well known to the child because he has been
with them so often in the mother's presence and has observed
her friendly contact with them. The most meaningful beginnings of these new relationships indeed take place from the
safety of mother's arms or lap or while she feeds, bathes, or
cleans the baby. During these times the infant watches dad
sitting nearby, touches brother's face, or laughs at sister's
somersaults. The interested and available father then soon
develops special interactions with the now older baby which
are enjoyed by both: a finger game, a song, a chance to hold
dad's pen or to touch his watch, to chew on his jacket buttons,
ride on his knees. The father's participation in the baby's
bodily care does not enhance or speed up this new relationship. Father as mother-substitute is different from father as a
loved person in his own right. Far from becoming "spoiled"
by mother's continuous care, the baby's trusting experience
of it actually furthers his mental growth and enables him to
seek and enjoy new relationships all the sooner.(Burlingham,
1973).

THE FATHER'S RELATIONSHIP WITH
HIS TODDLER

As the infant grows into a toddler he acquires new functions
which help him to be less dependent on his mother and to
approach the father actively. Through self-feeding and
enjoyment of a variety of foods he joins the family meal and
asks for bits of what mother as well as father eat; by walking

and running he can seek out Dad and climb onto his knees; with the help of his beginning use and understanding of speech he can engage father in verbal communication. The diminishing urgency of his needs and the ability to keep mother with him in mind because he now carries a loved mental image of her, make it possible for the toddler to leave mother for short periods and to participate in more advanced father–child activities: driving to the drugstore to get the Sunday newspaper, going for a walk up and down the street, riding on his shoulders or in the stroller, rolling the ball to and fro, getting in the way while Dad cleans the car, looking at a book together. Many of us can recall one or another such activity with our fathers from the later preschool years, although we are likely to have forgotten its beginnings when we were one-and-a-half or two years old.

In this additional and separate relationship the father is spared the full impact of the toddler's relationship with his mother, his clinging possessiveness and provocative rebellion, his fierce controlling love and quick explosive anger, his testing and teasing. When the mother is the main recipient of this tyrannical toddler love she can best help the child to grow beyond it toward a more mature considerate relationship for which the less intense and less conflictual bond with father already acts as an incentive. By contrast, when the father regularly doubles as mother, the toddler relates to both of them in his stormy, contrary way and finds it harder to leave it behind and to become considerate toward loved people.

WHY ARE TODDLERS INCONSIDERATE AND HOW ARE THEY HELPED TO CHANGE?

The toddler's close but primitive relationship with the mothering person contains a kind of love which derives pleasure not only from mutual kindness but also from mutual irritation and conflict. The child actually enjoys doing and saying teasy or contrary things that will "rile mother up," "get her goat," draw her into an excited interplay, or reduce her to helplessness and an ensuing struggle for power. At times, hurting and being hurt are sought and felt as a form of being intensely close to each other. We see remnants of this kind of loving in the later more or less good-natured teasing between people who like one another, or in the intense arguments and fights of couples who are, in this way, closely bound to one another, or in people who feel that something is missing in life when there is no chance for a good old fight.

However, not all of the child's contrariness and lack of consideration stem from his special way of loving. His anger too is primitive and unmitigated in response to the slightest frustration. Mother's "no" to the child's demands, her leaving of him or inattention to him, her inability to arrange life according to his wishes, all are experienced as intolerable, deliberate insults or injuries deserving of total rejection or banishment. This is even true when the mother's restrictions are imposed for the sake of the child's safety and well-being ("No, you mustn't climb on the window"; "No, you may not put stones in your mouth"); or when circumstances beyond her control make it impossible to meet the child's demands. For example, she cannot change the weather so that the child can play in the sandbox nor can she avoid leaving him with a sitter when she has to keep a doctor's appointment. In his angry frustration the toddler does not hesitate to wish mother away, to turn his love to others in the hope that they will prove more compliant, or to attack her and her things in an outburst of temper. He may even "punish" her by doing things to himself which he knows worry her, such as not eating, messing in his pants, or running into the street or other unsafe places. At these times the child's love and need of mother are temporarily forgotten. His actions distress him only later when he wants her again and fears that she may retaliate in kind and not be available to him.

As long as the mother remains the main continuous caring person, the child learns that his angry wishes do not materialize (she stays although he sends her away), that mother's ability to provide satisfactions outweighs the moments when she frustrates, and that she does not retaliate in kind but continues to love and protect her child even though she gets angry at him or her at times. He also learns that, at least most of the time, she does not respond with angry excitement to her child's provocations and does not share his fun in teasing, arguing, and fighting but prefers a more mature way of showing love. These experiences and mother's model help the child toward giving up his demands for loving–hurting tug-of-wars and toward achieving a new way of toning down hate or anger for the sake of love. He will not stop getting angry but, like mother, will begin to temper the nature of his anger in such a way as to preserve his love and his loved one in spite of it. "I am very angry at you but I still care about you and won't harm you." It is a difficult and slow process, determined by many factors but dependent above all on the relationship with the mothering person.

HOW DOES THE FATHER HELP HIS TODDLER WITH THIS STEP?

The father's newly developing specific relationship with his child usually centers on activities which do not involve bodily needs or bodily pleasures. They involve the child's interest in experiences outside himself, offering glimpses of the world at large. The toddler finds a new kind of enjoyment in them, looks forward to them, and is eager to repeat them. They serve as an incentive to branch out from the intense mutually focused interaction with the mother. They are a taste of things to come and whet the appetite for growing up. The times with father may also serve as a respite for child and mother.

Caring for a toddler is, in many ways, even harder than caring for a baby. Mothers need occasional little breathers. The toddler's twenty minute walk or quiet play with Dad can be heaven when dinner is to be got ready. As during the child's babyhood, the father's support and appreciation of the mother's task is vital, both privately and in front of the child. He helps mother and child a great deal when he praises what she does ("That's a fine dinner Mom made"; "I like your nice new shoes. That was kind of Mom to buy them for you"), when he stands by her rules ("Mom says it's nighttime, so we have to stop now"), when he refuses to be hoodwinked into playing the better parent ("No, if Mom doesn't let you have candies now, I won't either"). Moreover, the father's considerate, appreciative behavior toward the mother as well as toward the child sets up a helpful model of what a more

mature relationship is about. For the mother this adult relationship, and the companionship it entails, provide the
necessary antidote to her life with the toddler and a perspective on its stresses. In short, the father's help, once again,
enables her to be a good mother. (R. A. Furman, 1983).

The father's role is both important and difficult to fulfill.
With the provocative, forever-on-the-go toddler, it is all too
easy to be critical of the mother, to minimize her job, and
refuse to help out, or to take over and "do better" (for a couple
of hours). It is also tempting to join the toddler at his level, for
example by playing excited games of tussling, tickling, and
chasing, and then hand back to mother a thoroughly overstimulated child who will ultimately vent his excess tension
in irritability at her. It is much harder to find calm, age-
appropriate activities.

CAN A STEPFATHER OR OTHER PERSON SUBSTITUTE FOR THE BIOLOGICAL FATHER WITH THE TODDLER?

As far as the child is concerned, his need for additional relationships can be met by a variety of other household
members—older siblings, grandparents, uncles. Stepfathers,
adoptive fathers, and foster fathers can often invest themselves fully in their paternal relationship with the child and
love him as if he were their own, because it is a mental rather
than bodily bond. By the same token, some biological fathers
may not be able to develop their relationship with the child,
either through lack of opportunity or due to psychological
interferences in their personalities.

The other aspect of the father's role, namely that of supporting and assisting the child's mother in her task, can
sometimes also be fulfilled by nonbiological fathers, but this
is more difficult for them. If it isn't possible this represents a
big loss, directly to the mother, indirectly to the child.

CAN MOTHER AND FATHER REVERSE ROLES VIS-Á-VIS THEIR TODDLER?

As far as the toddler's well-being and development are concerned, it does not matter who fulfills the main caring role

and provides the opportunity for the ongoing one-to-one relationship. The difficulty lies with the adult. With toddlers, though to a lesser extent than with babies, the capacity for investing oneself fully in the child's care, empathizing with his feelings, and meeting needs is usually easiest for the biological mother for whom the child still represents a bodily part of herself or for the woman (adoptive mother, step-mother, grandmother) who has mothered the child during his first year and made him her own with the help of her special motivation. A father usually has neither the natural mother's close bodily bond with the child nor the adoptive mother's special motivation and preceding first year experience. However, under exceptional circumstances these handicaps could be overcome to a sufficient extent: for example, if the father has been the primary caretaker from the very start.

WHAT HAPPENS WHEN BOTH MOTHER AND FATHER SHARE IN THE TODDLER'S CARE?

We have already talked about the father as a baby-sitter and the father as the provider of an additional relationship which, in contrast to the primary relationship with the mothering person, is focused more on enjoying joint activities and less on bodily need-fulfilling care. When the father shares equally or substantially in the ongoing care, his toddler relates to him more like a second mother. His youngster receives "double" or "split" mothering, an arrangement similar to the alternating care by mother and nanny, mother and grandmother, or mother and professional substitute, such as a day care worker. The changeover in care may follow the child's wishes ("Today I want Daddy to stay with me—to put me to bed—to stay at home with me") or, as is mostly the case, it occurs according to the adults' needs and convenience.

How does alternating mothering feel to the child and how does it affect his ability to master phase-appropriate developmental tasks? Those of us who have worked with such families during the child's toddler years and have traced the effects of shared care through treatment of the child at a later age, appreciate that this is a big topic and too full of individual variations to do it justice in a brief discussion. But we can at least look at some outstanding general features, keeping in mind that "general" is not necessarily "individual" (E. Furman, 1984a).

Perhaps the most obvious thing is that the mothering father invites and receives the same fiercely loving and conflicted investment as the mother and, at the same time, loses out on providing the important special additional relationship. The child now has to outgrow double the amount of gratification, and has less incentive to progress toward newly satisfying relationships because there is no different relationship with the father to pave the way. Sometimes this handicaps the child's later relationships. He continues to relate to others as though they were mothers and he were a toddler.

However, having two mothers is not more gratifying in all respects. When the toddler is with one parent, he does not have the other, either because he dismissed one parent in favor of the other or because he was left by him or her. One of the main tasks of this phase is to take over bodily self-care, to become mother to oneself, in toileting, dressing, or self-feeding. The child with one mother accomplishes this by "leaving" the mother figuratively to do for himself while counting on her continuous availability, much as later on adolescents venture out into the world but rely on the old home being there to touch base with in case of need. The mother's role is to be there to be left (E. Furman, 1982b). By contrast the child who is left by the mother, cannot count on her being there, and this makes becoming independent harder. Likewise, the child who "sends her away" and turns to his other mother or mothering father for care, is not on the way to independence, but intent on changing mothers. Children with double mothering often lag in their wish to care for themselves. The changes in caretaker tend to make it more desirable to preserve the being-taken-care-of relationship than to relinquish it for the sake of independence. These children sometimes have to be cajoled or pushed to do for themselves and regard self-care as a chore instead of preferring to be masters of their bodies and resenting it when the adults don't let them ("Me do, me do").

Double mothering also makes it more difficult for the

toddler to cope with angry feelings and to achieve that most important step of taming anger for the sake of love which makes consideration for others possible. The child who controls which parent should care for him, enjoys the power of summoning the current favorite and banishing the one he currently dislikes. But this does not help him to learn to accept and get along with the parent even when he is angry at him or her ("I'm mad at you, but I still love you enough to want to keep you and even to forgive you"). Nor does it help him to cope with the inevitable times when the parent has to leave him, a fact he is then apt to interpret along the lines of his own experience: "He leaves me because he doesn't want me, doesn't like me, or wants someone else more"—a scary and unsettling thought. It makes the child dread the parent's anger as much as he enjoys the omnipotence of his own anger, and it thwarts realistic understanding of the many reasons for leaving and being left. When the decision about who takes care is in the adults' hands, the toddler feels forever frustrated in his longing, and helpless to influence or bring about the closeness of his loved ones. Loving two mothers also means missing both and resenting the absence of either. This immeasurably increases the child's anger and makes it once again, though now for different reasons, harder to tame.

Another reason why shared care makes it harder for the toddler to master the conflict of loving and hating the same person, is that the similar relationship with two people invites splitting them up into a good one and a bad one. The "good" one receives all the love and is invested with all the virtues, the "bad" one gets all the hate, can't do anything right, and is blamed. Such a division of loving and hating may switch at a moment of frustration from one parent to the other, but it may also lead to permanent preferences and difficulty in liking people according to their real merits. Both like and dislike are, in these instances, based not only on what the parent actually does but on the opportunity to divert anger to someone else instead of modifying it and tempering it with love. In fairytales and Westerns we reexperience these early solutions to loving and hating in our attitudes to the all-good and all-bad characters, the "good guys" and the "bad guys". In real life it is not helpful when we need to safeguard our love and loved ones at the cost of hatred for others. When we cannot rely on our love for others to hold the fort against damaging anger, we also cannot trust that others can truly love us. Such unresolved toddler conflicts are not always the outcome of equal care by two mothering persons. They can also result from other experiences, such as separations over longer periods or a relationship with a mother who herself suffers from this difficulty, and cannot tame her anger at her child out of love for him.

The child who remains plagued by unmastered mixed feelings may later experience difficulty in separating from his parents and in enjoying relationships with others.

As a toddler Jane had been cared for by mother and father in alternating shifts due to the parents' work schedule. At that time she showed most difficulty when both parents were at home. She would either play up one against the other or was irritable and unhappy unless she commanded both parents' full presence and attention. She was very slow to become clean and had wetting and soiling accidents for a long time. She also did not like to dress herself and went about it so slowly that it often ended up being the parent's job. When Jane started nursery school at four years, she clung to her mother. For many weeks she could not feel comfortable at school without her and could not allow herself to like her teacher or to enjoy the school activities. She worried that mother might not come to pick her up and that mother might enjoy herself without Jane so much that she would prefer to stay away. At home, however, Jane spoke of nursery school in glowing terms and wished she could go to school on weekends and holidays. Whenever she felt dissatisfied with mother she declared that the teachers were much nicer and the school toys were much more fun. In working with Jane and her family on this difficulty we learned that Jane's unresolved feelings about mother's and father's alternating care now affected her relationship to home and school. She viewed the teacher as a second mother rather than as a person with whom she could form a special additional relationship. At home, when she was assured of mother's presence, she vented her anger by stating her wish for that second "better" teacher-mother; at school she warded off her temptation to be disloyal to mother by not allowing herself to enjoy school, and was plagued with concern that mother would be disloyal to her and abandon her. She expected her mother would get rid of her if she proved unsatisfying, just as she, Jane, wanted to exchange mothers when her mother displeased her. Jane had failed to temper her toddler anger, had not yet learned to love a person even though she got angry at him or her at times.

Shared care does not have to produce adverse effects. When the parents are aware of the stresses and potential pitfalls it entails, they can help to minimize and overcome them. There are many ways to do that. For example, it helps when one parent takes the role of sitter and supports the child's relationship with the main mothering person; it helps when times of absences and takeover are regular and prepared for so that the child always knows what to expect, feels less helpless and angry; most importantly, it helps when the parents can feel with the child and assist him in recognizing and expressing his anger, sadness and other feelings about the arrangements so that he can better master them.

WHAT HAPPENS TO THE TODDLER'S RELATIONSHIPS WHEN HIS CARE IS SHARED EQUALLY BY SEVERAL PEOPLE?

Sometimes this means that others help with the care in the presence of the mother, so that she retains the primary relationship with her child, as in a big household. The child can then turn back to her at all times and treats the others as part substitutes and part additional persons to relate to. Even when the mother is not always there, she may still remain the main caretaker whose relationship helps to mitigate the stress of changes and separations. In extreme instances of multiple care, however, there is a danger that the child's relationships will be spread so thinly that none of them will be sufficiently close and meaningful to influence the toddler's mental growth, to help him overcome his primitive self-interest and intolerance, to modify his anger, and develop appropriate concern for others. Children who become arrested at this developmental point may never be able to maintain a mutually caring or trusting relationship and may act on their sadistic or violent impulses for personal gains, for perverse satisfaction, or in response to frustration. This makes it difficult for them to maintain a marital relationship or to parent consistently, may lead to spouse and child abuse, and may jeopardize adjustment to the wider social community. Some adult psychopathic criminals suffer from this kind of pathology, as illustrated, for example, in Truman Capote's book, *In Cold Blood* (1965). With young delinquents of this type the most effective correction lies in providing a new opportunity for a close long-term relationship which may, belatedly, fulfill the parental role with the toddler. Such help consists of many years of skilled devotion, but may prove only partially effective. It is not known exactly at which point a person can still benefit and correct earlier deficits. There are many individual variations. In general, the younger the child, the better the outlook.

Similar difficulties may result from serious disruptions or inadequacies in the toddler's relationships; for example, when the mothering person is permanently lost without adequate replacement, or when the continuous caring person provides insufficient loving experiences for the child (Aichhorn, 1925; Bowlby, 1944; Friedlander, 1947).

5

Mother–Father–Child

THE YOUNG PRESCHOOLER AND HIS PARENTS

As the two-year-old toddler gradually grows into a three- to four-year-old preschooler, the nature of his relationships change and they serve new functions in the child's developing personality. Needs become less urgent and the preschooler is more able to meet them on his own, be it getting a drink of water, putting on his coat and shoes, or tolerating a feeling. He also considers himself more clearly and stably a person in his own right. Bodily and mental dependency cease to be the main tie to the loved one. The child becomes more interested in people as people: how they look, what they do, and how he compares to them. Mother and father now assume a new and more equal importance and meaning in the child's life, and their roles change.

Even in casual encounters, preschoolers impress us with their intense personal curiosity about people and with their spontaneity in sharing equally personal information about themselves.

Accompanying her mother at the supermarket, three-year-old Jenny suddenly asked the checkout clerk, "Are you a mommy?" When the startled woman replied that she had two children, Jenny upstaged her with, "We have lots of children—me and John and Bill and my Mommy even has a baby."

At the bus stop, four-year-old Jeremy observed to his Dad

in a loud whisper, "Why does that man have a cane? Is he a grandpa?"

In the doctor's waiting room Heather told everyone that she was going to get a shot with her checkup. The one woman who evinced interest was treated to additional impressive news, "And my sister got her shot last week. And I got a big doll for Christmas and she makes wee-wee if you put water in her. And these are my new shoes," and Heather showed them off to good advantage.

Some people are put off by the children's lack of respect for privacy, some react defensively, especially when the child's observation or question exposes their vulnerable spots, but many people sense that the youngster invites them to participate in a specific way of relating—a kind of mutual admiration society—and they respond in kind. When a nursery school teacher, attuned to this kind of relationship, meets a new pupil, she usually says something like, "I am glad to meet you, Charlie, you have very handsome big cowboy boots on. I bet they are quite new." Or, "So you are Susan. Your Mommy told me about you and I like the blue ribbons in your hair." And while Charlie or Susan beam coyly, the teacher generally proceeds to show off a bit herself and invites the child's admiration, "Now we have some very nice toys here for you to see. You might especially like our big new blocks in the corner here and the dollhouse over there."

Wherever preschoolers live, play, and learn, their focus is on watching and finding out what others are about and on drawing their admiring attention: "Look at me"; "See how high I can jump"; "I have the biggest ball." This type of behavior is so commonplace that we often take it for granted and do not fully appreciate that it represents a phase-specific way of loving and being loved which would strike us as inappropriate if we encountered more than a touch of it in the relationships of adults. (Can you imagine the nursery school teacher meeting the child's mother with a comment on *her* clothes?) We are not even surprised when the youngster's unhappiness with or anger at his loved ones manifest themselves in the same vein; when he feels envious and inadequate in the face of their prowess or when he tries to inflict these feelings on them by boosting himself up a notch: "*You* don't even get to go to her party!"; "My candy is bigger than yours"; "Our car is more fancy."

Inevitably, gratifying one's curiosity entails opportunities to make comparisons which may arouse admiration, envy, or cause blows to one's self-esteem. How intense such feelings are and how well they can be tolerated and mastered depends on whether one also feels appreciated and loved for one's own qualities ("Yes, John is a very good ballplayer but you are especially good at block building. That house you built yesterday was just great"), whether one is allowed, or even invited, to share in the other person's desirable attributes ("I got a new board game and *you* can play it with me"), and whether one can see one's way to achieving the same or similar accomplishment. ("I've been cutting out cookies for a long time and that's why I'm so good at it, but now you can start practicing and you'll see that very soon yours will turn out very well too. Look at this last one. It is much better than the one you did before.") The more chances there are for becoming like the loved, admired person or to share in their desirable "greatness," and the more their appreciation of one's own qualities helps to soften the hardship of one's envy and inadequacy, the more gratifying is the relationship of the "mutual admiration society" and the better it serves its functions in the preschooler's personality growth: to provide knowledge about the world, models to emulate, and ways of making them a part of oneself. It is in the nature of this, and to some extent of all relationships that when we love and admire someone very much we want to become like him or her, at least in some respects. Many of our attitudes, interests, values, and ideas stem from identifications with loved, admired persons. Most of us remember, perhaps from a later period in our lives, a friend or beloved teacher who instilled in us the beginning of a new interest or way of looking at life which have now long since become an integral part of ourselves. Some of us also remember occasions when the wished-for ideal seemed all too far away and hopelessly unattainable. In this vein a young woman recalled a commercial for cameras which she used to watch as a four-year-old. It showed next to one another a snapshot of a little girl with her doll, then one of her graduating from college in full regalia, and finally one of her wedding where she appeared in white, accompanied by her handsome groom. "I watched it over and over," she commented, "and wished so desperately that I could get there just as fast. It seemed that for me it took forever."

Of course, some changes lie far in the future and some things one can never have for oneself. It is very difficult for young children to content themselves with having to wait or with having to do without altogether and still be able to enjoy what they are and have now. This is especially true when the youngsters' curiosity and admiration focus on what is closest to home, namely their own bodily attributes and functions and those of their most important loved ones, their parents, and perhaps siblings. We noted earlier that even babies perceive many of the differences between mother and father—their different looks, voices, smell, feel. The toddler's observations and experiences with his parents amplify and deepen this knowledge and children early on start to compare themselves with the adults, often with painful awareness of their own helplessness and incompetence in contrast to the grown-ups' power and seeming perfection. During the preschool years the child becomes particularly aware of the sexual differences between people. Who is a man? Who is a woman? What is a boy? What is a girl? How are they alike and how do they differ? Understanding the facts is quite difficult, but it is perhaps even harder to accept and feel comfortable with one's own sexual identity and immaturity. Children inevitably perceive that others are not only differently endowed but may be bigger, stronger, and more capable. Although the little boy and girl may know in which ways they are like the adult of the same sex, the differences between boy and man, girl and woman, are almost as impressive as the differences between the sexes. Such discoveries pose a threat to the child's bodily and mental self-esteem and cause envy and anger. The child's concerns and misgivings may be helped by intellectual understanding, but they are tolerated and mastered only through the relationship with the parents.

When we say, "The father shows a boy what a man is about," we mean that, in order for a boy to understand and like himself as a boy and to want to grow up to be a man and father, he has to have a father who enjoys being one and who serves as a model. Indeed it takes that, but also much more. The son's wish to adopt the paternal model depends very much on the nature of the father–child relationship and on the father's attitude to his son's manliness and growing up in all areas of daily living. If a boy is to feel that he wants to become a man, that he has a chance to reach this goal, and that he still amounts to something worthwhile now although he is little and less competent, he has to experience the kind of relationship that most ordinary, devoted fathers provide. He has to experience the mutual bond of shared activities in which the father enjoys and encourages the child's participation ("Hey, want to come and rake leaves with me? It's more fun when we do it together."), the trust that the father will help him learn the admired skills and appreciate the child's efforts and successes ("What a great job you're doing. You've really learned to handle that rake well."), and the opportunities for sharing in father's "greatness" ("Dad and I raked all the leaves"; or "My Daddy can count to a thousand"; or "My Dad won't let you bother me").

However, it is not only the relationship with the father and the model he offers that help a boy to consolidate and like his sexual identity. The mother's love of her boy and of her man are equally important.

Likewise, the little girl needs a supportive relationship with a mother who enjoys being a mother and a woman, and she needs a relationship with a father who loves and admires little girls. She too needs to know "What a man is about" in the widest sense. When a girl merely views a man as a person with a different body but lacks the context of a close relationship to know how he feels, thinks, and acts, she is much more likely to feel angry and deprived. Her self-esteem is immeasurably enhanced by his appreciation of her and of her achievements and by the opportunity to include him in her self-love: "*my* Daddy" becomes a part of the "me" and lends it the sometimes essential boost at times of feeling inadequate.

Assisting the preschooler in consolidating and accepting his sexual identity and immaturity as well as helping the young child to develop new interests, skills, and goals are important functions of the relationship with both parents, but they are not the only ones. Actually, when we ask people what the parents' main role with their children is, they usually answer: "Make them mind"; "Discipline them"; "Tell them how to behave"; "Stop them from being naughty and getting into trouble." In other words, we tend to think of the areas in which the parents' and children's wishes conflict. And this happens quite often.

Sometimes it happens when the child wants very much to be like the parents but cannot bear to wait and acquire laboriously the necessary know-how (Johnny "borrows" Dad's pen and letter paper and scribbles busily, using up page after page—"just like Dad"), or when the child wants to be grown up in ways inappropriate to his mental or bodily capacities (Mary refuses to go to bed because she wants to join Mom and Dad at a concert; Brian insists on lifting the heavy shopping bag, like Dad, drops it and spills the contents). At other times the parent-child conflict arises from the child's need for independence and his wish to gratify his needs and impulses directly, immediately, and without interference ("I don't want to wait for dinner, I'm taking my cookies off the tray now"; "I want to play in the sandbox and I don't care if my clothes get all muddy"; "But I like to run around naked, it's fun!"; "I like to jump up and down on the couch, whee!"; "No, I won't stop and if you won't let me, *you'll* get it." And the parent often does "get it," in word and in deed).

It is said that education consists of "Not this but that; not here but there; not now but later." Teaching and learning how to tolerate frustration, how to delay gratification, how to accept compromises and substitutes are a tall task for parents and children. We shall talk about its complexity in more detail later. Suffice it to say at this point that all measures are doomed to failure unless they are taken in the context of a close relationship. Its ties reward the young child's efforts and help him soften his resentment. Much hardship can be borne for the sake of gaining the parents' loving appreciation ("Now there's a good girl. It's hard to wait but I knew you could do it") and many a temptation can be resisted with the help of the parents' spoken, or implied, appeal to the child's wish to become like them ("*Daddy* waits for his dinner"; "*Bigger* children take care of their clothes").

THE OLDER PRESCHOOLER AND HIS PARENTS

In time the preschooler's "mutual admiration society" bond with the parents also paves the way toward a new and more adult relationship with them. Thoughtful love for another person takes the place of the earlier self-centered demand for attention, and sexual and other differences between people serve as a source of attraction and pleasure rather than of discomfort and competition.

Five-year-olds and kindergarteners often astonish us with their spontaneous helpfulness which stems from genuine loving concern—"Mom, I cleaned up the playroom. I wanted to give you a nice surprise"; "Dad, you look tired. Did you have a hard day at the office? I'll get you the newspaper"; "Mom, I let Sally play with my blocks so she wouldn't bother you." Their occasional gifts begin to be chosen with a view to what the recipient might enjoy and bear less often the mark of seeking admiration for oneself. We are apt to hear, "I made you a picture for your kitchen so you have something to look at when you cook dinner," instead of the earlier, "Isn't this the best picture of a house you ever saw? You can have it." The change is neither sudden nor complete. Features of the child's earlier levels of relationship persist to some extent. The five-year-old still enjoys mother's fulfillment of his needs and her bodily and mental care. He still indulges in occasional teases and toddlerlike tugs-of-war, and there remains a good deal of wanting to impress others and be admired by them. But there is a new ability to give of oneself in love and to seek a partner to complement rather than to enhance oneself.

Father and mother become additionally significant in their roles as husband and wife. Children have now reached the point in development when, through their own feelings for each of the parents, they can understand the parents' mutuality, the complementary and cooperative nature of the marital relationship, the capacity to give to one another, and to create something jointly. This applies to the parents' sexual relationship and ability to make babies as well as to their many other activities; for example the way they share and complement one another's daily tasks to make a home. The child not only likes to share in that relationship but may want now this, now that parent as his or her exclusive partner. It is frustrating and disappointing to feel left out of some aspects of the parental relationship, to experience the fact that two is company and three is a crowd, and to realize how one falls short compared to one's rival. Some of us recall such moments in our own lives. One young man related, "I used to always get into my parents' bed in the morning, right in the middle between them." One woman remembered how she always "hung on my Daddy's arm," and another still felt half-pleased, half-ashamed for "talking a mile a minute so that Mom and Dad couldn't talk to each other."

When I once asked a group of high school seniors why a five-year-old girl needed a father, one woman student replied, "She needs him to learn what it is like to be loved by a man." Freud made a related comment many years ago, "A mother's task is to teach her son how to love." These are indeed important experiences. It is only when the child is thus loved that he or she can appreciate and come to terms with the fact that the parents' love for their son or daughter differs from their love for each other.

I should like to touch on another aspect of father's and mother's role, namely how they combine within their own personalities, or complement in the relationship with one another, the universal bisexual elements which exist in each of us along with our specific sexual identity. It is widely recognized that men and women can usefully integrate their masculine and feminine, passive and active tendencies into their individual lives and activities; for example, men can find satisfaction in taking care of people (as fathers, physicians, nurses, chefs, etc.) and women can be efficient and effective with machinery (as drivers, engineers, scientists, etc.). Some societies restrict their members' opportunities for such activities (e.g., Kikuyu women are not allowed to hunt); others make definite provision for them (e.g., Samoan men do most of the cooking); and others yet expect each person to make full use of his or her individual potential. This latter pattern is becoming more prevalent in the United States and Europe. Our children observe that some mothers enjoy doing woodwork and others do not, some fathers like to prepare a meal and others do not. In their preschool years children begin to learn about these preferences in their parents, they take part in many of the activities, and test which ones appeal to them.

It is sometimes thought that when a society restricts its members' activities according to their sexual identities (men can only do this, women can only do that), it imposes severe frustrations on the individual and may cause them to resent their sexual identity or to envy the other sex. It is often forgotten that we can achieve gratification not only by doing things ourselves but also by enjoying vicariously what others do.

When one young girl transferred from an all-girl to a coeducational elementary school, her parents asked her, after some time, how she liked her new school. She replied that it was wonderful because she now never needed to be naughty, the boys did it all for her and she could just sit back and enjoy it. Vicarious gratification assumes a special dimension when it occurs in the context of a close relationship. Many men gratify their femininity by gaining pleasure from their wives' lives—their appearance, activities, mothering, feeling, and thinking (R. A. Furman, 1983). Similarly, many women have for centuries gratified their masculine strivings through the lives of their fathers, husbands, and sons. Women who, by choice or necessity, restrict themselves to the roles of housewives and mothers are not *necessarily* frustrated, bitter, or depressed but may complement their direct satisfactions with those they indirectly experience in their closest relationships with their men. Pride in one's child's achievements is taken for granted, deep satisfaction in one's spouse's pursuits or accomplishments is equally possible. This is of course also true in areas that are quite unrelated to sexual identity or bisexual tendencies. Most of us are not "best" at everything and, although we may sometimes envy others their accomplishments or gifts, we often derive pleasure from their performances, be they artists, athletes, politicians, scientists, or just the clever man next door who always gets his roses to bloom. In the ordinary family, the parents' division of labor is not based on superiority and inferiority, or on strictly apportioned pseudo-equality, but derives naturally from what and how each can best contribute to the common goal of the whole family's well-being.

THE PASSING OF THE PRESCHOOL YEARS

Although children forget the specifics of these early impressions, the feeling tone of their experiences with their parents as a couple and as father and mother, remain with them, become a part of themselves in the form of interests and goals, ideals and values, and affect their perceptions of themselves and others. They determine, to a considerable extent, the children's later comfort with themselves and with their sexuality as well as their capacity to maintain satisfying relationships with men and women, to enjoy a marital bond and a family, and to parent.

Whereas these effects become evident in the child's future life, others manifest themselves in the present. Painful lessons are learned of what the child can and cannot have now, of tolerating being left out of some aspects of the parental life, of appreciating that one will have to wait a long time and master many things before one can become adult like the parents. Older now, and wiser, the child gives up some of his intense all-consuming investment in his parents. His horizon widens to include new relationships and new pursuits outside the immediate family. Teachers, friends, school, sports, and hobbies become much more important and meaningful.

In this as in the earlier phases of the child's development, the parent–child relationship serves a double role. On the one hand it meets the child's current bodily and psychological needs, on the other hand it becomes a building block in the growing structure of the child's personality. This means that the child, at each developmental level, gradually internalizes—takes into himself—the parental function. What was done for and to him becomes a part of himself. When the end of a developmental phase is reached, the child becomes able to do for himself what the parents used to do. In this way he comes closer to being an adult with each step. Of course phases overlap and do not start or finish on a certain day. The child's taking over of parental functions and building his own personality takes place piecemeal and extends over a long period. By the time children are ready for elementary school, they are able to take care of many of their bodily needs, have established their sexual identity, have acquired many skills, and mastered many tasks. Toward the end of the preschool phase the child takes a particularly big step. He takes in the parental morals, their "rights and wrongs." These become the basis of his own conscience, of his standards for and judgments of himself. From this time on, and forever after, when we do something "right" (in accord with the demands of conscience), our conscience makes us feel good about ourselves, and when we do something "wrong," it makes us feel bad or guilty—even if nobody praises or scolds or even knows about the deed. Although the conscience is not an exact replica of the parental values, ideals, and admonitions, it does, to a considerable extent, represent them inside the child's mind and this lessens his dependence on the "outside" parents. We shall discuss the conscience and its role again at a later point.

WHAT HAPPENS WHEN THE PRESCHOOLER'S MOTHERING OR FATHERING PERSON IS NOT THE BIOLOGICAL PARENT?

As we already know from our previous discussions, adoptive parents, stepparents, or foster parents can often invest themselves fully in the parental relationships with the child and substitute very adequately for the biological parent(s). We know also that some biological parents are unable to function as parents. When the nonbiological parents are also marital partners, it is particularly helpful to the child's development, allowing him or her to relate to them not only as mother and father but also as a couple. The preschooler, however, in contrast to the younger toddler, is likely to become aware of the reality that one or both of his parents are not his progenitors, even if he has never known the biological parents. His phase-appropriate curiosity about the functions of people's bodies, the origins of babies, and the relationships between people lead him to question and find out about his own history, or, if he knows it already, to intensify his interest. As the child learns the reasons for not living with his biological parents, he is usually confronted with sad or frightening events; for example, the biological parent died or was killed, or divorced from the marital partner, or was unable to parent and decided to find another home for the child. Such happenings may be painful and difficult to understand. They may be experienced as threatening and may increase the child's sense of being helpless because he had no control over them or, as one little boy put it, "And they didn't even ask my permission" (E. Furman, 1974; Wieder, 1977).

Although nothing can altogether obviate such distress, children can be helped to cope with it and master it sufficiently so that it does not impede their healthy progressive development. The best way is to help children through their trusting relationships with their substitute parents who can discuss these matters with the child, assist him in understanding them, empathize with his hurt, and soothe it with their love (Krementz, 1982). It is a difficult task for substitute parents but one that serves to strengthen their relationships with the child as well as to help him. Experience has shown that in instances where children cannot ask their parents, or do not get truthful answers, or cannot get parental help with the mastery of facts and feelings, it is much harder for the children to come to terms with the realities, and their relationships with the substitute parents may suffer to an extent. This can be a great loss for the children and the substitute parents.

WHAT HAPPENS WHEN THE PRESCHOOLER HAS ONLY ONE PARENT?

In families where one parent has died, or permanently disappeared, the child is often helped very much by a substitute who maintains a relationship with the child and fulfills some of the absent parent's functions. For example, when there is no mother, an older sister, female relative, or housekeeper may take on this role, or when the father is deceased, an older brother, uncle, grandfather, or male friend of the family may be of help. Such substitute relationships provide opportunities for getting to know what a man or woman are "all about," they serve as models for identification, and they bolster the child's self-esteem by enabling him or her to share in their adult status. At best, however, the child still misses out on living with and learning about the parents' husband–wife relationship. This is a considerable loss for him at the time as well as for his future life and presents him with a special stress to overcome. There is also the additional stress of having to understand and cope with the reasons for the absence of the parent (R. A. Furman, 1980, 1983; E. Furman, 1983).

Children who cannot avail themselves of a substitute relationship have a much harder time. They miss out on the gratifications and functions of the relationships with parents of both sexes and often feel themselves diminished in comparison with more fortunate peers. In lieu of a realistic image of the unavailable mother or father, they fill in the gaps with their fantasies which tend to picture the missing parent as ideal or potentially threatening, as too "good" or too "bad," or both.

Five-year-old Henry had initially been cared for by his unmarried mother and from age one-and-a-half years on had lived in a small children's home, staffed entirely by women and located in isolation on the outskirts of a little village. He was well loved by the matron (director–nurse) who came rather close to being a substitute mother. However, he had hardly any access to men and no chance at all to relate to one. When I knew him, just after the Second World War, there was as yet no television, so that he rarely even saw pictures of men. Yet Henry talked about men almost constantly, in part asking about them, in part describing his vivid ideas about what they could or would do. The mailman, seen at a distance from the window, and the milkman with whom he occasionally exchanged a greeting, became figures of great importance in Henry's life. Sometimes he fantasied that they would take him to their homes and lavish their love and gifts on him, but at other times he feared they would attack and hurt him or appear in the dark of night to frighten or kidnap him.

At times he boasted about what he would be like when he grew up, the fantastic feats he would perform, and the unrealistic favors or punishments he would bestow on others. In reality Henry was quite lovable at times but lacking in self-control and quick to anger. He also was a bully—the mark of the child with little self-confidence. He attacked the weaker ones but became fearful and submissive when he knew or suspected that someone could really stand up to him.

Henry's situation was extreme but not unique. He and others like him helped me to recognize how great a thirst there is in children for the "other" parent, even when they are loved by one parent and when they have little opportunity to compare themselves with children in other families. It was also impressive to see how difficult it is for children to form a realistic idea of a man in the absence of real experience.

Usually children cared for by one parent have much more access to men and women and, given their own wish and the parent's permission or encouragement, it is easier for them to get to know people and to build relationships with them. The more satisfactory these turn out to be, the better it is for the child. However, some measure of stress is probably unavoidable (E. Furman, 1981b).

Andy's early experiences were more fortunate than Henry's, although he too was without a father, the latter having died when Andy was a baby. Andy lived with his devoted mother who appreciated and supported his growing boyishness. She had loved her husband and often talked with Andy about his father so that the boy formed some idea of what his father had been like. They also discussed the father's death, and with his mother's help, Andy learned to cope with the difficult facts and feelings related to it. Andy maintained a close relationship also with his grandfather and the two enjoyed many activities and social times together. There were also many contacts with families of friends and less intimate experiences with people in the wider community. As a preschooler Andy was well developed and capable. When Andy entered nursery school, however, he experienced difficulty. He compared himself unfavorably to his boy peers. They appeared bigger, stronger, and more competent to him and he feared that he could neither compete with them nor be accepted and liked by them. In order to hide his presumed inferiority and to gain friends, he limited himself to copying the ideas and behavior of others, did not utilize his own abilities, and at times withdrew from activities altogether after half-hearted efforts. When other fathers visited or picked up their children, Andy either pretended not to notice or watched with wistful awe and longing. He reproached his mother for not providing a father for him, yet resented her attention to male friends. At the start of elementary school his standards for himself were unrealistically high, and when he inevitably failed to live up to them, his early conscience was very harsh. Guilt feelings lowered his self-esteem and self-confidence.

Single parent families, due to separation or divorce, vary greatly. In some the children continue to maintain close and satisfying relationships with both parents, in others they hardly ever see the parent who does not live in the home, in others yet the parents' remarriage requires that the children adapt to two families and several new siblings. The individual circumstances and relationships vary so much that it is impossible to generalize. It is fair to say, however, that the breakup of the husband–wife relationship and the dissonance between them constitute a special stress for the child (Wallerstein and Kelly, 1980; Goldstein and Solnit, 1984; E. Furman and R. A. Furman, in press). It also constitutes a special and difficult task for the parents to help their child, to feel with him, and to understand his hardships at a time when the parent him or herself is embittered and upset or elated and relieved.

In general it is more difficult for children to feel good about themselves and to develop realistic inner standards and expectations when one parent is physically or emotionally unavailable to them (and this can even happen in two-parent families) and/or when the paternal and maternal figure do not maintain a marital relationship. When at least one parent recognizes that the situation is stressful for the child and is willing and able to help, these difficulties can be modified and mastered to a considerable extent. By contrast, the child's chances of a healthy development are further impeded when the parent(s) fail the child in this respect, either by denying the impact on the child or by expecting his feelings to be the same as theirs.

CAN A PERSON RAISED IN A FAMILY WITHOUT A HUSBAND—WIFE RELATIONSHIP HAVE ONE HIMSELF AND CAN HE BE A PROPER PARENT?

The child's experience of the parents' marital relationship plays an important part in the adult wish for and comfort with this kind of relationship, and the ability to parent indeed depends on having been parented, but these are not the only determining factors. Other early and later life experiences also matter, as well as each person's unique ways of coping with them. Early stresses may be overcome or compensated for and an individual's weak points in some areas may be balanced by strengths in other areas. Being able to maintain a relationship with a spouse and parenting are not all or none pursuits; at best they are not perfect. Sometimes an unhappy experience with two parents can cause as much or more difficulty as not having one parent.

In discussing this topic, one young man, in his late teens, related how distressed he was by his father's repeated mention of the fact that he, the father, had grown up without a father, had suffered much hardship because of it, but had worked extra hard and supported his bereaved family, and paid for his own education. Holding himself up as a model, the father complained that his son failed to achieve as well and did not make good use of the advantages he enjoyed. The son, our young man, felt sorry for his father's deprivation and bad about his own shortcomings but, he sighed, "My father had one great advantage that I never had. He didn't have a Dad who was constantly criticizing him and telling him how lucky he was."

CAN ONE ESCAPE OR MODIFY WHAT IS PASSED ONTO ONESELF BY ONE'S PARENTS?

One cannot altogether escape what is passed on because the full development of one's personality depends on taking in aspects of one's parents. However, one need not take into oneself everything, and one can and does modify many features to a considerable extent. Moreover, we often take in what the parents seemed like to us or what we wished they were, rather than how they actually acted. No parent is perfect. Recognizing and accepting one's parents' fallibility, quirks, and unhelpful traits, is an essential part of growing up which starts already in the later preschool years. The parents often help the child with this process when they are aware of their shortcomings and encourage the child explicitly to avoid repeating them in their own personalities. ("I am not good at being punctual and it makes it so hard for me and for others. I hope you will be very different and much better in that way than I am.") Sometimes we become aware much later that we are just like our parents and can work at changing our attitudes. Often, what we have taken in from our parents is altered or overlaid by subsequent identifications with other people who have become very meaningful to us. But there are always some parental aspects, helpful and unhelpful, which we perpetuate in ourselves without even knowing them. However, it is also important to remind ourselves that we do not simply consist of what is passed on to us by our parents. Each person's individual endowment, his propensity to develop special gifts, or to be subject to special deficits, also assert themselves and interact with the environmental influences in such a way as to produce a unique personality.

WHAT HAPPENS TO THE PRESCHOOLER'S SEXUAL IDENTITY WHEN MOTHER AND FATHER REVERSE ROLES OR WHEN THEY KEEP STRICTLY TO MALE AND FEMALE "STEREOTYPED" ROLES?

A boy's or girl's sexual identity relates to gender; that is, their male or female characteristics and functions. They compare themselves in this respect to each other and to the adults. They learn that, as they grow up, they will come to be like the parent of their own gender. A person's gender is not determined by his activities, clothes, manners, or by nonsexual

bodily attributes, such as gait or facial expression. Such
characteristics may be associated with masculinity or femininity in some societies or in the minds of some individuals,
but they do not define sexual identity. We realize how true this
is when we remind ourselves that a woman in pants may be a
fully functioning wife and mother and that very manly Scot-
tish men wear skirts. When little Mary tells us that her friend
is a girl because she has long hair, we know that Mary either
does not yet appreciate the real nature of sexual differences or
prefers not to think of them.

A young child is helped to conceive correctly his or her
own sexual identity by understanding what really makes a
person a boy or a girl, a man or a woman. Children are helped
to feel good about their sexual identity when both parents
appreciate them for what they are and when the parent of
their same sex feels comfortable with his or her own sexual
identity. As long as this is the case, it does not matter whether
the parents reverse roles in nonsexual activities or keep to
"stereotypes."

The difficulty for the child arises when the parents are
not comfortable with their sexual identities, when they feel
inadequate as men or women, or dissatisfied with their
gender. When such emotional overtones determine a parent's
insistence on or avoidance of certain activities, clothes, or
other attributes, they convey their inner discomfort to the
child. Such parents are also likely to have difficulty in appreciating the child's sexual identity and in helping him or her to
understand and value members of both sexes. Thus, the problem does not arise from whether mother or father fixes the car
or washes the dishes, but from the way they feel about it in
relation to their sexual identity. Children are very astute in
sensing their parents' feelings and respond to them.

THE ROLE OF THE PARENTS WITH
THE OLDER CHILD

For the schoolchild and adolescent the parents remain essential figures. They not only provide for the growing individual's physical well-being but help consolidate and enrich the
foundations of his or her emotional growth which they laid,

almost singlehanded, during the child's earlier years: taking care of oneself, relating to others, establishing and maintaining ideals and values, acquiring interests and knowledge, learning new activities, and, eventually, growing away and becoming more than ever like the parents as self-supporting adults with a mate and family of their own.

In the child's mind, however, the parents, from school age on, lose some of their earlier all-absorbing significance and intense emotional investment. People and activities outside the immediate family circle increasingly gain in importance and contribute their share to the development of the child's personality (A. Freud, 1958; R. A. Furman, 1983).

6

Friends and Relatives

WHAT IS A FRIEND?

Many of us know what it feels like to have a friend, yet when we are asked to define it we often falter. "A friend is someone who helps you when you are in need, who keeps you company when you feel lonely, who stands up for you when others are against you, who listens to your troubles, who visits you when you are sick, who loves you in spite of your short-comings." Yes, but so does a mother. Isn't there a difference? "Oh yes, a friend does more. He enjoys things you enjoy, he shares some of your interests and activities, he goes to the movies with you or to a party." Yes, but so does a companion, a colleague, an acquaintance, even a parent or sibling. "But a friend is more someone your own age, a peer." Yes, but a peer is not necessarily a friend and a friend need not be a peer. Indeed, a friend is all these things and can be of any age—someone who can empathize and sympathize with our feel-ings, who shares some of our interests and activities, who helps and supports us even when it causes him inconvenience or requires some self-sacrifice. But surely the most important characteristic of a friendship is its mutuality, the fact that we do all these same things for our friend. This sustained give and take, this reciprocity, distinguishes a friendship from all other relationships and as such requires a considerable degree of emotional maturity in each partner.

WHEN CAN ONE BEGIN TO HAVE A FRIEND?

Babies certainly can't make friends. They may be intently interested in other babies, stare at them, follow their movements, even smile at them, but they do not turn to another baby for help or comfort, do not extend themselves to others, and would not even be able to engage in a joint game. Toddlers sometimes enjoy playing alongside another child. In a sandbox, and with mother safely nearby, two or even three toddlers may fill and dump their buckets, quietly aware of and content with each other. They may even enjoy copying one another's efforts and ideas. However, the moment one toddler takes a special liking to another's little shovel, he may just grab it for himself, quite unconcerned by the perplexed consternation or howling cry this produces in his companion. Moreover, when he is intent on getting out of the sandbox, he may think nothing of using his playmate's body as a stepping stone, and when his mother brings him a cookie he would not dream of sharing it, much less of going without for the sake of pleasing his "friend." Insofar as babies or toddlers render services for others (even their mothers) or give to them of their own belongings, they are not motivated by generosity or selfless concern. They either take pleasure in doing instead of being done to, such as putting their food or spoon into mother's mouth as she has done to them, or they part with their things because they happen not to want or need them at the time. Even very young preschoolers' social attitudes are still marked by parallel play, lack of true consideration, use of others for his or her own ends, minimal appreciation of the feelings of others and association by convenience.

During the nursery school years, however, we see some prestages of the capacity for friendship: There are brief periods of give-and-take play ("I'll be the mommy and you'll be the child and then we'll take turns and you can be the mommy and I'll be the child"). There are incidents where one's ideas and wishes are compromised for the sake of continuing the desired joint activity ("We don't have to make a parking lot. Will you go on playing if we build your garage?"). A gift may be shared or given in order to gain a playmate's admiration or willing participation in an activity ("Come

look at my new game. You can play it with me"; or, "You can
have one of my candies and then we'll play firemen"). We see
even true episodes of empathy and concern for others.
("Jimmy's crying for his mommy. There, you can hold my
teddy, Jimmy.") Such moments in the nursery school are as
encouraged and praised as they are rare because, at this stage
in their development, children still are more often focused on
the exclusive one-to-one relationship with the parent or
teacher. It is mainly for the sake of the loved adult that other
children are tolerated or even liked. The bond with the adult
gives rise both to feelings of rivalry with other children and to
the wish to be nice to them and interact with them in as
friendly a fashion as the beloved grownup does (A. Freud,
1963).

In the preschool years we see also the beginnings of other
forms of association between children which are sometimes
mistaken for true friendship. Among these are associations
sought and maintained for self-aggrandizement, for status,
for acceptance and relief of feelings of inadequacy. For
example, a child may follow another, perform services for
him, share his possessions with him, and say nice things to
him in order to gain his good will and thereby share in his real
or assumed admired qualities, and the "admired" partner
may return favors because having admirers and being in
demand enhance his self-importance. This self-serving one-
sided or mutual arrangement between star and fan is not a
friendship.

Another type of early association is that of being accomplices in wrongdoing which has the advantage of shared
guilt seeming like half the guilt and it indeed binds people to
each other but is not a tie of friendship. Young children
sometimes accept or seek out partners-in-trouble. When "we"
spill the paints or snitch the cookies, it does not feel half as
bad as when "I" do it and, when apprehended by the authorities that be, "we" feel more powerful and less threatened by
them than "I" alone. A related form of pseudofriendship is
the association based on shared sexual interests. For example, children may team up to "play doctor" which is sometimes a euphemism for investigating each other's bodies or
engaging in mutual sexual manipulations. Or children's

excitement may be expressed less directly in high pitched chasing, tumbling, and fighting which, as the adults usually predict, tends to end in somebody's tears or in damage to property.

Of course, such associations are not limited to preschoolers. They are common at all stages of growing up and persist even with some adults, but are always indicative of emotional immaturity and/or inability to cope adequately with inner conflicts and impulses.

This does not mean, however, that a real friendship excludes any other form of relationship between people. For example, a teacher or parent can also be a friend, especially in later years, and a husband and wife may be friends as well as sexual partners. Similarly, two young children may at times be companions in trouble or in excitement or serve to enhance each other's self-esteem, but at other times they may interact as real friends. It is a matter of degree as to which relationship predominates.

A real, sustained capacity for friendship develops toward the end of the preschool years and during the first years of elementary school. It is a period when boys and girls have grown to be loving and thoughtful in their relationships with their parents, and have aspired to achieve an exclusive mutually satisfying bond with one or the other parent. They will have eventually resigned themselves to the inevitable disappointment that such an exclusive bond is not possible because a parent–child relationship cannot also be a husband–wife and father–mother relationship. When children are in the process of coming to this realization we often see it reflected in their relationships with peers. We may, for example, see a touchingly attentive and considerate attempt to "woo" another child and to establish a loving boy–girl relationship. The pair may act like mature friends but the undertones of a hopeful erotic tie show themselves in the occasional earnest statement: "When I grow up I'll marry her (or him)." Or we may see children who are always intent on having an exclusive "friend" but the main purpose of it is to exclude a third party: "*We* won't play with *him*, will we?" Here the frustration and anger at the home situation, where the parental twosome feels like a rejection, shows itself in the child's turning the tables on an innocent peer: "He is left out, not I."

When the inner acceptance of one's status in the family has taken place, it becomes possible for the child to sense that other children are in the same boat, that they find themselves in the same circumstances, and suffer the same hardship. This common bond of experiencing the same feelings enables the child to empathize and sympathize with his peer, to extend to him the thoughtful consideration learned in the relationship with the parents, to accept the other child's proffered kindness and comfort, and to enjoy the shared togetherness. And thus friendships come to be.

Nobody ever has many friends, and even the best friendships may end as personalities and circumstances change. A great deal may depend on the capacity of both partners to surmount obstacles, to forgive shortcomings, to tolerate disappointments and differences. No friendship, however, can flourish unless the foundation has been laid in the context of the late preschooler's relationship with his parents and his or her ability to come to terms with the limitations inherent in it. There are people who do not fully achieve the level of a giving, considerate relationship to their parents or who do not master the necessary disappointments it brings. They may remain at the prestages of friendship limited in nature and continuity, and/or their friendships may repeatedly end in frustration or disillusionment because they are invaded by other interests and motivations. Sometimes such complications are phase appropriate; for example, friendships among adolescents are readily affected by the young person's strong sexual and aggressive impulses or by his or her sense of inadequacy. In the former case a friendship may also become a sexual relationship or be interrupted for the sake of a sexual partner, or may turn into a partnership of accomplices in wrongdoing; in the latter case the need for acceptance or enhancement of self-esteem may determine the choice, or change of companion; for example, an adolescent may choose a "wrong" friend because he feels that no one "better" would accept him. At later periods in life, in adulthood, interferences in the ability to have a friend are usually a sign of personality difficulty.

**IF ONE HAS NOT GONE THROUGH THE
EXPERIENCE OF LOVING ONE'S PARENTS AND
OF ACCEPTING BEING LEFT OUT IN SOME
WAYS, CAN ONE STILL LEARN TO HAVE
FRIENDS LATER?**

Making friends is not learned in one day or even just at one
time in one's life. Inner growth enables people to improve
their friendships and to make them more lasting. At some
periods in life friends may be more important than at other
periods. At each phase of life, shared experiences and interests provide new opportunities and impetus for friendships,
such as attending the same school, liking the same hobbies,
working at the same job, serving together in the armed forces,
living through a period of hardship, rearing a family at the
same time. However, without experiencing an early give-and-
take love with one's parents and without mastering its limitations, a child does not begin really to seek a friend and does
not know how to give of himself to a friend.

DO FRIENDS INFLUENCE ONE'S CONSCIENCE?

That depends on the meaning of this question. If one means
whether "friends can lead one astray," the answer would be,
"Yes, they sometimes can lead one astray but that does not
affect the nature of one's conscience." Allowing oneself to be
led astray may be due to one's conscience tolerating whatever
misdemeanor one is indulging in, or it may be due to one's
conscience not serving as a reliable inner guide to behavior.
In either case, those that have led one astray have not influenced one's conscience. We have either chosen to go along
with them because their values and precepts are similar to
our own or because we have not listened to our conscience.
School children need much practice in learning to live with
their consciences and to utilize them appropriately as an
inner guide. Adolescents too sometimes experience trouble in
this respect. When parents say, "Don't go out with so-and-so,
he'll get you into trouble," they simply mean that they do not
trust their child's conscience to help him resist temptation.

In another way, however, friends can influence one's conscience, in the sense that all long-term meaningful relationships can add to or modify some aspects of our values, ideals, and standards. The basic "parental" conscience always remains a part of a person's conscience and additions or modifications are most likely to be integrated when they are not too much at variance with it. After all, our very wish and ability to maintain meaningful relationships with others and to take into ourselves admired aspects of their personalities is part and parcel of our early relationship with our parents and of the conscience that grew out of it. Those who could not be influenced by their parents in such a way as to develop a conscience, cannot acquire a new or different one from others in later phases of life. It may sometimes seem that our values are very different from our parents' but, on closer inspection, we may find, for instance, that our very ability to find individual solutions to life's problems is the principle we took over from them. Perhaps they too chose to differ from their parents' precepts.

RELATIONSHIPS WITH SIBLINGS

Living in the same family and sharing the same parents constitute a special mutual bond between the children but does not lead to a uniform or constant type of relationship between them. Even a limited glance at any ordinary family quickly reminds us that the relationships between siblings are complex, ever changing, and individually varied. The D. family may serve as an example. Yvonne was the third child in the D. family and was barely two years old when a baby sister was born. Yvonne was evidently fond of her eight-year-old brother Charlie. He often helped his mother to take care of Yvonne, even baby-sat with her for brief periods, readily let her play with some of his toys, shared his candies, and played little games with her. But since he spent most of his time with his own friends and activities, Yvonne did not see very much of him, and even when he was around, Yvonne often preferred to be with her mother and did not like it at all when

Mom and Charlie did something together that meant she had to wait. In fact, she often protested and interfered between them or interrupted them by getting into trouble. Charlie, for his part, sometimes couldn't be bothered with Yvonne, could get quite cross with her, and complained when Mom couldn't do something for him because she had to take care of Yvonne.

Relations between Yvonne and four-year-old Jack were less smooth. Jack too occasionally "mothered" Yvonne but his attentions were less appropriate and thoughtful, and Yvonne was much less cooperative with him. Sometimes she teased him and wouldn't allow him to do things for her, sometimes he was too forceful and strict, so that their interactions often ended in struggles and cries for mother's immediate help. At times Jack and Yvonne played together contentedly for a while, usually with *her* toys, and she enjoyed his companionship and tried to copy his inventive ideas and superior skills. B   these moments too tended to deteriorate. Either he becan. too bossy and she too frustrated, or he wouldn't allow her access to his toys and she grabbed back her own and destroyed what he had made. Again mom's help was needed. Jack and Yvonne were also much more rivalrous of one another in regard to their parents, demanding more exclusive attention for themselves and resenting love, time, and energy spent on the other. It was a good thing that Yvonne's naptime freed Mom for Jack and his morning at the nursery school freed her for Yvonne. The times when Jack and Yvonne seemed least desirous of their parents and most satisfied with each other's company were the very times when Mom and Dad hurried to them most urgently. They knew that such quiet episodes indicated that Jack and Yvonne were partners-in-trouble and that they had to "Go see what the children are doing and tell them not to."

With her newborn sister Yvonne really did not yet have a relationship at all. She had shown clearly that she had not been in favor of Mom having another baby. She was both sad and angry at mother's care of little Janie. Although Yvonne sometimes watched the baby with interest and helped Mom by bringing clean diapers, Mom had to watch very closely to make sure that Yvonne's tentative gentle touching of Janie would not suddenly turn into a push or pinch. For the most part Yvonne's interest focused on preoccupying mother. Indeed, she seemed to need mother more than before Janie was born and was less willing to accept Charlie's or Jack's care.

The brothers were less perturbed by Janie's arrival. At times they resented Mother's times with her but more often they were proudly helpful and disappointed that Janie paid as yet no heed to their attentive smiles and coos. Their interaction with one another sometimes included give-and-take play, sometimes rivalry, and sometimes they seemed to live apart in different worlds. But when they were not with their parents, for example, when playing with other children in the neighborhood, Charlie was often quite protective of Jack and the latter relied on his brother for help and comfort. Just recently they sometimes talked with each other seriously about other children, or TV programs, or football players.

At this time in the D. family the siblings' relationships were certainly far from simple or uniform. Janie was just beginning to form a relationship with her mother, and her brothers and sister would not play much of a part in her life for many months. Yvonne viewed Janie as a mere intruder into or rival for her relationship with her mother. The rivalry elements were also marked in her relationship with Jack, less so with Charlie. He was regarded mainly as a parent substitute or additional parental figure, whereas Jack was more of a playmate and perhaps partner-in-trouble. To Jack, Charlie was some of each—playmate, additional parent, rival—but there were also little beginnings of friendship. If we were to follow this particularly fortunate and loving family for some years in their development and on into adulthood, we would no doubt note many changes in their relationships. However, in the future as much as in the present, each child's level of personality development and individual circumstances would affect his or her view of the siblings.

The younger the child and the more exclusively he or she still needs the parents to maintain basic physical and mental well-being, the less welcome are brothers or sisters who are "new" or very close in age. No advantage is felt to derive from them, on the contrary, they are more likely experienced as a threat to oneself and as a sign of rebuff by the parents. It takes time and reassuring words and experiences for a young child to realize that the sibling is not an intolerable interference. It takes even more time and a loving relationship with the parents before the child can identify with the parents' love and care for all. As the young child increasingly wants to be like Mommy and Daddy and enjoys doing for someone else what has been done for him or herself, it becomes possible to "be nice" and to "mother" or "parent" the little sibling.

Preschoolers as well as younger children tend to regard new siblings as a threat to be dealt with, as the following memories of young adults illustrate. "I am the oldest in our family and I was just over four when my first brother was born. After he'd been home for a week I helped my Mom get the wastebaskets ready for the weekly garbage collection and I said to her, 'Let's put the baby out in the trash. He's been here long enough.' My mother said, 'No, we don't put babies in the trash. Bobby is going to be with us always and you'll see there'll be enough love for everyone.'"

"I was three-and-a-half when my mother had my younger sister. I remember one day a neighbor came to see the baby and I wouldn't leave my Mom alone and kept hanging onto her and asking for things. Then the neighbor lady said, 'Your Mommy has a baby now so she won't have time for you.' But my Mom hugged me and said, 'That's ridiculous.' My mother told me that soon I began to try to amuse my little sister by dragging her around on a blanket and now we're great friends."

When children learn to like and care for their younger siblings in a parental way, the younger ones relate to them as additional, or substitute, parents, as we saw with Yvonne and Charlie and, to a lesser extent, with Yvonne and Jack. The children's feelings for and with their parents are, in this way, a great help to their relationship with each other even though it can bring some drawbacks; for example, the children may direct at one another feelings from their relationship with their parents that are less helpful to their interaction, such as anger, envy, or wishes for exclusive closeness.

The siblings' common bond with their parents as well as their joint experiences may increasingly promote other types of association among them—as playmates, as accomplices-in-trouble, or as mutual "boosts" for extra "power" vis-à-vis outsiders or even vis-à-vis the parents. For example, "*We* don't like stew," or, "*We* don't want to go to bed," promises more impact on Mom than "I don't," especially when one worries a bit that being the only rebellious one may send one's share of Mom's love to the brother or sister who is "good." When the children reach the stage of being able to engage in friendship, siblings may become friends. They may empathize with each other's feelings and support one another or find comfort with each other at times when the parents have proved disappointing.

Usually, however, children form friendships first with peers outside the immediate family. There are several reasons for this. When siblings are very close in age, their rivalry for the parents' relationship tends to interfere. When there is a considerable age difference, they lack shared interests and the parent–child bond between them may overshadow their feeling of being in the same boat. Also, as they grow from one phase to another, their relative closeness changes, for example, an eight and ten-year-old may feel they have much in common but three years later, as eleven and thirteen-year-olds, the younger one is still apt to be an elementary school child, whereas the older one may consider himself a teenager. Also, the intensity of their togetherness and the intimacy of daily living, so similar to their feelings with the parents, introduces elements of conflict. As siblings grow older, as their age difference becomes less significant, as their emotional dependence on the parents lessens, and their relationships outside the family become more meaningful, their chances of being friends increase.

WHY DO SIBLINGS SOMETIMES NEVER BECOME FRIENDS?

Many factors may contribute to this, some of which we have touched upon, for example their age difference may be too great for the mutual feelings of parent–child to be overcome; their very closeness in age may accentuate and perpetuate their rivalry for the parents; their individual experiences within the family may differ so much that it may be difficult for them to empathize with each other (one sibling may suffer serious illnesses or separations from home, or may maintain a very different relationship with the parents, or may have very different individual gifts or deficits); being of the same or opposite sex may also play its part, sometimes facilitating a relationship and sometimes creating an interference; a child's position in the family may, but need not be a factor.

One of the most important and ever present factors is the nature of the siblings' relationships with their parents. Sibling relationships are greatly helped when the parents are able to form a satisfactory relationship with each of their children and when they can help each child to express to them both his positive and negative feelings (anger, frustration, disappointment, competitiveness, jealousy, envy, etc.). When feelings toward the parents are deflected from their true targets and diverted to brothers or sisters, they cannot be appropriately mastered and tend to burden the relationships between siblings. For example, anger at the new baby is, to a considerable extent, anger that really belongs to the parents who are responsible for the baby's arrival; envy of the older brother's possessions and accomplishments is, to some extent, envy of the parents' even more superior attributes; jealousy of sister's friends may, likewise, become excessive when it also includes jealousy of the parents' love for each other and their exclusive relationship. It is not easy for parents, or anyone, to acknowledge to themselves that they cause hardship to their children and to accept the children's blame. Children, for their part, find it much easier to divert their "unacceptable" feelings from parents to siblings. In doing so they avoid antagonizing the parents ("You don't bite the hand that feeds you") and gain a ready opportunity for direct discharge (it is easier to hit or snatch something from a sibling). As a result parents and children are often inclined to take troubles between siblings at face value instead of viewing them as a sign of trouble between parents and children.

Sam and Bruce, aged eight and five, were always in trouble with each other when the parents went out together. Bruce would interfere with Sam's activities and Sam would belittle Bruce, often to the point of loud arguments and fist fights. Their irritability with each other would continue throughout the evening and, on their return or the next day, the parents often had to help resolve the boys' quarrels and accusations of one another. The parents eventually realized that their sons' hard feelings for one another at these times really related to their unhappiness about the parents' outing. They shared this idea with the boys and suggested they could tell Mom and Dad when they didn't like being left, or felt left out of a nice time, instead of taking it out on each other. As Sam and Bruce, with reminders, began to complain directly to their parents ("Yah, you always get to go out"; "I wish I could stay up late. It isn't fair"), they had less trouble with each other and could often support each other in a friendly way.

DOES IT HELP ONE TO MAKE FRIENDS IF ONE HAS BROTHERS AND SISTERS OR ATTENDS A NURSERY SCHOOL?

Living with other children inside and outside the family helps one to get to know what others are like, how they are similar or different, and which are their good and bad qualities. With the help of parents and nursery school teachers, children also learn the necessary social rules of interacting with one another, how to ask someone to play with you, how to take turns, how to offer and accept ideas, how to settle quarrels. These are very important aids in choosing a friend and in getting along with him or her but they do not produce friendship. The crucial factor is the child's experiences in his relationships with his parents and teachers which lead to his wish to like others as the loved adults do and to have a caring partnership.

An only child without access to peers may lack opportunity to make friends or may lag in the know-how of interacting with others, but he would still develop the wish and capacity for friendship through his relationship with his parents, and this would prompt him to long for a friend and to seek one.

ARE TWINS' RELATIONSHIPS DIFFERENT FROM OTHER SIBLING RELATIONSHIPS AND ARE TWINS MORE LIKELY TO BE FRIENDS?

The personality development of twins poses a special task for the parent–child relationship. It is difficult, but not impossible for a mother to invest herself equally and at the same time in two babies and to meet their simultaneous demands in such a way that each child can develop a fully differentiated independent personality. Insofar as the parents succeed in this task, identical as well as fraternal twins' rivalry may be exaggerated but their eventual chances for becoming friends may also be enhanced. The danger lies in parents not relating to each twin fully and individually. This may cause inadequate personality development in one or both twins and impairment in their functioning as independent individuals. When twins unduly depend on each other it may not be a sign of friendship but an indication of insufficient self-differentiation or unresolved rivalry (Burlingham, 1952; Burlingham and Barron, 1963).

RELATIONSHIPS WITH GRANDPARENTS

Societies assign different roles to grandparents. In North American and European countries the grandparents' function varies considerably from group to group, from family to family. In some cases, the grandparents carry the main parental authority. Their wishes and decisions are binding on their adult children and may significantly affect the handling of the grandchildren. Other groups conceive of the ideal grandparent as an ever-available, yet never intruding, additional parent, who is a little less strict and more tolerant than the parent, who supports the child a bit against the parent, and somewhat softens the parent's authority, but who never interferes in the parent–child relationship.

Be their role that of additional parent, substitute parent, or "superparent," the grandchild may look to them for comfort and support when he is a bit at odds with his parents, or needs some respite from them, or when he simply enjoys the satisfactions of an additional and different relationship. This may, in a helpful way, enrich the child's experience and lessen his or her total dependence on the parents. In practice it is rare for all four grandparents to be alive and available. They may be ill or live far away. Moreover, grandparents may be unable to maintain appropriate relationships with their children and grandchildren. They may be intolerant and critical of the parents' parental functioning, causing resentments and loyalty conflicts between the generations; they may be so demanding of their children's care and attention that they become the grandchild's rival; or they may be disinclined to participate in any way in the lives of their children and grandchildren.

Yet, regardless of individual circumstances, grandparents still play a special part in the grandchildren's lives, and relationships with them are eagerly sought as soon as children are developmentally ready for relationships beyond the basic parent–child bonds. The parents' close relationship with the grandparents forms an important link. As is the case with mother's fondness for father, and with both parents' fondness for the other siblings, children want to get to know and love those who share in the parents' affection. But the parents' parents are important also in another way. They represent the continuity of the changing generations, the proof that parents were once children and that children grow up to be parents. They afford a look into the past (it is comforting to know that parents were not always powerful and perfect) and a look into the future (there is room in the world for parents and children when one grows up). Children rarely tire of hearing grandparents' stories of their parents' childhood, especially if they include some of the parents' early shortcomings, and they are always glad to know that their parents will become grandparents in time, because sometimes it feels to little children that their own growing up may leave no place for their parents.

All this is especially significant and welcome for the preschooler who struggles with finding his place in the family and in the order of things, and who tries to come to terms with what he is now, whence he came, and whither he is going in life. At later phases in their development, and under specially fortunate circumstances, grandchildren and grandparents may even develop a relationship that comes close to friendship.

DO CHILDREN MISS GRANDPARENTS WHEN THEY HAVE NEVER HAD ANY?

Yes. When children, usually as preschoolers, become interested in growing up and learn that their parents were once little, they inquire into who took care of them. This brings the wish to get to know the grandparents, the joy in finding that one has a special tie with them as grandparents, or the disappointment that one does not. Many youngsters spontaneously seek out other older people when their grandparents are dead or absent. They may take a special liking to other relatives of the grandparents' generation, to elderly neighbors or friends of the family. Many families have such unofficial "adopted" grandparents who fill the important links between the generations.

7

The Teacher–Pupil Relationship

Up until now we have looked at the development of the infant's first, crucial, and all-inclusive relationship with the mothering person, at the growing child's increasing ability to form additional and different relationships with the father and other members of the family, and at the later beginnings of friendships which usually extend into the wider community. All these relationships are based on powerful mutual emotional bonds: they embrace all of the loved person—looks, actions, thoughts, likes, and dislikes. They provide many satisfactions, immediate bodily pleasures intermingled with more sophisticated joint interests and activities: there is hugging and kissing, giving and receiving of affection, togetherness around eating, sleeping in the same home (what a treat it is to spend the night at grandma's or at a friend's house!), caring and being cared for at times of need. There are shared hobbies, games, sports, learning things from and about each other, discussing matters of joint interest. Another hallmark of all these relationships is their continuity. Once established, we expect them to last, day in day out, year after year. They endure and adapt to many changes in the partners and in the circumstances of their lives. When a family relationship or close friendship is interrupted (through death, separation, conflict, or withdrawal), we consider it a major distress, regardless of how old we may be.

TASK-ORIENTED RELATIONSHIPS

Let us now look at a kind of relationship which is so different

that it may appear strange at first sight: its main focus is an
activity or task which the partners jointly pursue. Their relationship revolves around it. They do not share other parts of
their lives and may know little about them. They work toward
a common goal, and, in contributing their share toward
achieving it, they are more likely to look in the same direction
rather than at one another. Their relationship provides only
mental rewards and excludes bodily contact and gratifications. It is limited in time, in the sense that the partners only
meet for agreed, relatively brief periods of the day or week,
and in the sense that they expect the relationship to termi-
nate after a period of months or years. And when the anticipated end does come, they expect it to cause minor not major
distress. In spite of its special characteristics and limitations,
this kind of relationship may be deeply felt and very meaningful. At times it may even be preferred to the intensely
emotional family relationships, or may provide a welcome
respite from them, because of its relative ease and calm.

Who maintains these very different task-oriented relationships? As adults we often enjoy several of them—with
colleagues in our job or profession, with co-workers on various projects, or with men and women with whom we regularly get together to pursue a hobby. In childhood, the first
such relationship usually is the teacher–pupil relationship.
Even a brief look confirms that all the essential elements we
listed apply to that relationship. The child entering elementary school and the teacher who welcomes him into the classroom accept the fact that they will spend a certain number of
hours together five times weekly (i.e., they expect to meet only
at specified times). The child wants to learn to read and the
teacher is eager to help him do it; that is their common goal.
Both feel that reading is a desirable and perhaps enjoyable
skill, worth a lot of hard work to achieve, and each pitches in;
the teacher with lesson plans, board work, teaching aids,
worksheets; the child with concentrated attention, with
laborious sounding out of letters and words, and with pencil
tightly grasped to reproduce the difficult shapes. Both partners take it for granted that each has to contribute his or
her share to the joint work in pursuit of their goal, neither
finds it easy going. Each has to face mistakes, frustrations,

and setbacks. Patience sometimes threatens to run out. But together they experience the thrill of the first word recognized or sounded out, of the worksheet correctly completed, of the primer read aloud haltingly, of the news "I read a word in my Dad's newspaper." These shared pleasures cement their liking for one another as do the hard times when the teacher's encouraging word helps the pupil to overcome a sense of failure, or when the child's appreciative, "Gee, I *like* that worksheet" lifts the teacher's spirits on a hard day. They build their relationship through their joint work and derive their satisfactions from it as well as from the hard won piecemeal successes which bring them closer to their goal.

Yes, it all sounds very austere. Yet, for many of us, this relationship, tied to the first pains and pleasures of learning to read, is so important and so deeply felt that our elementary school teacher forever retains a special, fond place in our hearts, even if we never see him or her again in later years. It was, after all, a relationship discontinued as planned after a certain time.

There are, however, also many among us who do not treasure these early experiences. Learning with a teacher may have never brought satisfaction or success, only boredom, or shame and failure, or an unbearable sense of a chore from which we could not wait to escape. In some instances all this changed for the better in later years, or felt better with some teachers or with some subjects, or outside a school setting, such as in a job or in extracurricular activities. With others all learning may have remained unhappy and such people avoid being a pupil at all cost.

We often blame unsatisfactory learning experiences on poor teachers, lazy pupils, lack of adequate equipment, disinterested parents, and we suggest and try many remedies. Perhaps teachers should be nicer, or more demanding, or more punitive; learning should be made exciting with the help of games, or more rewarding with the help of candies or prizes; or it should focus more on the basics, or be enforced with structure and discipline; parents should be involved in the school and with the child's homework, or they should stay out of the way altogether and leave the child's schooling in the hands of the teacher.

It is rarely recognized that learning depends primarily on a true teacher–pupil relationship. It is even more rarely appreciated what this kind of relationship is about, what each partner has to contribute, and when and how a child develops the capacity to engage effectively in such a relationship. So let us now think about all this and what it entails.

THE CHILD'S READINESS TO FORM A RELATIONSHIP WITH A TEACHER

Three- or three-and-a-half-year-olds are usually ready to take the difficult developmental step of entering a nursery school. During their few hours of regular attendance there they learn to form the beginnings of a teacher–pupil relationship. How do we know when this is accomplished? Many signs tell us: The child is eager to go to nursery school, comfortable in leaving mother and in functioning at school without her, yet glad to welcome her at the end of the session, and ready to return home. He differentiates parent from teacher, home from school, and accepts certain differences between them— differences in rules, in behavioral expectations, in the type of activities and available materials, in traditions, such as how holidays are celebrated. The child is also able to bridge the gap between home and school; for example, by sharing with the parents what happened at school (he does not expect them just to know without having to be told). He shares with the teacher what happens at home in appropriate ways (an account of an outing, a new toy to show and share, a feather for the science corner) rather than inappropriately (a garbled story of his night fear, a baby blanket, an object from home which nobody should touch). His or her fondness for the teacher shows in eagerness to join in the activities she offers, in enjoyment of the materials she provides, and in efforts at mastering the skills she demonstrates. The child admires the teacher's know-how, accepts her suggestions, welcomes her encouragement and praise, but also takes pride in his or her own work and achievements. The child rarely gives or expects physical affection or demands bodily care, is independent in toileting, eating and dressing for outside play or for going home. He may enjoy a snack at school, may solicit the teacher's help with a hard zipper, may allow her to put a Band-Aid on a scratch, but does not consider these services her main function, and takes it for granted that the teacher attends to all the children. Sharing her love and attention with them is no special hardship.

In all these ways the child often behaves "better" at school than at home, a fact that mothers and teachers sometimes erroneously attribute to the teacher's better educational methods. Actually, the difference in the child's behavior stems from the difference in the nature of the relationship. The longstanding, intense emotional closeness between mother and child makes for more conflict in their interaction but it also paves the way for the child's ability to relate to a teacher and to behave like a pupil. No child is capable of these advanced achievements without having experienced, and benefited from, a great deal of good mothering.

The mother's part starts years before entry to nursery school. As we know, her continuous caring relationship with her baby enables him to grow into a person in his own right in the first place and, gradually, to develop skills and interests which make it possible and enjoyable for him to be more independent and to relate to others on new terms. In order to be ready to form a teacher–pupil relationship and to contribute his share to its joint task, the child must have mastered many steps with the help of his relationship with the mothering person. Let us list these steps in personality growth and group them under a few headings:

1. *Taking Care of Many of His Own Bodily Needs:* self-feeding, dressing, control of elimination, and ability to avoid common dangers, such as electric outlets and hot stoves. As long as the child depends on a mothering person to meet these basic bodily needs, he or she cannot be comfortable without her. Such children either require the mother's presence in addition to the teacher or they relate to the teacher as a mother substitute.

2. *Mastering His Urges and Feelings to a Considerable Extent:* being able to wait, to accept substitute gratifications, to use words for needs, feelings, and thoughts and to communicate them to others, to tolerate some disappointment or failure. Babies and toddlers want what they want, now, be it

getting their dinner, reaching for their teddies, seeing their Moms, building a block tower, or using a hammer. The urge is so strong and immediate that the infant cannot postpone it, or give it up, or do something else instead. Very young children pursue their wishes with all the verve they can muster, and if something proves unattainable they tend to become overwhelmed with rage and despair. It's a long way to being a youngster who is sufficiently master of himself to learn with a teacher in a classroom!

3. *Achieving a Measure of Consideration for Others:* so that one's anger at them will be tempered and sufficiently restrained to safeguard them and the relationships with them. When we remind ourselves of the toddler's unmitigated outbursts of temper, of his "bearhug" mixture of affection and destruction, and of his actual disregard for his peers, we realize how far he is from being able to participate in cooperative work and social interaction.

4. *Enjoying Activities That Involve a Measure of Effort and Skill and Aim Toward Achievement:* (such as building with blocks or making sandpies). For a long time youngsters can appreciate and sustain such activities only for very limited periods. The sandpies soon deteriorate into mud baths and the blocks are knocked down or thrown around.

5. *Building Relationships Around Companionship and Shared Activities in Which the Loved One, At Least At Times, Is Not Regarded as a Mother Substitute:* these relationships, usually with family members, still include bodily closeness and an all-embracing emotional interest in one another, but they are a stepping stone toward the later teacher–pupil relationship, with its specific purpose of learning in the narrower goal-directed sense.

How do youngsters accomplish all that? Slowly. Parental help in all these areas starts early on and continues all along. Learning to relate to a teacher and to contribute appropriately to that relationship is by no means easy, even when children have maintained a good relationship with the mothering person (E. Furman, 1969b, 1977a,b; R. A. Furman and A. Katan, 1969).

Preschoolers and some young elementary school children are apt to view the teacher initially as a mother-substitute or family member. This may show in inappropriate expectations of the school (always wanting to sit by the teacher, hold her hand on walks, or kiss and be kissed) or in a loyalty conflict between mother and teacher (teasing mom with "I like Mrs. A. better" or worrying whether one likes the teacher better than mother). Children also sometimes lag in self-care (expecting the teacher to help with toileting, with dressing, or with wiping runny noses). They are not always masters of their urges and feelings (fidgeting during stories, running around the room at snacktime, grabbing materials from others, refusing to compromise on using crayons when their heart is set on painting just then, sitting forlornly in a corner instead of telling the teacher of a tummy ache or of a hurt inflicted by another child). Anger is occasionally still expressed in loud yells, punches, or destruction of materials when the teacher's rules feel too annoying, when another child gets a first turn at the new game, or when the child's frustration at not being able to make the scissors cut out-reaches the limits of his tolerance. Immediate bodily plea-sures are sometimes still preferred to the hard-to-achieve taste of success with skills, as when the paint is gleefully smeared over table, child, and floor instead of being labor-iously worked into a picture, when the blocks are made to crash loudly instead of being used to construct a building, or when a baseball practice deteriorates into an angry–excited free-for-all. In short, at the start of nursery school and even at the start of elementary school, the young child is still learn-ing to be a pupil, learning to make his contribution to the joint task, and learning to appreciate the teacher's role.

THE ROLE OF THE TEACHER

But what is the teacher's role? That is simple to state but difficult to appreciate fully, even for teachers. It consists of liking the subject or skill one teaches, and of wanting to learn ever more about it. It also consists of liking the process of teaching and learning, and of supporting and enjoying the pupil's learning. Last but not least, it includes deriving satis-faction from the pupil's work and from the successes he achieves. These contributions by the teacher are as crucial to teaching how to cut with scissors or build with blocks as they are to teaching reading and arithmetic, or astronomy and history, or child development.

Let us take a closer look at what these statements imply. Is it really important for a teacher to like his subject? Is it even possible for him to like it and to want to learn ever more about it? How can one like counting to 100, or simple addition, or printing letters? How can one go on liking such things year after year? Yes, one can like these activities and one can continue to like them. Every good kindergarten teacher indeed does like them, just as every good nursery school teacher likes building with blocks and playing Lotto, and collecting leaves or acorns, and just as every good mother enjoys bathing and dressing her child. There is no skill too humble to like, too unimportant to merit interest, or too simple to execute well without dedicated effort. And those who choose to teach it need to consider it worthwhile, need to like and respect it. Unless they do, they cannot derive satisfaction from their work, nor can they convey their positive interest to the pupil. One of the reasons children sometimes don't like to do household chores is that they are asked to do the chores the parents don't like to perform, but when the parents do enjoy a chore (yes, many mothers enjoy doing dishes and folding laundry!) the children are eager to learn it with them and to take it over.

As for liking the process of teaching and learning, is it really true that a teacher has to like both? Is it not enough to like the teaching part of it? Is it not the whole point of being the teacher that one is the one who knows all about it? No, it is not. Teachers who only like to teach cannot want to learn more about their subject or more about the methods of teaching it. They cannot empathize with their pupils or learn from them. Pupils teach the teacher a great deal about his subject as well as about how it is learned and how it is best taught. Above all, a teacher who does not enjoy learning can never help a pupil experience pleasure in learning. He can, at best, make him feel that it is superior fun to teach and inferior misery to learn.

What does it mean "to support and enjoy the pupil's

learning"? Learning is an arduous task which requires many
skills, some general (like concentration and frustration tolerance) and some specific (like small muscle control for writing
or ability to think with symbols for doing arithmetic). Each
skill has to be learned, applied appropriately, and perfected.
This makes up the process of learning. A teacher who does
not appreciate all aspects of this process and does not support
and enjoy its unfolding and development in the pupil misses
out on much of what teaching and learning are all about.
Getting there is half the fun. A baseball player who only likes
to win and has neither interest nor enjoyment in the technical
intricacies and skills of the game is not a truly dedicated
sportsman. Similarly, the good teacher not only wants his
students to achieve well but is interested in how they learn,
assists them with the learning process, and appreciates their
struggles.

The results, however, are important too. Here we come to
the teacher "deriving satisfaction from the pupil's work and
from the successes he achieves." A teacher can and should be
pleased with his contribution to the joint task but he must be
clear in himself that the goal is the pupil's acquisition of
knowledge for himself. Insofar as this goal is reached, the
success belongs to the pupil. The knowledge or skill the pupil
has gained by dint of his own efforts, and with the teacher's
help, is his to use, to enlarge, or to set aside and forget as he
wishes. It is also his to enjoy. The teacher can share in it only
by enjoying the fact that the pupil is pleased with his
achievement. This implies that the teacher enjoys the pupil
becoming more of an equal or even surpassing him—a pleasure similar to that of the parent who enjoys seeing his child
grow up without having to claim the child's success for himself or having to compete with him.

Whenever a teacher usurps the results of the joint work,
the teacher–pupil relationship becomes distorted and ultimately affects the pupil's chances for wanting to learn for
himself. Such distortions can take many forms; for example,
assignments may be treated as a task the student performs
for the teacher rather than to further his learning. ("*I* am very
pleased that you handed in a correct worksheet" instead of
"You did a fine job with your worksheet. I hope you are

pleased with it.") Time and effort expended on learning may be viewed as a way to satisfy the teacher rather than to satisfy the student. ("I like children who work hard" instead of "You'll really get good at that when you work so hard at it. That'll make you feel very good about yourself.") A good grade may be given as a reward for producing what the teacher demanded rather than as a measure of the extent of knowledge or skill the student has acquired ("If you are a good boy and do everything I told you to, I'll give you an A" instead of "If you work hard at it you will achieve at A level"). The words themselves do not matter but the attitude they convey counts.

Of course, all this applies to the student's failure as much as to his success. The failures and dissatisfaction are the student's too. The teacher can sympathize with the pupil's unhappiness with himself, he can help him plan how to improve his work, or he may question the student's lack of seeming concern, but a pupil's failure should not be regarded as an insult or injury to the teacher, nor should it be countered with threats and punishment.

Does this mean that pupils should never be praised or receive awards for their legitimate achievements? Not at all. Everyone likes to be appreciated and receive recognition, and everyone sometimes likes a little deserved respite from hard work. By the same token, teachers need to feel and express dissatisfaction when the pupil's contribution to the joint work is inadequate or when he loses sight of the goal. But these are not the main incentives for learning.

Learning and achieving have to be one's own thing. They have to provide their own satisfactions and make us feel good about ourselves, otherwise we will not continue to learn when the external rewards or punishments cease or when we do not like the teacher. Above all, we would not enjoy learning itself, would not like what we learn or develop a lasting interest in it. The role of the teacher–pupil relationship does not include inducing the pupil to learn out of love for the teacher or out of fear of his disapproval, nor in order to be loved or to avoid punishment, nor in order to gain rewards which have nothing to do with learning, such as candies, free time, or parties. The teacher–pupil relationship does contribute an important part to the pupil's *wish* to learn, but that works in different ways.

Now we have come to the most important driving force in learning, the pupil's wish to learn. Even when pupil and teacher are able to contribute appropriately, they cannot successfully work together unless the pupil wants to learn, unless he is "motivated." Where does this wish to learn come from?

THE WISH TO LEARN

As with all developmental steps, the wish to learn comes neither automatically nor suddenly. Personality development resembles the growth of a plant in many ways. Just as the inherent potential of the seed is released by the available sun, water, and nutrients, so the development of the child's personality is shaped by the mutual interdependence between his maturational potential and his emotional and educational environment. With the wish to learn, as with every other stride, the environment—and especially the child's relationship with the parents and, later on, teachers—facilitates the unfolding of his or her endowment and helps bring it to fruition.

When we talked about the mother's relationship with her baby and toddler we saw that her role of meeting the child's needs and ministering to his body is gradually taken over by the child himself. The more consistent and satisfying the mother's care has been, the sooner does the child become a person in his own right and the sooner too does he signal, and often insist, that he wants to do for himself the very things mother had done for him. In the second half of the first year, we usually see one of the first steps in this direction—the baby grabs for the food, takes hold of the spoon or cup, and wants to be the one who does the feeding. When he is present at the family meal he may impatiently sideswipe his little dishes and clamor for bits from the parents' plates. Given a chance, he not only tries to feed himself but often tries to feed mother and his teddy or dolls. "Me do, me do, all by myself" is the healthy toddler's constant refrain. He pushes mother away and wants to dress himself, wants to reach his own cookies, wants to walk rather than be carried. Within months he also wants to become clean like his parents and learns to use the toilet as they do. In all these activities the child's wish to learn and do as his mother and father do, stems primarily from his love and admiration for them which prompt the drive to become like them.

We have already talked about this role of the parent–child relationship with the preschooler. There we saw how the love and admiration of the parents as a man and woman inspires the child's wish to be big, to look and do as they do. And we also talked about how the child comes to appreciate that he cannot be and do just like the grown-ups right away and resigns himself to work toward that goal slowly, by learning their skills and by acquiring their knowledge for himself. The most desirable parental attributes and activities are usually those which the parents appear to value most in themselves and which seem to contribute most to their status in the child's view.

In this way the parent–child relationship fosters the child's wish to learn to become like the parents and provides a special incentive for him to learn what the parents like and enjoy. This is especially true when the parents offer the child an opportunity to learn and support his efforts. After the child has really mastered a new activity it gradually ceases to be "Something I can do like my Dad" and becomes a part of the child himself, a part he enjoys, is proud of. It enhances his self-esteem.

Let us take reading as an example. John, a preschooler, observes closely all his beloved dad does. He notices that dad likes to read the newspaper when he comes home in the evening. John knows a bit about what reading means because now and then Dad reads out a paragraph to share with Mom or he tells her about what he has read. Now and then too, Dad or Mom reads a book to John. John handles the book, looks at the pictures, picks up the newspaper, and can't make sense out of it. He may feel something like, "I wish I could read like Dad. I'd really fancy myself if I could read!" Next we find John pretending to read, turning the pages, and perhaps repeating phrases from a favorite story or jabbering away big nonsense words the way dad sounds when he talks in big words to mom. John feels great when he pretends to read like dad, but after a while this good feeling gives way to one of disappointment or inadequacy when something or someone reminds him that he is not really reading like dad. Mom and dad probably notice John's wish to read. Perhaps they print out his name on a piece of paper by way of helping him to recognize this most important word, or they may show him letters in an alphabet book. Perhaps they just smile at him indulgently. Sooner or later, they are likely to say, "You'll have a chance to learn to read when you go to school. That's what school is for and there will be a teacher to help you." They offer him a realistic setting in which he can fulfill his wish to learn to read—in school, with a teacher When learning eventually gets under way, John finds it slow and arduous but every letter and word mastered bring the glowing inner feeling, "Now I am closer to being really like Dad." This powerful motivation helps to bear many frustrations. In time, reading gets to be enjoyable in its own right. It becomes John's own thing, not just a vehicle to becoming like Dad. He gets satisfaction from his achievement, from the new world books open up for him, and from his independence in being able to explore this world without having to beg or wait for others to read to him. He may then feel something like "I like reading and I like myself when I read. It feels good." If and when John comes to that point, we say that he has identified himself with his parent in regard to reading. Reading is now a part of him. He gains satisfaction from it and it helps him to be a more adult member of his family and community.

The young child's wish to learn skills and to advance himself to more grown-up status stems primarily from his relationship with his parents, but this wish may not always include knowing how to read; for example, one kindergartner I knew showed no interest in reading. He was thought to have a learning problem until the teacher realized that the boy's father was illiterate, a fact the family kept secret. The boy's attitude changed markedly after the father acknowledged his illiteracy to his son, told him that he had not had a chance to learn but hoped very much that his boy would read and surpass him in this respect. Even in instances where the father takes pleasure in reading, however, the child's wish to emulate him depends on the nature of their relationship and on the father's support for his son's growing up.

Already early on, and increasingly so during the child's growing up, relationships with teachers (not necessarily in a school setting) serve a similar role of inspiring the wish to learn. Within the framework of these relationships it is no longer the loved person's grown-upness which is admired, but his or her mastery and love of a particular subject. When a teacher really enjoys, say, science, is good at it, and finds it fascinating to study, and when he is also willing to share his knowledge with us and to help us enjoy it too, we often want to make his interest our own. We may feel, "Gee, I never knew bugs could be so interesting. I wish I knew more about them too. I'm going to get to work on that." Our new wish to learn about bugs may only last long enough to give us a glimpse of the new vista the teacher opened for us, or it may develop into a lasting hobby or even career. In either case, our new knowledge and skill is viewed as an end in itself; it enriches our lives. It is not, as with the very young child, a means of acquiring adult status.

Sometimes even very little children are motivated to learn something as an end in itself when the offered or available activity brings special satisfactions; for example, many preschoolers want to learn to use scissors and thoroughly enjoy cutting out shapes; many love to draw or to work with clay. Now they may have admired these activities when performed by a parent, teacher, or older sibling, and they may have got help from them in learning how to go about it, but they enjoy working at it for the fun and satisfaction it brings them. Their absorption, genuine pleasure in the process, persistent effort at creating new, better, and different products, all tell us that they are engaged in doing their own thing for its own sake, that the process of learning gratifies so much as to be a motivating force. There are other, much older children and even adults who are not interested in what they learn and do not get satisfaction from the process of learning, yet they do want to learn because they see it as a stepping-stone toward some desired end or achievement; for example, to achieve a high school diploma or college degree we may need to take courses we would not choose in order to accumulate enough credits. With this kind of motivation learning becomes much more of a chore, and we can hardly wait to get it over with and to enjoy the end result. Of course, learning is most enjoyable when the process as well as the goal are satisfying.

THERE MUST BE MANY PEOPLE WHO NEVER FORM A RELATIONSHIP WITH A TEACHER AND NEVER ENJOY LEARNING IN THAT WAY

We have described a perfect teacher–pupil relationship. In real life nothing is perfect and indeed should not be. All teachers, parents, and pupils make mistakes and get "off the track" at times. They also tend to overlap their relationships somewhat, so that elements from one extend into the other. A father is sometimes also a sitter, a teacher acts on occasion a bit like a mother-substitute or family member, and children, especially young children, inevitably cast them all into mixed roles now and then. Often enough, this enhances rather than interferes with the specific relationship between the partners; for example, a school party on special occasions is not strictly speaking a function of the teacher–pupil relationship but can serve to cement it through a friendly good time enjoyed together. Difficulty only arises when the essential aspects of the teacher–pupil relationship are not predominant; for example, when teacher and/or pupil altogether mistake the nature and purpose of their relationship (such as when the child treats the teacher as a mother who is there to take care of him and love him, or when the teacher treats the child as his or her offspring and mothers instead of teaching). Or they may misunderstand what teaching and learning are about, for example, when they assume that it is like force feeding or like a fight over who controls whom. Many people do maintain good enough, though not perfect teacher–pupil relationships. They make mistakes, correct them, and learn from them.

There are, however, people who truly fail to form a relationship with a teacher. When this is due to a lag in their development, or due to a current stress in their lives, or due to an unhelpful teaching situation, they may well come into their own at a later time. If it is due to a difficulty within their own personality they may, in some instances, be able to overcome it with the help of psychological treatment. But some may indeed never be able to relate to a teacher as a teacher. Regardless of what may cause this, it still does not necessarily preclude all learning. Much can be learned even with the wrong methods and in far from ideal circumstances. Such learning, unfortunately, is often limited in one or another way. It may provide less satisfaction and add little to self-esteem. It may not be assimilated as a lasting part of our minds. It may not pave the way for a wish to learn more and may not prepare for later learning in higher grades, or may fail to serve as a means of adapting to a job in the community. It may be experienced as a waste of time and effort, and may even leave an aftertaste of bitterness.

DON'T MOST CHILDREN LEARN FOR THE "GOLDEN STAR" RATHER THAN FOR THEMSELVES?

It is nice to have both. Learning for oneself makes one independent and brings a deeper, more lasting satisfaction, but it is quieter and less spectacular than the "golden star." This makes learning for oneself the easily forgotten pleasure. Many children, from early on, do actually enjoy learning but they are not always aware of it, especially when the adults stress the "star." Often children also prefer not to notice what they feel about their work because they are critical of it, more critical than the grown-ups. However, parents and teachers who recognize their own pleasure in learning and appreciate how great it is not to have to depend on others, often help children to know their inner feelings, good and bad, and to value them.

When children appear not to look at their own work but right away rush it to the adult for praise and reward, they often do so to avoid self-appraisal. Perhaps in their own eyes their work would not be judged as favorably as in the eyes of the teacher or parent, and they therefore use the "Band-Aid" of adult acceptance to cover their own misgivings. When we ask children to assess their own work, we often hear an embarrassed "It's too sloppy," or "Jack's is better," or "These big letters are yucky" where we would have judged their efforts as very good. At such times we can help children to be less harsh with themselves, to better their self-esteem, and even to enjoy the "star" more, by talking over with them the discrepancy between their assessment and our own: "I think you are a bit too hard on yourself. To me your work looks better than to you. After all, you have only just begun to practice this and therefore I wouldn't expect it to be perfect. I think it's a very good first effort. In time it will get better yet." Praise which tallies with one's own assessment is much more appreciated than praise which substitutes for, or hides, self-criticism.

ARE THERE NOT MANY PEOPLE WHO LEARN ON THEIR OWN, PROMPTED BY THEIR SPECIAL GIFTS OR INTERESTS WHICH ARE DIFFERENT FROM THOSE OF THEIR PARENTS AND TEACHERS?

Superior intellectual or athletic endowment and innate artistic gifts do indeed provide motivation and gratification, and so do individual interests which, as we shall discuss later, are derived from the child's early bodily urges and feelings. However, none of these operate independently. The persistent, successful pursuit of an activity usually involves extra hard work and a good ability to learn from others. When Bach was praised for his genius, he is said to have replied, "Anyone who chooses to work as hard as I do, could produce the same or better music." We do not quite believe him but he does remind us that genius does not imply "it comes without effort and without learning" and both these attributes are closely related to upbringing.

Also, a person's gifts and special interests are usually affected by his or her relationships with parents and teachers; for example, loved adults may appreciate and support a child's activities without being good at them themselves. Some children identify with a parent's attitude; for example, the parent's interest in nature may help to develop his child's special interest in physics although the parent has no knowledge of physics in particular. Sometimes children take up interests just because they differ from the parents'; for example, a child's literary predilection may be related to the very fact that his parents have no interest in literature and present no competition to him in this field or will be unable to intrude upon his studies, but even such an indirect link with the parents is still significant as a motivating force. Moreover, teachers are not necessarily schoolteachers. A child's interest in drawing may stem from his relationship with a neighbor who "taught" him. There are also many early events, experienced with the parents, which stimulate special interests; for example, an interest in medicine or nursing may stem from experiences with illness and death in the family. Close and deep insight into an individual personality often reveals unsuspected links between specific activities and early relationships.

IF CHILDREN HAVE NOT HAD A SUFFICIENT ONE-TO-ONE RELATIONSHIP WITH THEIR MOTHERS, CAN THEY STILL BE HELPED TO HAVE A RELATIONSHIP WITH A TEACHER?

Unfortunately, it is not possible to build a second story onto a house which has no foundation or first floor. I think we would all agree that the first order of business would be to erect the missing substructure. Likewise, a child cannot start out with a teacher–pupil relationship. If a youngster has missed out on the necessary relationship with a mothering person, we would have to try and provide that first and hope that he or she could utilize it belatedly and make up for the earlier deprivation. The teaching situation, however, is not well suited to serve this end. Even a very kind, helpful, "motherly" teacher makes a poor mother-substitute. After all, what kind of mother is it who never shows up on weekends or vacations, who never cooks meals, or cares for her child during sicknesses? These inevitable limitations interfere with a teacher's attempt at mothering and cause the child who regards the teacher as a mother, too many disappointments and frustrations.

There are, however, some children who experienced some

mothering but whose development has fallen a little short of reaching the stage of a teacher–pupil relationship. These children relate to a teacher as a partial mother-substitute and use the relationship to achieve some learning. Certain forms of individual tutoring and teaching in small groups with much individual attention are geared to help children with such difficulties.

AT WHAT POINT CAN A CHILD NO LONGER MAKE UP FOR STEPS MISSED IN HIS DEVELOPMENT?

We don't know a general answer because there are so many individual variations—different children, different past experiences, different ways of making up. Many children have missed out only on some aspects. Usually, the sooner a child can get help and the more suited such help is to the child's specific needs, the better are the chances of repairing early misfortunes. Unfortunately, there are some who never get the right help or for whom it comes too late.

IS IT NOT IMPORTANT FOR A TEACHER TO LOVE CHILDREN MORE THAN TO LOVE HIS SUBJECT?

In every community children are a minority group, perhaps the most helpless and vulnerable of all minorities. Like other minority groups, and sometimes even more so, children are a ready target for prejudice and as such are unrealistically loved or hated, favored or mistreated. If a teacher's love of children springs from such a prejudice, it is usually not helpful because it has little to do with the qualities and needs of real individual children and gets in the way of building appropriate relationships with them. In the same way, a teacher who hates or detests children as a group cannot appreciate and relate to an individual child sensibly.

If, however, a teacher's love of children means that he or she respects and treats each child as a person, is able to feel with children and enjoy the give-and-take of relationships with them, then we shall probably find that such a teacher likes some children more than others, depending on the teacher's and child's particular personalities. It is not necessary to love one another in order to get along and work together. It is necessary to be civil, respectful, and appreciative of each other's contribution to the joint undertaking. This applies to pupils too. A child's successful learning does not necessarily depend on his like or dislike of a particular teacher as a person. It tends to depend more on the child's willingness and ability to apply himself and on the teacher's ability to convey his liking of the subject and to kindle the child's interest in it.

HOW DOES THE TEACHER–PUPIL RELATIONSHIP CHANGE BEYOND ELEMENTARY SCHOOL?

There are some changes but they happen only when the earlier relationships provided a good basis for further growth. The child's capacity for sustained work increases, as does the range of his interests and goals. Attitudes to learning and to the teacher which were still developing in the younger child and required much fostering, become more firmly established; for example, learning for oneself, working toward one's own goals, understanding and accepting the teacher's role. Ultimately some people (and some children can even do this at times in elementary school) are able to learn without a "real" teacher. They may use books as a substitute or utilize experiences to teach them—observations, experiments. We sometimes even speak of life as a great teacher, but people can only learn from life if they know how to learn and want to be taught.

SHOULD A TEACHER NOT BE INTERESTED IN THE CHILD AS A WHOLE PERSON RATHER THAN CONCERN HIMSELF ONLY WITH THE CHILD'S LEARNING?

It depends on the nature of the interest and the reasons for it. The interest is appropriate if the teacher wants to know about all aspects of the child's personality in order to be able to help him better with his learning and to adapt the joint work and goals to the pupil's current capacities; for example, a child's chronic illness or temporary stress in the home may affect his learning and may require changes in teaching methods and goals.

The teacher's interest is less appropriate and helpful if its aim is to establish an all-encompassing, close emotional tie for its own sake or in order to help the child with those concerns which are not within the teacher's proper domain; for example, unhappy relationships within the family or emotional problems. This could encourage the child to relate to the teacher as a family member or as a therapist and would then interfere with the teacher–pupil relationship and with the tasks it pursues. It is preferable to be a good teacher than a poor substitute for other people in the child's life. Often a teacher helps most by sympathizing with a child's distress and, if necessary, by alerting the parents or caretakers to his need.

IS IT NECESSARY FOR A CHILD TO GO TO A NURSERY SCHOOL TO LEARN HOW TO RELATE TO A TEACHER?

No, it is not essential. This developmental step can be taken at the start of elementary school. A good nursery school can be very helpful and facilitate entry to public school. A bad nursery school can be a harmful interference in the child's maturation.

RELATIONSHIPS

Basic Concepts

• Our personalities grow gradually, stage by stage, in innate developmental sequences. Each maturational spurt forms the base for the next stage in growth.

• The child's emotional and educational environment nurtures maturation, helps it to unfold and to achieve its full, harmonious shape at each successive level.

• Relationships make up the child's emotional and educational environment.

• A continuous good enough relationship with a mothering person is crucial to the baby's physical survival, forms the roots of his or her personality, and the base from which all other relationships grow.

• Through relationships the child learns to care for himself and others.

PART II

LEARNING SELF-CONTROL AND

COPING WITH DAILY TASKS:

CONTROLS AND MASTERIES

8

When and How a Child Gets to be Master of Himself

We rarely reflect on all it takes to function as an adult member of one's community. Depending on our circumstances and stage in life, we usually focus on what appears to us as the most difficult undertaking at that point. It may be a major aspect of life, such as earning a living, working out a harmonious relationship with a spouse, bringing up children; it may be a special stress, such as coping with an illness, a bereavement, or a loss of property; it may be one of the many smaller tasks which periodically confront us, like taking exams, or shopping for Christmas presents, or putting up the storm windows, or finding one's way to an appointment in an unfamiliar section of town. At such times we tend to become aware of all the knowledge, skills, and self-discipline it takes to accomplish these tasks. We may surprise ourselves at how many strengths we can muster in ourselves but we may also recognize and bemoan our inadequacies—our lack of good judgment or of patience, or difficulty in grasping the issues or in explaining them to others, our poor physical stamina or insufficient dexterity, our inability to compromise and adapt our wishes to the demands of reality.

What we usually don't do is to list for ourselves the many areas in which we master life's situations adequately and just what enables us to do so. We take our know-how for granted. Yet to a different or younger person, the very accomplishments that seem so easy and natural to us may seem extraordinarily difficult because he or she has not acquired the necessary personality "tools" to achieve them. To the twelve-year-old who still struggles to make a go of his paper route, running a business seems miles beyond his capabilities. One nine-year-old, after cooking a full family breakfast for the first time, said, "It was the hardest thing I ever did in my whole life and I didn't even think I could do it"; to her mother it was a simple daily routine requiring hardly any effort. The preschooler we talked about earlier was in awe just at his Dad's reading.

Now some people might say, "That's just a question of time and of learning. The younger ones or the less skilled ones still have to learn how to do things. They haven't been taught or they haven't had enough practice, or both." Yet, we recall that when we discussed learning we found that learning itself is a big achievement, that a child must have mastered many developmental steps in order to be able to be a pupil and to learn with a teacher's help, and we found that, unfortunately, some people's personalities never mature sufficiently to know how to learn effectively.

We also noted in our earlier discussion that the developmental masteries which underlie the ability to learn with a teacher, in or out of school, are not simply related to a child's innate potential but are achieved with the help of the adults with whom the child maintains an ongoing relationship, especially the parents. We listed some areas of personality achievements necessary for working with a teacher—independent basic self-care, a degree of mastery of urges and feelings, a measure of consideration for others, with appropriate control of aggression, enjoyment of interests and activities that do not provide immediate or bodily pleasures, and a capacity to relate to people on the basis of a cooperative endeavor.

These are not just big words, they stand for big achievements. They determine to a considerable extent whether a child gets to his elementary school on time, remembers to bring his homework, sits still, understands his lesson, completes his assignment and takes pride in doing so, and waits to go to the bathroom at the appropriate time. They determine whether he doesn't fight with his classmates, takes his proper place in line, doesn't steal another's candy, pays attention, corrects his mistakes, and doesn't giggle with his pal while the teacher explains something. These same achievements also form the basis for the adult's ability to hold a job and earn a living—his ability to get to work on time, to remember his uniform or equipment, to get along with the boss and colleagues, to work persistently and avoid undue coffee breaks or other distractions, and to derive satisfaction from a job well done.

We could draw similar connecting links between a youngster's care of his body and belongings and the adult's ability to look after his health, home, and property; between the first grader's ability to accept his place in his family and to maintain cooperative relationships with teachers and peers, and the adult's ability to be a considerate spouse, friend, colleague, and parent. Essentially the same personality achievements are required for coping with life's small and big tasks, in relation to ourselves and to the world. The difference is only one of degree. The means our personalities utilize for mastery develop early on and have to be tended carefully. They are, as it were, the building blocks of which our personality achievements are constructed.

There are two kinds of these building blocks or means for mastery: the "tools," that is, the functions we use to accomplish tasks, and the inner "monitors" or "helpers" that direct, guide, and judge our efforts. Among the former, the tools, are such functions as motility (large and small muscle motor control), speech, thinking, observing, and frustration tolerance. Among the latter, the inner monitors or helpers are self-esteem, conscience, and self-discipline.

HOW THE TOOLS AND INNER HELPERS DEVELOP

Neither the tools nor the inner helpers develop automatically. They are not manifest in the newborn human being except, in some instances, in very rudimentary form; for example, the baby's undirected waving around of arms and pushing of legs is the beginning of motility, his cry may be seen as the start of speech. Some of the functions are altogether absent at birth; for example, we cannot observe any signs of self-esteem or of conscience. Instead, the baby seems to carry within him or herself an innate developmental potential with an approximate timetable; that is, at certain periods in his or her growth the child becomes capable of learning to do certain things; for example, some time between about eight and eighteen months children usually become capable of learning to walk, an important manifestation of motor control. Some children learn to walk early, show a lot of intense inner "push" to move; others walk late and are not particularly keen on getting around. Some insist on being active with their large muscles by crawling, walking, pushing, and throwing things; others are more intent on exercising small muscle control by handling objects and using their fingers. We think that these differences in children's motility are due at least in part to variations in endowment. We assume that some children have it in them to develop motility earlier than other children and to control and coordinate their large and/or small muscles more effectively. I say we "assume," because we really cannot prove it since factors other than innate potential are always at work.

The differences between children are also related to bodily health (sickness or malnutrition may affect the start and intensity of motility) and to the intactness of the organs (malformed legs may interfere with movement). Beyond that, however, the unfolding of each function, including motility, is also from the very start codetermined by the child's environment, by the caring adults. The effect of their relationships with the child and of their attitudes and handling may delay or accelerate the development of functions, may contribute to a function flourishing or becoming stunted, may cause a function to be lost, at least temporarily, and may prevent some functions from developing altogether.

This may be difficult to believe. Many people are only now beginning to appreciate, for example, that a person's tested IQ is not simply a measure of his *inherent intelligence* (a term itself difficult to define) and is not a constant. It may vary considerably at different periods during a child's growth and is subject to the environmental influences which make up the child's total experience. Moreover, even a high intelligence measure in no way guarantees that a person can effectively utilize it for himself. He may not be able to learn well or to apply his potential in his job, nor may it serve him to make sensible decisions in his private life.

If it is hard to think in these terms about intelligence quotients, it is perhaps even harder to recognize that something like motor control is so complex and so closely linked to a child's experiences. After all, one might say, "Once he walks, he walks!" or "What an athletic gift that kid has. He'll be good at any sport." Yet there are children who learn to walk and then revert to crawling after an illness or separation and perhaps never regain their initial zest for movement. There also are very energetic early walkers whose motility never becomes gracefully coordinated and who never learn to channel it into the pursuit of athletic skills. They just remain toddlers in regard to their motility—"all over the place," forever into everything with their bodies, dashing around, but incapable of controlled directed skills and therefore hopeless at sports.

In humans each function takes years to develop, years before it unfolds fully, and before it takes its place within the personality and begins to serve it as a tool for mastery. During these years there is a constant close interaction between the child's potential and the environment which facilitates its fruition. Sometimes perhaps a strong potential can withstand and overcome environmental handicaps, sometimes a weaker potential may be so well nourished and tended that it thrives beyond expectation. In extreme cases, the finest potential can, no doubt, be irrevocably damaged by an unhelpful environment and a lack, or near-lack, of potential cannot be compensated for by the best environment. The fact, however, that no child can grow independently apart from caring adults, makes it impossible fully to isolate and measure the exact contribution of either the child's endowment or of the effect of the environment. What really counts is their harmonious interaction, step by step, all along the way.

The role of the caring adults starts before the child's maturational timetable has begun to operate, before the baby can move purposefully, before he can observe and make sense of what he or she perceives, before there is communication in words. For this reason the initial task of the parenting persons is to take over the child's functions and to perform them for him. But it is also their job, right along, to watch for the beginning manifestations of each function, and, when the first little signs show themselves, to foster and encourage it, to give it as much scope as possible, and to help the child to exercise it, enjoy it, and utilize it for his own independent growth. During the years when a function gradually matures, the child and the caring adults in many ways share it. On the one hand that means that the parent often still has to take over when the child's own functioning is insufficient to a task (even the most active toddler, walking along on his own, sometimes needs to be carried the rest of the way when he has gotten too tired to continue). On the other hand it means a different kind of sharing; namely, a sharing of the pleasure in the child's achievement, because every function needs to bring satisfaction to the child *and* to his loved ones, in order to develop well. Newly acquired functions are not ready to thrive on their own. It takes a long time before a function is "independent," before it is really part and parcel of the child's personality and available to serve him or her as a tool, regardless of the support of the environment.

A toddler may look like a competent walker and talker, having fun with his accomplishments, yet when a longer separation from the mothering person intervenes, he may lose it all. Sometimes mothers tell the day care center before enrollment that their children can walk and talk. When the children are first left at the center, however, they may not be able to communicate verbally and may even revert to crawling. The day care personnel are then apt to think that the mothers lied and portrayed their children as more advanced than they really were. But the child's regression may be as much of a surprise to the mother as to the day care center and she may even blame the staff for not handling her child well. While mother and day care worker put the blame on each other or feel bad, reproaching themselves or the child, they tend to forget that the child's functions still depend on the relationship with the mother and are easily affected by separation from her.

When we were discussing the role of the teacher–pupil relationship we noted some similar ways in which the pupil shares the learning process with the teacher, builds and deepens his relationship with the teacher in doing so, and only eventually may make learning and interest in a subject his own thing. We stressed that the teacher's interest and pleasure in the subject as well as in the process of learning it were important. This applies also to the parental attitude to the child's developing functions. The mother who herself enjoys talking as well as enjoying her child's learning to express himself in words, is of much greater help to his speech than the mother who is taciturn or ill at ease with language, or who chatters a lot but does not really use words for effective communication. Wanting to do as the loved person does, identifying with the admired, caring, and cared for parent, plays a considerable part in stimulating the child's potential for developing and investing his own functions and for making them a lasting part of his own personality. All this applies in equal measure to the development of the child's inner helpers, self-esteem, conscience, and self-discipline. We have touched on this when we talked about the ways in which the child takes in the parents' rules and values and forms a conscience, and about the ways parents and teachers help build the child's own good feelings in regard to learning and achieving, a part of self-esteem.

With the inner helpers it is more often recognized that their development depends on the caring adults. However, we often do not appreciate all that goes into helping a child to develop self-esteem, conscience, and self-discipline, how slow a process it is, the many steps it entails, and that even the most helpful parents cannot accelerate it at will but need to take into account the child's maturational timetable. For example, parents and nursery school teachers often bemoan the fact that they have told their youngsters "a thousand times not to take another's toy" but he still does it, although "he knows it isn't right." The adults' minor annoyance at this is understandable, but when they feel intensely frustrated, their anger is due to a mistaken idea about the preschooler's developmental capacities. He or she knows the rule but does not yet have a fully formed conscience to serve as a guide nor the self-discipline to restrain strong impulses. At that age the child can only use his knowledge of the rule with the loved adult's help in the form of supervision, reminder, and shared pleasure in the accomplishment. Nor will just any helpful participating adult suffice. When I once visited a nursery school I was left in the playground with two four-year-olds while the others had already gone into the building with the teacher. The two boys started to fight and I tried to intervene, "You must stop fighting. It's against the rules, you know." They did not stop but yelled at me almost in unison, "You can't tell us. You're not the teacher. You don't even know the rules here." Of course, as soon as they heard me call the teacher they got themselves in control.

As we now come to take a closer look at the growth of some of the child's tools and inner helpers, we shall over and over return to the role of the facilitating environment; that is, the part played by those who maintain the closest and most meaningful relationships with the child. In the context of these relationships, the work of each function and inner helper is first performed *by* the loved one, then *with* the loved one, and ultimately *like* the loved one.

9
Doing (Motility, Motor Control)

This is a good function for us to start with because we have already talked about it a bit and because it is one of the first to unfold in the baby's maturation process and one of the earliest to reach independence and integration within the child's personality. We can easily observe its beginnings in the first year (grasping, turning over, standing up, reaching, keeping hold of objects and directing them toward oneself), then see the main developmental thrust in the toddler (when walking gets really under way and when all the large and small muscle activities are exercised as if suddenly charged with energy), followed by a period of increased coordination and of beginning flow and grace in movement. Toward the end of the preschool years most youngsters are literally doing their own thing. Motility is by then a well-established function, has become essentially independent of the relationship with the caring adults, does not require thought or praise. Now the child just feels good to be moving around and doing things, and is ready to use motility as a tool, to get things for himself and to use them, to go to people or to get away from them, and to enjoy the many activities that have been mastered, be it pumping on the swing, or throwing and catching a ball, cutting paper or painting, zipping up a coat, or spreading a sandwich.

This does not imply that the five-year-old is capable of doing everything or of learning all motor skills. The maturational timetable of his muscle coordination will release new and more advanced levels of potential during the early years of elementary school and again in adolescence. This together with the developing ability to learn with a teacher will make it possible to acquire many skills that could not have been mastered earlier, such as writing, sports, playing a musical instrument, typing, sewing, woodwork, and many more. But success with these later motor activities depends to a considerable extent on two earlier steps: (1) the child's initial basic investment of his motility with zest and enjoyment; and (2) learning to use it as an effective tool. We can see that this second step has been sufficiently mastered when motility is no longer pursued for its own sake and no longer depends on being shared and supported by a loved one, but is used in the service of a skill or goal. School-age children don't run and jump up and down aimlessly or throw things around like toddlers (at least not most of the time!); they play baseball or basketball, they jump rope in ever more intricate ways, and even cops-and-robbers involves rules and techniques. The social aspects of these games bring much satisfaction, but many a youngster spends hours practicing them on his or her own, for the sheer fun of becoming proficient at a skill. Once the function is well integrated and feels comfortable in daily use it continues to serve a person all his life, way beyond the energetic years of youth. It contributes to the difference between the adult who enjoys physical activity and the one who prefers his armchair, and between him who pursues a dexterous hobby or work and another who is "all thumbs." The foundation is laid in the first years of life.

HOW DO THE PARENTING PERSONS ASSIST WITH MOTILITY?

Many mothers encourage and enjoy their babies moving and doing from the start. They prolong their baths and diaper changing times to let them kick their legs unencumbered; they allow them to move their arms freely during feeding and welcome their babies touching and holding on to the breast or bottle; they appreciate their babies' struggles in guiding their thumbs or fingers into their mouths and their eventual successes in keeping them there, which is usually the baby's first achievement in deliberate and purposeful motor coordination. Within a few months there is more to be fostered and to be thrilled with. As the baby reaches for things, mother hands him or her safe things to grasp and to mouth. She seemingly never tires of picking them up when they are dropped and holding them out again with a smile. She even laughs with her infant as he pokes at her eyes and pulls her to him by her hair. She also provides hard crackers or other food items to chew on and helps baby's hands to guide the cup, praising his efforts and putting up with the spills. By that time a number of mutually enjoyed games usually get under way, such as holding his arms to provide support for pulling himself up to stand or clapping hands and playing pat-a-cake.

In the last part of the first year the real job starts when suddenly the child propels himself from place to place and finds a whole new world within his reach. Almost all of the child's waking hours are spent on the go, getting a hold of some things and throwing down others. The mother who enjoys being physically active herself is most likely to take pleasure in her toddler's energetic mobility and to provide safe scope for it by being in constant attendance and by "clearing the decks" of valuables and breakables. She applauds his crawling though she needs to retrieve him time and again from under the couch when he gets stuck because he can only move forwards but does not know yet how to back up. She allows him to toddle along at his own pace instead of carrying him to save time and trouble, and she stands by patiently as he conquers the stairs. At best, the youngster's early motility is an exhausting business, particularly since it tends to head the child away from the mother, in fact in the opposite direction as a rule, and is as yet heedless of common dangers like electric outlets, table corners, standing lamps, stoves, not to mention street traffic. It's the mother's task to be on the lookout so that the child's pleasure in his movement is periodically curtailed with a "not safe" injunction rather than brought to a shocked standstill with yellings, spankings, or self-inflicted injuries. There is bound to be some conflict of interest. Most mothers cannot squeeze all their other work into the toddler's nap and sleep hours or into the usually brief periods when father can help with supervision. For this reason, the playpen may come in handy as a short-lived, more or less acceptable, "cage," and a gate across the stairway may at times be needed to block access to the Everest of upstairs.

Small muscle motor control poses its own challenges for the mother. It is so much more efficient to feed, wash, and dress toddlers than to pick up on their signals of wanting to do for themselves, especially since these signals are usually ill-directed at first—grabbing the spoon or dish, dripping the washcloth outside the tub, protesting mother's efforts at putting on garments, or running off with the shoes. Moreover, mothers usually enjoy ministering to the child's body and may not feel ready to exchange this gratification for the new one of sharing the child's pleasure in taking care of himself. Yet, many mothers put up with the mess of spilled food and splashed water, and they buy clothes which the child can more easily learn to take off and put on himself. They patiently assist his attempts, and they transfer their satisfaction in doing for the child to appreciation of his efforts at mastery. They soon feel rewarded by the joint glow of pride at "You are such a good spoon eater," "And such a good foot washer," and "Such a good shoe putter-on" when occasional successes are finally achieved. These same mothers often supervise their toddlers' play with pots and pans from the lower kitchen shelves, or they keep boxes with spools and jar lids handy for his small muscle practice while they prepare dinner, ever careful of the obstacle course under foot. And in freer moments they enjoy such ubiquitous toddler games as rolling a ball to and fro.

When mothers are unable to provide sufficient safe scope for and appreciation of the unfolding motility, it may come to harm. Young toddlers who have to spend excessive time in their cribs, playpens, or harnessed in baby buggies, may become quite passive, or they may find unhealthy outlets for their activity in headbanging and rocking. Sometimes children's motility remains jerky, impulsive, and ill-coordinated if severely restricted during the initial zestful period. For example, Anne's motility, interrupted at seventeen months by a hospitalization during which she was tied down, remained clumsy, wild, and aimless so that, as a kindergartner, she was a regular bull in a china shop and miles behind her peers in mastering motor skills.

Not surprisingly, a similar arrest in the development of motility can be due to a lack of relationship with a parenting person; for example, studies show that young toddlers in institutions who were given ample scope for motility did not achieve a coordinated flow and grace of movement until they established a consistent one-to-one relationship in a foster family. This was in contrast to their peers who remained institutionalized and whose movements continued to lack integration (Provence and Lipton, 1962).

The late toddler's and young nursery school child's motility needs a great deal of shared enjoyment for the gradual development of skills. Sometimes mothers think that as soon as the child knows how to feed or dress himself, or how to stack blocks or make sandpies, he no longer needs them and can entertain himself. Actually the child can only enjoy and perfect his skill when it does not lead to mother's withdrawal but, on the contrary, when she continues her support as an appreciative audience and, at times, participant. Left to himself, the newly acquired activity withers away, as a plant wilts without water. Quite often, when children enter nursery school, they initially lose all the skills they seemed to be capable of at home. They don't show interest in drawing, although at home they wielded pencils and crayons with zest; they throw sand around, although they used to make nice sandpies with Mom; they refuse to put on their coats or hats, leaving the task for their embarrassed or irritated mothers at pickup time. These children are not naughty or stubborn, it's just that, without mother, doing is joyless. When activity brings no pleasure it won't be practiced and there will be no wish to do it better or to learn something harder. Usually, a gradual separation from mother at the start of nursery school and a chance slowly to build a relationship with the teacher avoids such setbacks or helps to overcome them. Sometimes even a young kindergartner's skills still depend on the relationship with the parents, especially those that started with the wish to become like the parent. One young, very articulate woman had great difficulty in putting her ideas into written form. She was aware of this and claimed that she had always had trouble with writing. She attributed this to the beginning of her schooling: "I used to write my name with my mother and I remember loving it and being so proud of myself. But when I went to kindergarten there were so many children and I felt the teacher hardly knew me. I just didn't like writing the way she did it and I think I never got to like it again." Perhaps her mother discontinued her interest in the daughter's writing, perhaps other factors also intervened, but there is no doubt a kernel of important truth in the young woman's own thinking about this.

Usually children's motility becomes truly their own toward the end of the preschool years, in the sense that it is not likely to be "lost" altogether due to temporary restriction or separation from the parents and is now ready to serve the personality as a tool for doing things. Throughout the school years, however, the acquisition and perfection of new motor skills depends, to an extent, on the chance to learn, practice, and enjoy them with a loved person in the family, school, or community.

CAN EARLY INTERFERENCES IN MOTILITY BE MADE UP OR TREATED?

Unless they are especially marked, early interferences in motility are often not noticed or attributed to variations in endowment. In adulthood, such differences are accommodated by individual life-styles, reflected in a person's work or leisure activities. During childhood, parents and teachers notice that some children are more graceful and others more clumsy, that some possess mastery of many motor skills and easily learn new ones, whereas other children have few skills and are not interested in acquiring more. They may even be aware that some children enjoy "doing" more than others. Educators' efforts are usually directed at helping children with specific motor skills, such as sports or writing. This means that they do not attempt to affect the early developmental phase of the function or to undo interferences that affected it in its initial unfolding. Rather, they pick up at the point where the function is already the child's own and where it serves him as a more or less adequate tool, with the aim of helping the child to achieve adequate age-appropriate mastery in certain skills. The question then is whether or to what extent a child's learning of a specific skill with a teacher (the teacher may be the parent) and the pleasure he derives from it, can compensate for the earlier deficiencies. The answer varies with individuals. Sometimes children become very efficient with specific skills and enjoy their mastery greatly. Sometimes even their general coordination improves, but rarely is there a real change in the function itself; that is, rarely do their movements develop flow and grace and rarely does their enjoyment of some skills spread to an enjoyment of all motility. For example, one may become a very good swimmer without being lithe and without a wish to engage in other sports or physical activities when swimming is not feasible. Also, with some skills, flow of movement is more important, such as dancing, whereas with others, such as football, strength and practice play a large part. It is easier to make up for deficiencies in strength and practice, grace is harder to achieve belatedly.

Attempts to affect or treat the function itself are usually most effective when they are undertaken while the child is very young, a late toddler or young preschooler. At that time the caring adult's encouragement of and shared pleasure in the child's motility still play a special part. We do not know the exact time when such help ceases to be effective. It seems to vary with individuals and to depend on many related factors in the child's overall development.

Sometimes motility is interfered with by emotional factors at later stages in a person's life. A specific, well-established skill or even all movement may become inhibited for psychological reasons; for example, a person may not be able to walk, or to move his or her arms, or to play a musical instrument. Such symptoms of emotional difficulties can be treated psychiatrically.

WHAT IF A MOTHER DOES NOT KNOW SHE SHOULD HELP HER CHILD WITH MOTOR CONTROL?

Mostly a mother's relationship with her little child enables her to be in tune with his needs and to meet them adequately.

Her support of his motility is a part of her interaction with him and she usually helps him without specifically knowing that she should do so. This also applies to the father whose relationship with his toddler often includes most especially support of motor control, such as going for walks, helping with stairs, playing roll-a-ball, assisting with push toy activities.

What mothers and fathers often don't know is just how valuable and important these activities with their toddlers are. Such knowledge could increase their self-esteem as parents when they do support their child's "doing." It could help them to make an extra effort when they are tired or pressed for time. It might also alert them to avoid or minimize practices that unduly restrict the child's movements; for example, when parents realize how hard it is for young children to stay in bed when they are ill, they allow them to be up and about as much as possible.

Parents are more often aware that their school-aged child benefits from physical activities with them, such as playing baseball or swimming together. These skills, however, can be acquired with other loved adults, whereas the early support of motility itself is primarily in the parents' hands.

10

Observing Reality

We often pity those who cannot fully perceive what is going on around them because they are blind or deaf, and we appreciate to some extent how difficult such a handicap makes it for them to assess the world and to adapt to it. Even a temporary cold makes us aware how much pleasure we are missing out on because we can't smell and taste as well as when we are healthy. If, for some reason, we cannot use our hands to touch, to feel things, we notice how important these perceptions are to us, how much we usually rely on them. When we have an opportunity to be acquainted with people who are mentally ill, who are not deprived of perceptions but deprived of the ability to interpret them correctly and to judge what is real, inside themselves and outside, we realize how helpless we are without this mental tool. More often, however, we just take it for granted that we are able to observe, and to make sense of what we perceive. We think that this special ability has always been a part of us and we rarely notice how much it contributes to our sense of well-being. Yet even in those of us who are healthy, it develops only gradually, needs a lot of parental help, and hardly ever reaches its full potential. For example, most of us see only a fraction of what we could see and quite often misjudge even that. How many of us think we know what our house looks like, but when we try to draw it we notice how much we have overlooked, how many details we have not noticed, and how poorly we have assessed its measurements and proportions. What distinguishes the artist is, above all, his acute ability to observe, and this is equally true of the really good physician, scientist, naturalist, or businessman. It is also a most important tool for parents and others who care for or work with children, serving as a guide to understanding and educating.

HELPING CHILDREN TO OBSERVE AND ASSESS THE REALITY OF THE WORLD AROUND THEM

As with motility, however, special skills in observing and assessing reality are mastered later, after the function itself has developed and become well established within the child's own personality. Originally the mother watches and listens and judges for her baby and, at the same time, helps his or her functions to unfold. A baby's senses need the right kind and amount of stimuli. Most observant mothers soon learn that too many or too loud noises upset her infant as do too many different faces and things milling around within his sight. Some skin contacts interest or soothe him, for example a bath in water of the right temperature, and others are intensely irritating, such as a cold hard table surface. When there are too many perceptions or when they are too intense, babies become overstimulated, fussy, cranky, and confused or they "tune out" and withdraw, often into sleep, in the midst of turmoil. Neither reaction is helpful to their developing capacity to observe and to make sense of what they perceive. It is equally unhelpful when the baby receives too little stimulation, such as when he is rarely picked up, is not held during feeds but sucks from a propped-up bottle, and does not hear voices. Along with the quantity of sensory stimulation, it matters what kind of perceptions they are and whether they can be used to understand what goes on.

Since the mothering person is the most important part of the child's environment, it is not surprising that a baby's vision is equipped to seek out and focus especially on the shape of the human face, his hearing is especially tuned to pick up the range of the female human voice, and his movements and muscle tone respond to that of the mother's holding body and to the rhythm of her speech. The most

significant and meaningful perceptions are thus related to
the caring interactions with the mother and to the need satisfactions they bring. Given good enough care, these perceptions also have the great advantage of being consistent, so
they can be more easily remembered and eventually used to
assess and even anticipate events. Within a few weeks after
birth babies often know that mother's voice signals soon-to-
be-received comfort. Mothers are rightly thrilled when their
baby stops screaming on hearing her talk to him as she
approaches the room. Sometimes people go to great lengths to
provide toys, music, wall decorations, and similar items for
their babies' earliest "education." They forget that mother is
the best-equipped provider for and stimulant of the child's
mind. Toys become more meaningful later, but even then
they interest, please, and help the child most when they are
enjoyed *with* mother rather than *instead* of her.

The baby's first understanding of reality is, however,
quite tenuous. Mothers are often startled to realize just how
upsetting it is to the baby when his perceptions deceive or
disappoint him. This happens, for instance, when mother
shows up with a changed hairdo. Baby takes one look at her
and starts screaming. He didn't recognize her and it may take
a while of soothing, talking, and holding, to convince him
that it is mother after all. When different people with different
faces and voices, with different ways of holding and of going
about things take care of the baby, his or her perceptions are
so varied and so hard to link to specific results that the baby
may take a much longer time to sort out what's what and/or
may not get to feel that his perceptions are a worthwhile
means of gauging reality at all. Of course, inadequate, inconsistent, and unresponsive mothering has similar disadvantages.

It is not too long before the baby also notices and assesses
things which mother sometimes wishes he didn't, for example in the second half of the first year, and sometimes even
earlier, children's acute perceptions alert them to mother's
intention to leave. Sometimes the mere sight of her coat or
purse or the different rhythm of her voice and movements,
enables a baby to draw that conclusion and sets off his vigorous howling protest. Since the baby's world *is* the mother, her

leaving threatens to shatter it. Some mothers welcome the child's alertness and help him or her to understand the reality of their absence a bit better. They show the child their preparations for leaving, show him who will take care, talk to him about it simply and calmly, and wave bye-bye. Afterwards they signal their return with a happy "hello." If the absence is not too long, children soon make the link that bye-bye is not forever but is followed by a bearable interval and by eventual reunion. Games of peek-a-boo, of "Now I see you, now I don't," help with the idea. It does not prevent the child's upset at mother's leaving but it helps him observe, understand, and master it. If, however, mother sneaks out in the hope of the child not noticing and being spared an upset, he is likely to be taken by surprise and be more upset or, worse yet, he won't get to feel that his perceptions give him reliable information and can help him figure out events that concern him. Why bother to look around and listen and think? If the world is quite unpredictable, if there is no hope of figuring things out, if it is overwhelming and mostly unpleasant, if one's efforts are forever foiled and go unappreciated, there is no encouragement for the developing capacity to perceive and to assess reality. By contrast, the baby who is helped to perceive and to understand, begins to experience the special joy of noticing things and of finding that he can trust his senses. Few things make a person, even a very little person, more solidly "with it" and more confident in himself than the feeling "I am right because I know what is true." It is a steady anchor for oneself and for the world in which one lives. In the baby and young child this trust in himself depends intimately on the mother's cooperation, confirmation, and shared enjoyment. For the most part, mothers' in-tune observations of their infants are good enough to enable their children to develop a good enough ability to observe and to observe correctly, and to enjoy their mastery so that they want to observe more and more.

The well-developed toddler's intense alertness and ability to perceive everything is often underestimated by the parents: "I had no idea he knew where I'd put his ball"; "He couldn't have heard me talk to the sitter on the phone. Why, he was in the other room!"; "It doesn't matter about the TV being on; she doesn't notice yet what they are showing." It certainly is often very inconvenient to take into account the toddler's powers of observation. It puts lots of restraints on parental sayings and doings and requires much explaining. Yet most parents are willing to make the effort because they are also proud of their youngster's "smartness" and appreciate it with him or her: "Why you little so-and-so, you really figured that out, good for you!" And when his observations lead him to make mistakes of judgment, they usually do not laugh at or belittle them but help him to understand better. For example, when little Jessica heard her mother comment, "I wonder how she got that miserable flu?" she answered quite seriously, "From jumping on Mommy–Daddy bed." Her mother, surprised and bemused, explained to Jessica that people do not get ill from doing naughty things, not even from jumping on Mommy's and Daddy's bed. She did not, however, go on into a complicated account of viral infections because she gauged correctly that Jessica would not be able to make sense of it. Sometimes it is sufficient to know what does *not* cause events and to bear the thought that one will perhaps be able to understand it better later. It can be quite frustrating not to know and not to understand but that frustration is easier to learn to bear when children are helped to appreciate that the adults also don't know and understand everything.

Some parents, unfortunately, deliberately fool children, perhaps to "spare them" upset: they tell them "Grandma went on a trip," when Grandma is ill in the hospital and everyone is upset about it; or to coerce them ("The boogey man is waiting outside to get you if you don't go to bed"). To avoid being pestered parents may say: "The ball went bye-bye, all gone" when it was really hidden out of sight because it's time for dinner; or to provide a surprise ("No, I didn't buy anything for you" when the birthday present was just stashed away in the closet). However kindly the intent, when the caring adult's stated assessment of the reality is at odds with the truth and with the child's own potential observations, the capacity for observing and understanding is diminished. Even unpleasant realities can be mastered with parental help and are preferable to confusion.

Damage to the child's developing functions may occur when the child is led to disregard his own observations and to abide by the parent's faulty assessment. The parents' false or mixed-up picture of reality may not be due to their deliberate misrepresentation of facts. It may be caused by their own difficulty in observing and assessing situations. For example, two-year-old Laura's mother viewed their baby-sitter as very competent and failed to notice that she was too harsh and neglectful of Laura's needs. She accepted the sitter's reports of Laura's "naughtiness" and punished Laura without realizing that Laura was simply reacting to inadequate handling. She did not think to solicit and respect Laura's limited verbal accounts and reluctance to go to the sitter, trusting the adult's "truth" more than the child's. Laura, in turn, could not complain about the sitter because she felt that she, like her Mommy, had to like her caretaker and had to accept her as being in the right and herself as being in the wrong.

Some of the worst damage to the child's ability to use and trust his senses results from his relationship with a psychotic parent whose illness interferes with competent observation and judgment and prevents support for the child's developing function (Anthony, 1970).

During the nursery school years children's inquisitiveness is especially pronounced. Their observational abilities have advanced, are more independent of the caring adults, and are fueled by growing interest in the sexual differences between boys and girls and the sexual functions of men and women. The youngsters' insistent "researches" and their endless questions of why and how pose as much of a problem to parental handling as does their as yet limited capacity for understanding. In this, as in earlier phases, parents are most helpful when they can gauge appropriately what is too much and what is too little food for the senses and just what amount and kind of knowledge their children can absorb. When youngsters are not supposed to ask and are not given any answers, their important developing capacities for observing and understanding may be stunted, but this can also happen when parents take the extreme opposite approach, exposing the children to observations that overwhelm them and give them explanations which far exceed their understanding. This applies not only to observations and facts of a sexual nature, but to everything the child perceives and attempts to make sense of. The observant parent is at a great advantage in learning how to meet the child's needs because he can use the child's behavior and verbalizations as a guide.

Three-year-old Danny was quite insistent on watching a number of TV shows in the late afternoon. Since he seemed to like them and since mother found it easier to prepare dinner without Danny underfoot, she allowed him to watch. She noticed, however, that Danny's behavior during and after dinner became quite obstreperous. He was excessively noisy and bodily active, could not settle down to enjoy the family meal, and would not heed reminders. She suspected a connection between Danny's behavior and the preceding TV programs which she mentioned to him and asked him to tell her more of what he had seen and heard. His accounts and her own later viewing with him made it clearer that Danny felt overwhelmed and confused by the antics of the actors that were intended to be funny. In his obstreperous behavior Danny displayed a caricature of their performance and gave his own "show," which made his parents into as much of an uncomfortable captive audience as he had been in front of the TV. With one of the programs mother's explanations helped Danny to make sense of it, with the other she felt it was too stimulating and difficult to understand. She told Danny so, decided against his watching it, and arranged to have him help her with dinner instead. Danny was indignant at first but also relieved, and his behavior during the evening hours soon improved.

HELPING CHILDREN TO OBSERVE AND ASSESS THE REALITY OF THEIR INNER WORLD

Young children have great difficulty in distinguishing real from pretend, which often adds to their misunderstanding of TV and also of stories, books, and theater. In part this is related to their immature mix-up between reality and fantasy, between perceiving and knowing what is true outside themselves and what is true inside their own minds. When they wish something, good or bad, they often expect it to happen. When they fear something in their minds they tend to see it materialize outside—the witch who hides in the closet or the bear who threatens from under the bed. Helping youngsters to observe and evaluate their inner reality is as important a parental task as their support for the child's understanding of the world around them (Hall, 1982a). Indeed, observing oneself and what goes on inside oneself is often more difficult. Yet knowing what one truly feels and thinks, though sometimes unpleasant, brings a sense of certainty and mastery in itself as well as a good guide to what to do or not to do about the situation. Initially in this area too, the mother observes for the child.

It takes a lot of in-tune looking and listening to note little differences in a baby's cry, expression, and body posture before one can gauge correctly whether his inner sensations indicate hunger, pain, fatigue, cold, and so on (A. Freud, 1953). Sometimes even the skilled mother makes a mistake, offers the wrong comfort, and has to observe the baby further to come up with a better answer. The mother's correct observations and assessment not only help to meet the child's need and to comfort him, they also entail respect for his communications to her and help him to learn to know and gauge for himself. One of the problems that may arise with on-demand feeding is that the mother may respond to all of the baby's cries with nursing instead of distinguishing between different signals and offering need appropriate comforts. The baby, in turn, may learn to accept her judgment and demand food whenever he feels inner discomfort—eating when he is tired, or when he is lonely, when he is cold, sad, or angry. Such failure to know what goes on inside contributes to later problems with overeating or addictions.

As the infant gets older he can begin to observe inside differences between needs and feelings. For example, Terry, only fifteen months old, was irritable, threw her toys around, pushed at her mother, and looked distressed. Mom said, "Terry feels angry." Terry repeated "angry, angry" and looked relieved as though something had suddenly made sense. A bunch of bewildering inner sensations had become a definite something, a something that Mom knew and didn't get alarmed about. It was a beginning step for Terry in observing and knowing about her feelings, and in time, of course, she learned to know many different feelings—happy, sad, excited, jealous, disappointed.

Around the start of elementary school, when the child's conscience is new and its voice feels unfamiliar and harsh, children often have difficulty in recognizing that it comes from inside them. They tend to complain unjustly that the teachers and parents yell at them. They feel criticized and punished by the mildest rebuke, and may view the most reasonable school principal as a vengeful monster. At this time it helps when parents point out that perhaps the "yelling" and criticism is really an "inside" feeling, that it is not the people outside but the conscience inside that makes them feel bad about themselves. When one knows that one feels guilty one can begin to figure out what one reproaches oneself for, and can perhaps put it right or make amends. The parent or teacher then ceases to be an "ogre" and may even appear supportive and reassuring.

Jimmy, a well-functioning kindergartner, complained that his teacher was "ever so mean" and didn't like his work. The parents were surprised when, during a joint conference, the teacher praised Jim for his efforts and achievements and spoke with him in kindly fashion. At home, the parents pointed out to Jim the discrepancy between Jim's feeling about the teacher and her actual behavior and puzzled with him about the reason for his feeling. They then noticed that Jim often spoke disparagingly of his own school papers and very much admired and envied his older brother's more advanced homework. They could then wonder with Jim whether perhaps it was not the teacher but Jimmy who criticized himself because he expected so much of himself.

The ability to observe, within and without, and to assess both realistically, becomes only gradually the child's own tool and, to some extent, does not lose its dependence on the relationship with the adults until adolescence. Teachers influence it most helpfully when they themselves enjoy observing, appreciate the pupils' observing and help them practice it.

When observing is enjoyed and valued, it is easier to steer

clear of the many pitfalls that tend to interfere with it, such as the wish to see what one wants to see rather than what is really there, or the need to cut short observations and arrive at snap judgments because it is hard to bear the uncertainty of not knowing, or the need to impose values of "good" or "bad" on what one observes instead of viewing the facts in a neutral manner.

LEARNING SPECIAL SKILLS IN OBSERVING

As the child's observational ability becomes increasingly his own, he also learns to develop it in specific areas of study, such as observation of machines, of animals, of chemical processes. In different societies individuals are expected to exercise their powers of observation and judgment in varied ways and in certain fields. The primitive hunter and gatherer needs to develop special observing skills which, in their accuracy and goal-directed efficiency, appear almost like magical know-how to the city dweller of a Western culture. On the other hand, democratic urban societies make it very necessary for individuals to be observant of all their needs, feelings, and ideas in order to function independently. Many of us also need to develop specific observing skills in our chosen work or profession. Those of us who have made observation our own valued tool, still have to learn these skills with a teacher and perfect them on our own.

For those of us who work with children or care for them, learning how to observe children is a most important part of the job. We cannot really understand how children develop or how we can help them without knowing how to observe them. Yet, although children can readily be seen and heard everywhere, observing them is probably harder than observing anything or anyone else. There are many reasons for this. Among them is the tendency not to respect children, either because we were not respected as children or because we did not respect ourselves as children. Among them also is the fact that children, and all they do and say, touch off our own feelings and threaten to throw us off our adult balance. They do not yet abide by our adult social rules, their direct remarks ruffle our feathers, and the undisguised intensity of their feelings takes us aback. We cope with our discomfort by belittling or disregarding children's words and behavior, by imposing our controls and restrictions on them before we have a chance to understand them fully, or by attaching moral values to their actions. How often we say that "John was bad last night" when closer observation would have revealed that John was worried or upset or even angry at us for understandable reasons. When we can allow ourselves to observe children, however, we reap rich rewards. We may not always grasp why a child does what he does or what the full meaning is of all he tells, but we can feel the thrill of looking at a new world or, better yet, of getting back in touch with a world we once inhabited and had almost lost. Children can teach us a lot too (Out of the mouths of babes . . .) and often their assessment of reality is superior to ours, as illustrated by the well-known story of *The Emperor's New Clothes* in which only the little boy dared to observe and state that the emperor was nude (Andersen, 1837).

HOW CAN ONE OBSERVE CHILDREN WHEN ONE KNOWS THEM AND INTERACTS WITH THEM?

It is often assumed that the personal feelings which are part of an observer's relationship with a child may prejudice and distort his observations, and that his give-and-take activity with the child affects the child's responses and interferes with a chance to see what would happen if there were no interaction. There is no doubt that both these factors have to be taken into account. It is not uncommon for a fond parent not to "see" the son's troubled behavior, or for a baby-sitter not to notice that her little charge's inability to go to bed relates to the excited hide-and-seek game she played with him just before sleep time.

The competent observer minimizes these interferences by being aware of his own feelings and actions and of their effect on the child. He observes himself as well as the child. This is not as difficult as it sounds. It is just a part of learning the skill of observing. One keeps it in mind, practices it, and, if possible, gets help with it from one's teacher. The potential disadvantage of making mistakes and of having some "blind spots" are heavily counterweighted by the great advantages of gaining more valuable observations and of understanding them better because they are part of the relationship and can be fitted into the familiar framework of the child's life.

To illustrate this we can remind ourselves of what happens almost daily in many families where the father, on returning home in the evening, is often unable to make sense of his child's behavior without being filled in on what had transpired during his absence. For example, father observes that his nine-year-old, Kenny, is disgruntled, hardly says hello, and hides away in his room. Some fathers might simply consider Kenny ill-mannered and tell him off. Many fathers, however, would rely on their knowledge of Kenny to recognize that something is bothering their son. They might turn to the mother to ask her, "What's up with Kenny?" and perhaps be told, "He's been uptight ever since he got home from school because he messed up his spelling test. He feels really bad," or they might use their own relationship with Kenny to ask *him*, hoping that he would tell them what's troubling him. If Kenny were then to respond only by shrugging his shoulders and turning away, Dad would know that this is Kenny's characteristic way of indicating that the topic is too painful to talk about just then. If Kenny were only two years old and had an obstreperous evening, father would have no choice but to turn to mother to see whether she knows what the upset relates to, because the two-year-old is unlikely to give father an understandable account himself, either in words or in behavior. Since even a kindly and interested father needs that much help to understand his child, what sense could an "objective" outsider make of either nine- or two-year-old Kenny, given a limited observation period, no additional knowledge of the boy or his experiences, and no relationship with him to elicit trusting and trustworthy answers? True, he might not be tempted to get annoyed at Kenny, but his observations would be so out of context as to preclude any assessment of the situation. That is the great disadvantage of the "objective outsider." His handicap is the more prohibitive the shorter the period of observation, the younger the child, and the more it excludes both relationship and interaction.

Objectivity is best attained by being a competent observer of self and others, rather than by excluding data and depriving them of a meaningful context. Also, it is sometimes overlooked that the "outside uninvolved" observer still affects the situation he observes. Children are acutely aware of and react to both a one-way mirror and a bystander. This interference is considerably helped when the purpose of being observed is discussed with the children; for example, "This is Miss So-and-so. She is here (or she will watch through the mirror from the other room) because she wants to learn about what children do and say."

The observer who knows the child can often correct his "blind spots" by comparing his observations with those of others who observe the child, either at the same time or at another time; for example, when parent and teacher compare and complement their observations. The "outside" observer is helped to understand his observations by learning more about the child from "inside" observers; for example, a baby-sitter who first meets the child asks the parent for clarification and additional information to understand better what he or she has observed.

WHEN ONE IS IN CHARGE OF CHILDREN AND RESPONSIBLE FOR THEIR BEHAVIOR, IS IT NOT MORE IMPORTANT TO ACT THAN TO OBSERVE?

In some extreme instances this is true; for example, when one sees a young child standing on the windowsill one needs to help him get off at once rather than to observe what prompted him or what he might do next. The observant caretaker, however, is not likely to find the child on the windowsill because his ongoing observation usually helps him to notice that the child may make himself unsafe before the situation gets that far. When action is based on observation and goes hand in hand with it, there is a better chance that it will be appropriate and well-timed. For example, seven-year-old

Lionel and his nine-year-old brother Justin have an argument about their game of checkers. Whether and how the sitter should intervene will depend on his or her observations of the children's personalities, of what had taken place during the preceding hours, and of the cause and nature of the argument. Do the brothers usually quarrel? Do they resolve their arguments peacefully or end up in a fight? Did Lionel tease Justin all evening (or vice versa) so that the argument is a culmination of their interplay? Has Justin not been feeling well and is particularly touchy that day? Are they arguing about the rules, or over one brother's cheating, or because one of them cannot bear to be the loser? These and many more observed facts will determine the sitter's correct action, along with an assessment of his or her own part—perhaps her own impatience that day, her tendency to "jump in" or to let things go on too long, or the fact that she was on the phone and partly neglected the boys, so that their argument related also to their not feeling properly supervised and taken care of.

Actually, many sitters would wisely rely not only on their own observations but would ask the children to help, by soliciting their observations of themselves, of the others, and of the situation; for example, they might say, "I can't quite figure out this argument, so why don't each of you in turn tell me how it looks to you." Or, "You know, it's unusual for the two of you to get into such an argument. You are usually quite nice with one another. Let's see what you think got in the way today. Perhaps we can then understand it all better together and figure out a good way to settle it." Or, "Justin, it's looked to me like you've had a hard evening all along. Have you noticed that too? Is something the matter? Is this argument a part of it? Perhaps we can work things out better if you could figure out what bothers you and tell me about it." It is always helpful to find out what the child has observed and to encourage his observation of himself at the same time. This may not only assist one in understanding and resolving the immediate situation, but it also supports the child's developing function and, last but not least, improves the relationship between child and adult because he and his opinions are respected and appropriately considered.

**HOW CAN ONE HELP CHILDREN
TO OBSERVE THE RIGHT THINGS SINCE,
SO OFTEN, ALL THEY WANT TO LOOK AT
ARE THE WRONG THINGS, FOR EXAMPLE AT
THE MISBEHAVIOR OF OTHERS RATHER THAN
THEIR OWN, OR AT EXCITING AND VIOLENT
TV PROGRAMS RATHER THAN AT
EDUCATIONAL ONES?**

Children of all ages, and adults as well, find it easier to observe what is wrong with others than what is amiss in themselves, and to advise and correct others rather than themselves. A lot depends on how much it hurts one's feelings to look at oneself, and on the extent to which one feels that admitting one's shortcomings would destroy all one's self-esteem or would just dent it a little.

Annie, aged three-and-a-half years, was reprimanded by her mother for leaving her toys in a mess. She looked chagrined and was very quiet for a moment, then replied, "But in most ways I am very nice," and ran off to pick up her toys. Annie felt hurt but not devastated. She could summon her good feelings about herself to counterbalance the hurt and to see it in proportion. Had she felt in danger of being too hurt, she would have protected herself by denying that she had done anything wrong, or by getting mad at her mother, or perhaps by some other way characteristic of her. The nature of the mother's reprimand also played a part. A stinging criticism hurts more than a more gently worded one. A louder or harsher rebuke tends to make it harder for a person to accept it, although parents and teachers often mistakenly assume that the opposite is true (i.e., they fear a child won't listen unless they come down hard). The mother's attitude in her relationship to Annie also mattered. When a parent always presents him or herself to the child as perfect and brooks no criticism, the child adopts a similar way of handling shortcomings. If, however, the adult acknowledges his or her own mistakes and imperfections and allows the child to lodge complaints properly, the child has a chance to model himself accordingly.

Children's, and sometimes even adults' propensity for preferring to be interested in excited and violent happenings is a very different matter. It applies not only to TV programs but to wherever such events might take place—in the home, street, playground, in books, movies, comic strips, newspapers. It relates to our instinctual impulses and to the gratification they seek. The young child's curiosity is an important part of these impulses and has not yet had a chance to be diverted to other, more neutral aspects of life. The older child, in elementary school and beyond, has usually invested a good part of his "looking and finding out" energy in intellectual pursuits, although even then there remains a part of him that wishes to look at the more immediate bodily things.

The developmental step from wanting to find out mostly about the "wrong" things to becoming interested also in the "right" things is slow and difficult. It depends to a considerable extent on the environment's help and model and is not always achieved to a sufficient extent.

11
Using Words

Why talk of "using words"? Why not say "speech," "talking," or "language"? I chose the term *using words* because, in discussing the development of personality tools, functions, we are concerned with the ways in which words serve a person rather than with the many different aspects of language or speech in general. Specifically, we shall look at the use of words for the purpose of communication, of thinking, and of mastering feelings, and we shall highlight how these uses of words help a person to be master of himself, to cope with his environment and to get along with others.

COMMUNICATING IN WORDS

When, as adults, we find ourselves among people who speak a foreign language, or when we have had some dental work done and can't talk because our mouth is anesthetized or sore, we suddenly can't use words to make ourselves understood. This can be most frustrating and infuriating, or frightening to the point of panic. If we are ingenious with bodily gestures, point, make faces, or demonstrate in action, we can often still get across what we immediately want or need, but we feel pretty much stymied when it comes to exchanging ideas or relating events, and we usually have to forego altogether the pleasure of a give-and-take companionable conversation. After some time of this we may end up feeling lonely and isolated. Our handicap of not being able to use words becomes

155

much easier to bear when we are with people with whom we have a close relationship. Our knowing them well and their knowing us facilitates nonverbal communication and helps bridge the gap. Even little gestures and slight changes in expression are more readily "caught" and correctly interpreted. A mere look may convey a feeling or want and evoke an empathic response. Indeed, close friends or marital partners often are so much on the same "wavelength" that they understand each other's thoughts and feelings in a situation without having to say a word. This kind of mutual understanding, however, is not really wordless. Both think in words, both have talked with each other at other times and often talk about an event afterwards ("I knew what you were thinking and I could hardly wait to talk with you"). They also find it important and helpful to discuss in words situations which are new or complicated, or on which they do not see eye to eye.

Then how do mothers communicate with babies who can neither talk nor think in words? In talking about the early mother–infant relationship, we found that mothers have to learn to recognize the baby's nonverbal signals, and that they are greatly helped in this by being with the child all the time and by loving him or her, which means caring a great deal about understanding what the infant needs, wants, feels, and experiences. When the mother is able to meet her baby's demands in the right way, she communicates in her turn: "I have understood you and I feel with you." Very soon then the baby begins to understand mother's signals, gestures, moods, sounds, and responds to them. Within weeks and months they communicate with each other nonverbally. Even at its most empathic and harmonious, however, this kind of communication runs into difficulty when something new comes up, say the child gets ill. The mother does not understand right away what is wrong; she may misunderstand what is going on, and she may say in desperation, "If only he could tell me what he wants. I can't wait till he can talk. It'll be so much easier." The baby in that situation just finds himself not understood and, like the adult among foreigners, gets angry, frightened, and helpless. A mother who doesn't understand is almost as bad as a mother who has disappeared—both situations may feel like the end of the world. As the baby grows into a toddler, his ability to communicate is increasingly helped by the addition of verbal signals. This is particularly necessary as understanding each other no longer revolves just around basic needs and concrete wants but begins to include exchange of ideas and a greater variety of feelings. But the step to real communication in words is a slow process. We are often startled to realize how much the toddler still relies on nonverbal communication within the framework of the relationship with the mother when a new sitter or day care person takes over. These newcomers have great trouble understanding the child's communications, even the few words he may use, and he, in turn, can't make out what they are trying to convey because their gestures, movements, and even words may seem quite incomprehensible—like being with the foreigners again.

So we see that while nonverbal communication is possible and can even provide some special emotional satisfactions, it tends to be limited to the setting or to a close empathic relationship, and works best in conveying feelings and needs. The more we have to communicate with people who are strange to us or with whom we are less close, and the more we want to communicate abstract and complex ideas, the more do we have to use words. In our highly diversified Western societies words are therefore especially important. We live and interact mostly with people we know little and whose backgrounds, experiences, interests, and ideas are different from our own. In small tribal societies, where families always live in the same community, share the same experiences, and hold the same values and ideas, all speak literally as well as figuratively the same language and can more easily understand each other without words.

For us it is not only important to use words but to make quite sure that the words we use convey exactly and clearly what we want to communicate. Sometimes we find ourselves among people who speak our language, speak it distinctly, and use a large vocabulary, but what they say makes no sense to us. We might comment on such an experience with "He's just a politician—a lot of words but no meat," implying that the man's words are not intended for meaningful communication but to befuddle us or to show himself off and make us think he is great, or to sway our feelings and make us go along with him without our even knowing whether we agree with his ideas. In short, the man is not using but misusing words. In some ways, though not deliberately, this can happen between mother and child. For example four-year-old Diane said a lot of words but made no sense. In psychotherapeutic work with her and her mother it was learned that the mother, when anxious or angry, talked, as she put it, "a blue streak—just a whole lot of words streaming out." The words were real words but did not serve to express specific thoughts or feelings. They were a meaningless discharge and either overwhelmed or turned off others instead of communicating with them. Little Diane misused words in similar fashion. She knew how to talk and knew many words but had not learned to use her words as a tool for communication.

Whereas not being able to talk or not being able to talk well are handicaps, proficient speech in itself is not necessarily a personality tool that serves communication.

USING WORDS FOR THINKING

This applies equally to the role of words in thinking. Words are symbols (i.e., they stand for, or represent, something). We don't usually look at them in that way. We may think of a country's flag as the symbol of the nation or, as all kindergartners learn, we look at the letter "a" as the symbol for the sound "a," and we know that the printed sequence of the letters "a-p-p-l-e" stands for the word *apple*. That word in its turn represents a real thing, a thing we can see, touch, taste, and smell. We *can* think of an apple without knowing the words for it, for instance by having a visual image of it in our mind, but usually we think of it by its name without visual or tactile images, or, if we do have accompanying images, they are vague, fleeting, in the back of our minds. Now if we think of *fruit*, we think in a kind of shorthand. The word does not represent one thing but many. It is a lot quicker and more efficient to think the verbal symbol *fruit* than to line up images of apples, pears, and oranges in the mind's eye. When, however, we come to verbal symbols that do not stand for concrete things, for example the word *friendship*, we would have great trouble in substituting images for all the experiences and feelings and ideas which that symbol stands for. To think about "friendship" without its verbal symbol is very difficult indeed. And it is even harder to think without words about concepts like "because" or "past" or "future." When it comes to fitting ideas together in a relation of cause and effect, or of time sequences, we can hardly do it without thinking in words. Similarly, words are indispensable when we try to figure out how something works or when we try to think through how we are going to make something work. Sometimes we are not aware of using words to think things out, at other times we find ourselves actually talking to ourselves. ("How can I get that suitcase to fit into the trunk? Suppose I put it lengthwise. No, that won't do, the tire is in the way. Maybe I can take out the box and push the suitcase in first. Ah, that'll do it.") When we figure out something in this way, thinking saves us the experimental doing. Thought used for trial action is an enormously helpful tool, saves us a lot of effort and trouble, enables us to plan and to decide whether and how to act. Although sound thinking depends on many things, words (verbal symbols) are most useful in the process.

Thinking is not only advanced by the silent inner use of words but by being expressed in words. In this way we can learn from the thinking of others and correct our own thinking. Perhaps all of us have had times when we assumed we had thought something through quite well in our own minds, but it is only when we try to tell someone about it or to write it out in words that we realize, or are told, that we made mistakes or got muddled or skipped some of the connecting steps. Sometimes we find that we could not think something out correctly because the words we used did not represent the right thing or idea. ("Oh, I didn't know that if you pay for it in installments you have to pay more! I had figured it out all wrong.") With young children this happens all the time and it is only when they tell us their thoughts in words that we can help them correct and improve their thinking; for example, two-and-a-half-year-old Andy looked in awe at a garbage truck in operation. "Gee, it sure eats a lot," he commented. His mother explained that trucks are not people and don't eat, that the man makes the truck squash the trash and then drives it to a special place to dump it out, just as Andy fills his little truck with leaves, pushes them down, and then dumps them out. If Andy had not used words, mother might not have known that he needed help with his thinking about animate and inanimate things.

USING WORDS TO COPE WITH FEELINGS

The area where the use of words is usually least appreciated is that of mastering feelings. In infants, feelings are experienced as bodily sensations, pleasant or unpleasant, and discharged in bodily actions (screaming, crying, vomiting, diarrhea, and, as motility develops, in kicking, pushing, hitting, running). Older babies and young toddlers become aware of specific feelings through their interactions with the mothering person. They respond to her changes in mood and she feels with their emotional states. They do not, however, easily recognize that certain sensations within themselves represent definite feelings like anger, sadness, or happiness. Their vague inner turmoil prompts immediate action or need of the mother, or may indeed overwhelm them temporarily as they disintegrate in a temper tantrum, in a screaming spell, or in a heap of helpless despair. Often even nursery school aged children do not know clearly what they feel. Instead they may become irritable, whiny, or tired, listless, hyperactive, aggressive, or they may still experience bodily discomfort, as one four-and-a-half-year-old boy did who almost threw up when I prohibited his mistreatment of a toy. "You make me sick," he shouted. He was angry at me but did not experience his anger as a mental feeling.

When one does not know clearly what one feels, one cannot be master of one's feelings. One cannot recognize and tolerate it sufficiently to stop it from overwhelming one, or to stop oneself from discharging it in actions that might get one into trouble. One cannot decide what best to do about it—keep it to oneself, share it with a friend, do something about the situation that causes it. Each and all of these steps are greatly facilitated if one has a name, a word, for one's feelings and if one can use different words to represent those inner sensations which make up the different feelings. The verbal symbols, "I'm mad" or "sad" or "envious," help us to assess what is going on inside us and this is the first necessary step toward figuring out what causes our feeling and what we had best do about it. The words also enable us to cope with our feelings by substituting verbal expression (in thought to ourselves or aloud to others) for physical discharge.

Many people misunderstand what "telling one's feelings" is about. It is not a way of getting rid of them, nor do we need to get rid of them, because feelings are not poisons. Appropriate expression of feelings in words means above all being in charge of them, being master of them, knowing them, experiencing them inside, and choosing a purposeful way of channeling them. One decides when one tells, to whom one tells, how one tells, and why. That is how words for feelings are used as a personality tool.

HOW DO WE DEVELOP THIS AMAZING TOOL, THE USE OF WORDS?

Barring instances of organic damage or anomaly, all of us are born with the potential for speech, just as we are born with a potential for motility, observation, and thinking. However, whereas these other functions develop to some extent without a relationship with a caring person and depend on the assistance of that person only to achieve full unfolding and flourishing, speech stands alone in that it does not develop at all without contact with people. In the few cases on record where youngsters were found who had apparently survived altogether on their own, speech was conspicuously absent.

A most important factor in speech development, therefore, is the mothering person, the way she uses words, and the way she uses them in her relationship with her infant (Hall, 1982b). One pediatrician, when asked by mothers when they should start talking to their infants, always replied, "From day one on." He advised this because babies always understand words long before they can say them. Since nobody knows exactly when they start to understand, it is best not to wait and perhaps miss out on the beginnings of their ability to understand. The process works also the other way round; namely, the sooner infants are talked to, the sooner they understand. Most mothers don't even ask about it. They talk to their babies spontaneously from the start and the babies listen very soon because they are especially attuned to hearing the female voice range and because hearing mother is an important way of getting to know her and the comforts she brings. Nor does it take too long before the baby "talks" to the mother or "joins" her in conversations. For example, when a mother has an interview with me and we talk to each other while she cradles her infant or has him lying on a blanket beside her, the baby usually becomes quite vocal. In fact, he ends up making so many loud sounds that the mother needs to focus on him to see what may be the matter. As soon as our conversation stops, however, the baby quiets down too and eagerly looks from one to the other. Mothers then often say, "I guess he wanted to get a word in too," or, "Well now, it's your turn, Johnny. What did you want to say?" That kind of early "talking" between mother and baby is not talking in meaningful words. Mother does not expect the child to understand her exact words and the child does not really say things to her. It is a part of their nonverbal understanding and enjoyable interaction. It sets the stage for the next big step when words begin to have a specific meaning and when talking to each other serves new pleasures and masteries.

In the latter part of the first year mothers usually begin really to talk, in the sense of using words or simple phrases to communicate a specific something to the infant: "hi," "bottle," "night-night," "bye-bye," "Mommy," "Daddy," "Mommy come back," "no, no." The child's babbling too becomes more specific though often only mother can pick up what the child "says" and interpret its meaning. Just as the child attentively "drinks in" mother's explanations or preparations or reassurances, so the mother makes every effort to understand what the baby articulates and rewards him or her with a joyful smile or hug or verbal praise. Apart from these intent beginnings at true verbal communication, mother and baby usually have periods of talking for fun, making mouth noises at and with each other, and laughing together. Increasingly the baby also "talks" to himself when mother is not right there, in part perhaps because making these noises brings back the memory of being with mother, in part because it's just fun.

Hearing mother talk, making sounds with her, babbling for the sheer fun of it, and beginning to understand certain words and phrases that help the infant to anticipate events and make sense of them, these are the first year experiences which lay the foundation for the next big step in speech development when the use of words comes into its own during toddlerhood.

To the young toddler words must seem like magic—say "Mama" and she comes, say "cookie" and it is handed to you. The words themselves seem to have the power to make things happen. It is the period in life when many of us could, as in the story, say "Open Sesame" and gain access to the treasures of the world. And that's indeed how the infant should experience it if he is to regard words as a helpful tool and if he is to feel that more and more words will be useful to him in making an impact on his world, in getting it to understand him, and him to understand it. Most mothers sense this without having to be told and, as much as possible, respond to the toddler's words as if they were all-powerful. Not only do they produce what the child wants, they add, for good measure, their thrill and praise for his ability to say what he wants. Children whose words do not bring results, neither in the sense of getting what they ask for nor in evoking their mothers' interest and pleasure, may learn to talk but are unlikely to use words as a tool for mastery. By contrast, children whose words are listened to, responded to, and enjoyed, are also likely to pay heed to the words of others and make them count. Of course the parents help by talking to the child sensibly, understandably, and truthfully. When mother says, "I'll go bye-bye and I'll come back," it will really happen. The more talking matters, the more eager children are to learn new words and to use them. Parents usually welcome the toddler's interest and gladly name for him everything he encounters.

Where speech development or effective use of words is

delayed or inadequate, it is often related to the fact that there has not been a good enough continuous relationship with a caring person, especially during the most crucial period for speech development, roughly between six to twenty months of age. Among such cases are children who grew up in institutions with changing caretakers, children who suffered bodily and emotional neglect, children whose mothers were depressed or withdrawn, children who needed to spend their early months and years ill in hospitals without sufficient access to a parenting person. Similarly, lack of timely speech, loss of speech, or setbacks in its progressive development, are often evident in children who experienced separations from the mother or who changed from one to another mothering person, or who were affected by mother's emotional withdrawal. Many of these children are able to catch up and begin to talk, or resume talking, when their opportunities for a close one-to-one relationship are restored (A. Freud and Burlingham, 1943, 1944).

LEARNING WORDS FOR FEELINGS

When the adults appreciate the importance of words for mastering feelings, they name them for the child and encourage him to express his feelings in words. Saying what one feels does not require a big vocabulary. It is as easy to say "Mad at Mom," or "Mom bad," or "Betsy ang'y," as it is to say "Nice kitty" or "Cookie." The difficult part is that parents do not like children to be angry at them. In spite of their reluctance, however, most parents recognize that their children do get angry at them. Many are not happy with the child's physical expressions of anger (hitting, kicking, screaming, attacking things, or having a tantrum) and they realize what a tremendous step in mastery and self-control is taken when a youngster can begin to know what he feels and can channel it into words. It is comparable to dealing with an international crisis by discussion instead of taking up arms, or, on a smaller scale, settling a family feud with words instead of a fist fight.

Sometimes a young child's special difficulty in putting unpleasant feelings into words may interfere with his overall

use of speech. At the Hanna Perkins Therapeutic Nursery
School in Cleveland* some children who did not talk or only
talked nonsense, progressed toward appropriate use of
speech when helped with expressing feelings in words (R. A.
Furman and Katan, 1969).

Alice talked a rapid streak but made no sense. Phrases
from TV commercials and songs could be heard but did not
enable anyone, even her mother, to understand her. Careful
observations showed that Alice's "speech" became especially
agitated when her own or another child's mother was about
to leave. With the therapist's help her mother told Alice that
perhaps she was sad when Mommy went away and that
Mommy was sad too and would miss Alice. Within a few days
Alice was seen to watch intently when a peer cried at school.
She then said her first meaningful sentence, "Boy cry, boy
sad, boy want Mommy." It was her first step toward recognizing this and other feelings also in herself, linking them to
their appropriate cause, and expressing them in words. Her
speech began to make sense and her syntax improved.

Margot did not talk at nursery school at all although her
occasional statements at home indicated that she had the
ability. She scowled in a corner while her peers busied themselves with toys, and she refused to participate or answer
questions. She repulsed all advances with such intensified
sullenness that it became clear she was very angry. Eventually her teachers told her that she seemd angry, perhaps she
didn't like school. They added that she did not have to like
them, that it was okay to be mad and to say so. Margot's
speech soon began with a vehement swearword in response to
her teacher's refusal to leave her in the classroom during
outside playtime. She began to voice more verbal protests and
along with them came talk about what she needed, wanted,
and thought. This made it possible in time also to understand
with her the reasons for her great anger.

*This school has, since 1950, operated a special program for young children with
emotional difficulties. Their parents, assisted by teachers and childanalysts, work
together to understand and resolve the causes of the youngsters' troubles through
treatment-via-the-parent. If necessary, children are also treated directly by a child-
analyst. In addition to these services, the school is also a research center and has
published its many findings on normal and pathological child development.

In his play *The Bald Soprano*, Ionesco sensitively and amusingly portrays the role of feelings in verbal communication (1950). In the first act, the characters use fluent, flawless speech but it is so devoid of feeling that a man and woman, while conversing at a party, accidentally notice that they are married and share a home. In the second act, all is reversed. The actors speak only in letters "a," "b," "d, e, f," but they put so much feeling into their vocalizations that their relationships to each other and a complicated unfolding plot are clearly understood not only by the actors but by the audience.

Feelings, especially uncomfortable ones, are not the only things that are sometimes omitted from the vocabulary parents teach and children learn. Some parents do not like to talk about some topics and do not like to listen to children's ideas or questions about them. In some families certain areas of life remain unmentioned. The children quickly sense this and tend not to persist in pointing them out or asking about them but, without the help of words, they are handicapped in ever coming to grips with them in their thinking and feeling. Just as in some families it is taboo to feel scared, sad, or angry, in others this prohibition or avoidance applies to everything related to death, sexuality, illnesses, or financial concerns. For example, in working with children who suffered the loss of a parent through death, we found that this serious stress could be mastered more readily by children who had been helped to understand what "dead" means, who were told how the parent died, who could ask questions about it all and receive truthful answers (E. Furman, 1974). At the same time, the surviving parent's ability to talk with his child depended to a considerable extent on whether his parents had been able to talk with him about death when he was young. Unfortunately, many very intelligent and verbal adults would not talk with their children about the death or its circumstances because they themselves had never had a chance to discuss these matters and, as a result, their own thinking about it had remained confused and shrouded in infantile fears and misunderstandings. It is both tragic and frustrating to find that, in spite of knowing how to talk and being able to talk about all kinds of subjects, one suddenly comes up against situations one can't cope with at all because "words fail" us. It may happen with a bereavement, a sexual problem, an illness and need to talk with a doctor, or with just a day-to-day difficulty in discussing differences of opinion within the family.

The trouble with not talking about feelings and not talking about certain topics that engender feelings is, however, not limited to the fact that these areas may be left out of speech development and may remain unmastered. There is always the danger that a taboo on the use of words for one thing may spread and interfere with communicating in words about other things.

IS THE CHILD'S SPEECH DEVELOPMENT ALL UP TO THE PARENTS THEN?

The emphasis on the parental role does not imply that all children speak early and well as long as they have a good enough relationship during their first two-and-one-half years and get the parents' help with talking, nor does it mean that all delays or difficulties with the use of words are related to the relationship with the parents. Quite apart from physical or neurological handicaps which may impair speech, the child's endowment and other experiences matter too. There are no doubt variations in individual children's maturational timetable. Some develop speech somewhat earlier, others later. Children also vary in their preference for one or another function; for example, some children appear so fully invested in mastering motility first that they seem to put off speech for a bit, or vice versa, some focus on speech and delay motility. But there are also many who manage to invest themselves in all functions simultaneously.

Another factor within the child is the degree of "mouth pleasure" he or she has experienced earlier. Children who have enjoyed their mouths for sucking, chewing, and making sounds, also enjoy forming words. Some of the fun in talking comes from the sheer pleasure in using one's mouth, rolling the words around in it and bringing them forth. Many of us recall even from later childhood years the thrill of pronouncing fancy nonsense words or of chiming nonsense phrases in the rhymes of games. By contrast, children whose early mouth pleasures were minimal or who actually suffered pain in their mouths, perhaps due to illness, do not find it fun to move their mouths for forming sounds and words.

Ricky, from birth on, could not enjoy having anything in his mouth. The moment he took in the nipple and swallowed, he pushed it out again and screamed. He thrived very poorly until a postnasal allergic drip was diagnosed which caused him to choke when his mouth was closed. The difficulty could be corrected with medication and he was able to drink without discomfort in his fourth month. Although he then gained weight, his pleasure in mouth activities never developed. He preferred the cup and spoon, never sucked his thumb, and did not babble. By the time he was four-years-old, his appetite was still poor and mealtimes were a chore for him. He knew words but did not enjoy talking or singing and communicated his needs and wants by pointing.

There are also children who develop psychological problems which inhibit their speech. They have developed speech and know how to talk but cannot speak at all, or cannot speak in some places or situations because conflicts in their minds interfere. Such difficulties in the use of words require psychological treatment to be resolved.

WHEN WORDS REALLY BECOME THE CHILD'S TOOL

During their nursery school years, children's speech usually becomes much richer and clearer. They learn to use it with people outside the family, people with whom there is little or no additional nonverbal communication. They increasingly also use their own and others' words to learn about the world around them, how it works, and how to deal with it.

During this period the earlier magical power of words has to be set aside. Words remain important and useful as a tool, but children have to learn that words, like all tools, have their realistic limitations. Although children's words still are, and deserve to be, listened to and taken seriously, just talking no longer brings the kind of admiration and concrete results which the toddler enjoyed. Children often find it quite difficult to learn that things don't happen just because we wish them.

Four-year-old David felt so terrible because he had told his Mom to "get out of the house and don't come back" that he could not fall asleep that night. When his mother understood what worried him, she assured him that wishes in words don't come true and he could not make her leave him. For a moment David was greatly relieved and hugged his Mom. But then he suddenly asked, "Don't even the *good* wishes come true?" "No, not even the good ones." David did not like that at all. He got angry all over again, except this time he could afterwards go to sleep.

During the elementary school years, the use of words truly becomes a child's own mental tool, a permanent part of his personality. Although it still benefits from being fostered and encouraged by parents and teachers, children with a solid base in the use of speech can now communicate appropriately and think independently, can master their feelings well enough to know when to say them only to themselves, in the privacy of their own minds, and when to express them to others. They also enjoy talking enough to want to become ever more proficient—be it through learning new words or new languages, or learning how to express their thoughts and feelings in writing, or learning how to appreciate the literary work of others.

DO CHILDREN LEARN TO TALK FROM PEERS? IS IT TRUE THAT CHILDREN WHO LAG IN SPEECH DEVELOPMENT ARE HELPED BY ATTENDING NURSERY SCHOOL?

Children can learn to talk from and with peers and speech does sometimes progress when the child atttends a nursery school. However, speech acquired with peers, in or outside the home, does not further the use of words for the purposes we have discussed. When speech does not grow out of the relationship with the mothering person it tends to remain cut off from the emotional side of the personality and does not serve effectively for communication and mastery of feelings. It may only serve us like a dress we put on for certain occasions instead of being our skin which is a permanent part of ourselves and grows with us. For this reason, developmental lags or early interferences in the use of words are best helped by understanding and correcting the difficulty with the help of the mothering person. A teacher can support a mother in helping her child and can assist her by handling the child's speech appropriately at the nursery school, but a teacher–pupil relationship or peer relationship alone cannot substitute for the mother–child relationship. Even therapeutic nursery schools focus, in this respect, on helping the mother help her child and on dovetailing her efforts and those of the school.

Sometimes children develop two kinds of speech—one is the home speech, serving communication in close relationships, the other is the "official" speech, serving superficial contact with outsiders. This may happen with children who speak one language at home and another one at school, for example, Spanish at home, English at school, or Black English at home and standard English at school. Such splits serve well to an extent but may cause difficulty when they interfere with using speech as a tool for linking home and school, feeling and thinking. This does not apply to children who grow up bilingual within the home or to those who learn a new language later, after the mother tongue has become their tool.

WHAT ABOUT SWEARWORDS? HOW CAN
ONE HELP CHILDREN TO SPEAK POLITELY?

Essentially, children will use the words and phrases which are used in their families. If the parents use swearwords, the children will too, however much their elders might wish them to "do as I say, not as I do." In some families swearing is acceptable and children can learn that home and school have different rules in regard to swearing, as indeed they have different rules on many other things.

Sometimes, however, children's use of swearwords is not due to identification with the parents. A child may repeat to the adults a new word he has learned or overheard to find out what it really means. If the parents can explain it calmly and tell their child that they prefer to use other, more polite or appropriate words, there is little chance that the child will persist with swearing. If, however, the child's swearword produces great upset and excitement in the adults, the child is likely to continue with swearing because he now knows that he has hit upon a powerful tool for angering, defying, teasing, humiliating, or exciting others. This happens not infrequently because, for many adults, swearing is not just a matter of using unsuitable words but carries powerful sexual and aggressive meanings from their own childhood as well as the prohibitions against them. The issue at stake then is not the words but the underlying attitudes to these instinctual aspects of life and to ways of dealing with them. When swearwords are used to evoke an emotional response (shock, giggly excitement, horror, anger, laughter) they turn into a means of sexual or aggressive interaction and do not serve well as a tool for mastery, thinking, and communication.

HOW DO DEAF-MUTE CHILDREN DEVELOP TOOLS FOR COMMUNICATION AND HOW ABOUT NORMALLY ENDOWED CHILDREN WITH DEAF-MUTE PARENTS?

This is a complex topic to which we cannot do justice here and which even experts in this field are still struggling to understand better. Let us limit ourselves then to a few aspects of the question.

The nonverbal relationship between parents and children, regardless of who is deaf-mute, need not be impaired, and serves as the basis for the development of communication by sign language which uses verbal symbols, each sign representing a phrase, word, or letter. Signing is a visual language which, as a personality tool and means of communication, is as effective as the hearing person's oral language (Klima and Belugi, 1979). Nevertheless, deaf-mute children are likely to experience special interferences in their development (Terhune, 1979). They also have to overcome difficult hurdles to learn spoken language without hearing, but many succeed to a remarkable extent. The hearing child of deaf-mute parents learns his spoken words from others but helpfully combines his speech with an often unusual degree of sensitivity to nonverbal clues derived from his relationship with his parents.

12
Thinking

In many ways our mental tools depend on one another and their development overlaps. Our ability to think is closely connected with observing and with the use of words. Yet thinking stands out on its own too and is often judged to be *the* mark of a fully functioning, independent personality. That is what we mean when we say, "He really thinks," or "Think, man, think!" We value our freedom of thought very highly and zealously guard our right of access to information so that we can think things through for ourselves. We often look down upon those who take over and merely parrot the opinions of others, "You can talk him into anything. He doesn't think for himself." We abhor brainwashing, depriving people of their capacity for independent thinking, because we see it as the destruction of a person's human dignity and individuality. Many people belittle children and treat them as second-class citizens because children's thinking is immature and often makes them seem gullible and easy to fool.

The thinking we prize so highly is that which serves a person as a tool for figuring things out correctly in his mind. This means finding out facts that are true, relating them to one another logically (in terms of cause and effect and in sequences of time), and drawing conclusions from them which are in accord with reality. When we think in this way, we are able to make sense of what is happening within us and in the world around us, how it came about, where it is likely to go, and how we can make the best of it or change it. When we reach that point, we are into planning; that is, using thinking for trial action which, compared to doing, saves us a lot of time, energy, and trouble, and enables us to avoid making mistakes. Most of us wished at times that we had thought things out a little harder or better, even such simple things as going to the corner drugstore, "I should have made out a list, then I wouldn't have forgotten what else I need"; "I should have thought to bring along extra money"; "I should have this . . ." and "I should have that . . ." and, not least of all, "I should have figured out that they would be closed at this hour."

For many people thinking is also the main tool in their line of work, in business, education, science, or art. In fact, most jobs demand some thinking. Indeed, it is often felt that work cannot be satisfying unless it involves thinking, and the lack of it is considered one of the reasons why assembly line work in factories is so tiring. Although this is perhaps not true for all people, it reminds us that thinking can also be a great source of enjoyment and satisfaction, quite apart from its amazing usefulness for coping with all the small and large tasks of life. Many of us have fun with thinking for its own sake or as a mental exercise. We play games that mainly use thinking, such as checkers, chess, bridge and other card games, word puzzles, anagrams, and we pursue "thinking" hobbies.

It is generally agreed that people's potential for developing realistic thinking varies. As with the other mental tools, however, the successful unfolding of the maturational capacity depends on the way it is nurtured. This does not mean that children who do not receive sufficient help from their parents simply don't think. Even very young infants think, but their thinking differs in many ways from the realistic thinking we talk about in terms of adults. It's the gradual step from infantile to mature thinking which requires so much help. Although realistic thinking has usually been achieved to a considerable extent around the beginning of elementary school, it continues to depend on the support of the caring adults, parents and teachers, for many years. Thinking becomes a person's own, fully independent personality tool only during adolescence. This does not mean that it happens to a teenager on one day or even in one year. Children can use their thinking on their own in many areas long before then, but in some areas they tend to remain dependent. To think for oneself, to be able to trust one's thinking, to know that it will serve one truly at any time, is the mark of a mature adult personality. It is not often achieved, even among the best endowed. One reason for this is that infantile thinking is never altogether superceded by realistic thinking but inevitably persists in parts of ourselves and, in the form of fantasies, daydreams, night dreams, and art, continues to serve us in its own way. Another reason, perhaps, is that realistic thinking is usually not nurtured as well as it might be.

WHAT IS INFANTILE THINKING LIKE?

Annie, a well-developed three-and-a-half-year-old, was quite distressed when her mother arrived ten minutes late to pick her up at nursery school. Annie hugged her Mom and was glad to see her but her main concern seemed to be with the car. "Where's the car?" she asked quite anxiously. "In the parking lot," replied her mother. Annie rushed out and spent some time checking over their car. During the ride home, Annie suddenly asked, "How did you put it together again?" "Put together what?" "The car! The teacher said the car was broken." Mother could then begin to figure out Annie's worry: Mother had called the school and asked the teacher to inform Annie that she would be a little delayed because of car trouble. The teacher told Annie, "Mom's car broke down. She'll be late," and Annie understood this to mean that the car had literally broken to bits. She was greatly relieved to learn that "broken down" only meant that something in the car was not working right and that the garage man fixed it.

Five-year-old Henry, sitting at the dinner table, suddenly slammed his hand over his glass and exclaimed gleefully, "Got you, God." He explained to his astonished parents that he had learned in Sunday School that God was everywhere and that he had tried to find Him in all sorts of places in vain to get a closer look. "So God must be in the glass too and this time I can really catch Him." Henry carefully removed his hand as he peered into the glass, puzzled and annoyed to find it empty. His parents had a hard time explaining to him that God could only be thought about, not seen.

Three-year-old Richard had seen a TV movie of King Kong on a visit with his friend. During the night he woke his Mom to tell her that King Kong was in his room and scared him. Mother walked back with Richard who tried to point out to her just where King Kong had stood. He even searched around the corner, in case King Kong had moved. Mother realized that Richard had dreamed about King Kong. It took her many days to explain to her son that a dream is something we think about when we sleep, that King Kong in the movie was a dressed up person, and that both differ from real living people or animals.

Two-year-old Ellen covered her ears in fright when a noisy motorcycle rushed by. "Don't worry," explained her four-year-old sister, "they make a big noise but they are not angry—at least most of the time." Mother added that motorbikes were never angry because things don't feel, they are neither angry nor happy.

These are not unusual incidents. Most parents and others who are close to young children can recall many similar incidents. Annie's worry about the "broken" car and Henry's "catching" of God simply illustrate that their thinking is literal and concrete, bound to the reality their senses experience. Figurative and abstract concepts are not yet within their ken. Richard's King Kong and Ellen's and her sister's angry motorcycles point up another characteristic of infantile thinking, namely the inability to distinguish inner mental experiences from external reality. The children also did not yet fully know what was animate and inanimate, real and pretend in the outside world, nor could they demarcate dream from fantasy in the inside world of their minds. Infantile thinking is always literal and concrete, does not distinguish between inner and outer reality, and confuses facts and fancy. But these are not its only characteristics.

Children's thinking also operates with a different concept of time sequences. Today, tomorrow, last year, next weekend, not to mention dates and calendars, are all foreign ideas. We have earlier talked about the baby's inability to gauge time and how this makes him or her feel that a separation from mother (which may be very brief in adult terms) or a wait for a meal (which may be only five minutes) are never ending, and therefore unmasterable experiences.

Three-year-old Sharon cried inconsolably, "My Mommy is going away." When her Grandma pointed out, "But she is only going away for two days and one night and then she'll be back," Sharon, amid sobs, retorted, "When *my* Mommy goes away, it's a million years."

Parents are often startled when their preschoolers, apparently out of the blue, refer to a trip of two years ago or to a statement a neighbor made last month. It is difficult, even for parents who are so used to their children's ways, to appreciate that when youngsters think of something, they think of it as *now*. When past events surface in their minds, they treat them with the immediacy of the present; when they focus on a future experience, it too is thought of as right now. Many parents avoid promising a treat for "later" because they know they will be pestered from that moment on: "When can we go get our ice cream? You *promised*!" Sometimes parents get quite annoyed at their youngsters' inability to think in time sequences, for example when parents ask their children for an account of what happened. It is nearly impossible, even for kindergartners, to relate coherently what they did at school that day. In reply to mother's question about it, they may say, "Nothing" or, if pressed, they may dutifully report a general sequence which fits most days. The real news of the day, such as a fire alarm, a teacher substitute, or a special test, usually surfaces suddenly in the midst of a shopping expedition or at bathtime, often not until days later. Yet young children are not forgetful. A five-year-old's memory often reaches back into his first year. It's just that their thinking about past, present, and future events does not follow our familiar dimension of time.

Young children's causal relations also differ from the objective basis we adhere to in mature thinking. In figuring things out children do proceed from cause to effect, but they assume that everything that happens, all causes and effects, are related to their own person. If mommy goes away, it is "because she does not love me," or "because I was naughty," or "because I wanted her to leave me alone." Unless mommy takes time and trouble to provide different, objective reasons it is just about inconceivable to a young child that mother's leaving has nothing to do with him but is caused by, for example, mother's need to go to the bank, or to work, or to the hospital. Often enough the child clings to his own cause-and-effect line of thinking even when other reasons are mentioned.

Margaret was eagerly anticipating her fouth birthday. She planned to have her party in the backyard. Mother approved but added that it would have to take place indoors if it rained that day. "But it won't rain," insisted Margaret, "because it's *my* birthday." She was lucky and enjoyed the nice day with an air of "I told you so," brushing aside impatiently her mother's explanations that we can't boss the weather. Had it rained, Margaret might have blamed her mother for spoiling her day, or blamed herself either for not wishing hard enough or for having been naughty so as not to deserve sunshine.

Many of us can, at least occasionally, catch ourselves with similar egocentric thoughts, such as regarding nice weather for an outing as a personal special favor, or feeling that the red traffic light is a personal insult, or pretending to make it change to green with a special magical word or gesture. It is just so hard to appreciate that the world does not turn around *us*, that our lives are affected by forces over which nobody has control, and that even our parents (or, later, other authorities) who seem so utterly powerful are not in command of them. Young children's self-focused thinking is tied to their lack of knowledge about the world and what makes it tick as well as to their need to feel important and in charge of everything that touches their lives. When we, as adults, lack adequate information about an event or when it makes us feel especially helpless, we too tend to fall back on these infantile ways of thinking; for example, sometimes, when there is a death in the family, people think they or others did something to cause it or could have prevented it, even if there is no objective justification for their reasoning. The stress of circumstances makes it difficult to think realistically and the impact of strong emotions throws us back to infantile ways of assuming that events that touch us personally are caused personally.

Young children look for the causes of events not only in what they and others do. As we have already seen, they also think that wishes, thought or spoken, have the same power as action to make things happen. Margaret wished for a nice day and assumed that her wish could bring sunshine. Since hers was a "good" wish it caused her no qualms. A sunny day is welcomed by most people. Some wishful thinking, however, is "bad," calls for mean or harmful things to happen. As long as one thinks it can produce real effects, one might regret it, feel bad about it, or worry that one will be "paid back" in kind. Many a young child's fears stem from expecting retribution for bad thoughts. In spite of that, young children find it hard to give up their imaginary power.

Three-year-old David's mother had once again explained to him that wishing does not make things come true. "Not if I wish real hard?" he inquired. "Not even if you wish real hard." David didn't like that at all. "Well," he said triumphantly after a moment's thought, "*your* wishes might not come true but mine do because I can wish harder than anybody. That's why I *will* get a bike for my birthday."

Sometimes the step toward more mature thinking is welcomed, at other times it is not. And this brings us to the ways in which parents and others close to the child, can foster the development of logical, realistic thinking.

HOW THE CARING ADULTS HELP A CHILD WITH HIS THINKING

It is a great help to parent and child when the parents realize that the child's way of thinking is different. That in itself enables them to bridge the inevitable gap in communication, to attune their words and behavior to the child's comprehension, and to gauge his readiness for steps toward realistic thinking. Parents who know how their child thinks are not necessarily parents who have been taught this, although learning about it may help them. Most certainly they are not parents who work from a list of do's and don'ts, of what to say and how to act. Most parents' understanding derives primarily from their emotional closeness with their child and from their respect for him as a person, which includes his thinking.

This manifests itself in their thoughtful attentiveness to the child's behavior, in their listening to what he says, in soliciting his ideas and feelings. In short, they treat him as an important, worthwhile person and learn from him. When they misjudge, and of course they do, they are helped to realize their mistake by the child's responses. They apologize, clarify, or correct themselves as best they can and have learned a little more for the next time. This kind of common decency means a lot to the child and does a great deal for his developing thinking.

Unless parents are respectful of the child's own thinking and eager to observe and listen to it, they will not know what and how he thinks, and will not be able to help him alter it by offering their ways of thinking in a timely and appropriate manner. More important yet, when the parents try to understand the child's thinking, he or she is likely to want to understand the parents and to adopt their modes of thought. Realistic thinking cannot be superimposed on a child—"This is the way to think"—it has to be acquired little by little, by way of comparing infantile and mature thought on the many small and big occasions that arise daily. Only the parent who is intimately in touch with the child's thinking can gauge what and how much the child can understand and absorb at any given time. Above all, however, the parents' thoughtful respect for the child's thinking implies a caring relationship of which thinking together and exchanging ideas is an important part. And it is just this kind of relationship which is the essential nutrient for the growth of the child's thinking. It assures that the interest, importance, and enjoyment which the parents invest in thinking will be taken over also by their child. Thinking has to be practiced, valued, and appreciated in order to flourish. When children's infantile thinking is stifled, belittled, or laughed at, and when their steps toward more mature reasoning go unnoticed, they have little incentive to think and to enjoy thinking.

With babies, respect for and help to the child's thinking is a matter of acting more than of talking; for example, many mothers appreciate that regularity in daily care provides the infant with repetitive rhythms of bodily activities which in turn become his first sense of time. When sleeping, eating, bathing, playing with mother and other family members, do not follow a routine but happen at different times and in different sequences each day, the baby has no way to learn "After this comes that," the basis of past, present, and future. Parents also appreciate that their baby's upset over mother's short absence is not due to his being spoiled but stems from his inability to gauge time. Preschoolers still depend very much on a predictable daily schedule but also begin to think in terms of weeks, when the weekends too bring a repetitive routine which alternates with that of the weekdays. They rely for their sense of time on this established pattern and gradually build on it to comprehend longer time sequences. Mindful of this, parents may tell their youngsters, "I'll buy you an ice cream *after dinner*," rather than "later," or "I'll be back *after your nap*," rather than "at 4 o'clock." At a later point calendars on which each day can be marked off are a big help in helping children anticipate future events, such as vacations, special outings, birthdays, or medical checkups.

Parents are similarly thoughtful of the child's concrete thinking. They avoid figures of speech, such as "the car broke down," without giving special explanation. They do not overburden him with ideas that are beyond his comprehension, be it a detailed account of a complex operation, or the intricacies of how a machine works, or a philosophical lecture. They help with distinguishing real from pretend, may monitor his TV viewing, choose stories and books to match his mental grasp, assist with understanding what people dressed up in costumes are about, such as at Halloween and Christmas. Above all, they enjoy the child's own steps toward thinking things through realistically.

Five-year-old Chuck was playing with rubber bands which he stretched in patterns across a board with projecting nails. His Dad watched him run his fingers over the bands and asked why he was doing that. Chuck replied, "When they are tight, they make a high sound and when they are loose they sound low." "Chuck, what good thinking! You figured that out all by yourself and, by golly, you're right. That's just great"! Chuck and his Dad beamed. They were sharing a happy moment on the upward path of Chuck's growth in reasoning.

THE ROLE OF EXPERIENCE

Chuck had indeed figured things out for himself, with the help of his advancing ability to observe and reason and with the help of experience which is a great teacher too. Quite often it is not the parents' words but the repeated lessons of experience with reality that further the child's developing thinking and enable him to correct earlier ways of understanding events. For example, David, who was so sure that his wishes would bring him a bicycle, or Margaret, who was so sure that her wish brought about a sunny day, would no doubt find by repeated experience that their wishes don't work. One doesn't always get the wished-for presents and birthdays are sometimes rainy. However, experience alone can take a long time to make its point and sometimes it can seem to confirm rather than correct the child's infantile ideas about cause and effect. Unfortunately, mothers sometimes have a car accident, get ill, or leave the child. Had this happened in the wake of a youngster's angry wishes, his experience would have tended to confirm his thought that he caused this outcome. In psychoanalytic treatment with young bereaved children we found repeatedly that they related the parent's death to their own "bad" wishes or behavior, a burden of unnecessary guilt so hard to bear that it interfered with their personality functioning and development (E. Furman, 1974). They could have been spared some of their suffering if, at the time of their bereavement, the caring adults had helped by explaining the true causes and circumstances of the parent's death. Although this is an extreme instance, which fortunately occurs rarely, less momentous occasions happen all the time in which experience itself is not a sufficient guide to mature reasoning. Whereas in some situations the child's experience, or experimenting, helpfully contribute to his understanding, in many others there is no way for him to find out on his own; for example, how concentrated orange juice gets into cans. In other situations it would even be unsafe for the child to conduct his own investigations. (Do people float in water? Do knives cut everything?) In fact, preschoolers' curiosity about the workings of everything in their world is so compelling that parents and teachers are constantly either preventing children learning from experience or guiding their experimentation into safe and constructive channels. Thus, even the teachings of experience have to be guarded, selected, or corrected by the caring adults.

SOME DIFFICULTIES ALONG THE WAY

Children don't always find it easy to progress to mature thinking and parents do not always find it easy to help them along. For children, as we have already seen, the hardship sometimes lies in having to face harsh facts and in having to accept their inability to control them. Although at times children may be glad that their wishes don't come true and that they are not the cause of all the bad things that happen, perhaps even more often it is an unwelcome realization. Real events can be disappointing, painful, worrying, dangerous and it feels terrible to have limited power, or no power at all over them. If Mommy goes away because you are naughty, at least you have had some say in it and could change it; if she goes away for reasons that have nothing to do with you, it leaves you helpless—but not altogether. We can remind ourselves that realistic reasoning does not deprive us of all control over events. It brings us power through understanding and figuring out ways of doing things which work truly and effectively, although they do not have the omnipotence of magic.

For the helping parents the difficulties are greater. All the observing and listening and careful adapting of their own behavior takes a lot of patience and is sometimes very inconvenient. But that's not all. It is downright unpleasant, annoying, and unnerving at times to have to realize that the child thinks and asks about topics that one would rather have him leave alone. For some parents such touchy topics may be death, or sexual matters, or arguments among grown-ups. It can be taxing to have to correct children's misunderstandings by providing them with some of the real facts, causes, and consequences; for example, Addie, aged five, needed help in understanding the reasons for her uncle's jail sentence. She thought he had been imprisoned for yelling at Grandma.

Her parents needed to explain that people are not put in jail for angry yelling but that her uncle had done something that nobody is allowed to do. Although he is a nice person in many ways, the wrong thing he had done was to steal someone's car. On other occasions it may be equally hard to learn that the children have actually figured things out correctly and to need to acknowledge this with them; for example, Robin, at four-and-one-half years, told his Dad that he knew why Dad was late for dinner; Dad had got a ticket for speeding. Dad said it was true, he had made a mistake and done the wrong thing and would be going by the rule next time. And there are other times yet, especially as the children get older, when one is unable to help a child's thinking because one has not even thought things through for oneself or has not yet learned about it; for example, seven-year-old Bill's parents were unsure about their religious beliefs and told him so when he asked them about God.

Notwithstanding their own discomforts and embarrassments, many parents do their conscientious best to think with their children about difficult topics. They very much want to help their children to think well and they sense that this cannot be accomplished by forbidding thinking in some areas or by deliberate deception. Even kindly and well-intentioned fooling, such as the tooth fairy or Easter bunny, can be quite bewildering for very young children who cannot yet tell real from pretend. Make-believe only gets to be fun when children are sure enough of their own knowledge of reality. Pretend is enjoyed most when one really knows it is pretend.

Four-year-old Cecily could not go to sleep for several nights. She told her mother eventually that she was afraid of someone coming into the house. When assured that all the doors and windows were locked, Cecily retorted, "It doesn't help. They can all come in through the chimney, just like you said about Santa Claus."

As long as children's thinking is not their own mental tool it has to rely on the parents and teachers to provide reliable truths. It is most unfortunate when the caring adults fail the child.

IF A CHILD HAS NOT BEEN HELPED WITH
HIS THINKING, CAN HE USE HELP LATER?
HOW LATE?

Since the development of a child's thinking depends for a long time on his environment, it is often possible to influence it for many years, certainly throughout the years of elementary school, and, in some ways, much longer, perhaps throughout the years of early adulthood. It will depend on the individual child's potential and personality, on how far he was able to progress before he received additional help, and on the kind of help he received later on. Relationships with teachers, in and out of school, and methods of teaching, are important factors.

Justin was thirteen years old when he changed schools. In his old school he had achieved good grades by memorizing his assignments and producing the answers his teachers requested. In his new school, he and his teachers found to their dismay that he could not do his work because he could not think for himself. It was a new task for him. One day he read an assigned story about astronauts and conscientiously answered the comprehension questions about it by looking them up in the text. But one question floored him: "Have you ever wanted to be an astronaut?" He told his teacher that he had looked through the entire story but could not find the answer. He was not accustomed to using his thinking and did not expect to be asked what *he* thought. With the help of the teachers and an individual tutor, Justin understood what was missing and began to develop his thinking and apply it in his studies. He made great strides during the next two years and improved his thinking considerably.

Some interferences in the development of thinking cannot be helped educationally but can be helped through psychological treatment.

CAN A CHILD THINK TOO MUCH?
CAN PARENTS PUT TOO MUCH EMPHASIS ON
THINKING?

Yes, in the sense that thinking, like every other tool, can be misused. Unbeknownst to them, children and adults can use thinking for nonadaptive purposes.

Ten-year-old Jeff, for example, did a great deal of thinking about basketball, knew all the rules and plays, and was a whiz on national teams and scores, but he played rarely and poorly. As soon as he made a mistake he gave up practicing to improve his skills and turned instead to one of his sports books to read and think about it some more. He did not realize that he misused his good thinking ability to avoid his difficulties with motor control.

Jack, also ten, misused his thinking in a somewhat different way. He worked out complicated and detailed plans and schedules of all he would do that day, that weekend, that vacation, or that school year, but he never got round to accomplishing what he had thought out. It remained a good plan but did not get him anywhere. He did not know that he indulged in thinking as an end in itself but could not use it as a means toward realistic achievement. His thinking only served his wishes of what he would like to be able to do and, though quite sophisticated, was really infantile.

There are also more or less deliberate misuses of thinking, such as thinking up excuses for wrongdoing, or schemes for cheating, or tall tales for showing off and impressing people.

Parents may contribute to their children's difficulties with thinking, not by putting too much emphasis on it but by putting the wrong emphasis on it. One would hope that they would notice the child's problems with thinking and would help him correct it or, if necessary, get professional help for him. For when thinking is misused it cannot develop into the mental tool that serves us with the tasks of living.

SHOULD CHILDREN NOT BE TOLD FAIRY TALES OR OTHER "PRETEND" STORIES EVEN WHEN THEY ENJOY THEM AND ASK FOR THEM?

Parents need to gauge the child's readiness to understand and cope with every kind of "pretend." When the child is sure in himself that a story is "pretend," or when the parents can help him to be sure, then he is ready for it. Whereas in general, children of elementary school age are more ready for "pretend" stories than preschoolers, there are some stories that confuse or upset older children and there are other stories that even very young children can master. The one thing that is not helpful is to fool children, in the sense of telling them, or letting them assume, that something is real when it is not, or that it is pretend when it is not.

Parents can often learn from the child's behavior and words whether he has been able to cope with a fairy tale. His enjoyment at the time, however, or his asking for it to be repeated, are not very reliable indicators. Children sometimes do enjoy a story or program, or profess to enjoy it, but their behavior suggests that it also bothered them; for example, a child may not be able to calm down afterwards and follow his usual routines, or he may have bad dreams which relate to the story, or he may need to tease and scare others with parts of the content. The child may be aware of the part of him that enjoyed the story, but unaware of the scare, upset, or confusion experienced. He may indeed be quite angry when the parents do not want him to be exposed to the experience again. It sometimes helps when parents can share their observations with the child: "I know you liked it but I think it also bothered you and made it hard to go to sleep. So we'll let it go for now. As you get older, there will be more of the fun and less of the bother and then we'll try reading it again."

Often children insist on having a scary story told over and over. This does not necessarily mean they like it so much. It may actually reflect their wish to control the scare by making it happen and by being able to anticipate the shock. Sometimes such repetition can indeed serve mastery, sometimes it fails. Again, only the observant parent, or teacher, can decide what is best. In making his decision, the adult will not be guided solely by the child's wish and enjoyment (there are many things children want and enjoy that are not helpful to them) but by his assessment of the child's overall responses. The child may consider him a spoilsport in the short run; the caring adult has to keep in mind the child's welfare in the long run.

13

Coping with Frustrations

Each of us probably has a different situation in mind when we think of frustrations and of ways of coping with them. Life indeed is full of things that don't go the way we want them to and dealing with them is no small matter, be it a rainstorm in the midst of a picnic or losing one's job, or even just struggling with a zipper. The ability to cope with frustrations, little ones and big ones, is a personality tool that is rather different from the ones we have discussed up until now. It is not tied to a particular part of the body, like speech or motility. In fact, when we cope with a frustration we often use all the other tools combined—observing, thinking, talking, and doing. It also includes feelings. When things don't go the way we want them to, we feel helpless, angry, disappointed, or sad. Whatever the feelings, they are a part of every frustration and of our way of coming to grips with it. Moreover, it is a tool which, more than any other tool, depends most intimately on the child's experiences, on his relationships with his loved ones, and on their ability to assist him in developing it.

Let's start our thinking about frustrations with a simple example, one that many of us have experienced. Late in the afternoon, seven-year-old Michael barges into the kitchen and wants a sandwich, but his mother refuses. His wish is not fulfilled and he feels frustrated. What does Michael do about it? He may just shrug his shoulders and leave the kitchen. He may add a "shucks" to register his annoyance. Or he may start yelling at his mother and berating her as mean; he may slam the door and throw down his jacket; he may attack his mother with his fists and smash her things; he may have a real temper tantrum, flailing, kicking, and screaming; or he may dissolve in helpless, unhappy tears. He may do any or many of these things, and more besides, such as disregard mother's prohibition and help himself to some food, either from the refrigerator right in front of her or from a secret cache of goodies in his room. Most likely, he will start a more or less angry discussion with her, aimed either at persuading her to relent ("But I'm so hungry, Mom! Couldn't I have half a sandwich? I didn't have much lunch. I really need something now!"), or at ascertaining how long his wait will have to be ("How long till dinner? What are we having? Couldn't I have dinner early so I can watch the special on TV?").

If I asked which of these ways of coping are the "best," some people might say, "Shrug his shoulders and leave," for that makes Michael a "good" boy who gives up on his wishes when necessary. Others might say, "Get his own food in his room," for that makes him a kid who goes for what he wants without creating a big fuss. And others yet might say, "Persuading his Mom" or "Figuring out how long his wait will be for dinner," for that shows that he doesn't throw in the sponge at the first hurdle, uses his faculties to assess the whole situation, and works out the best possible compromise.

I hope, however, that someone would say, "Hey, wait a minute. We can't tell the best way unless we know more about the situation." You may want to know more about the nature of the frustration. How hungry was Michael? Was he perhaps just bored and wanted a sandwich for lack of anything else to do? Was he a little hungry because he had a light lunch and had used up much energy playing outside? Or was he really very hungry because the family's income made sufficiently nutritious meals impossible? And how hungry does a seven-year-old get, anyway? After all, hunger varies at different stages in life and between individuals. Most mothers know that their growing adolescents consume fantastic amounts of food, because they get so hungry, and that an adult would soon grow in the wrong dimension if he or she were to eat anywhere near as much or as often. In order to assess just how big a frustration Michael is up against, we will also want to know how long he will have to wait for a meal (a short while or several hours), and will the meal he eventually gets satisfy his needs? The answers to these questions will make quite a difference to how we would expect Michael to cope with his predicament. If he were quite hungry, had to wait for many hours, and could not anticipate a proper meal even then, we might expect him to protest a lot, to do all kinds of things to get at some food somehow. We also might not be surprised if he cried desperately, or even just slunk away dejected. But if he were a little hungry, had to wait only half an hour or so, and could look forward to a good dinner, we would think he could take it in stride because he will have learned to handle that kind of frustration.

What means does a seven-year-old have for dealing with a moderate temporary frustration? He can observe, reason, and talk, which helps him to find out about when and how his hunger will be stilled. He has probably learned to tolerate the minor bodily discomfort that a little hunger brings. He has probably also learned to bear the mental discomfort which comes from his anger at the frustration, so that he will discharge it either by just thinking a few choice words to himself or by grumbling a little under his breath. No doubt he can also do quite a few things to take his mind off his hunger and to provide some nice entertainment for himself during his wait. He might play a game, or watch TV, or phone a friend, or even finish his homework. How different it would be for a baby, or indeed for Michael just a few years ago! He couldn't ask about anything, couldn't understand it if he were told, would not know how long half an hour was, would feel miserable with his aching tummy, furious or desperate in turn at the frustration, and could only suck his fingers to make himself feel better. If Michael had not grown up and learned how to cope with such a frustration, he might still cope with it like a baby. He would scream and kick, or cry desperately, and feel quite overwhelmed and helpless.

Perhaps some of us would object to the idea of the helpless baby. "Surely," we would say, "a mother would help her baby. She would not let her baby go on screaming for his feed. If she can't give it to him right away, she would hold him and rock him and talk to him and he would see her get it ready and would remember that she always feeds him." Yes, a lucky baby would get that kind of help. By the same token, we may now wonder what our seven-year-old's mother did to make the situation more or less tolerable for Michael. Did she make a reasonable demand and help him deal with it in a kindly way? For example, "Mike, I'm very sorry you are hungry but dinner is but half an hour from now and I want you to enjoy it with all of us. So try real hard and wait. Perhaps you could sort out your baseball cards in the meantime, and if it gets too bad you can ask me for a piece of celery to keep you going. That won't spoil your appetite." Or did she arbitrarily reject his request and expect him to comply without protest? For example, "You get nothing and off with you. Don't bother me." Or did she explain, "Mike, I'm sorry but I have nothing in the icebox. We have to wait till Dad gets home with the car and with his paycheck. Then you can come to the store with me and we'll get things for dinner. It shouldn't be long now. Let's play a game together and that'll help us wait." We all know that Michael's response is likely to be affected by the manner of his Mother's refusal and by the reasons for it, insofar as he understands them. A frustration tempered by sympathy and help is always easier to take. It does not add insult to injury and makes us less angry.

Of course, we also know that Michael's way of coping with this particular frustration will depend a lot on all the frustrations he experienced previously, how they were handled by his parents, how they helped him to develop means of coping, and what their own attitude to frustrations has been. For example, his mother's "Off with you" reaction may be rather unusual, and if so, Michael would figure that something is upsetting her and he would deal with the situation differently than if she always brushed him off.

Have we made too big a deal about Michael's sandwich? Isn't it just an unimportant event in a young boy's daily life? Many people think that little children experience little frustrations and that the bigger and more real frustrations only come as one gets older. By contrast, most children believe that it's the other way round, "The grown-ups have it made. They can do what they want." Who is right? I guess both are right, in a way. No yardstick measures frustrations equally for all. For a baby, a fifteen-minute wait for his food or a few hours absence of his mother are major frustrations, comparable perhaps to many days of starvation or to a spouse's desertion, for an adult. How big and how real a frustration is depends on what it means to the individual and what measures he has at his disposal for coping with it. There are as many cherished wishes in childhood as in adulthood. When these are denied, the frustration is big and real, for child or adult. Where the child is at a disadvantage is that he has not yet acquired ways of dealing with frustrations. This makes many childhood disappointments feel especially big.

HELPING CHILDREN LEARN TO COPE
WITH FRUSTRATIONS

If then young children are so ill-equipped to cope, should we spare them such hardship, not expose them to frustrations? Or, to the contrary, should we let them be frustrated as early and as much as possible so as to toughen them for later on when life won't fulfill all their wants? Parents may lean one way or the other, but their educational approach will only work if they take into account the ways in which their child responds and if they keep in mind that many frustrations life inflicts are beyond their control. It is impossible never to frustrate a child. For his own safety, many of his wishes can't be fulfilled: Can you let a child jump out the window because he wants to? Many frustrations cannot be prevented: Who can control illness? Moreover, when there are no frustrations there is no learning to cope with them and that would assure that even the smallest frustration would forever be experienced as a major stress because the child, and later adult, would face it without inner resources. A "spoiled" child is not one who gets all he wants but one who falls apart when the least thing does not turn out to his complete satisfaction. Similar results stem from the opposite approach of imposing too many frustrations too early. When a child can never achieve what he wants or get what he needs, when feeling helpless and overwhelmed is the rule rather than the exception, in daily living, there also is no chance to learn to cope. The severely frustrated child, like the spoiled one, experiences each little frustration helplessly. In extreme cases, he may even become hopeless, may give up wishing and wanting, with no will left to make his life better and more enjoyable, and with no trust in being able to achieve it by himself or with the help of others.

So how can parents help their child to become competent and sensible in dealing with frustrations? How can they make sure that he will not give up all aspirations nor pursue every whim relentlessly, but will learn to judge each frustrating situation realistically, to gauge what can be done about it or whether anything can be done about it, and then to act accordingly? To be sure, it's not an easy task and, like all of parenting, is in itself quite an exercise in coping with frustrations. To start with, however, it helps to recognize that coping with frustrations is essential throughout life and that children don't learn it on their own. It also helps to appreciate that it is not just a matter of giving up or giving in. Coping competently involves much more, and that makes it easier and harder, all at the same time.

In every person's life there are some situations in which he needs to hang onto his wish, in big things like fighting for his safety, and in littler things like keeping on practicing a skill he wants to acquire. And there are other situations in which he needs to give up his wish, in big things like accepting the laws of nature, and in littler things like ending his vacation when it's time to return to work or to school. Coping with a frustration may involve working away at making a wish come true, and it may mean giving up a wish altogether, and of course both include bearing many unpleasant feelings in the process.

For the most part, however, it's not a matter of all or none but of working out compromises, postponing gratifications, and accepting substitutes. We already know that education is often said to consist of not this but that, not here but there, and not now but later. When Michael could not get his sandwich, we did not assume that he should fight for it at all cost, nor did we expect that he should give up eating forever. We thought he could manage to wait ("not now but later") and accept a substitute—a piece of celery or an enjoyable activity ("not this but that"). Such delays or substitute satisfactions are not necessarily welcome or easy to take, but they make life's many inevitable frustrations more palatable, avoid a lot of trouble for ourselves (if Mike had gone at his mother with his fists he might have ended up worse off by far), and often they even enrich life in the long run. Perhaps playing a game and enjoying a good dinner with his parents afforded Michael so many gains in actual pleasure and in the good feeling from his parents and for himself that it more than compensated for the gratification of eating his sandwich.

By now we have already seen that learning to cope with frustrations works best when the frustration is manageable, when it produces the kind and amount of hardship a child can bear by mustering his own resources. In this sense it is similar to building up bodily strength. When we want to "get in shape," we would not start out with fifty push-ups and work to the point of collapse, nor with one push-up which would not add strength to our muscles. A good exercise program gauges the right number of push-ups to start with and increases them gradually. We would feel some discomfort each time but, as our muscles toughen, we could tackle ever harder tasks.

With babies and young children it is the parents' job to gauge the "exercise program," to gauge what kind of frustration the youngster can handle, and when and how. It's a difficult job because so many factors determine the proportion between frustration and resources at any given time. Yet most parents do not need to think through each situation to work out the proper balance. When they are in tune with their child, they usually sense what seems appropriate, and when they misjudge they are likely to recognize their mistake from the child's response and correct their handling.

Sometimes gauging consists of selecting the right size of frustration, in keeping with the child's available means of coping; for example, expecting the two-year-old to bear his mother's absence for a couple of hours when he has a familiar sitter, or expecting the four-year-old not to grab items from the store shelves, or expecting the seven-year-old to do half an hour's homework before playing.

At other times gauging means reducing an inevitable frustration to manageable size by dealing with parts of it for the child or by compensating for the stress it imposes on him;

for example, when a five-year-old feels very envious and left out on his older brother's birthday, his parents often lessen his frustration by giving him a "favor" (a small token gift), by letting him help with the cake baking and other preparations, and by including him in the festive meal. Or, when a young child is ill and uncomfortable, his mother will stay with him, soothe his pain as best she can, prepare his favorite foods, and read him stories. When their first-grader complains that older children threaten him and grab his belongings on the way home from school, the parents may suggest what he can do about it, but they may also help by accompanying him or by speaking to the other children or their parents.

These kinds of parental help address themselves to the frustration itself, but parents also help by focusing on the child's means of coping. They may do this by supporting the child in using his own ways of handling a frustrating situation or by suggesting new ways. This is another aspect of the gauging job. Each parent goes about this task in his or her own way, to fit the occasion, to fit the individual child. The following examples are not *the* way but *one* way.

Ginny's mother supported her child's own means: When her friend suddenly canceled a promised visit, five-year-old Ginny told her Mom that she was "so mad and so sad." The mother sympathized that it was hard, that she would also feel disappointed if a friend let her down, and that she was glad Ginny could tell her how she felt. After a while Ginny asked if she could invite another girl the next day. Her mother agreed, told Ginny what a good idea this was, and later helped her to make the arrangements. In this instance the mother first supported Ginny's ability to have the appropriate feelings and to express them in words. The mother knew, or sensed, that in order to deal with a frustration sensibly you have to recognize how you feel about it and you have to be in charge of what you feel. If Ginny had avoided her distressing feelings ("I don't mind, fine by me"), she might have given up her wish for a friend—if you don't mind when you don't get something, why pursue it? If, however, Ginny had let her disappointment overwhelm her, she might have had a temper tantrum, with not enough calm judgment left to figure out what to do about the frustration. A young child needs to learn to bear and be master of the unpleasant feelings that accompany a frustration so that the feelings can serve to assess and resolve the situation realistically. Ginny's plan of inviting another friend on another day shows a very mature capacity for accepting delayed and substitute gratification. It probably goes hand in hand with her good tolerance and mastery of hard feelings. Her mother recognized and supported Ginny's compromise of not this but that and not now but later, and assisted her in working it out. She also praised Ginny for it, complimented her on her good idea, which no doubt helped Ginny by making her pleased with herself and by letting her bask a bit in mother's appreciation.

Adam's Dad helped by suggesting new means of coping: Adam very much wanted a "two-wheeler" and was overjoyed when he got one for his sixth birthday. He showed it off to his buddies and then began to ride it. A few minutes later he was back in the house. Tears were running down his cheeks, his knee bled, the bicycle was lying on the sidewalk, and Adam shrieked in fury, "It's a lousy bike. It doesn't steer. I don't want it." His Dad put a Band-Aid on the knee and waited for Adam to calm down. It took some time. Then Dad said, "Adam, we need to talk this over. I guess you're ready now to tell me what happened." Adam was still irritable and a bit incoherent, but Dad could piece together the story: Adam expected to get on and ride, but he could not balance himself, the bike wobbled to and fro, Adam fell off, his friends added insult to injury by jeering, and Adam was not about to touch the bike again. "I am very sorry," said his Dad, "and I can understand how you feel. But there is a mistake. The trouble is not with the bike, the trouble is with you wanting to be an expert cyclist right away. Nobody is. When I want to do something new, I have to learn and practice and practice, even now at my age. And when I first had a bike, I had to practice for a long time and take quite a few spills. It's not fun but it's the only way. The fun comes from getting better at it slowly. It doesn't matter how fancy the bike is or how long you wait to get started, you'll still have to practice. Right now you need to pick up the bike and store it safely in the garage, and then we'll make a plan for learning to ride it." Adam put away the bike and, somewhat reluctantly, cooperated with a plan for practicing with his father fifteen minutes every night after dinner. The first few times he had to be reminded and felt miserable all through practicing time. But as his skill improved he picked up courage and conceded it wasn't so bad after all. Needless to say, he ended up a good cyclist and enjoyed himself and his bike. Adam's Dad knew that one can't cope with a frustration when one is overwhelmed with disappointment. He sympathized with Adam's feelings when the boy had them in better control and then offered him more sensible ways of dealing with the situation. They would entail discomfort and hardship but they would help Adam achieve a realistic goal, "not now but later."

The parents of Ginny and Adam, like may other parents, did not merely support their children in coping with the frustration in a realistic manner. They took it for granted that a realistic resolution depends on a realistic assessment of the situation. For this reason they also helped their children to assess their frustrations sensibly. Ginny's mother agreed with her little girl's idea that the friend had let her down, a judgment seemingly warranted by the way the friend canceled the visit. Adam's father corrected his boy's assessment on many counts—the trouble was not with the bike, nobody can be an instant expert, learning is slow and hard, bikes need to be taken care of.

THE ROLE OF THE PARENT-CHILD RELATIONSHIP IN LEARNING TO COPE WITH FRUSTRATIONS

Isn't it enough to make frustrations manageable for the child, to sympathize with his feelings, and to help him to assess and work out each situation realistically? Not really. The parents' role extends further. It involves their own attitude to frustrations, their ways of dealing with their own frustrations, including the many frustrations the child imposes on them. It also involves their overall relationship with their child. Learning from and with someone always takes place in the context of a good enough relationship and is helped by the model the teacher sets. Without a relationship there is no incentive to follow someone's suggestions. Without an appropriate model even the best suggestions may not be taken in as a lasting inner guide to action. The relationship with the parents and the example they set are particularly important in learning to cope with frustrations because frustrations make one angry and so do suggested ways of coping because they are often hard and require painstaking effort. All this anger tends to be directed at the parents who make the suggestions or who even impose the frustration in the first place. It takes a lot of loving on the child's part to go along in spite of his anger and a lot of love on the parent's part to make it possible for the child to do so. The parents convey their caring not only during happy times but perhaps especially at times when the child has to deal with a frustration.

How do they do that? We all know that frustrations are most infuriating when we feel they are imposed arbitrarily, or for the convenience of others, or out of their anger. It helps a great deal when parents impose frustrations and expect them to be coped with in certain ways for reasons dictated by reality and for reasons that benefit the child. Among the former reasons are such situations as "I'd like to play with you but I have to get dinner ready"; "I like you very much and I'd like to pick you up but I can't because my back is sore"; "I'm sorry I can't get you a swing set like the Jones' because we don't have enough money." Among the latter reasons are the many necessary frustrations imposed for the sake of the child's health and safety, for the sake of avoiding unfortunate consequences, for the sake of furthering the child's intellectual and emotional growth, for the sake of preserving his loving relationships and his self-esteem. These are of course the frustrations that children often view as spiteful interferences with their wishes and pursuits. "No, you can't play with Jim. You need to finish your homework first, otherwise you'd be in big trouble at school tomorrow. Your teacher would be angry and you'd feel bad about yourself." Or "No, you can't grab your sister's toy. You need to ask her. Nursery school children like you are big enough to ask for things. You wouldn't like it if I let her grab your toys." Or "No, you can't come with us. Tonight it's 'Mommy–Daddy time' and we'll go to a movie for grown-ups. I know it's very hard to be left out and I'm sorry. I still like you very much and I'll think of you."

Nor is it enough for just the parent to know the good reasons for frustrating the child. Unless these good reasons are explained to the children and they are helped to understand them, they assume that there is nothing that parents cannot change or bring about, and that parents impose frustrations only because they "don't love me" or "are angry at me." Without simple and clear explanations even the most essential frustrations may be seen as merely "mean." It helps even the littlest toddler when the parent says, "Not safe" as he restrains him from running into the street after his cherished ball. When the child is helped to appreciate that the parents act out of necessity or because they have his or her welfare in mind, the anger is mitigated and the frustration is not experienced so much as a matter of "you against me." At the same time, of course, this provides a chance for the child to learn about the realities of life, the fact that even grown-ups are sometimes helpless to change things, and that by giving up some immediate gratification one can enjoy different pleasures in the long run. If Adam had not endured his daily practice sessions, he would never have had the fun of riding his bike well.

The child's anger is also lessened when parents are consistent in the frustrations they impose because this helps the child to anticipate these situations and to accept them. When the same wish is, apparently arbitrarily, fulfilled on some days but thwarted on others, it is more difficult to give it up and makes one more angry, "But you let me do it yesterday"!

When it is not the frustration itself but the difficult ways of coping with it that make the child angry, the loved parent's praise and appreciation of the child's efforts can add the necessary spoonful of sugar to the bitter medicine, "Gee, you managed that well, and it was hard too! I guess you're really growing up." Parents admire every little step in frustration tolerance and successful coping: "How well you've learned to wait," "What a good sharer of toys you are," "What a hard worker you are, good for you." They convey that the difficult job of bearing disappointments and of coping with frustrations brings love, enhances self-esteem, and most important of all, it is an admirable and desirable quality, a mark of being grown-up. It is a lot easier to work at coping with frustrations and to overcome one's anger when it makes one feel more like a somebody. It is just about impossible when it feels like a humiliation that only little and helpless people have to put up with. With this, as with other things, when children love and admire their parents, they want to become like them, and the closer they get to achieving it, the better they also like themselves.

Actually, the consistent caring relationship with the parents not only makes handling frustrations easier, it makes it possible in the first place. Without that relationship, a child simply does not learn to tolerate frustrations and does not learn to assess what he can and cannot do about them realistically. The relationship makes it worth the effort.

HOW LONG DOES IT TAKE TO DEVELOP THIS TOOL AND TO MAKE IT ONE'S OWN?

In one way, learning to cope with frustrations takes a lifetime. There is no specific age or stage when one has, so to speak, made the grade. Step by step, we learn to cope better and to deal with more demanding situations. To some extent, each period in life brings its own specific frustrations—being a little child, when one wants to be adult, can be as hard as growing old when one wants to be young. There are always new and hard frustrations, even for the most fortunate among us. We are forever challenged and forced to practice and perfect our tolerance and skill in dealing with disappointments.

However old we may be, frustrations are always easier to bear when they are not inflicted in anger and intended as personal insults, and when there is sympathy and appreciation from loved ones. That does not mean, though, that our ability to cope with frustrations forever depends on the support of loved ones. The parents' or parent substitutes' help is crucial at first. With the transition into the school years, this tool becomes a part of the child's own personality to an extent but still needs reenforcement from parents, teachers, and other trusted adults. Support is also helpful—for many even necessary—during adolescence. The better our early learning has been, the greater are our chances of learning more later.

CAN ONE START LEARNING TO COPE WITH
FRUSTRATIONS LATER? HOW LATE?

It is possible to get a later start and still learn. The later a person starts, however, the harder it gets and the more limited are his chances of success. It depends not only on the age, but on the opportunity for a consistent helpful relationship. Later learning stands the best chance when people have had a close, good enough relationship early in life and can use this relationship as a base for forming a relationship later with a person who assists them in coping with frustrations over a long period, perhaps years. The early relationship may have been interrupted or may not have helped the child with frustrations, but it did bring about the ability to form relationships and that is a crucial factor. The other crucial factor is of course finding the right person later who can help them for long enough. And there are also some to whom a later relationship is of no help because they cannot utilize it due to their early deficiency in meaningful relationships. Many people, however, fall between these two unhappy extremes and do achieve some success in coping with frustrations in later childhood or even in their adult years.

WHAT HAPPENS WHEN LIFE FACES
CHILDREN WITH UNUSUAL FRUSTRATIONS
THAT PARENTS CAN'T CONTROL, LIKE
SERIOUS ILLNESSES OR BEREAVEMENTS?

The parents' and child's tasks are made much more difficult when unavoidable frustrations far exceed the child's normal limits of coping. Unfortunately, this happens all too often with serious illnesses and losses of loved ones through death, as well as with many other stresses, such as physical handicaps, chronic diseases, injuries, painful medical and surgical procedures, separations and interruptions of relationships, extreme poverty and deprivation, and many more (Anthony and Koupernik, 1973).

Just how serious any one frustration is depends on the age and personality of the child, on his specific circumstances at the time, and on his other life experiences before and after the event. To a major extent, however, it always depends on the parents' ability to extend themselves to their child. There are many amazing and admirable parents who manage to support their children in such ways that even great hardships are mitigated enough to be coped with in a healthy and realistic manner. When parents are in tune with their child and aware of his needs and feelings, they leave no stone unturned to ease the child's stress even a little and to help him bear it by sharing the burden and by allowing him to lean on their strength. The frustration is much worse when the parents themselves are afflicted and unavailable for support. Even then one parent can often take over for the other one, or a familiar parent substitute can help out. The worst frustrations are the ones children have to face alone. This happens when there are no loved ones available or when they can't appreciate how the child feels.

WHAT HAPPENS WHEN PARENTS THEMSELVES CAN'T COPE WITH FRUSTRATIONS SENSIBLY?

No parent can cope sensibly with all frustrations all the time. Parents try their best and succeed with many frustrations much of the time. As long as they watch for, and recognize, many of their mistakes and correct them, lasting harm is usually avoided. When parents tell their child that they mishandled a situation, perhaps apologize, the child can learn something from them about dealing with his own mistakes.

Some parents can't cope sensibly with certain frustrations because of isolated difficulties in themselves. For example, some mothers can't bear to be kept waiting although they may be very patient in working on skills and in other areas. It helps the child when parents recognize their problem and discuss it with the child: "I have a trouble with waiting. It makes me more angry than it should. I try to do better and I'm sorry when my trouble makes it hard for you. I hope you'll get to be good at waiting and won't have a trouble like mine." One such mother took a further helpful step with her four-year-old. They agreed that the daughter could remind her mother with a "Mom, time!" when she felt Mom got too angry and impatient about waiting for her. Quite often it worked well and helped both of them.

A number of parents have a much more widespread difficulty in coping with frustrations. This does not mean that they can't deal with frustrations at all (just taking care of a child well enough to enable him to live and thrive takes plenty of frustration tolerance), nor does it necessarily mean they don't have any means of coping and find themselves constantly overwhelmed, helpless, or furious. Usually they do cope, but not realistically. They may not assess the situation sensibly, may not know appropriate ways of dealing with it, and cannot help their children to do differently, although they may wish that he or she could get along better. Unless the child has additional close relationships with other adults who are more helpful and provide a more suitable model to counterbalance the parental attitudes, the child is most likely to adopt his parents' ways of coping.

AREN'T CHILDREN MORE OBEDIENT AND ACCEPT FRUSTRATIONS BETTER WHEN THEIR PARENTS AND TEACHERS ARE VERY STRICT, MAKE THE CHILDREN DO AS THEY ARE TOLD, AND DON'T WASTE TIME TALKING AND SUGGESTING THINGS?

Some parents are very strict, expect a great deal from their children, and don't waste many words, but they may, at the same time, be quite realistic in assessing and handling frustrations and aware of the child's feelings. If so, the child is likely to find it hard but will learn well.

Sometimes, however, "strict" means subjecting the child to unreasonable demands, making him submit by use of force and threats, and being unaware or intolerant of his feelings. Such handling does produce obedience to the parents but it does not help children to accept and cope with frustrations realistically. Instead, they are apt to learn less adaptive attitudes. They may become timid and unable even to protect their safety and rights. Or they may conform in the face of superior force but harbor great resentment and take cruel revenge when and where they get the chance to have the upper hand—on weaker or younger people, on animals, behind the back of the "authorities," or even on the parents or society in later years. They may avoid either of these two extreme adaptations, but they are not likely to avoid a measure of identification with the parents' attitude to frustrations and with their inability to assess and handle them realistically.

Some time ago I worked in therapy with a mother who wanted help with her young daughter's behavioral difficulties. The mother acknowledged that she was very harsh with her child, sensed that this contributed to the little girl's troubles, but she did not know what else to do "to bring her up right." She beat, punished, yelled, and threatened three-year-old Lisa into submitting to excessive frustrations in daily life—to eat certain things, not to suck her thumb, to stay in her room when mother had company, not to protest when mother left for work, and many others. At the same time, the mother felt bad because she could not fulfill some of Lisa's extravagant expectations of her. She could not buy her a big house, or a big dog, nor could she change Lisa's dark curls into long blond silken braids. When Lisa insistently demanded these things, the mother would respond with silence or with a vague "Maybe one day." She bought Lisa many, too many clothes and toys to make up, but she feared that the child would forever resent her for not having fulfilled her hopes, just as she never forgave her own mother for her deprivations.

In the course of our work the mother came to appreciate that she was harsh like her own mother, on the one hand frustrating her child as she had felt frustrated, and childishly unreasonable on the other hand, wishing to spare her child all frustrations as she still wished for herself. One day she summed it up, "I guess I don't know whether a good mother never disappoints or always disappoints." Later, when she could relent on her excessive expectations of the child and clearly refute the child's excessive demands on her, she added, "A really good mother helps her child with the right kind of disappointments."

14

Self-esteem

If it's the "tools" that give us the know-how of mastery, it's the "inner helpers" starting with self-esteem that guide us to use them to do well by ourselves, within our family and community. We cannot do well by ourselves, unless we think well of ourselves and like ourselves. Our good opinion and feeling about ourselves make up our self-esteem. It contributes so much to our sense of general well-being, and is therefore so important to us, that we are usually willing to expend a lot of effort to protect it, preserve it, and even enhance it.

We are not born with self-esteem. Newborns only have the potential to develop it, step by step, with the help of their environment. And the first and most important environment, as always, is the caring parents. The first important step is for the baby to get to like his or her body, in the sense of liking it to feel good. The infants' basic bodily well-being then gradually extends to what they own and what they can do and to the kind of persons they are, with all their traits and pursuits.

LIKING ONE'S BODILY SELF

So let us start where the baby starts, with learning to like it when his body feels good.

We discussed this at some length earlier in connection with the role of mothering during the first year of life. We said then that the baby's bodily and mental survival depends on the mother meeting his needs in such a way that he can feel good enough often enough. The consistent pleasurable experiences in the need fulfilling relationship with the mothering person help the infant to remember them, to seek them out, to want to repeat them. In time, these experiences join together and help to create an image in the mind, an idea of "me," the start of the baby as a person in his own right. If this "me" is made up of many good enough experiences, the baby likes it, likes him or herself. "Me" then means feeling good, wanting always to feel good, and not liking it when one doesn't feel good. This first "me" is primitive and represents the infant's body parts and functions only insofar as he has come to know and feel them, but it serves him already to do well by himself—to bring about the fun and satisfaction of need fulfillment and to protest or avoid uncomfortable and painful experiences. In the second half of the first year we can observe this development in many ways: The baby screams purposefully to alert his mother to his needs, and enjoys their gratification intensely; he also cries vigorously when he is deprived or hurt. Unlike the newborn's nonspecific distressed screaming or crying, the older baby knows what he wants and what he likes and what he doesn't like; he enjoys sucking his thumb or fingers but does not bite, pinch, or hit himself. Instead, he directs his attacks outward, against people and things; he keeps a close eye on mother, whose presence assures his satisfactions, and protests her leaving. In short, he is engaged in the business of doing well by himself and looking out for number one.

When there is no consistent good enough mother or when she cannot meet the baby's needs in a good enough way (perhaps because he is too ill to experience pleasure or because she cannot be in tune with him), the first "me" may develop belatedly and may not feel so good. "Me" may mean "feeling uncomfortable" or even "feeling pain." When such an idea of "me" is the only one and is taken for granted by the child, it does not spur him on to change his state of well-being for the better by seeking pleasures and by protesting discomforts. Such an infant may be listless much of the time, his appetite may be poor, he may show minimal reaction to discomfort and pain, he may bite, scratch, bang, or otherwise hurt his own body, he may lack interest and pleasure in exploring and touching his own body and that of his mother, he may whine indiscriminately, and may not care about mother's presence or absence.

The early loving investment in a bodily "me" that feels good is the lasting underpinning of our later inner guide to keep our bodies safe and to provide them with comfort and pleasure. It is also the core of our later mental self-esteem. Many more developmental steps have to be taken before all parts of body and mind are included in a loved image of ourselves and before we learn more mature ways of caring for and protecting ourselves. However, these later developments, good or bad, can never altogether override the earliest attitudes to our bodily pleasures and safety. People with a solid self-love from the first year are not likely ever to inflict real physical harm on themselves nor will they willingly allow others to do so (unless they fall ill with a mental disorder which destroys most of their personality functioning). By contrast, people with an early weakness in bodily self-love remain prone to self-injury and to inadequate self-protection, especially when later developments and experiences favor such behavior.

The first loved idea of "me" and the satisfying need fulfilling experiences that underlie it are, of course, closely linked to the one-to-one relationship with the mothering person. Along with it, however, both parents contribute to their child's growing self-esteem in other ways and these become increasingly important.

LEARNING TO PROTECT ONE'S BODY

Liking one's body derives not only from the good feelings it gives us. Learning to be kind to our bodies, to care for them appropriately, and to protect them has a lot to do with the way our parents love and treat our bodies. First they do for us, then we gradually take over their attitudes and make them our own. Their treatment of us, to a large extent, becomes the model for how we treat ourselves. Most mothers and fathers consider their child's body beautiful and precious. They love every bit of it. They admire it, fondle it, respect it, and handle it as gently as possible. When the child is ill or hurt, they soothe and comfort his body. Most youngsters, loved in this

way, know that the best remedy for every injury is when mom
"kisses it better." Even when parents have to submit the child
to unpleasant treatments to help his body get better, they
convey their solicitude, show how sorry they are, enlist his
active participation, and manage to keep the child's trust in
their kindness and goodwill toward him. When a toddler
shows distress at being hurt or not feeling well and seeks
comfort from his parents, we take it as a very important sign
that he likes his body and wants to do well by it (E. Furman,
1984a). With a preschooler we would expect him also to be
able to turn to other caring adults, like his teacher or doctor, to
cooperate with them, and accept the minor discomforts of
necessary treatments, but to protest painful ministrations.
By the same token, we are concerned about a young child who
does not notice when he is hurt or ill, does not complain, does
not solicit care, and is a "good" patient, in the sense of submitting passively to all manner of treatments without protest. Such a child either has not developed sufficient love of
his body to mind when something is wrong with it, or has not
learned to expect that it can be made better; for example, the
parents may have habitually brushed off the child's complaints and refused comfort ("That's nothing. Don't make a
fuss!"). Alternatively, their treatments may have been experienced only as adding to the discomfort instead of helping
it, so that the cure seemed worse than the disease, or they may
even have tended to scold or punish the child for getting hurt
in the first place. Of course, they may also be children whose
illness and medical care subjected them to such an extent of
prolonged discomfort that the parents were unable to as-
suage it.

This does not imply that a child's development is awry
unless he carries on in anguish over every tiny scratch. Caring parents do show pity for their child but they also differentiate big hurts from little hurts and help their child to do so.
They also support him in tolerating a reasonable amount of
pain without expecting undue bravery or stoicism. What
counts is that the child recognize his discomforts, seek help
and solace, and trust that he will receive sympathy and helpful care. This paves the way for his own future attitude to
himself, his ability to watch out for his health and bodily

well-being, to notice signs of illness or injury, to take care of his body sensibly and kindly and, if necessary, to turn to a competent professional with the expectation of good and thoughtful care. Truly independent care of one's health is usually not fully achieved until early adulthood. The toddler has a lot to learn before then.

One of the difficult steps for parents to teach, and children to learn, is that of preventing harm to one's body, what to do or not to do to stay safe and well and avoid pain. Even when little children want to feel good, they do not know how to assess danger realistically. In most situations it is not possible to let them find out for themselves, such as letting them burn their hands on the hot stove so they'll learn to keep away from it. Most parents take it for granted that they need to protect the child from harm either by removing the danger or by removing the child, and that at the same time, they need to help him learn to protect himself by explaining what is unsafe. The child learns most easily when the explanation is simple and calm, "No, not safe," or "No, makes an 'ouch,'" from which he takes in the ideas, "The stove can hurt and she doesn't want me to get hurt." Oftentimes parents cannot handle it in this way because they are so worried. Parents' anxiety may prompt them to rattle off all the possible horrible consequences in gory detail, which scares, excites or overwhelms the child but does not help him to understand and master the reality. Children are then often driven to do the dangerous activity to test it, or become panicky themselves. Worried parents may also get very angry and punitive, from which the child learns, "It's naughty to touch the stove and it makes Mom mad." To this he may respond by being obedient to please the parents, but at another time, when he is angry at them, he may well want to tease them or be mean to them by doing the very thing because it will make them mad. He may also do the forbidden thing when they are out of sight and he does not have to fear their wrath. Looking out for oneself works most reliably and sensibly when one does it to please oneself rather than to please others, and when one sees the facts as they are, rather than viewing them through a haze of terror or excitement.

Around three years of age children are usually able to

avoid common danger, that is, dangers which are a part of their daily living, such as electric plugs, stoves, and irons. By this time, too, children walk around furniture and people without bumping into them, do not climb onto or jump off from high places heedlessly, and are cautious of traffic, though not independently safe outdoors. In addition, their idea of "me" has come to include many more body parts, even some they cannot see, such as their behinds. It took a lot of experience and learning. For example, mothers frequently notice that their toddlers don't know where to wipe themselves when they first struggle to master their toileting. Mothers have to give them directions, guide their hands, and advise them to check the toilet paper for smears. Eventually the youngsters locate the right area and add these outer limits of their bodies to the inner concept of the whole body, the liked self. Yes, even the behind has to be liked in order to be cared for and protected. And so do internal parts of the body which the child gets to know mainly because they hurt, such as the sore throat and the infected ear. In fact, we need to like a painful or ill part of our body most especially in order to protect it from further harm. Most children do just that and it is therefore rather a good sign when they are "bad" patients who protest painful and overwhelming medical procedures.

A most important step in the preschooler's growing bodily self-esteem is getting to know and like his sexual organs and their functions. To some extent, children can get to know them through looking at and touching themselves and experiencing sensations, but only simple verbal explanations from the parents can clarify the basic internal organs. Liking oneself as a boy or girl at that stage is an important prerequisite for learning to like oneself later as a young man or woman during the adolescent years when the body image has to be adapted to major changes in size, appearance, and functions. Also, when children like their sexual body parts, they are better able to protect themselves from molestations and to guard against allowing their bodies to be promiscuously misused. Those who do not properly know and appreciate their sexuality are prone to be careless about how it is used and by whom. An early sense of bodily respect and dignity are crucial to later care and responsibility in sexual matters. A child or adolescent with basic sexual self-regard can utilize intellectual information on sex for his welfare and protection. Without such self-esteem, sexual enlightenment is apt to confuse, overwhelm, and excite. Needless to say, the parents' respect for their own and the child's sexual parts and functions plays an important role from early on and right through the growing years, as does their attitude to all aspects of the body.

Beyond the initial crucial steps the child takes in building respect and liking for his own body, there are many years during which parents and child share in the process of continuing growth. As the child's self-esteem increasingly serves him as a guide for doing well by himself in a realistic fashion, the parental task shifts from caring for the child to supporting him in caring for himself. It is not always easy for parents to gauge the child's capabilities and to hand over to him the loved and loving business of caring and protecting. However, the healthy child wants to look out for himself and even though the parents may lag behind a bit, usually it isn't too long before they enjoy his new independence with him and help him along. This gradual shifting of responsibility often manifests itself, for example, around the issue of "what to wear." Mother insists on bundling up her schoolboy in sweaters, boots, and scarves, only to watch him arrive back home after school bareheaded and with his jacket casually dragging behind. Sometimes the boy is too careless. He acts in protest against mother's imposed care but does not yet know how to go about it sensibly himself. At other times the mother misjudges her boy's needs, as the children put it, "When *she* is cold, she wants *me* to wear a sweater." Some mothers soon resolve the difficulty; for example, they work out reasonable guidelines, relating what to wear with weather conditions and temperature. The child learns to check the weather forecast and to choose his clothes accordingly—perhaps with a little license now and then, just for the fun of it.

Anna Freud (1952) reports a touching observation of a little boy struggling to do up his coat and saying to himself, "Button up carefully, darling." This happened during the Second World War in Britain when he, along with many other children, had to be placed in the Hampstead Nurseries to be safe from the most dangerous air raids. He missed his mother's loving care of his body and made up by being mother to himself. His was a precocious step, forced by circumstances, and does not suggest full independence in self-care, but it points up the way by which a mother's caring becomes the child's own. When children's bodies have been well loved and respected in their very first years but are then deprived of this care, the youngsters tend, prematurely, to take over themselves, but at a cost. They may continue to "baby" their bodies as the parents used to and may remain overly solicitous of their bodies as though they forever needed the special protection accorded helpless infants. A person's healthy bodily self-esteem is always appropriate to his bodily state at the time. It is flexible and adapts to the person's age, stamina, health, or sickness, and individual strengths and weaknesses. When we know and respect our bodies, we take into account their changing needs and meet them accordingly.

This kind of flexible and adaptive, sensible bodily self-esteem implies that we are realistic about our bodies, that we neither over- nor underestimate them. The ordinary devoted parents at first quite properly overestimate their child's body. Everything about it is seen as wonderful and admirable. This enables parents to tend to it as a precious treasure. As the infant takes over their attitude, it helps him to build up a solid base of self-worth which will serve as a buffer against later inevitably disappointing encounters with reality. For example, even the healthy toddler, who does not have to accept a physical handicap or limit his activities because of illness, soon finds that his body is inadequate compared to those of his parents. It is not as strong or tall or skillful. Later on, when the child compares his sexual organs to those of the other sex and to adult males and females, he or she may also feel inadequately endowed. Moreover, each of us has individual bodily characteristics, such as facial features, hair, shape of limbs, and so on, which we may compare unfavorably with those of others. A good early bodily self-love allows a child to recognize and accept these shortcomings for what they are and to like him or herself despite them. This is especially likely to happen when the parents can help the child sort out real from imaginary inadequacies, can adjust their own early overestimation, and can love the child as he really is.

For example, four-year-old William came home crestfallen. The older boy from next door had laughed at him, called him a midget, and told him he would never grow bigger. William indeed was small for his age, so small that his parents had been concerned. They had worried that William's short stature might be caused by some illness or anomaly, and they had also been disappointed because, to them, being tall meant handsome and manly. They had asked their doctor who told them that William was healthy and developing normally but that his growth and weight rate indicated he would always be below average in height. Although this relieved the parents on one score, they were distressed that their boy would not measure up to their hopes for him. However, they accepted the facts, struggled with their disappointment, and sorted out for themselves that a boy's or man's height bore no true relation to his masculinity. They came to terms with the issue and realized that they could love their son regardless of how tall or small he was. Now they had to help William with his loss of self-esteem. They sympathized with his hurt feelings and worry about himself. They clarified that he was not a midget because he did not have the kind of illness that makes people midgets, and they assured him that he would indeed grow. However, they also added that he was smaller than some other four-year-olds. Nothing was wrong with him, people just are made differently. Nobody can choose how tall or small they are and nobody can change the way they are. Last, but not least, they said, "We love you the way you are and we hope you'll like yourself too." Maybe other parents would just say, "Oh, come, come! You're okay as you are and we love you," giving less explanations, but conveying a similar spirit of realistic acceptance.

When the child's early self-love is shaky and when the parents cannot help because they too have difficulty in loving the child's body as it really is, the child's self-esteem is apt to crumble when faced with disappointing shortcomings instead of adapting to a more realistic self-image. And so it happens that one person hates all of himself because his nose is not to his liking, another believes himself to be the handsomest ever and cannot acknowledge what the mirror tells him about his nose. But another yet can say, "My nose is too big, but in most ways I'm okay." He is the one who likes his body in a realistic way.

LIKING ONE'S MENTAL SELF

The process of getting to feel good about what we do, think, and feel, is similar to that of getting to like our bodies. In many ways these two aspects of our self-esteem are related, affect each other, and overlap, but they are not identical and do not necessarily go together. A person who likes and respects his body may not feel good about his work and his behavior, and a person who has a low bodily self-esteem may like his intellectual abilities and his character traits. Mental self-esteem, like bodily self-esteem, is not a "given" at birth, nor does its development depend on a realistic assessment of our qualities at the start. A toddler does not get to like his ability to climb the stairs because he is actually better at it than most other people, nor does a kindergartner feel proud of his beginning reading skill because he is the best reader or because he is unusually smart. As with the development of bodily self-esteem, we get to appreciate our mental qualities and accomplishments because they bring us pleasure and because our parents and other caring adults love them. It takes many years, much help, and many, one hopes not too humiliating letdowns, before our mental self-esteem is more or less in keeping with reality. For the beginnings we need to go back to the infant's first years.

LEARNING TO FEEL GOOD THROUGH TAKING CARE OF OURSELVES

Actually, we have already discussed many areas in which the mothering person, and later both parents, help their baby and toddler build love and respect for his activities. We talked about the infant beginning to participate in caring for himself. He holds his cup, feeds himself with his hands and becomes adept with the spoon, reaches out with his arms and legs to assist with dressing, gets on his shoes (usually the wrong way round), manages to pull off his pants and master his own toileting, and so on. The mother welcomes each little step, encourages his efforts, praises and admires them, sharing and reflecting the infant's own joy and pride in his accomplishments. Of course his "Me, all by myself" efforts take much longer and their outcome is usually much less perfect than if mother did it all by *her*self, but most of the time her satisfaction in watching him grow and feel happy seems worth it. Doing for himself as his mother has done, and joining in her admiration of himself, become the cornerstone of accepting himself as worthy and serve as an incentive for independent self-care. This helps youngsters to enjoy fulfilling their own needs, and they prefer it to being cared for, except at times of illness, fatigue, or special stress. Preschoolers who always want to be fed, dressed, and cleaned, show that they lack self-esteem in this area. This is often due to a difficulty in the mother's loving investment of the child's self-caring efforts. She may have been away too often or too long; she may not have allowed the child to do for himself or been too critical of his poor skills; she may have insisted on his doing things before he showed that he was ready; or she may have left him to do his own thing but did not remain with him to be his appreciative audience. Sometimes mothers do not realize that they are needed when the child wants to be independent—needed to love him and to applaud him. The transition period of sharing the activity, in the sense of "I don't need Mom to do it but I need her to love me doing it," is an essential step toward making it fully one's own and liking oneself for it. Earlier we mentioned that children often "lose" what they had learned and enjoyed doing at home when they enter a day care center or nursery school. The skill or function was not yet fully part of the child's own self-esteem and was given up when mother's loving presence was lost with separation from her.

An older schoolchild's or young adolescent's love of self-care usually is more independent. Preparing a meal for himself or being his own "sitter" is fun and adds to his self-esteem. The earlier parental appreciation is now part and parcel of his good feeling about himself. Their "Good for you!" now speaks to him inside.

HOW OUR PERSONALITY TOOLS AND ACTIVITIES CONTRIBUTE TO OUR SELF-ESTEEM

Similarly, when we talked about the development of personality "tools" (doing, observing, using words, etc.) we noted how the parents welcome new steps in the child's functioning, praise them, infuse them with their own enjoyment, and enhance the child's pleasure and good feeling about himself. Everything he does is admired—babbles and first words, crawling and walking, noticing the world around him and recognizing himself in the mirror, figuring out how a toy works, or waiting patiently for a few minutes. As the use of each tool progresses, so does the parents' and child's shared pride and enjoyment until, gradually, it becomes the child's own to use and to feel good about. As we grow older, parents no longer admire us for walking or talking nor do we congratulate ourselves on being able to do so, but in a quiet way, just exercising these functions continues to fuel our self-esteem. We only become aware of it when we lose the function or have no opportunity to use it; for example, when once again we cannot walk because of an injury or because our work commits us to long hours of sitting, we become uncomfortable with ourselves, nothing seems right with us or the world, in short, our self-esteem is diminished. Then, when we get to walk again, we suddenly feel so good and the world seems a better place—our self-esteem is on the increase. We may even say, "Now that I've had a walk again I feel more like a somebody." Whenever handicaps, illnesses, or other circumstances interfere with our normal functioning we are deprived of a valued loved part of ourselves and our self-esteem is lowered. Those who could never attain a liking for their "tools," either because of physical handicaps or because of lack of parental praise and pleasure, are deprived of important sources of self-esteem.

The same process of initial loving parental investment,

shared pride, and ultimate independent self-esteem applies to all our activities and interests, to play as well as to work. Unless young children experience the shared pride and pleasure, it does not make them feel good to play with toys, to learn new skills, to develop and pursue interests, to draw or paint or sing. They may be fascinated with a new toy for a while but soon it will be boring, broken or lost. This holds true even for things or activities the child seeks out himself, but it is, of course, especially marked with the many pursuits which require effort and patience. We have earlier talked about the role of the teacher in helping children build self-esteem in learning and achieving. This is helpful to a student at any age but is especially important for the young schoolchild. For example, Karen was thrilled when her kindergarten teacher assigned homework. She worked hard at it, was quite pleased with her results, and eagerly anticipated the teacher's praise. However, the teacher did not ask for the homework. When Karen told her about it, the teacher suggested she keep it in her desk or locker. After a few days, Karen began to lose interest in doing homework, expended no effort on it, and threw away unfinished worksheets. She could not yet sustain self-respect for a job well done without her teacher's participation. She might have had a chance to turn it into a lasting source of self-esteem if the teacher had regarded her work as important and had shared her pride in her good efforts.

Once self-esteem is well established in relation to some of the things we do, it tends to carry a momentum of its own, "Gee, if I can do this well, maybe I can succeed at that too." It spurs us on to include more things among our goals and accomplishments, gives us the confidence to try, the trust that we may achieve, and the resilience to weather disappointing setbacks.

So far we have talked about areas of self-esteem in which, from the start, parent and child essentially strive in the same direction; for example, the parents are pleased to see their child start walking and the child's innate growth "schedule" as well as his wish to be big, propel him toward walking. This is the case with all the developing personality functions and with most of the activities and interests. In many instances the child has, in addition, special abilities or gifts, such as good intelligence, advanced muscular coordination, or perfect pitch for music. Such endowments make it relatively easy for him to become quite adept at certain skills and to enjoy them. As long as the child's and parents' goals more or less coincide, self-esteem in functions and activities develops so harmoniously, so devoid of friction in the parent–child relationship, that we are hardly aware of the process. We don't even think of all the ordinary things we do as a source of self-esteem, much less realize how crucially important they are to feeling good about ourselves.

GAINING SELF-ESTEEM FROM ACHIEVEMENTS THAT ARE HARD TO COME BY

More often, when people think of self-esteem, they have in mind things that were hard to come by—qualities of feeling and behaving, such as being nice, kind, patient, conscientious, polite, or clean, or difficult achievements that required a lot of effort. Our parents always wanted us to have these attributes but we did not naturally strive for them. Very little children don't mind being dirty, are rarely kind or considerate, never patient, and unable as well as unwilling to accomplish major tasks. Their inclinations tend to the opposite of their parents' wishes. Children have the developmental capacity to give up their liking for dirtiness, or satisfaction with selfishness, and to exchange them for an opposite inner ideal, but this happens only with the help of the parents. At best, it takes a long time before we are really pleased with ourselves for being clean or considerate, and chagrined when we let ourselves down. However, once the ideal of "I like myself clean, I don't like myself dirty" becomes established in the child's mind, it serves him as a reliable guide to his behavior and as a source of self-esteem, insofar as he lives up to it. And when he does get dirty, it at least helps him to clean up and restore the good inner feeling. Even as adults we sometimes say to ourselves, "I have to clean up my room (desk, house), I just can't stand myself living in such a mess." And after we get it all done, we look proudly at the completed task with an "Ah, that feels better." All of us achieve the ideal of "I like myself clean" at least in regard to elimination. People who soil or wet themselves feel ashamed and bad about their trouble and wish they could control it. We take it as a serious sign of mental deterioration when a person loses his wish to keep clean in regard to urine and feces. However, beyond this basic cleanliness, our ideals in regard to it vary greatly. For some, the slightest contact with dirt causes a loss of self-esteem, for others, dirty clothes and belongings, or even dirty skin or hair, are of little concern. With some of us, a part of being clean is not to please ourselves but to gain approval from others; for example, we may clean house before guests arrive but would not bother to do it for ourselves, or at least "not yet." Just how high our standards of cleanliness are and to what extent they are truly internal, depends for the most part on the way our parents helped us when we were little.

When we talked about parental help in tolerating frustrations, we touched on many factors that apply also to other areas where the child learns only gradually to like in himself what the parents like in him and in themselves. We said that the parents help by gauging their expectations according to the child's ability at the time, demanding neither too much too early nor too little too late. They set a helpful model and maintain a good enough relationship with the child so that he will love and admire them and want to become like them. This wish is the first big step toward parent and child sharing the same goal. From then on the parental task is to help that wish become a lasting inner ideal and to learn how to live up to it. Parents do so with praise and support for the child's efforts. They enjoy every little success with him and hold out trust that he will have further successes. For example, toddlers usually take months to learn to like themselves clean, and then it takes many more months before that liking is independent of the loved adult. When two-and-a-half or three-year-olds lose the parent or suffer temporary separation, they tend to revert to having toileting accidents.

Oftentimes those attributes or activities which took longest to become our own ideals and which are hardest to live up to, provide us with the most self-esteem, or at least with the kind of self-esteem we are most aware of. To achieve a difficult thing makes us feel especially good. These are, of course, also the areas where we are most acutely aware of suffering loss of self-esteem when we fall short. The more sources of self-esteem we have the more chances do we have to make ourselves feel good. It also helps us to compensate for setbacks, for areas where we can't achieve as well as others, or don't come up to our own expectations, and where others disappoint us or are unjustly critical.

When our behavior and activities are not guided by our self-esteem and do not contribute to it, we lose out on feeling good about ourselves and may forever depend on supplies of esteem from others. Children may be clean and do their schoolwork in order to gain praise or to avoid punishment, but without ever feeling good about it for themselves. This may happen when they were not helped to value and enjoy their own accomplishments, when the adults stressed, "You have to be clean to please Mommy" rather than to be proud with yourself. Or, "You have to do your work so the teacher won't give you a detention," rather than "You can be proud of being such a good student." In such cases the child, or later adult, is likely to drop the activity when nobody praises it or when nobody threatens him with punishment, because the activity of itself provides no gain in self-esteem for him.

Is it wrong then for the adult to give "gold stars" or good grades, or to show that he is pleased with the child's performance? Of course not, but it depends on the attitude. If the attitude implies only "to please the adult," it will not work. If it implies a shared pleasure in the child's own satisfaction with himself and an appreciation of how pleased *he* must be, it helps build the child's self-esteem.

Moreover, the adult's pleasure in the child's achievement counts for little when it is not in keeping with the child's own satisfaction with himself. Recognition from others does not really make us feel good when we think to ourselves, "It's not as good a job as I'd like to have done," or "If only he knew how much I goofed on that job." Even with young children, praise only feels really good when it parallels self-praise. In many instances, children set their standards too high, despair of ever living up to them, and cannot use their actual achievements as a source of self-esteem (E. Furman, 1969a, 1985a,b).

Six-year-old Alan was doing quite well with his skating lessons and received much praise from his teacher and parents for his good beginning skills, but he was always disgruntled after lessons and even wanted to give them up. When his Dad asked him about it, Alan said, "It's because I'm no good at it." How come? Hadn't he been praised? Hadn't he seen that he was skating better than some of the other pupils? "I am not as good as the teacher," replied Alan wistfully. Obviously, Alan's expectations of himself were quite unrealistic. His parents had to help him tone them down and learn to enjoy the smaller successes he could achieve. No amount of praise would have helped Alan. At the same time, self-esteem is never wholly independent of the opinions of others, especially of those we care about most. When we feel pleased with ourselves, their appreciation makes us feel even better, and when we feel bad, our self-esteem is bolstered by their satisfaction with us.

PARENTAL SELF-ESTEEM

Perhaps it has seemed throughout this discussion that I have ideal parents in mind who possess all the virtues, all the patience and good sense, and no end of love to pour into their children. No, I have millions of ordinary parents in mind, rich and poor, in all walks of life, parents who make mistakes and who do better in some areas than in others, but who nevertheless manage to convey their deep caring for the child to him or her in such a way as to foster the development of the child's self-esteem. What enables parents to do that? There is no simple answer, but a very important part relates to the parents' own self-esteem.

When we earlier talked about the beginnings of the parent–child relationship, we noted that it is a unique kind of bond in which the partner is not only a loved person but also represents a part of oneself. This is easy to see in the child's tie to the parent because the parent actually functions for the child in so many ways for so long. It is less obvious in the parent's relationship to the child, yet equally important. The mother and father only become parents in the true sense when they view the child, to an extent, as a part of them-

selves, and usually the child represents the best part of themselves. His or her person is a big source of their own
self-esteem as is their parenting. To have a child and to be a
good parent to him or her, is a deeply rooted wish with most of
us. When we can realize it, it makes us more proud and
pleased with ourselves than most other things in life. This is
particularly true during the child's early years when he or she
is more a part of the parents than later on. It enables us, as
parents, to exert ourselves on the child's behalf and to give to
him to an extent beyond even what we might do for ourselves
because it makes us feel so good. That does not mean that
children are always a source of self-satisfaction (they bring
many disappointments), or that parents do not get angry at
their children, envious of them, and competitive with them. It
also does not imply that the child "belongs" to the parent,
that the child's achievements are the parent's. Allowing the
child to become him or herself is part of the self-esteem in
parenting.

When parents do not seem to love their children, cannot
see good things in them, cannot do well by them, it usually
means that their own self-esteem is so low that the best they
can invest of themselves in the child is not good enough. They
dislike their child as they dislike themselves. The best way to
help them with parenting is to raise their self-esteem so that
they have something better to invest in their children. When
we help children to have a sense of their own dignity and to
establish a realistic sense of self-esteem, we lay the foundation for them to become good parents.

CAN WE MAKE UP EARLY DEFICITS IN SELF-ESTEEM LATER ON?

To an extent we can and do make up such deficits. As we get
older, some of the things that used to make us feel inadequate
really change; for example, many of us like ourselves as
adults better because we are bigger, more competent, less
helpless. As we mature we also revise our ideals and adapt
them more appropriately to our capabilities and life circumstances. As a result we can live up to them more often and feel
good about ourselves. For example, like little Alan, men-

tioned above, most of us cease to berate ourselves for not achieving professional skill in skating and are content with the fun of just skating more or less well. Fortunate experiences in later years can also help to heal early wounds of disappointment and humiliation and improve our self-esteem. And psychiatric treatment can help with overcoming early interferences in the development of self-esteem.

However, not everything can be put right later. The earlier the deficits and the more pervasive, the harder it is to change their effect on the total personality.

Sometimes people do not really make up for low self-esteem in early life, but find ways of coping with it to spare themselves conscious suffering. They may then not even be aware of not liking all or parts of themselves. For example, people may bolster their self-esteem by accumulating lots of possessions, or by buying ever "better" things, or by associating with people they consider superior in order to share, as it were, in their desirable status, or, alternatively, by seeking out the company of inferiors with whom they can compare themselves favorably. There are many individual ways of supplying oneself with esteem from the outside to compensate for lack of inner self-regard. Some of these ways are more adaptive, some less. In their attitude to young children, people often betray how they viewed themselves when they were little or perhaps how they felt others saw them. When we look down on children, scorn their stupidity, or can't be bothered with them, we probably do not value the child in ourselves.

WHAT HAPPENS TO ABUSED CHILDREN?

When children are abused from early on in their lives, they have little opportunity to build a first concept of "me" around feeling good. As we said before, when "me" is associated with discomfort and pain, it does not serve the child to seek good experiences and to protect himself from harm. Abused children, characteristically, do not complain about their hurts or about their parents. More often they feel they have it "coming to them" for whatever they may have done wrong, thus reflecting the parents' attitude to them. Many remain insufficiently protective of themselves, with low self-esteem. They are also likely to become abusive themselves, especially toward their own children. Abusive parents once were abused children—a vicious generational repetition that is difficult to bring to a halt.

A special danger lies in the abused child's tendency to get to enjoy being maltreated. They then seek out people who are apt to abuse them or they actively provoke abuse through their behavior. Those of us who enjoy feeling good find it difficult to believe that anyone can get a kick out of being done to, but it happens with some people. Among several reasons for enjoying being hurt is the fact that children often get to like whatever their parents do with them frequently, especially when it involves intense emotional interactions, even sadistic ones. For some abused children the parental assaults represent the closest form of relationship they ever experience, taking the place of kindly attention and affection.

DOES SUICIDE HAVE TO DO WITH LACK OF SELF-ESTEEM?

Many factors contribute to a person's suicide. Cultural traditions play a part (e.g., in Japan) and so do external real circumstances (e.g., suicide during the terminal phase of a painful illness). However, the most important factors lie within the individual's mind. When a person has a psychosis, a mental illness that interferes with his thinking and judgment, suicide may be one of his symptoms. Such serious sicknesses of the mind may come on gradually and be clearly observable for a long time before suicidal symptoms enter in, or they may develop rather suddenly, with suicide as one of the initial symptoms. In these latter instances, the suicide may come as a surprise to others and they may not realize that it is a part of the patient's illness. Many psychoses can now be treated and helped.

Suicide can also be a symptom of other, nonpsychotic, mental disorders. Their nature varies greatly and there are usually many internal causes. Low self-esteem and excitement in self-hurting can be among them. Two aspects, however, need always to be considered: (1) Current and recent distressing experiences (loss of job, loss of a loved one, unkindness from others, worries about exams, etc.) are "used" by the already present illness and may trigger it into action, but they never cause it. Many other people cope with such experiences quite differently. (2) As a rule, very early deficiencies in the loving investment of one's body play a part. They render the person's inner protection against self-inflicted injury inadequate (E. Furman, 1984b). Perhaps all of us have suicidal thoughts at times, or at least feel, "I wish I were dead," but we do not carry out our ideas when we have an inner protective barrier, our early established bodily self-esteem. We may not be aware of it, but it works for us.

DON'T PEERS OFTEN AFFECT OUR SELF-ESTEEM MORE THAN PARENTS?

Yes, peers already affect the preschooler's self-esteem to some extent and their impact increases as children get older. However, the relationships with the parents underlie the later development of relationships with peers and, in the same way, the early building of bodily and mental self-esteem with the parents underlies the child's responses to peers' attitudes.

When little William in our earlier example felt crushed by the neighbor boy's ridicule, he turned to his parents. At that stage their opinion mattered most. Insofar as they will have helped William to feel good about himself, he may well cope with greater equanimity with such ridicule during his later school years. By the time peers' acceptance or rejection matters as much or more than the parents', the child meets it with his own self-esteem, good or bad, such as his parents helped him build. This shows in the kind of peers the child chooses as companions, what his attitudes to peers are, and how he feels about their attitudes to him.

15

Conscience

Wandering through department stores and looking over the tables and shelves laden with fancy things, we find ourselves thinking, "Oh, I could use this," or "That would be nice to have," or "Boy, I really need such-and-such." We may even handle the article or try it on, we may consider buying it if we have enough money, but most of us would not steal it. Are we afraid to be caught and punished? Yes, but that is not what really deters us. We just don't do it. It isn't right. Something inside tells us so. We usually call that something our conscience. It is our inner monitor, reminds us of right and wrong, good and bad, warns us to keep to its rules, and makes us feel good when we take heed. But if we stray, it punishes us with guilt. We may experience guilt as feeling miserable and hating ourselves, or as dread that something horrible may happen to us, or as fear of specific punishments by God or man, or as being undeserving of love and kindness from others, or of enjoying the good things in life. With these pangs of conscience may come remorse, wishing we had done right, wanting to confess our wrongdoing, or wanting to undo it or make up for it.

I took the inner rule of not stealing from a store as an example because it is a situation in which many of us have been aware of the conflict between "I want it" and "I mustn't," and because most of us resolve it by not stealing. What this means is that in our society most people have an inner law that prohibits stealing from stores and they abide by it. However, even this inner command of "Do not steal" is not the same for all of us. Some people have no qualms, no conscience, about stealing from stores. Many of us who feel it is wrong to steal from stores, allow ourselves to steal in other situations without feeling bad. We may help ourselves to paper and pens from the office where we work; we may keep gloves we find on the sidewalk; we may misrepresent our income to pay less taxes; we may use another person's ideas and pass them off as our own without acknowledgement, in an exam or in a composition. And there are others yet whose conscience does tell them they should not steal under any circumstances but it does not guide them to act accordingly, and so they steal, perhaps even from a store.

We are born with the potential for acquiring a conscience, but our upbringing, and especially our relationships with our parents, determine whether we really will develop a conscience, which rules it will include, and how effective it will be in influencing our behavior.

HOW OUR CONSCIENCE DEVELOPS

Parents, sitters, indeed all who take care of very young children, know only too well that youngsters' behavior is guided by their wishes for immediate satisfaction rather than by inner rules of right and wrong. They attack other people and grab their possessions, they destroy property, they want to be first and have most, they disregard fairness, in short, they are quite uncivilized and, far from feeling guilty, they are usually very angry at anyone who interferes with their pursuits. Yet, by the time these same youngsters are in first grade, they are generally most eager to be kind, considerate, polite, and hardworking pupils. They regard being unfair as a crime, and rules are so important to them that many a game with peers can hardly get under way because so much time is taken up with discussing the rules to be followed. They are mortified when they make mistakes, very touchy about criticism, and often expect much more of themselves than others demand of them. Our society, like many others, recognizes the timing of this big developmental step in conscience formation and gears its institutions to it. Formal schooling and religious training usually start at around age six.

HOW DOES THIS BIG STEP
IN CONSCIENCE FORMATION COME ABOUT
AND WHAT LED UP TO IT?

Initially, children's behavior is monitored from outside rather than inside. The parents set the standards and rules for their children's actions and restrain their behavior accordingly. When the crawling baby reaches for the vase, they say "No, no," but they also quickly pick up and remove either the child or the vase. From the second year on we see increasingly that the children themselves modify their behavior in response to the parent's requests; for example, mother's "No, can't touch the vase" is likely to stop the toddler, though he may reach toward it and give it just a little tap. He may even look at mom as he heads toward it, anticipating her prohibition. By two-and-a-half or so, he clearly knows that the vase is off limits and may stay away from it, at least in his mother's presence. His self-restraint cannot be fully relied on even then, however, and it is apt to vanish in his mother's absence. But the fact that the child knows and obeys the rule at times, shows that there is a beginning wish and ability to modify his behavior in accord with the parental expectation. The reason, of course, is the child's wish to please his parents and to be in their good graces. Toddlers have learned that all their bodily and emotional satisfactions depend not only on their parents' presence but also on the parents' loving good will. When mom approves, all goes well, when she disapproves, everything that makes life good and safe is in danger of being withdrawn. There is no way the young child can get it from anyone else or provide it for himself.

Parents tend to underestimate the enormous power their loving approval wields over the young child. When he can elicit and preserve that loving approval it ranks above other satisfactions; when he loses some of it, the desolation is so great that he would do anything to bring it back. For its sake, children forego other pleasures and want to learn what makes parents approve and what causes them to disapprove. And so it happens that rules are remembered and behavior is modified. At first this only applies as long as the parent is actually there. When a stranger takes the parent's place, the child no longer behaves according to the parent's rules. Even the familiar baby-sitter knows that her effectiveness is greatly enhanced when she reminds the children of the parents' "mental" presence, "This is your Mommy's rule. She will want to know whether you put away your toys. She won't like it when she hears you left them lying around." In time, the child himself becomes more able to keep the relationship with the parents in mind when they are temporarily absent. This helps him also to keep in mind the parents' rules and to anticipate their approval or disapproval on their return as well as to conform to the rules of others to whom the parents have specifically delegated their authority. For example, on entry to nursery school many children need the parent's sanction or support to go by the teacher's different rules. Some children, fearing mother's disapproval of messing, refuse to handle the unfamiliar clay or paint until the parent says it's okay to work with these messy materials at school. Other children still have difficulty in keeping parental rules in mind and mistake the nursery school's new rules for "no rules"; mindful of mother's disapproval they are clean at home but abandon themselves to messing at school, smearing clay and splattering paint on furniture, floor, and themselves instead of using them to make objects or pictures. They then need mother's and teacher's reminders that home rules about keeping clean still apply at school, even though different materials are available. To an extent, the loved person's loving approval continues to affect children's behavior even many years later. During the school years, the substitute teacher's lot is rarely a happy one as there are always some students who test the rules or resent a change in rules.

WHEN DOES THE CHILD ACCEPT THE PARENT'S RULES AS HIS OR HER OWN?

Here again the parental relationship plays its crucial part. As we have seen with many other developments, when the relationship is consistent and good enough, the child mostly loves and admires his parents. He then wants not only to please them but to become like them. Their standards and values become his. Of course parents support this, implicitly and explicitly, welcome the child's wish to be like them, and approve his every effort in that direction: "Big people don't mess with their food"; "Soon you'll learn to be big and eat neatly"; "Isn't it nice to see you eat like a big boy. You are really growing up. Now you can tell yourself how to eat."

Preschoolers begin to take into themselves parental expectations and struggle to live up to them. Oftentimes their lapses in behavior are not caused by an absence of inner rules but by an inability to muster the self-control necessary to follow them. When they tattle on others, "Jimmy is hitting" or "Jessica took Mary's book," they are usually confessing their own recent transgressions in this way or their temptation to do the wrong thing. Criticism of others at this stage shows that they know the rules and are close to self-criticism. Parents and teachers sense this and tend to keep a special eye on the tattler to help *him* do the right thing or to help him put right what he has already done wrong. Young children's lying is similarly often an indication that they wish they had done the right thing and feel uncomfortable about their wrongdoing, rather than that they deliberately want to deceive others in order to "get away" with their forbidden acts. Another sign of early inner conflict about being "bad" is nighttime fears which so often plague young children. Some of these result from the child's inner misgivings about his naughtiness or temptations. They come home to roost when he is alone in bed and make him fear punishment from mean imaginary beings, the external representatives of early guilt.

As the preschool years draw to a close, children make a more stable and successful transition from conforming to the parents' rules to gain and keep *their* loving approval to accepting these rules as their own and following them in order to approve of themselves. The parents' disapproval is replaced by self-criticism, shame, and inner dread. Along with the growth in self-esteem, and related to it, these are the forerunners of conscience.

Then around the age of six, children take a very big step in conscience formation, the biggest step they will ever take and the most important one. Whereas in the preceding years they gradually took in one or the other piece of the parents' standards and rules, now they almost suddenly seem to swallow a whole big chunk of parental do's and don'ts and set them up inside their own personalities. And this is the core and basic substance of their conscience. Parents are often amazed how, within the span of a summer or of a few months, their excitable and somewhat unruly underfive turned into a reasonable schoolboy. He has grown up, but he has also grown away. Now that a good part of his parents watches over him from inside, he is less close to them, less involved with the real parents outside. Their earlier intimacy with him subsides. Schoolboys find too much overt affection a bit embarrassing and don't go in for kissing and hugging with their parents, and schoolgirls likewise don't sit so much in laps, draped around the parent's neck. The boy or girl who not long ago wanted nothing more than to be with his parents and go places with them, now often prefers the company of peers. And whereas previously the parents' say counted above everyone else's, now their ways are questioned and what "my teacher says" often ranks above anything they say. The earlier years are almost suddenly forgotten and parents as well as children are surprised when the vacation of a year ago, or the neighbor at the old house, now exists only in the parents' memories. Pieces of remembrance remain, and jut out like islands in the sea of the past, but the continuity is broken and many of the infantile pleasures and pains are now left behind.

WHAT ACCOUNTS FOR THIS BIG CHANGE? HOW CAN WE EXPLAIN IT?

No doubt many maturational factors are at work simultaneously but the most prominent one is a profound upheaval in the parent–child relationship. It may help us to look at it from two sides.

One important aspect of the underfive's love for his parents is his admiration of them and wish to be big and grown-up, just as they are. In the earlier years, as he began to take over some of their attitudes and skills, each step represented to him the achievement of "Now *I* am big" and the expectation of "Soon I'll be big in every way." Many young children actually assume that they will *be* the parents and that they will reverse roles, so that the parents will become the children. Quite often we hear comments from them to that effect. The world looks, in their view, like a place with a fixed number of adult spots and of child spots, and when the child grows up, the adult needs to grow down. It is only around the age of five or so that children really sort out the sequence of generations—"Mom was Grandma and Grandpa Smith's little girl and Dad was Grandma and Grandpa Jones' little boy; when I grow up, we'll all be grown up at the same time; then Mom and Dad will be my children's Grandma and Grandpa." With this new understanding of the reality comes the awareness that one cannot *be* Mom or Dad, that one can only learn to become *like* them, and that it will take a long time. In one way this is a big disappointment, in another way it is an impetus to learning, in a realistic way, all the things that will take one along the road to adulthood, step by step, and without expectation of getting there very soon. The schoolchild's relationship with his parents is focused on learning to become like the parents and sharing interests and skills with them. In the process the child acquires more and more of the parents' attributes, values, and standards. They become his own conscience and he measures and judges his conduct by its moral precepts.

The other important aspect of the underfive's relationship with his parents is the wish that they gratify all his emotional longings in an exclusive partnership. In keeping with the young child's developmental needs, the parents are the recipients of almost all of his feelings and he expects them to reciprocate. Sharing does not come easily. We know how difficult it is for youngsters to believe that Mom and Dad can love them as well as their siblings: "All *my* love is for you. How come yours is divisible?" Parents usually help the child to tolerate their love and care of brothers and sisters by assuring him that he is not forever left out, that he too either has already participated in the same kind of loving interaction with them or will soon do so: "When you were a baby I used to feed you in this same way," and "As soon as you start school I'll visit in your class just as I now do in your brother's." In a good enough relationship the child also knows that he need not passively wait for the parents' love but can actively bring it about by pleasing them. We have seen how this motivates him to modify his behavior and to adopt their standards, at least to an extent.

During the last period of the preschool years, however, the child comes to realize that there are some kinds of loving which the parents refuse him or her but give to each other only. We discussed earlier how at that time children firmly establish their male or female sexual identity and try to understand the sexual functions. This brings a new context to the child's emotional demands on the parents. He or she wants to love and be loved as men and women love one another. Preschoolers often say that they will marry mom or dad, often show their wish for loving intimacy in their behavior with one or the other parent, and also try to interfere in the relationship between the parents, such as by interrupting their private conversations, insisting on sleeping with them, or objecting to their going out together. The parents reply, in action and/or words, "This kind of love we have only for each other, not for you. It's for grown-ups, not for little children." Children are keenly aware of being left out of the adult relationship and of being unacceptable as a partner, however much they try to please. This faces them with a painful frustration and an inevitable but necessary disappointment. It seems that the maturational forces pave the way in which children resolve their predicament. They give up on achieving a union with the parents, and instead take them into themselves and make them a part of their own personalities. From now on the "inside" parents, the conscience, tells them what they should and should not do, loves them when they do right and disapproves of them when they don't. In mind, the parents are now closer than ever, actually a part of the child; in reality, they are at a greater distance as the child no longer depends on them so much. The relationship with them becomes less close and less exclusive and some of the wealth of feelings that used to be contained in it becomes available for investment in other people, peers, and adults outside the family.

When all is said and done, it still seems like a miracle that in this, as in some earlier developmental steps, the parents who exist outside the child become an inner part of him or her and serve as building stones of a growing personality. We do not know the exact pathways by which this transformation proceeds. We can only observe the manifestations of the process at work, and marvel at it.

The children too seem at first puzzled by their conscience (E. Furman, 1980). Its commands and reproaches feel strange to them and they often attribute the newly harsh inner "voice of conscience" to outside sources. As a result, kindergartners, first, and even second graders tend to view their parents and teachers as demanding perfection and as highly critical, and they expect them to mete out terrible punishments. When nothing drastic really happens, they are often quite surprised. They sneak by the principal's office as though it were inhabited by an ogre and are awed by the policeman as though he knew their every private sin. When the parents do issue a reminder, the youngsters may feel "yelled at," and when the teacher accepts their worksheet without special praise they may feel that "she didn't like it." Some children expect the ax to fall from the unknown. They worry that all kinds of calamities may come upon them, or they fear they might get ill. And if something unfortunate does happen or they do get ill, they think they have somehow caused it and that it is a just punishment. Many children become quite religious, fear God's watchful eye, dread His wrath, and frequently pray for forgiveness.

In other instances children do perceive the "voice" as coming from within but it still sounds to them like the adult's command, "I was just going to throw down my coat and then it was like Mom was saying, 'You have to hang it up'." Even at a much later age people may say something like, "I can't ever throw away leftovers. It's like my mother was still there saying it was a sin and you have to use them up."

Sometimes children's new conscience feels so harsh that they find it very difficult to live with. They may avoid the distress by, as it were, handing it back to the outside authorities who are more lenient even when they get angry. Such youngsters may seem to act as though they had no conscience but closer observation shows that they actually provoke punishment. Unwittingly they make sure that they are caught in the act of whatever "crime" or that they leave clues for the adults. (Children who are really without a conscience are much more clever at doing forbidden things. They are rarely found out, however alert their caretakers may be.)

In time children usually integrate their conscience better with the rest of their personality. It serves them better as a guide and as an inner friend who approves of their good efforts and achievements, and when it does cause them to feel guilty, they are more able to recognize what it is all about and can put things right again. The conscience too changes somewhat with time. Its high moral expectations are toned down and better adapted to reality, big, medium, and small wrongdoings are more correctly distinguished in the light of experience, and new aspects are added from relationships with meaningful adults within the family and wider community, such as teachers. In fact, our conscience continues to develop and undergo changes, especially in adolescence but also throughout life. It comes to include new precepts, in keeping with new responsibilities and tasks, and adjusts earlier ideals accordingly; for example, being a good parent or a loyal spouse does not figure much in the conscience of the fourth grader but becomes an important modification when we marry and have children of our own. To some extent these later developments of our conscience draw on our earlier experiences with our parents, to some extent they lean on more recent relationships. However, these later changes do not altogether overthrow earlier standards or create a new conscience.

When children fail to develop a conscience they cannot acquire one later. Such a developmental failure happens when there is no consistent and good enough relationship with parents or parent substitutes during the crucial early years. Without this relationship there is no wish to please, no wish to modify one's behavior and to become like the loved adult, and no attachment so profound that its disappointments can be tolerated and lead to a taking in of the partner's injunctions. This does not mean that such children do not learn the rules and do not obey the rulemakers whose punishments they fear. But their knowledge of right and wrong does not become an inner guide to or judge of their conduct.

Instead, this knowledge of the rules and of the punishments for transgressions serves them to decide when they can and cannot go against them with impunity. Not all delinquents and criminals are people without a conscience, but those who are usually know the law well—as an external force.

However, even people with a conscience are not all virtuous and law-abiding citizens. We do not always do as our conscience bids us and we do not all have the same kind of conscience. Each person's conscience is as individual as he or she is.

DIFFERENT KINDS OF CONSCIENCE

Earlier on in our discussion of conscience we noted that people have very different ideals about stealing, or even no ideals about stealing. We might have added that some people actually feel they ought to steal in certain situations. Robin Hood, who felt that way, is admired by many; stealing from the enemy in wartime is similarly acclaimed as moral and patriotic; and many revolutionaries risk their lives to steal because they consider it a legitimate means in the pursuit of their worthy cause. We also mentioned that some people's conscience, though it prohibits stealing, does not warn them effectively before they steal but seems only to "clobber" them after they have done it. We could look at moral values other than stealing and find similar variations between individuals, between groups of people, and whole societies.

These variations are, to a considerable extent, the result of our individual relationships with our parents and our experiences with them. The kind of conscience a child develops depends a lot on the parents' standards for the child, on the consistency of their expectations, on the way they enforce them, when and how they go about it. It also depends on their own standards for themselves, whether they live up to them, and whether they expect the same or different conduct from their children, "Do as I say, not as I do."

The effect of the parental model is so familiar to our thinking that we often take it all too readily for granted that the child's conscience will work just like the parent's. Sometimes people even think that the child's conscience is bound to be like the parent's. "What an honest boy! Just like his parents!" Or, "No wonder he's in trouble. His father is a real crook." Often this is quite true, even when the outsider cannot trace the connection. For example, the child who cheats without feeling bad may have observed, and taken in, aspects of his apparently virtuous father which others don't see—that the father cheats on traffic laws when there is no police car around, that he keeps the neighbor's shovel when he finds it in his backyard, that he adjusts his expense account in his favor, or engages in dubious business practices. Also, when the parents act differently with their child than they do with adults, the child may adopt their attitudes to himself; for example, parents who are very honest in their dealings with adults, may lie to their children (they may even do it for kindly reasons, but they are still lies), or parents who are very polite and restrained with adults, may be rude to their children, and yell at them or hit them when annoyed.

However, the parental model does not account for everything. What the parents expect of the child, and how they impart it to him or her, is at least equally important. Parents may, in some or all areas, set much lower standards for their child than for themselves, or much higher ones; for example, they may be very conscientious and hardworking themselves but may want their child to have an easier life and so don't expect him to do chores, or to take his homework too seriously, or to find jobs to earn some of his own money; by contrast, they may be rather lackadaisical themselves but very insistent that the child work hard. There are many other differences in approach. Parents may expect the child to modify his behavior very early in life and very quickly, or rather late and gradually. They may be very firm in their expectations or quite lenient, or even inconsistent, letting things ride one day and clamping down strictly the next. They may supervise carefully and prevent wrongdoings, or they may leave the child to himself but then punish him severely afterwards for not having behaved well. And of course the way parents disapprove varies enormously—how stern they are, how angry for how long, and how they show it, whether they punish, or expect the child to make up, or help him to do better next time, or simply brush it aside. The child's standards for himself will reflect many aspects of the parents' handling. It may decide whether his conscience "supervises" before he does wrong or "beats up" on him after it happened; whether it forgives everything, or nothing, or prompts him to make up as best as possible; whether it lets him do wrong one day but not the next. It may decide whether its demands are so exorbitant that they can never be reached and condemn him to continual self-deprecation, or whether they are within keeping of his ability to live up to them if he tries and allow him to feel pleased with himself; whether they permit him to enjoy all or some bodily pleasures and comforts or forbid them (some people feel that all fun is immoral and that they should not even eat what they like but only what is "good" for them). There are endless subtle varieties in parental handling and in its effect on conscience formation, but even this does not wholly account for the exact nature of the child's conscience.

In addition to all the parents stand for and do, the child's conscience also depends on him or herself, on how he perceives the parents and feels about them, on his life experiences with and apart from them, and on his individual makeup.

Children's perceptions are particularly subjective, colored by the haze of their own feelings, limited by their immature grasp of reality, and judged in the light of their smallness and helplessness. For example, when a frustrated, angry child looks at his angry parent, he sees the parent's anger magnified by his own anger and, taking into account his status vis-à-vis the parent, the parent's scolding, restrictions, or bodily attack may then seem much more dangerous to the child than the parent actually feels or intends. The perennial theme of David and Goliath, of vicious ogres in fairy tales outwitted by the youngest son, of space monsters subdued by crafty little humans, all recall such early childhood dread and attempt to undo it by reversing the roles, so that, contrary to expectation, the small triumph over the threatening big. As a result of the child's perception, the parental injunctions often seem much harsher than they really are. What he takes into himself is what *he* sees. This shapes the early conscience and contributes to its initial harshness.

Sometimes the parent is seen as punitive when he has

done nothing at all. For example, the parents' leaving on a vacation trip, or their leaving him in the hospital, may be viewed as punishment for naughtiness, especially since the child himself is so angry at the parents at such times.

However, the child's conscience is not only affected by his view of the parents' harshness but also by his unrealistic perception of their perfection. For many reasons children often idealize their parents and then take into themselves standards fit for angels rather than mortals. The real parents were not at all perfect and the child may later be quite disappointed in them when he measures them against the ideal he has made his own.

The child's well-being and self-esteem, his understanding of reality, and ability to deal with frustrations, his overall relationship with his parents, all his other past and current experiences, play their part in how he views parental do's and don'ts, which aspects he selects, and how he takes them into himself.

DO CHILDREN FROM SINGLE-PARENT FAMILIES DEVELOP A CONSCIENCE IN THE SAME WAY?

Yes, they do develop a conscience in the fashion discussed above. Some of the steps, however, are somewhat different, and perhaps harder, for them, and this may contribute to the kind of individual conscience each has. (R. A. Furman, 1983).

For many reasons, it is unfortunate when children have only one available parent. We talked about this also earlier in connection with the child's need to develop his or her sexual identity and to love and be loved by both parents. Single-parent families are not all alike, though, their circumstances vary. They may have consisted of two parents and one died, or the parents may be divorced and the child may or may not continue his relationship with the parent who left the home, or children with unwed mothers may have a male adult relative, or family friend, who acts as a father substitute to some extent. The relationship with a well-remembered parent, or with a frequently visited parent, or with a partial parent substitute, helps the children with their need to love and admire a man and a woman so that they can take in attributes and values from both. The better the children know them and the closer the relationships, the better they serve as realistic models.

When the parents, or parent substitutes do not maintain an adult love relationship, the children may not be as aware of all that makes up such relationships and may not feel left out in the same way, but they still have to accept the disappointing reality that their emotional demands for intimacy with the parent cannot be met. They cannot be husband or wife to either parent. Their conscience grows out of this developmental step, as it does with children from two-parent families, and incorporates the variations of each individual child's situation (E. Furman and R. A. Furman, in press).

HOW CAN DELINQUENTS HAVE
A CONSCIENCE?

In developing their conscience, children may take in the delinquent standards and values of their parents, standards which are not in keeping with their society's laws. Or they may take in some of the do's and don'ts their parents hold up for them, rather than for themselves. For example, parents may not engage in delinquent acts themselves, but may encourage and approve of the child's delinquent conduct, so that the child's conscience develops in accord with parental but not societal standards. Or children may have the kind of conscience which makes them feel guilty after the act but does not guide or restrain them beforehand. Also, some children have a conscience that includes all the expected rules but they lack sufficient frustration tolerance and self-control to carry out its commands. They cannot resist the temptation, at least not at certain times or in certain situations.

There are also delinquents whose guilt actually causes them to do wrong things in order to solicit punishment (Freud, 1916). Sometimes a conscience which forbids not only unlawful behavior but also "bad" thoughts and bodily pleasures may be too difficult to obey and cause constant inner distress. Some people may then feel miserable and be perpetually unsatisfied with themselves. Others may, without even

knowing it, escape their inner discomfort by being driven to
do something bad. They can, in this way, pin their vague guilt
on something tangible and get punished for it. For a while
this relieves them as though they had atoned, but in time the
vicious cycle starts all over again. We mentioned earlier that
such asking for punishment to "get it over with" often
happens with young children whose conscience is so new and
harsh that they have not yet learned to live with it and have
not yet modified it to realistic proportions. Such children
provoke punishment with their misbehavior and prefer a
spanking to feeling guilty. Adults help these children often,
not by meting out the requested punishment, but by pointing
out that the children are really asking to be punished, that
something is making them feel bad, and that they would feel
better if they put things right and got back in control by
themselves (E. Furman, 1980). Older children or adults who
are delinquent from a sense of guilt, stopped in their development at that earlier stage, and have not learned to utilize
their conscience to adapt to society.

DO PEERS AFFECT ONE'S CONSCIENCE?

Peers do not form a child's conscience but they may increase
or decrease the temptations a child has to resist, and in
adolescence and adulthood they may modify our inner
standards to some extent. "Good" companions, who try to
live up to their own similar standards, make it easier for a
child to keep to his inner rules; "bad" companions, who
engage in forbidden activities that seem fun, make it harder
to heed his own conscience. To an extent this holds true for
adults as well. Most people find it easier to go by their conscience when others in their community uphold the rules too.
When most cars drive within the speed limit we are more
likely to keep to it than when we notice all the other cars
passing us at excess speed.

  However, a person's own conscience is not simply at the
mercy of others. It not only guides us in our choice of companions but also helps us to determine just what we will or won't
join them in, and to what extent we will modify our standards, temporarily or permanently, to fit theirs; for example,

some of us may go along with inappropriate sexual activities but not with drug taking, or with drug taking but not with stealing, or with stealing but not with murder. Self-esteem has a lot to do with that. When we like ourselves, we also like our conscience and its values and are not likely to give them up. We take pride in what we stand for, trust ourselves, and feel good about it. When we do not like ourselves and consider ourselves unlovable, we don't think our standards are worth much either, and then we are apt to exchange them for those of others in order to be more acceptable to them. Children sometimes choose and go along with bad company because they do not feel that anyone better could like them.

WHAT ABOUT PUNISHMENT? IS IT NOT IMPORTANT FOR PARENTS TO PUNISH CHILDREN FOR WRONGDOING SO THAT THEY WILL KNOW WHAT IS RIGHT AND WRONG AND WILL NOT GO ON DOING THE SAME BAD THINGS?

We shall look more closely at the role and nature of punishment in our discussion of discipline. I shall therefore be brief and start with an anecdote: Our little five-year-old neighbor boy once arrived in our yard crying. "What's the matter, Billy?" we inquired. "My Daddy spanked me." "Why did he spank you?" we wondered, expecting to hear of Billy's misdeed. But the only reason Billy could come up with was, "Because my Daddy was mad."

Punishment, physical or otherwise, does not spell out right and wrong, words do; many parents and teachers know that. They usually do not think of punishing children who don't know a rule yet, but punish those who have transgressed a rule they do know. Punishment of itself may deter children, or adults, if they think they will be found out, but it does not make them want to take into themselves the rules of the punisher and to use them as an inner guide to behavior. When the do's and don'ts of the punishing parent or other person are taken over, it is because that parent or person is also loved and loving, in spite of the punishment he or she inflicts. What counts in building the child's inner standards, values, and rules of conduct into a coherent conscience is not the force of punishment but the power of the loved caretaker's clear and consistent disapproval (a partial withdrawal of love) for wrongdoing, his or her supervision and help in doing right, and approval for success in conforming to the expected standard.

16
Self-Discipline and Discipline

Self-discipline means more or less the same thing to most of us: to conduct ourselves voluntarily in such a way as to meet our demands on ourselves as well as the requirements of our community. To that end we restrain, modify, and selectively gratify our needs and wants. Regardless of where we live, as adults we hardly ever "do what comes naturally." Societies and individuals vary in the kinds of restrictions they impose and the types of pleasures they allow, but the world over, their expectations encompass every part of a person's functioning and therefore self-discipline affects all aspects of our lives. It determines what and how we eat, when and where we eliminate, how we care for our bodies in sickness and in health, what our sexual practices are and whom we select as partners. It determines what we learn, which interests and activities we pursue, how we spend our leisure time, whether and what kind of property we acquire, how we treat others, what kind and number of relationships we maintain. It determines how we handle disappointments and frustrations, or disputes with others, and so on. In each area there are some things we can do, some we cannot do, some we can do only at certain times, or in certain places, or under certain circumstances. All this takes a lot of self-discipline and an awful lot of learning how to exercise self-discipline. When we come to think of it, it is amazing that we are capable of changing and adapting our impulses in so many different ways and not surprising that it is often difficult, takes a long time, and does not always succeed.

In all culture patterns, nevertheless, people are expected to achieve a good measure of self-discipline and they are expected to learn much of it during childhood in their families. All societies view the adult members of each family as their representatives and entrust to them the task of teaching their children self-discipline. The family is the child's first community, whose demands he has to meet, and through whom those demands become his own. This is not a matter of chance, but is in keeping with the natural laws of personality development: Children acquire self-discipline through their most meaningful relationships. In early childhood these are the relationships with the parents or parent substitutes. Later, they come to include members of the wider community, such as teachers. Although in these respects all societies are alike, in other respects they differ.

We have already mentioned that their specific rules differ and therefore self-discipline has to be learned and exercised to fit them; for example, in our society children have to learn to eat with spoon, knife, and fork, to eat three or four meals daily, and to eat with all kinds of other people; in some African societies they have to learn to use their hands in certain ways for self-feeding, to eat one or two meals, to fast on certain days, and never to eat with members of the opposite sex.

Societies also differ in the extent to which they either expect all members to adhere to the exact same code or, as in this country, allow and even encourage individuals to develop and live by a variety of personal standards and values. In the latter case families have their own rules and expect their children to meet them; for example, in the United States many families have some of their own rules in regard to eating, such as keeping kosher or vegetarian diets. In some ways that can make learning self-discipline easier because a family may keep easy-to-follow rules; for example, family members may be allowed to eat what they want ("You don't have to eat it if you don't like it" or "You only need to taste it"), when they want (snacks any time), where they want ("I'll take my tray to the TV"). But in another way this makes self-discipline much harder. When one sees other people in other families following different and perhaps more desirable rules, it is more difficult to stick to one's own ("The Jones children don't have to finish what's on their plates, why do we?" Or "The Smith family always sits down together for a nice dinner at a nicely set table. Why do we eat catch as catch can, each at a different time in the kitchen?"). Also, when the family rules are very different from the community's norm, one may find oneself ill-prepared and lacking in necessary self-discipline (Johnny may be in trouble at school meals because he has not learned to handle knife and fork, to sit through a meal, or to wait to eat until all are served).

Furthermore, societies differ in the methods they use to teach children self-discipline, in the ways they help adult citizens to maintain self-discipline, and in how they deal with those who lack in self-discipline, who go against the accepted rules. In some societies the parents have to use the same specific methods of teaching self-discipline, and these methods are closely related to and prepare for the ways in which society enforces its rules with the adults; for example, many American Indian tribes rule out physical punishment with children as well as with adults. Such societies usually also provide a lot of help with self-discipline to their adult members all through life, mainly by means of constant mutual support and surveillance in well-defined, prescribed groups, such as groups joined by kinship, by puberty rites, or by shared work and activities. There is little opportunity for people to be alone when they want to or to associate with companions of their own choosing. By contrast, Western societies, and this country especially, represent the opposite extreme. Families can, to a considerable extent, choose their own methods of teaching self-discipline. These individual family methods may or may not be in keeping with those which society uses with adults; for example, physical punishment is still legal in regard to children but no longer legal with adults. People can and do live alone, may be unknown to their neighbors, need not belong to any prescribed group, and may choose anyone to associate with. The community exercises little control and gives little support. The police help relatively little in maintaining self-discipline (for the most

part they do not even know the citizens), and community
groups, such as church, business, or youth groups, are voluntary and meet only for a few hours at intervals of a week or
more. All this places a major responsibility on the effective
self-discipline of the individual, on the family whose task it is
to help develop such self-discipline in its children, and on
their choice of ways and means. This brings us to discipline.

WHAT DOES "DISCIPLINE" MEAN?

In regard to children, most people agree that discipline is not
an end in itself but a means toward inculcating self-discipline
(E. Furman, 1982a). It is not just a question of how one deals
with a child in a particular situation but how this will affect
his or her future behavior: "If he doesn't get any discipline,
he'll never learn to act right." The word *discipline*, however,
means rather different things to different people. This is not
surprising because, as we have just said, in our society people
use varied methods to teach self-discipline. To some, discipline means punishment (i.e., a consequence of, or retribution
for wrongdoing, for not meeting the required standards of
conduct). Thus, when discipline means punishment, it is a
method used *after* a failure in self-discipline, after things
went wrong. To others, discipline means measures that *prevent* transgressions. Making sure that nothing can go wrong
is usually achieved either by supervising children in such a
way that it will not be possible for them to do undesirable
things or by actually taking over and doing things for them.
For example, a mother may discipline her child's eating habits by watching him closely as he helps himself to food or by
serving him herself to ensure that he will take the required
kind and amount of food; or, parents may discipline their
child's leisure time by supervising his play or by choosing
certain activities for him, to make sure that he will spend the
time in what they deem an appropriate manner. And to others yet, discipline means measures that provide an environment which *facilitates* the child's learning and mastery of
self-discipline. For example, parents may find that consistent
rules and rules applied to all members of the family are more
readily learned and followed (e.g., coats are always hung up

in the hall closet and *everyone* hangs up his own coat); or parents may notice that their youngsters can better stay out of trouble when there are definite daily routines (specific times for getting up and going to bed, specific mealtimes, TV times, homework time); or, they may appreciate that their four-year-old is better behaved during their absence when he is prepared for it and cared for by a familiar sitter.

In practice most parents and educators use all these forms of discipline to teach self-discipline, but they may greatly favor one or the other approach. They also vary very much in the way they apply it; for example, when parents focus on discipline as punishment for wrongdoing, they may hit the child, or send him to his room, or deprive him of food or of pleasurable activites, or they may scold him, or make him repair the damage, or they may use several or even all of these measures at the same time. They may use the same punishment for all offenses or different punishments for different offenses. They may vary the punishment according to the child's age, or according to their own mood, or according to whether other people are present or not.

Before we look at the three areas of discipline more closely, let us remind ourselves of some of the things we already know about how children develop and learn, so that we can better evaluate the role and effectiveness of the various measures.

WHAT MAKES IT POSSIBLE FOR DISCIPLINE TO TEACH SELF-DISCIPLINE?

Above all we know that the important developmental process of taking into oneself a new attitude or way of doing things, and making them truly one's own, a part of one's growing personality, takes place primarily in the context of a consistent good enough relationship; this holds true equally for acquiring self-discipline. Without a consistent good enough relationship no disciplinary measure can lead a child toward adopting a demand and meeting it independently. Discipline without a sufficient relationship can at best act as an external control or deterrent, forever dependent on the vigilance of others. It will remain at the level of "I can't take Jeremy's chocolates because Mom is watching," "I won't take Jeremy's chocolates because somebody will see me and tell the grown-ups and they'll spank me," but "I will take Jeremy's chocolates as soon as I'm sure I won't be found out." It will never become "I won't take Jeremy's chocolates because I don't want to be a thief."

Let us also remind ourselves that, even when the disciplinarian maintains an adequate relationship with the child, it matters not only what kind of method he uses but how he himself behaves, for the child is likely to take into himself all aspects of the model, the said and the unsaid, the intended and the unintended. Teaching self-discipline depends also on exercising it. When mom leaves her things all over the house, lets them pile up in corners, and can never find what she needs, it will be very difficult for her to help her child acquire the kind of self-discipline that will enable him to keep his room neat and to take good care of his possessions. It is a well-known, tragically joked about truism that the parent who beats his child, saying "That'll teach you never to beat up on anyone that's littler than you," teaches his child just the opposite by what he does.

Further, we have recognized that children's personalities develop in maturational steps or sequences. They can only learn those things which are in keeping with their potential and its gradual unfolding at successive stages in growth. For example, it is impossible for a ten-month-old to acquire the self-discipline to sit quietly through dinner, to use a knife and fork, and not to touch his food with his hands; nor would it be possible for a five-year-old independently to complete two hours of homework. However, the child's ability to understand and carry out demands depends a lot on how much we have helped him to develop his personality tools—thinking, using words, motor skills, frustration tolerance. A demand may be easy to comply with when he has the "know-how" and very difficult when he lacks it. "Use your spoon, not your fingers" is no trouble for the dexterous youngsters, but spoils the pleasure in eating for the clumsy ones. It is comparable to an adult's difficulty in using chopsticks for the first time.

Strict or harsh disciplinary measures can force children to conform to expectations that far exceed their age-appropriate capabilities, but this is not likely to lead to reliable independent self-discipline or, if the child does internalize and meet the excessive demands, it may use up so much of his mental energy that other areas of personality development are restricted. For example, children who conform to a very early and insistent toilet training tend to respond in one or the other of two ways. Their self-discipline in regard to cleanliness may remain unreliable, they may be prone to later relapses to incontinence, may have periodic "accidents," may be untidy in their work habits or in the care of their possessions; or they may need to be so preoccupied with being clean that they may not be able to engage in other activities, may not allow themselves to play freely lest they get dirty, may refuse to use messy media, such as paint and clay, may dislike foods that appear dirty to them, such as gravies, stews, and some vegetables, and may be unduly worried about becoming contaminated ("picking up dirty germs"). On the other hand, when the adults' expectations are far below what the child could accomplish, he or she misses out on practicing the necessary skills, may then lag in developing self-discipline, or may even fail altogether in achieving it. Things that are not learned at the optimum developmental time are often much harder to learn later on or may never be learned at all. Timing and grading expectations appropriately to the child's developmental level and capacities play an important part.

Last but not least, we all know that we are much more willing to work hard at complying with a demand when we do not experience it as arbitrary, selfish, or humiliating but can actually see it as useful or advantageous to ourselves in some ways. For example, a law that prohibits driving when under the influence of alcohol may limit our personal freedom to do as we please, but we also see it as a help in protecting us from harm through accidents caused by ourselves or others. Similarly, when a nursery school teacher stops a child from hitting a peer, he may not like her interference, but perhaps after his anger has abated, he can also appreciate her rule, "I won't let you hurt others just as I won't let others hurt you. This has to be a safe school for everyone." In other words, when demands are geared to preserve our bodily well-being and when we have developed a sufficient bodily self-esteem so as to want to keep our bodies unharmed, the demand is in part in accord with our own interest. This helps us to want to go along with it even though it means restraining our immediate impulse.

Some demands are geared to help us feel good mentally, to contribute to our mental self-esteem. For example, when we have acceptable table manners, we are welcome companions at a social dinner. We gain appreciation from others and get a chance to do something we enjoy. When we are honest and conscientious, perhaps our conscience "pats us on the back" and we like ourselves better. Likewise, when a mother tells her five-year-old that he will not be welcome at the supermarket unless he stops running up and down the aisles, or that he will feel bad if he takes his brother's crayons without asking him, she appeals to the child's wish to be liked, to his enjoyment of shopping trips, and to his growing conscience.

Many of these and other demands prohibit an immediate gratification but offer another satisfaction later. Finishing his homework and doing a good job with it may be tedious right now and deprive him of a TV show, but it promises the later pleasure of a good grade, of feeling proud of himself, of being praised by the teacher, and of excelling in competition with peers. When demands are made in a spirit of helpfulness and worded in such a way as to remind the child of its benefit to him, he can better weigh both sides of the conflict. One eight-year-old described this as "You always have to choose between fun in the short run and fun in the long run."

The more we help a child develop his or her inner monitors—bodily and metal self-esteem and conscience— and the more we gear our demands to helping him feel good about himself, the easier it is for the child to comply with our expectations and to incorporate them as his own.

DISCIPLINARY MEASURES

Let us now look more closely at the three kinds of discipline: the environment that facilitates self-discipline, the measures that prevent wrongdoing, and those applied after wrongdoing has occurred.

The Facilitating Setting

Most parents and educators find that children of all ages, but especially the younger ones, behave better in some settings than in others. For example, children tend to have trouble with self-discipline in a home with irregular meals and sleep times and with many sudden haphazard changes (trips, house guests, parties, unfamiliar sitters, unexpected parental absences). We can similarly predict trouble, at least for some, at a six-year-old's birthday party for twenty youngsters, with one adult, which includes an overnight stay in sleeping bags and no structured activities. How can we explain that such settings are unhelpful? Some may reply "Too much going on," or "You don't even know if you're coming or going." In other words it is difficult, even impossible, to be in control of ourselves when too many stimuli impinge on us from without and within and when they take us by surprise. When a setting helps us to limit stimulation to a manageable degree, helps us to anticipate what is going to happen and to prepare ourselves for it, we don't get so overwhelmed (rattled, excited, frustrated) and can be better masters of our behavior. Even grown-ups lose their "cool" when there is too much noise, too many interruptions, too many sudden happenings, too many excited people talking and running around. Children are much more vulnerable, cannot absorb or screen out many stimuli, and have fewer means of mastery. A peaceful steady pace, predictable routines, consistent expectations, activities that do not take too long and are not too exciting or stressful, preparation for changes and unusual events, all make it easier for children, especailly younger ones, to conform. This holds true even for the smallest items in daily life, for example, a reminder "Five more minutes to play, then it'll be time to go shopping" is so much more readily obeyed than an unexpected "Stop playing and get in the car at once. I have to go to the store," which tends to provoke resistance or protest. Measures that facilitate self-discipline work well not only at the time. They also further the growth of self-discipline as they allow for ways of doing things to become firmly established, to take root, and to pave the way for mastering increasing challenges.

Is it possible to carry such a regime to excess and to defeat its own purpose? Of course, everything can be misused. Routines can be made so rigid as to enslave children rather than help them (for example, when the bedtime can *never* be extended by half an hour to allow the child to participate in a special family occasion or to finish watching a special TV show). Guarding against overstimulation can be made so extreme as to produce a sterile restricted life without room for fun, variety, or new experiences. Children may respond to such an environment by "kicking over the traces" as soon as they get a chance, or by becoming fearful of situations that allow more freedom and expose them to more stimulation. Also, the very measures that are helpful to the child at one period in his development, can become unhelpful if they are not altered and adapted to meet his changing needs and capacities at a subsequent period; for example, a 7:30 bedtime may be right for the three-year-old but restrictive and frustrating if still imposed when he gets to be nine years old; or, a shopping expedition followed by dinner in a restaurant may be "too much" for a three-year-old but can be an enjoyable treat for him at nine years.

In this as in many other areas, parents who are reasonably disciplined themselves and in tune with their child, readily sense what he can cope with. They also learn from the child's behavior when they have erred in exposing him to too much or too little. For example, they notice that the child is crabby and demanding toward the end of a car trip which has been too long, that he is unruly and "hyper" after an outing to the amusement park which has included too many rides, or that he is balky and angry at a change of plans he had not been prepared for. In these situations parents acknowledge their mistake to him, shoulder some of the blame for his misbehavior, and make better plans for next time.

Preventing Wrongdoing (Doing Things for the Child and Supervision)

It is quite common for a mother to spank her toddler for running into the street while she was chatting with the neighbor, or for her to scold him angrily for emptying the kitchen drawers while she was on the phone. Most of us, including the mother, know that such incidents are due to lack of self-discipline on the part of the mother rather than on the part of the toddler. Toddlers cannot gauge traffic but need an adult to do it for them. They cannot play safely on their own but need adult supervision. We also know that toddlers don't learn self-discipline in these situations from such punishments, don't learn how to watch for cars or how to take care of kitchen utensils. At best they learn that sometimes it makes Mommy very angry when they cross the street and play with saucepans. In short, most of us recognize that doing things for the child and supervising him are in these instances necessary preventive disciplinary measures.

What do we think of these also rather common occurrences: four-year-old Clara's mother spoon-feeds her little girl to prevent messes on the table and floor and she supervises Clara's toileting to make sure that she wipes herself properly and flushes the toilet. Eleven-year-old Irv's mother supervises his homework by sitting with him and checking each line. She also takes over for him by looking up his "new" words in the dictionary and rewriting his book report. I think many of us would consider these kinds of supervision and doing for the child excessive. We may regard Clara's mother as interfering unduly with her child's bodily functions and think that Clara should have been allowed to feed and toilet herself long since, and we may similarly expect Irv to be responsible for his own homework. In short, most of us recognize that doing things for the child and supervising him or her in these instances may prevent wrongdoing but at the cost of also preventing adequate opportunities for developing self-discipline and making some inevitable mistakes in the process.

But the lines are not always so clearly drawn: The W.'s live on a short block of a side street where youngsters of all ages play. Mrs. W. sends her children out to play too, four-year-old Jeff and seven-year-old Josh who is to keep an eye on his little brother. Almost an hour later Jeff runs into his house crying. His clothes are covered with dirt and his arm is scratched. Josh follows shortly, yelling something about "mean kids." Mother is upset and furious. It turns out that

Jeff was riding his tricycle and Josh joined his buddies in a ball game. At some point Jeff decided to play ball too and picked up a ball that was just "lying there." When the owner found that Jeff was using his ball and angrily tried to retrieve it, a scuffle developed in which Jeff was pushed to the ground and hurt. Jeff's crying then attracted Josh's attention and they ran home. Is this just one of those unfortunate accidents or was it the result of wrongdoing? And if so, who was to blame? Was it the fault of the "mean kid" whose mother should be told that he is a menace and that she should keep him off the street? Was it little Jeff's fault because he had been "told a hundred times not to take other people's things," or was he perhaps too young to be trusted with such self-control when alone, a bit bored, and a bit envious and left out of the bigger boys' ball game? Was it Josh's fault because he was to keep an eye on his brother but got involved in his game instead? Or is a seven-year-old perhaps too young to be a reliable baby-sitter while his peers are enjoying themselves? Or is the mother to blame? Did she misjudge her boys' capabilities? Should she have gone out to supervise them or should she, at least, have checked on them every few minutes? Is her anger at the children justified? Should she perhaps be angry at herself? Or should she tell her boys that she *and* they did wrong, have reason to feel bad, and need to learn from what happened so that it will not be repeated? Which way would be most helpful to teaching self-discipline?

And what about this situation: Zachary's third grade teacher has informed Zachary's mother that her son is in trouble with his homework. Some days he forgets to take it home, other days he fails to hand it in or returns it incomplete and poorly done. The mother was quite unaware of her son's trouble. Should Zachary be expected to take care of his homework altogether independently and does his wrongdoing therefore represent a lack of age-appropriate self-discipline? Should the mother have kept enough of an eye on Zachary's homework to be aware of what was going on? How should she deal with the situation now? Should she punish Zachary and expect him to take care of his assignments from now on? Should she start collecting his daily homework herself from the teacher, sit with him while he works on it, and make sure he carries it back to school? Should she only ask to see his completed work each night and remind him in the mornings? Should she ask him what *he* thinks gets in the way of his doing his work (perhaps he feels he doesn't know how to do it or doesn't know how to schedule his day to work on it), and ask him how she could help him to do a better job? Should she appeal to his wish to do well at school and to get a good report card? Should she combine several of these approaches and think of further alternatives?

The individual parents' own makeup, their knowledge of the child, and of past and present events in his life will no doubt lead them to different ways of handling such situations. Most parents will feel that some degree and form of supervision and/or taking over of the responsibility need to be included. The question is how much, in what form, and how will it best further the child's development of self-discipline. It is often difficult, and always necessary to gauge when too much supervision and taking over does not give the child enough chance to practice being responsible for himself, and when too little expects more of him than he can manage and therefore results in repeated wrongdoing without learning. Properly dosed supervision and taking over allow for learning and for step-by-step increases in responsibility.

What to Do After the Child Has Done Wrong

Can wrongdoing be prevented by a very helpful setting and by a correct amount of supervision and taking over? Certainly not. For every situation that works out well there is surely one that does not. Even the best parent and child are constantly faced with the question of what to do when the child's self-discipline failed. However, wrongdoing is not only an inevitable part of growing up and of life in general. Coping with mistakes is also a valuable aspect of learning self-discipline. But this can only happen when discipline is geared to this goal, when it includes correcting or making amends for the wrongdoing, when it helps the child understand what he did wrong and how it could be avoided, and when it motivates him to want to do better the next time.

I am deliberately stressing the correcting or making

amends because in our Western societies the consensus, and the laws that embody it, regard reparation as the main consequence of transgression. If I cause harm, damage or destroy something, I have to put it right or make up for it. If I cause a car accident, I am held responsible for the cost of repairing the car and of treating the injured person; if I steal something, I have to return it. We extend this also to mental hurt, for example, if I slander someone I have to retract my statements and compensate him for any damage to his reputation. With some transgressions, either because they occur repeatedly or because compensation cannot be made, the consequence is to deprive the offender of the activity which he exercised irresponsibly (e.g., unsafe driving may result in loss of driver's license) or to isolate him from the community altogether, for example by putting him in prison for a specified period). Moreover, our rules for adult offenders have to follow established guidelines. We forbid "cruel and unusual punishment" and this includes physical punishment and mental torture, and we aim to fit the punishment not only to the crime but to the criminal, taking his motives, circumstances, and personality into account.

In educating our children we need to keep in mind what the community will expect of them as adults and adapt our methods accordingly. Thus, even for very young children, punishments need to be geared to repair and compensation in a realistic logical manner; for example, when Jackie tears a book, she needs to be helped to mend it with tape; when Daniel kicks down another boy's block building, he has to rebuild it; when Ellie scratches or hits someone, she has to "make it better," perhaps by doing her victim a kind service or giving a little make-up present. When wrongdoings cannot be compensated for or are frequently repeated, the consequence would be to deprive the child of the specific offending activity; for example, when Minnie repeatedly misbehaves in the store, she cannot come shopping with mother for a period of time; when Bert causes repeated trouble at the dinner table, he may need to eat on his own; when Missie keeps pushing others on the jungle gym, she is not allowed to use it; and when Robin acts out of control, she needs to go to her room to collect herself. With children, as with adults, it helps to fit the discipline not only to the crime but to the "criminal"; for example there may be extenuating circumstances—unusual stress, provocation by others, or blame shared by them: "I hit him because he took my toy. He *always* does that." Or, "Josh didn't feel well today, so he's a bit more crabby and restless and less hungry."

Some people object to this kind of discipline because it's "too soft" on the child, "He was so bad at the store. Just not taking him shopping isn't enough of a punishment." Others claim that it is "too hard" on the child, "Sitting him down for all that time to mend a book is asking too much. It takes almost half an hour!" However, all who have applied such discipline agree on one thing—it is quite a job for the adult. First he has to figure out the realistic consequence in each instance. It's so much easier to think quickly of an unrealistic one, such as not being allowed to watch TV for hitting, or having to go to bed early for making a mess in the living room, or getting spanked. Then the adult has to adapt the realistic consequence to the child's capabilities; for example, Bob cannot himself fix the window he broke. To pay for it would cost him four months of his allowance. That seems too much. Would it make better sense for him to pay three weeks of allowance and to have to earn the rest by doing special chores? What chores could he do? Since it was partly not his fault, would it be fairer to have him contribute only half the cost? And last but not least, the parent has to supervise and help with the reparation. It takes a lot of the parent's time and patience to help a young child tape a torn book or mop up spilled paint, or keep track of Bob's payments and chores. Is it then, perhaps, primarily a punishment for the parent? One can look at it that way, but most parents don't. They see it as one of the many hard but inevitable parts of parenting, of helping their child toward taking responsibility for his or her actions.

Do such disciplinary measures help a child to appreciate what he did wrong? At least they provide a good chance for the child to do so, in part because the parent explains how the consequences are related to the wrongdoing, and in part because the time and effort spent on making up or being deprived of the activity confronts him with it. But there is another helpful factor: Realistic consequences are neither imposed nor experienced as an arbitrary vengeance, or humiliation, or expression of the parent's anger. They deal with the reality. This helps to reduce the child's anger too and enables him to assess the situation a little more objectively.

Will such measures help the child figure out how it all happened and how it could be avoided? Since the consequences are never over and done with in a few moments, the wrongdoing lingers. This gives the child a chance to recall how it happened and to think things through, and it gives the parent a chance to talk it over with the child after things have calmed down, to help with figuring out what went wrong and how it could be prevented. It's the time lapse that counts. When children are sent to sit in a chair and "think what they did wrong" right after they did it, they usually think only about how angry they are and how they'd like to get back at those who punish them. I am not implying that every little misbehavior needs to be on the agenda for weeks on end. This would be as unhelpful as forgetting all about it right away. What I do mean is that afterthoughts and calm cooperative discussion at a later point are often more fruitful than heated or righteous arguments and retributions at the time.

How do these disciplinary measures motivate the child to do better next time? To some extent, and often to a surprising extent, they act as a deterrent in themselves. For example, I heard a nine-year-old call out to his pal, "For Heaven's sake, pitch the ball to the other side. Last year I broke the window with it right here and it took forever to pay for it. You wouldn't believe how expensive these windows are." A little four-year-old, praised by his day care worker for his neat table area at lunch, replied, "It's because I don't like cleaning up. I like to do my puzzles after lunch."

However, this is not the only way in which they motivate the child. Perhaps more important is the loved adult's disapproval, and his or her appeal to the child's "inner helpers"— self-esteem and conscience. The mere demand that the child carry through with the consequences does not imply great anger on the parent's part but it always implies a measure of disapproval: "That's not as it should be." There are many wrongdoings which do not even cause damage or are not serious enough to require deprivation of an activity. Often enough it is sufficient to disapprove and to remind the child "Nursery school boys don't do that," or "How can you like yourself when you do that?" or "You'll feel bad."

Clearly and firmly stated disapproval ("I *don't* like that," "That makes me very angry," "That's *not* the way to behave") has, as we said before, a powerful effect, more so than parents and teachers often appreciate. The stronger and better the relationship with the adult, the more does his disapproval count. There is no need to reinforce it with angry outbursts, excessive punishments, or dire threats. Parents who feel that their disapproval, their temporary and partial withdrawal of love is insufficiently effective, are parents who underestimate the power of their relationship with the child and the child's dependency on their love. The child's wish to please the parent is his first motivation for compliance and always continues to play a part. From the very first years on, however, it is paralleled by the child's wish to like himself. This second motivation for doing the right thing, or doing better the next time, becomes increasingly important as self-esteem and conscience develop. Sometimes, when children are very angry at their parents and don't in the least feel like pleasing them they still want to like themselves and live in peace with their conscience. Already the toddler who makes a mess, either because it's fun or to show his anger at Mommy, takes note of "Oh no, big boys don't make messes! Mommies and Daddies don't make messes," which implies, "You want to be big and you won't like yourself when you don't measure up." His messy behavior diminishes his self-esteem. This and the later beginning of conscience become the parents' allies and representatives. The parent's disapproval is supplanted by the child's disapproval of himself, and the conflict between parent and child becomes a conflict within the child. When the parents remind the child that he does not altogether like what he has done, the child is more strongly motivated to do better than when the disapproval comes only from the outside. "It's not only I who doesn't like it when you goof, you don't feel good about yourself either when you don't get your chores done."

A young man in one of our child development classes

related the following incident: His eight-year-old brother would sneak into the young man's room and take little items. When the older brother complained to their mother, she was angry and, on several occasions, slapped the little boy's hands. But he would later tell his older brother that he didn't really care and this would further aggravate the young man who felt increasingly helpless. Then he took matters into his own hands and told the eight-year-old; "You know, you've got a conscience inside of you and it knows everything you do, and when you steal my things it says to you 'You are bad' and it'll keep on making you feel bad until you stop stealing." The boy became quite worried, ran to his mother to complain that his brother was telling him scary things. But the mother confirmed the idea of the conscience. There was no more stealing.

Physical Punishment

Punishing a child by hurting his body can take many different forms and may be done for different reasons. It may be a slap, a spanking or beating by hand, a kicking, shaking, or throwing down of the child, a whipping or flogging with strap, belt, hairbrush, or other implement. It may be an expression of the parent's minor annoyance, anger, or sheer fury, or the outcome of uncontrolled frustration and of not knowing what else to do, or it may be a deliberate and preferred form of discipline, administered in stern calm, or with righteousness, with a "This hurts me more than you but I'm doing it for your own good," or with sadistic satisfaction. It may be a daily punishment or a very occasional one. It may be applied at random for different offenses or carefully graduated to specific wrongdoings. These variations in parental attitude, in intent, in frequency, and in actual hurt or damage to the child's body and feelings are so great that it seems impossible to treat them as though they were the same thing.

There is only one element held in common by all kinds of physical punishment; namely, that any discussion of it quickly turns into an emotional issue, especially for those who use physical punishment and for those on whom it has been used. Many issues in child development and child rearing touch on people's feelings but none gives rise to as much pitched argument and provocative controversy, intense attack and defense, and an inability to consider the pros and cons calmly and thoughtfully. Nor does it ever seem possible, at least for some of the participants, to let go of the subject and to conclude the discussion. This in itself tells us how closely physical punishment is tied to early impulses and feelings in all of us and how deeply rooted it is in our society. In writing about it I hope to avoid this pattern of passionate, interminable argumentativeness. I have two advantages in doing so. One is that, in writing rather than speaking with my readers, I am insulated from their retorts. My second advantage is that I was never punished physically and have therefore found it rather easy not to do it to the children in my care. By contrast, those who have been hurt tend to favor physical punishment, but even when they are against it, they find it very difficult to restrain themselves.

I have already left no doubt that I am not in favor of physical punishment. I am, however, aware of how trying and provocative children can be and I can empathize with a parent's momentary minor loss of control. Parents make many mistakes, apologize to their children, and try to do better next time. A rare slap does not ruin a child's life.

What Good and What Harm Can Come From Physical Punishment?

Physical punishment is not an essential form of discipline. Many people in our society, and in other societies, have grown up to be upright, self-disciplined individuals without ever being physically hurt. Nor is there any evidence to suggest that physical punishment in childhood improves moral conduct later on. Those who favor hurting the child's body often think of it as a deterrent. Insofar as the child has come to like his body, he may indeed avoid wrongdoing in order to avoid pain and harm to himself. But is it necessary to use two deterrents? Disapproval is always a part of physical punishment, yet disapproval is a sufficient deterrent in itself. The addition of physical punishment may look like a stronger deterrent at the time, but it poses special difficulties for learning self-discipline in the long run because self-discipline involves taking in the model set by the parent. Though the punishing parent does not want the child to hurt himself or others, the child inevitably identifies with the parent. This may give the child trouble when he, like the parent, tries to impose his will on others by force or to settle his grievances against them by violent means. It may also give him trouble if he takes in the parent in the form of his conscience. Such a conscience may demand that the child hurt himself, or seek hurt from others, as a punishment for wrongdoing. Exposing oneself to bodily harm is not a helpful form of self-discipline.

Many parents and children prefer physical punishment because its emphasis is on external disapproval. It does not appeal to the child's self-esteem and conscience. A spanking "gets it over with." It avoids guilt feelings, avoids time and effort spent on reparations, quickly dispels the parent's anger, and allows the child to forget about his wrongdoing. When used in this way, physical punishment fails to promote independent self-discipline but does not avoid setting a model for the child.

However, the effects of physical punishment are not limited to discipline and self-discipline. Physical punishment has a lot to do with anger and how to handle it. Being hurt can make a child very angry and he is likely to discharge it in the way the parent demonstrates, namely by hurting those who are weaker and more helpless. Physical punishment also affects the child's bodily self-esteem. It is difficult to learn to take good care of oneself when the parent or adult who has to teach it inflicts pain. We often say of a person "He punishes his body" when he disregards what is good for it.

Perhaps the most dangerous effect of physical punishment is that children can get to enjoy it. It can become a source of a peculiar but intense excitement for children and they may actually come to "ask for it" by doing forbidden things. This kind of excitement may also contribute to the later development of adult perversions in which hurting and being hurt are a part of the condition necessary for sexual gratification.

LEARNING SELF-CONTROL AND COPING WITH DAILY TASKS: CONTROL AND MASTERIES

Basic Concepts

• Our personalities use many means for coping with the world around us and for being masters of ourselves.

• The child acquires these means of control and mastery gradually.

• The child's parents and educators facilitate the development of each innate means (observing, speaking, thinking, etc.). They help the child to use it as a tool for mastery and to learn the activities and skills which will enable him or her to function as an adult member of the community.

• Inner values and means of self-control are developed through identification with the parents and their means of education.

Part III

**Using Inner Resources
to Enrich Life: Needs,
Urges, and Feelings**

17

How the Child Channels Life's Energies into Well-being, Enjoyment of Activities, and Emotional Growth

We have already talked about the relationships which are so crucial to the child's survival and growth and about the ways in which the parents and other caring adults facilitate the unfolding of the child's personality and help him to cope with the world. We will now discuss the inner forces that give us "go," impel us to want and do things, and to search out ways of getting them. People use different terms for the momentum of life but we all recognize that, like all other living beings, we are endowed with energy that radiates from within us, fuels our strivings for preserving life, and gives impetus to the building and maintaining of our personalities. This energy manifests itself in needs and urges which we seek to relieve and gratify, and in feelings which are associated with them. Needs, urges, and feelings are always closely connected but they do not remain the same throughout life. At different developmental levels they vary considerably in nature and intensity and the growing child experiences and deals with them in different ways. Before we look at each more closely, let us clarify for ourselves what we mean by "needs, urges, and feelings," how they work together, and what part they play in the child's development.

WHAT ARE NEEDS, URGES, AND FEELINGS?

Our basic *needs* are bodily. They arise from hunger, thirst, elimination, fatigue, and pain. As the baby grows, other needs emerge as well, such as the need for activity, the need for protection and safety, the need for a loving, caring adult, and for companionship. Needs do not change, they are always with us and always have to be met. However, their intensity varies (e.g., children are more hungry during spurts of bodily growth and/or when they are very active) and we also learn to satisfy them in ways that are acceptable in our community (e.g., we learn to eat certain foods, use certain table manners, limit ourselves to eating at mealtimes).

The energies that manifest themselves as *urges* differ from needs in that they change in the course of development, can be transformed, diverted to serve different ends, and gratified in a variety of ways. We experience urges in their basic forms but can also be helped to put their energy to use in many activities in our daily lives. The energy of urges is so versatile that I find it helpful to think of it as though it were a river. Its source is in ever-gushing springs and all along its course it provides for our use and enjoyment. We swim, boat, and fish in it, we draw its water to drink and grow food, we use it to ship our goods. But its flow also carries potential danger—flooding and drowning. Yet by channeling the river's waters, by damming and piping them, we can tame their forces, widen and enhance their usefulness, transform them into electricity, and make them into a vital asset to many communities. In a similar way, our urges are neither good nor bad. They are there and it all depends on how we use them. Urges (also called drives, impulses, or instincts) may be viewed as twofold (A. Freud, 1949b):

1. The pleasure seeking urges are perceived in different bodily parts and we experience them as excitement or sexuality. The mouth, the anus and buttocks, the skin, the genitals are the main focus of these urges at different developmental stages. In time, the pleasure seeking urges are also channeled and invested in interests and activities that are no longer connected with specific body parts. The pleasure we derive from sports, playing, working, hobbies, and learning is still

full of zest and fun, but it is less intense and immediate than the bodily excitement. On the other hand, it lasts longer and enriches the whole personality. For example, young children's excitement in looking at each other's bodies and their curiosity about sexual functions later motivates them to learn about other things and to enjoy finding out how they work and why.

2. The aggressive urges, in their most primitive form, aim to destroy. In the earliest phases of the child's development they manifest themselves in screaming, biting, and in physically hurting people and things. Very soon, however, they also come to play a helpful and important part in furthering the child's zest for life. When we do not get what we want we feel angry and summon our aggressive energy to clear the obstacles that stand in our way. When something or someone threatens our personal safety and well-being we get angry and use our aggressive energy to defend ourselves. In these ways aggressive energy serves us to fulfill our needs and to gratify the pleasures we seek. As the child matures, aggressive urges are modified so that they can serve without causing actual harm; for example, angry words of protest take the place of hurting actions.

Almost from the start, however, aggressive urges are also transformed into activity and channeled into pursuits that retain the original impulse "to do" without the destructive goal. The same energy that fueled the angry screaming of the baby and the provocative kicking of the toddler later contributes to the older child's ability to work with a hammer, to excel in sports. It may ultimately even help him to become a skilled surgeon. Mental activities also require much of that determined activity, in learning and in working. Our language reminds us of this with phrases like "tackling a task," "grappling with a problem." And in elementary school, children are graded in "word attack," a part of learning to spell. In the form of activities and pursuits, aggressive urges contribute a great deal to personality growth and adaptation.

Feelings alert us to our needs and urges and let us know whether and how they are satisfied. Our memory of pleasurable and unpleasurable feelings leads us to want to repeat, change, or avoid the experiences that gave rise to them. The baby's feelings are very intense and very simple. Through them he perceives comfort and discomfort, pleasure and pain. By the end of the first year of life, and increasingly during the preschool years, the child acquires a wider range of feelings and they become more subtle and finely differentiated in tone—love, hate, sadness, happiness, envy, helplessness, anger, fear, jealousy, loneliness, delight, disappointment, enjoyment, fondness, shame, embarrassment, pity, guilt, and many more. The child also develops a greater capacity for recognizing them, tolerating them, expressing them in word and thought instead of action, and using them to understand himself and others. In this way feelings are essential to helping us know what goes on within ourselves and what to do about it. At the same time, they enable us to feel with others, to recognize true friend and foe, to know when to trust and when to beware.

HOW NEEDS, URGES, AND FEELINGS WORK TOGETHER

A healthy baby is born with the need of hunger. He feels discomfort when he is hungry, makes sucking and searching movements with his mouth, and readily "learns" how to draw food from a nipple. When the uncomfortable feeling gives way to a comfortable one, his hunger is stilled and he stops drinking. Nature reenforces such an important need as hunger by giving it a companion. During the first year of life a large share of the pleasure seeking urge is located in the lips and mouth, so that all the mouth activities are experienced as stimulating and exciting, provide intense pleasure, and are eagerly sought out. Touching with the mouth, sucking and drinking satisfy hunger as well as these early pleasure seeking urges. As the baby remembers the good feelings they generate, he builds the idea that eating is fun. This helps him to want to eat again and again.

Within a few months, when the teeth begin to grow and prepare the infant for chewing food, the aggressive urges too join in this new mouth activity. Chewing and biting on hard objects relieves teething discomfort, is soon used in eating solid foods, and helps the baby to enjoy new foods and new ways of eating. This blend of hunger, pleasurable excitement, and aggressive activity serves the baby's self-preservation. To an extent, it remains with us all through life, even when the mouth is no longer the main site of pleasure and aggression, when other parts of the body have become more exciting and gratifying, and when aggression and activity are expressed in new ways. As adults we still enjoy eating and chewing, but at times when we are temporarily deprived of these satisfactions we really appreciate just how much they mean to us; for example, a liquid diet or intravenous feeding may provide us with all the necessary nutrients but none of the fun. We get to feeling low and irritable and long for real mouthfuls of crunchy food, "something to sink your teeth into." When babies cannot derive sufficient pleasurable excitement from eating (perhaps due to illness or inadequate handling of their feeding by the mother) and/or when they cannot use biting and chewing in eating (perhaps because they are fed soft babyfoods instead of food to hold and chew on their own), their appetite is diminished. They become poor eaters and may not thrive well. Their early lack of zest in eating may also affect later developments which, as we shall see, are connected with the use of the mouth.

The baby's mouth pleasure exists also separately from eating. Babies suck their tongues, thumbs, fingers, or other objects even when they are not hungry, just for the fun of it, and they also use this kind of sucking to comfort themselves, to counteract and alleviate stress and pain. Some of this use of the mouth continues later on. It becomes a part of adult sexuality, for example in the form of kissing, and may be used for comfort even by grown-ups, for instance, drinking and eating without hunger, or smoking. Similarly, aggressive mouth urges surface independently of hunger. Babies scream and bite in anger. In later life too, chewing can serve to discharge aggression or irritability, for example, some of us use food or gum "to chew our little troubles away."

Soon, however, the urges already invested in the mouth in connection with eating, come to play a part in a newly developing mouth activity—talking. We have already mentioned that babbling and forming words is, in part, motivated by the sheer fun of using the mouth. Infants who have not experienced enough urge satisfaction in feeding are slower to vocalize and may never get to enjoy speech, but those who have relished their eating readily transfer the mouth pleasure they have felt to the new mouth activity. Making sounds, ever new and different sounds, is very exciting for the baby and toddler. As adults we still like to talk and sorely miss it when we don't get enough chance to talk, but our feelings about talking are more subtle. Some of us can come close to empathizing with the very young child's thrill when we can at least recall what fun it was in later childhood to pronounce new big words, to roll off the likes of "antidisestablishmentarianism," or to savor as catchy a mouthful as "expialidoscious" from the famous Mary Poppins' song. Anger too takes its place in speech. It may take the form of very sophisticated and contained verbal expression of annoyance or anger, but may also show in yelling, in "chewing someone out," or in "biting sarcasm."

Quite early on the bodily taking in of food is also channeled into mental taking in, a less direct satisfaction. When babies' needs and urges are satiated, their energy becomes more and more available for interest in their environment. Babies "hunger" for stimuli after the first few weeks and "greedily take in" or even "devour" people and things with their eyes, ears, and other senses. Whatever they can reach and grab, they bring into their mouths to explore, taste, learn about. In time, the basic bodily excitement and aggression in taking in become a more refined mental pleasure and activity. In this channeled form, taking in is an important part of all learning. It fuels it with motivation, pleasure, and persistence and gives rise to many subtle associated feelings. In psychoanalytic treatment, many children's learning difficulties can be traced to early problems with taking in by mouth or to obstacles in channeling the bodily mouth excitement and aggression into the mental pleasure and activity of learning.

Even the child's wish and ability to "take in," to "incorporate," traits and values from the loved caring adults are, in part, based on the early bodily urges connected with eating. As the growing child's primitive taking-in urges are newly channeled, they motivate the mental taking in of parental attributes and help build the child's personality. Yes, a good feed does a lot more for a baby than keeping him alive.

HOW THE ENVIRONMENT AFFECTS OUR NEEDS, URGES, AND FEELINGS AND HELPS US TO SATISFY AND CHANNEL THEM

Children are born with their rich heritage of life's energies but they have only a very limited ability to know them, to satisfy them on their own, and to regulate and channel them to best advantage for their well-being and personality growth.

At first the parents recognize and meet the child's needs and help him satisfy his urges. However, from the start, they also assist the child to become aware of them himself, to communicate and cope with them. They go about this task in many ways.

The most basic and important way is being in tune with the child. The mothering person, and later both parents, sense what their youngster feels, needs, and wants. When they are with him most of the time, when they are emotionally close to him, and when they are in good touch with their own feelings, they are able to empathize (i.e., sense correctly the child's feelings and feel with him). The parent's knowing not only helps him or her to do right by the child, it also paves the way for the child getting to know what goes on inside himself. Babies but a few months old at once look at the mother when they experience a strong feeling, pleasant or unpleasant. Her facial expression, body posture, and perhaps contact with the infant's body helps them to feel that she understands them, that she can tolerate and contain whatever it is they feel, that it is okay and will somehow work out. If mother is distraught or unresponsive, the baby does not feel understood, becomes bewildered, distressed, or panicky.

Most mothers talk with their babies. They put their understanding of the infant into words, "Oh boy, are you hungry," "My, you're real angry, aren't you?" "You are so sleepy," "Oh, that thumb tastes good," "You're getting all excited in the water; it's fun." The infants, in turn, understand mothers' words long before they can talk. As we already know, when children get to know the word, the *name* for what they are experiencing, they can take a big step toward tolerating the inner sensations. When children don't know what they feel and can't think about it in words, their feelings can't serve them well. To children they seem like an inside turmoil that may grow so big and intense that it over-whelms them (as in a temper tantrum); or that may propel them blindly to do things that bring them more trouble than satisfaction (as in grabbing things that could hurt); or that get them into the wrong situation altogether (as when they don't recognize that they are ill and get irritable and mean to others instead of asking them for help and comfort). As chil-dren begin to use words, they can also communicate their needs, wants, and feelings to mother and others which is a further big step toward taking care of themselves (Katan, 1961).

Just as it helps the child when the parents know what he feels and when they name it correctly for him, so it also helps when they do for it whatever may be appropriate. Their mini-strations, their ways of providing pleasure or comfort and relief, let the child know what he can do for himself; the toddler already knows to get the cookie tin when he is hungry, or to hug his teddy when he is lonely.

The parents also help by allowing the child to gain plea-sure and comfort in ways that are age appropriate and natu-ral for him, that he need not learn from them; for example, they let him suck his thumb or fingers, and they take care that his "blankie" does not get washed lest it lose its precious smell.

Gradually, they add to their handling new ways of cop-ing which involve control and mastery. They begin to expect that their child delay satisfactions and accept partial or sub-stitute gratifications. We have already discussed how parents assist their child in developing and enjoying some of his own inner means of control and mastery: Speech and thinking help him to know what he feels, to express it in words for partial relief, to plan and choose what he will do, and to postpone real action, motility enables him to do, and frustra-tion tolerance helps him not to do. Usually parents also wait until the child can enjoy new pleasures before they ask him to give up old ones; for example, the fun of feeding himself can take the place of nursing from breast or bottle, and parents expect the young child not to hit and kick when he begins to talk and can *say* that he is angry.

From early on too, parents help the child to channel his urges, to divert them from bodily to nonbodily or neutral activities and satisfactions; for example they don't let the toddler play with his urine and bowel movements but join his fun in water play at the sink and in the tub with toys, or they help him dig in the sandbox. Much of that play is "messing" too, but it is a step away from the body and a step toward such creative activities as modeling with clay and painting pictures.

All these are difficult and slow developmental steps and the child's success or failure depends a lot on the way the parents go about helping him—their timing, their preparation of the child for new expectations and new opportunities for expression, their pleasure in his tiniest accomplishment, their patience with his slowness and inevitable setbacks. Much of the time, parent and child work together toward the same goals; for example, a child who has really enjoyed his nursing months is eager to reach for the new pleasure of self-feeding and joining the family meal. Similarly, most toddlers don't mind much, and gladly help, when mother quickly removes their dirty diapers and they enjoy, almost as much, splashing around with their toys in the bath by way of getting clean. But there are always times when parents and child want very different things; for example, when the child wants to pull the cat's tail and the parents stop him and expect him to be "nice to the poor kitty," or when junior wants to sleep with mom and dad and they insist that he stay in his own bed. As we have already seen, how these conflicts are resolved, what disciplinary measures the parents use, and how the child is helped gradually to take into himself the parents' attitudes, has a lot to do with their relationship and with the building of mental self-esteem and conscience. Much of the important foundation for coping with needs, urges, and feelings is laid at home, in the preschool years. During this period the parents' handling helps the child's personality to allow proper room and scope for his inner energies so that they can serve him well.

WHEN DO NEEDS, URGES, AND FEELINGS
HELP AND WHEN DO THEY HINDER?

Some parents feel at odds with the child's needs, urges, and feelings. They do not trust that they can help the child to live with them and make every effort to control, oppose, or banish them as though they were enemies or competitors for the child's allegiance. They may think that children would never want to sleep or sleep enough unless made to, or that they would always stay in bed too late and get lazy unless they interfere; they control the meals as though children would never eat unless they had to, or would only eat the wrong foods, or would eat too much. Likewise they assume that children will indulge their bodily pleasures unless altogether forbidden to do so (for example, that they will always suck their thumbs if permitted to do so in infancy), and that the children's anger at the parents will destroy their loving feelings if they are ever allowed to express anger.

Their children may ultimately conform, may take over the parental attitudes, but at a cost. They may feel at odds with themselves, may need to restrict their zest in living, their ability to satisfy and enjoy themselves, and to pursue a variety of interests and activities. They may feel burdened with guilt and shame over the slightest indulgence or develop neurotic symptoms, the overt signs of inner conflict. However, there are many other possible outcomes; for example, the parents' prophecy may become self-fulfilling and the children may, secretly or in open rebellion, resist the excessive parental restrictions and follow the dictates of their feelings, needs, and urges. That does not necessarily spare them conflict and misgiving, nor does it enable them to put their endowment to their own best use.

By contrast, other parents feel that the child's feelings, needs, and urges should be given free reign and expression. They permit, even encourage, the child to follow his inclination of the moment wherever and whenever, sometimes in the hope that sufficient discharge will enable the child to "get it out of his system." This too does not lead to happiness. The children may come to feel unprotected and overwhelmed, at the mercy of their impulses, without means of mastery. They may fail to learn to consider their safety, to channel their drives into rewarding activities, or to fit them in with the standards of their community. This may create inner dread and outer conflict instead of satisfaction.

For better or worse, it is not possible to get rid of needs, urges, and feelings. We can neither push them under and deny them all gratification, nor can we expect them to redirect or exhaust themselves by allowing them unlimited gratification, nor can we really enjoy them if we do. It is only when we learn to use them wisely that we have a chance to use them well, so that they can help preserve and enrich our lives. Individuals and societies vary greatly in the kind of satisfactions they endorse, and when, where, and in what form they allow them to take place. However, there is no individual and no society, primitive or advanced, that can live and thrive without permitting some gratifications and without imposing some restrictions. It is the balance between them that counts, and it is their infinitely varied combination which is largely responsible for the many differences between individuals and between societal customs and mores. In each case it is initially the parents who influence the outcome.

ARE THE AGGRESSIVE URGES REALLY INNATE OR ARE THEY A RESPONSE TO FRUSTRATIONS?

Anger is indeed observed most frequently and clearly as a response to frustration. This may lead us to assume that anger arises *only* in connection with frustration. Whether or not this is really so is one part of the question; the other part deals with whether it is innate. Let us look at this latter part first.

When we say that a child "responds" with anger, we may mean one of two things: either that we are made in such a way that we get angry when frustrated (in which case our anger is part of our makeup, i.e., innate) or that we learn to be angry when frustrated (in which case we mean not only that we would not get angry if we were never frustrated, but also that we would not get angry unless we were taught this kind of response to frustration). Unfortunately, no life can proceed without any frustration. From early on, everyone is faced with at least some frustrations, like not being able to stick our fingers into electric outlets. This makes it impossible to test how a total lack of frustration would affect our feelings. Given the fact, then, that there are always some frustrations, we have much opportunity to observe that children do not have to be taught to respond to them with anger. Even during their first year, babies scream and bite angrily, and parents of toddlers are never in doubt that their youngsters know how to be angry even when they have not experienced the example of their parents' anger at them. There are few, if any, people who believe that anger is an acquired response, taught like table manners or like a conditioned reflex, by association through repeated experience.

Let us now turn to the other part of the question, whether anger is felt only in frustrating situations. Some years ago, when it became known that excessive frustrations make young children very angry, many educators hoped that we could greatly reduce children's anger if we kept their frustrations to a minimum. They gratified children's wishes as much as possible, made few demands on them, and adapted the environment to their needs. The children they thus raised became not less, but more angry. The least little frustration infuriated them. Obviously, relative lack of frustrations had not diminished their anger. It had merely diminished their chances of learning how to cope with difficult situations. They were as helplessly angry at small frustrations as the excessively frustrated children had been helplessly angry at big ones. Both were unable to use their anger as an impetus to purposeful activity because for each, though for different reasons, the frustrating situations were beyond their means of mastery.

A number of other experiences favor a view of aggression as an urge rather than as a mere reaction to frustration. Among these are many observations of young children's spontaneous unprovoked manifestations of anger; for example, maltreatment of pets and other animals who had neither harmed nor threatened them. Also, we have learned from the psychoanalytic treatment of inactive children that their difficulties resulted from aggression not being channeled into appropriate personality functions; for example, some children could not chew food, could not be bodily active in sports, could not defend themselves and their belongings, could not learn with zest and "tackle" problems until therapy helped them to reach their early suppressed aggression and to tap its energy for use (see also chapter 20).

We need to keep in mind, however, that the concept of aggression as an urge is not a religious dogma, to be believed unquestioningly. Like any other scientific formulation, it is merely a convenient framework for relating and understanding the available data in a comprehensive, logical manner. When new observations defy explanation within a given theoretical framework, it is time to change it. This may, some day, happen to the concept of aggression as an urge.

DO KIDS HAVE THE SAME FEELINGS AS GROWN-UPS?

As we have mentioned, during the first few months of life, babies' feelings are more on the lines of "good" and "bad," but after that they become more varied and are indeed like those of the adult. There are some differences: one is the young child's very limited means of tolerating and mastering feelings so that he or she always experiences them as very intense, even overwhelming; the other difference is the fact that every person feels most strongly about the things that matter most to him or her individually. The things that matter most to a child depend on his level of development and on his personal experiences. These are not necessarily the same as those of grown-up; for example, not being with his mother and feeling that she is irretrievably gone arouses very strong feelings in a young child but may not be of much concern to the adult who would feel a comparable feeling if he were to lose his job, spouse, and children. Of course adults too differ in the kinds of things they feel strongly about and in their ability to cope with feelings.

18
Needs

Many people assume that our basic needs (hunger and thirst, sleep, elimination) are so crucial to survival that they must assert themselves spontaneously and that we must be equipped with ways of meeting them. Surely babies know how to sleep when they are tired, how to eat and drink when they are hungry and thirsty (well, at least drink), and how to urinate and pass bowel movements. And, if it is true that pleasure-seeking and aggressive urges support these needs and participate in their satisfactions, then there is even more reason to think that needs present no problem for the child or adult.

Yet, when we take a closer look at the way things work out in life, we begin to doubt such an opinion: Babies know how to eat but not how to get food; toddlers eat stones and paint and even bowel movements but often refuse good foods, like stew and vegetables; older children sometimes eat much more than their bodies need so that they become obese, or they starve themselves, even to death (as happens in anorexia nervosa). Most parents complain, at one time or another, that their children eat too much, too little, the "wrong" foods, at the wrong time. They may also complain that their children do not learn to satisfy their hunger independently, that they want to be spoon-fed, that they don't want to fix their school lunch to take along, or help with preparing meals at home.

The need for sleep does not fare much better. Some children won't go to bed, or can't fall asleep, or won't sleep in their own beds. Many parents complain that their preschoolers wake up too early, that their teenagers sleep in too late, or that their children at any age "never get enough sleep." Many adults too are beset by sleep problems of one kind or another. Elimination is, likewise, a frequent source of difficulties. Some children soil their pants or wet their beds until they are quite old, others hold back bowel movements for days or wriggle and squirm instead of urinating.

In fact, children and even grown-ups manifest such frequency and variety of interferences in being able to recognize and meet their needs that many people go to the opposite extreme. They feel that there is nothing innate that prompts us to sense what is good for us or how to satisfy it. Acting on this assumption, parents then hold themselves responsible for prescribing what their children need and enforcing that they do as they are told: what and how much to eat, when to sleep and for how long, when to use the toilet and how much to produce.

In this area of child development, as in most, it is unrealistic and unhelpful to think in terms of extremes. So where is the true middle line? We have actually looked at it a bit already in connection with one need, the need for bodily safety. There we saw that children are normally endowed with a physiological pain barrier. When a newborn or very young baby is subjected to discomforts that exceed the limit set by the pain barrier, he experiences uncomfortable feelings and responds with discharges which serve as protest and SOS signals—crying, screaming, squirming, kicking, and hand waving. But we have also seen that this innate "security system" does not protect the infant adequately and does not automatically develop into a serviceable means of meeting his need for safety. Initially a mothering person has to be available who responds to her baby's signals, gauges what is wrong, and knows how to put it right. If she fulfills this task consistently and lovingly she enables her infant to feel good often, to get to know and like his body, to seek out states of pleasurable, safe well-being, and to avoid and protest pain. In other words, the mother's protective activity helps to link the innate pain barrier with the pleasure-seeking urges and to channel the aggressive urges into the service of self-defense. In this way she facilitates the process by which need and urges form a stronger and more effective mental pain barrier than the physiological distress of need alone could provide.

Nor is this all the parent helps accomplish. Then come the long years during which the parental know-how of meeting the need for safety is gradually handed over to the growing child. You may recall that we mentioned a number of things that can go wrong along the way. For example, the child's innate need for safety and properly developed wish to avoid discomfort may not suffice to protect him from dangers he cannot yet assess (like not knowing yet about hot stoves); or his innate need for safety may be interfered with and altogether "overruled" when he does not experience enough bodily pleasure (as may happen with neglected or abused children who cease to protest against pain and may even seek out hurts). The innate need for safety is there and it does assert itself from the start but, in the course of development, it has to be joined by other forces within the personality, and it has to be tended carefully from without; only then can it come to serve us well and only then can we learn to meet it adequately. The parents' role is crucial, but the mere fact that they and their relationship with the child have so much to do with the whole process can also make for difficulties.

We can similarly follow the developmental paths of the other needs and the ways in which they may be facilitated or interfered with.

RESPECTING NEEDS

Perhaps the parents' most helpful attitude to their child's needs is respect: "My child's needs are a part of his precious life force. They are the essence of his being alive. They are truly his and it is our job to help him use them for himself to his best advantage." Of course, parents are not likely to spell this out for themselves in so many words, but many parents feel it and act on it. So, the first thing they do is to learn and understand the initially primitive ways in which their baby signals his or her needs and they create an environment in which he can attain satisfaction.

The mother, or primary caretaker, watches out for her baby's hunger signs, tries to gauge them from his behavior,

from her knowledge of his feeding rhythm, and, if she breast-
feeds her baby, from the fullness of her breasts, because her
milk production is geared to the baby's hunger. When she
gauges his signals accurately and offers him the appropriate
food in a comfortable way, he will take it in. Mother will
watch and get to know her baby's own ways of eating—
slowly, fast, or intermittently with stops and starts. When he
has had enough he will stop eating altogether and mother
will find out how he acts when his hunger and thirst are
satisfied—perhaps he goes to sleep, or stretches and yawns,
or starts looking around, or wriggling around, or he may just
like to lie relaxed. In the beginning she may misjudge his
signals of hunger (perhaps change his diapers instead of
offering him food) and she will learn from his responses
whether she guessed right. She will also show her respect by
recognizing that he is sometimes more and sometimes less
hungry and allow his hunger to decide how much he needs to
eat. Later, when she introduces additional foods, she will
respect his taste and give him time to get used to new tastes.
She will offer a little of just one new food and see how he likes
it. If he doesn't, she may wait a few days and offer it again, or
she may try another food, or she may change the taste of the
first food by adding sugar or spice to make it more palatable.
In short, her respect tells her that her baby's hunger "knows"
when, what, and how much is good for him and will assert
itself unless she violates it and interferes with it too much.

   In the same way the mother learns her baby's signals for
needing sleep, the ways in which he can best go to sleep and
sleep well. For example, he may need quiet holding, or gentle
rocking, or a crib or wall decoration to look at, he may need
low lights or darkness, he may be bothered by the banging of
doors or other noises. She watches for the times and places
that help him sleep and tries to arrange her schedule accordingly; for example, if his crib and room are the best place, she
plans her errands with him at "awake" periods. She also
watches out for the ways in which he shows that his need for
sleep has been satisfied—perhaps when he wakes up gur-
gling, playing with his hands, looking around. In this way
she knows whether he is really slept out or had his sleep
interrupted—perhaps by a commotion in the house, by being

hungry, or having a tummy ache—in which case he will need to sleep again after the interference has been taken care of.

When it comes to elimination, the baby is usually able to complete the whole cycle on his own, from need signal to *relieving* himself, the word aptly describing both the expulsion of urine and feces and the good feeling of relief or satisfaction that follows it. The mother's help is needed only for cleaning up afterwards. But with this need too, she observes her infant's signals, how his face reddens as he squirms and twists, how he relaxes and smiles when he is done and ready to be cleaned. She gets to know his natural rhythm, whether he has several stools a day or one every other day, whether they tend to be looser or harder. She respects his ways, for example, by not trying to feed him when he is busy straining for a bowel movement. And when, at a time of minor illness, upset, or change in diet, her child is made uncomfortable by constipation or diarrhea, mother tries to assist his body with gentle means and refrains from interfering and taking over; for example, she may offer him fruit juices to soften his stools or mashed banana to harden them, rather then introducing purgatives, suppositories, or enemas that produce uncomfortably intense feelings and deprive the child of his bodily mastery.

This may all sound as if it takes the patience of Job and every minute of the day, but most mothers do it as a matter of course. One reason is that they enjoy it, as they enjoy most things about their babies, another reason is that they know it pays off. A baby whose needs are not heeded becomes cranky and irritable and is much harder to take care of.

When the mother comes to know well her infant's need signals and can help him become satisfied, the baby soon learns which feelings go with different needs and with different satisfactions. Within a few weeks or months, for example, a baby's hunger cry becomes specific and easily differentiated from other need signals, and he usually calms down as soon as the appropriate need satisfying procedures are under way, such as when mother shows him the bottle, or when she starts the going-to-sleep routine, or when she lays him down to change his diapers. Now *he* knows when he is hungry, or tired, or uncomfortably wet and dirty, and can let mother know. When this happens, mother and child have accomplished an important step in helping him to meet his own needs: His feelings of comfort and discomfort are no longer indiscriminate. He has begun to recognize his own needs, to know what it takes to satisfy them, and how it feels when they are satisfied. This will stand him in good stead as he grows older and becomes more independent. Even an adult's taking good care of his needs always involves respecting them, knowing what they are, what to do for them, doing all he can to satisfy them, and getting help if need be. The mother's respect and understanding of her child's needs becomes, in time, the child's and adult's own attitude to himself.

DOING FOR HIMSELF

As the mother lays the groundwork of respecting her child's needs, the next steps are also under way: Helping the child to become more and more proficient at doing for himself and at asking for assistance with what he can't do for himself. From the very start, the mother usually allows her baby to be as active as possible in meeting his own needs and watches all along for signs that he is ready for new ways of participating and for taking over more of the "doing" that is involved in attaining satisfaction. For example, during the second half of the first year, many babies become restless at the breast, may grab hold more persistently of the bottle and spoon, try to put things in their mouths. Mother sees these and other little changes in behavior as signs that her infant wants to feed himself. So she allows him to begin to wean himself, offers him foods he can hold, suck, and chew on. Self-feeding has started. During the same period she may notice that her earlier rocking and holding no longer help her baby with falling asleep. In fact, it may make him a little "wound up." But he calms and closes his eyes when he lies on his own, sucking his fingers, and perhaps rubbing his ear or blanket. In short, he is ready to put himself to sleep and knows how to soothe himself with his own body and blanket or soft toy. So mother gradually phases out her part, substitutes a little kiss-and-pat good night routine, and lets him do the rest on his own.

Likewise, she will let him take part in the cleaning procedure. She lets him hold the sponge or washcloth and, as he begins to toddle, she may let him bring the clean diapers and open and shut the pail to soak the dirty ones. Many mothers allow their child to stand up when they clean and change them because they notice that the child dislikes lying passively on his back.

The mother also talks to her baby more now and gives, him words for his needs: "You're sleepy. It's night-night time," "Boy are you hungry! Dinner coming up!" "That's a hard BM today. You are really working at it," "Let's get off these diapers. You'll soon feel clean and comfy." In his second year, the toddler will begin to use some of these words himself, tell mother when he is hungry, and ask for cookies, juice, or whatever. How often mothers encourage a child: "I can't understand what you want when you scream and cry, tell me!"

Actually, children whose needs have been respected, who have enjoyed need satisfaction, and have been allowed to be active participants, do not have to be made to want to do for themselves. They are very eager to take every possible new step toward independence and enjoy their accomplishments. And although mothers may miss their children's dependence, may miss being needed, they also appreciate the pleasures of their children's newly acquired know-how and enjoy it with them. The first steps may seem very small, but each is very important and leads to the next one, continuing throughout the growing years.

In learning to take care of his hunger, the child will go from self-feeding to helping himself to foods, to helping mother with shopping and cooking. Later he will also learn to anticipate getting hungry, will perhaps prepare his own luncheon sandwich and remember to take it along to school. And when he is close to being adult, he will buy his food and make sure he has sufficient supplies on hand. He will earn money and budget it to be able to buy his food. All along there will be times when he will have to enlist the help of others—with preparing and buying food, with money for food, with finding a job to earn money to buy food and, even when he is grown up, there may be times of illness or poverty when he will need to ask others for the kind of help he needed as a little child.

In taking care of his need for rest and sleep, the child will go from falling asleep with the help of his thumb or "blankie" to holding and playing with his teddy bear, to reading, or listening to the radio. He will learn to get ready for sleep on his own and will even tuck himself in. In time he will plan his daily activities so as to anticipate his need for sleep and allow enough time for it. Younger children often ask for help: "I'm tired," "Mom, run my bath," "Mom, come and kiss me good night." Older ones do not, unless they are ill or in unusual circumstances, such as when they can't use their usual room or bed.

And in taking care of his elimination, the child will progress from helping mother to clean him, to letting her know in words when he needs to be cleaned, to using the toilet on his own and cleaning himself. In time he will learn to plan for this need too, will go to the toilet before an outing or at recess between lessons, will find a bathroom before his need gets too urgent, and will fit it all smoothly into his daily routines and activities.

But is it all such easy going? Of course not. Mothers may not gauge the right times and ways for letting children do for themselves, and children contribute their share by either not wanting to take over their own care and demanding to be done for, or by wanting to be independent prematurely, insisting on doing things they can't yet do safely and well. Minor conflicts over dependence/independence arise often and can be resolved ("You can't serve the soup but you can serve the cookies"; "I won't undress you, but I'll be here and help with the hard T-shirt"; "Soon you'll know how to turn on the hot water on your own"). Major ongoing conflicts may interfere with the child's ability to take over need fulfillment. For example, many older children are not eager to do for themselves and do not enjoy it when they have to. This may happen when they were dissatisfied and felt deprived of mother's bodily care, or when their earlier attempts at independence were not appreciated. They then continue to de-

mand care, resent self-care, and even neglect their needs or
meet them inappropriately.

HELPING THE URGES TO PLAY THEIR
PROPER PART IN NEED FULFILLMENT

This is another aspect of the mother's task in regard to needs.
We have already looked at the ways in which pleasure seeking and aggressive urges join forces with the need for nour-
ishment and how the mother assists this process by making
eating a pleasurable experience and by providing foods to
chew, as soon as the child is ready. She also helps him channel anger into activity by allowing her infant to be an active
participant in meeting his hunger need, through early self-
feeding, and later through letting him help himself, take part
in preparing and cooking foods, in choosing the menu, and so
on. All this helps eating to be a good time, whereas lack of
pleasurable feeding, lack of opportunity for chewing and for
doing for himself, increases the child's anger, spoils his appetite, and reduces food to a necessary chore at best.

With sleep it works rather differently. Most people find it
impossible to go full tilt, then simply lie down, turn off the
light, and sleep. We usually need a transition period for doing
things that help us get ready, to deal with tensions and "let
down." We tend to slow down our activities, take care of our
other needs so they won't get in the way (washing, toileting,
having a bedtime snack or last drink of water), and we
arrange our bedding in individual ways to be "comfy." We
usually sleep best when our inner tensions are minimal, and
may have trouble falling asleep or sleeping well when we are
all "wound up," angry, and excited. Part of the process of
getting ready for sleep thus includes satisfying our urges and
reducing their claims. Children accomplish this by means of
self-comforting activities, using different parts of their bodies
at different levels of development, such as finger sucking,
rocking, rubbing their cheeks, ears, navel, buttocks, and genital organs. As they come to know other calming satisfying
activities, they may use them too, such as playing with their
soft toys, singing or talking to themselves, daydreaming, or
looking at books. All these practices help them discharge

urges in preparation for sleeping, but they only serve well for coping with minor tensions. When the experiences of the day, and especially of the period prior to sleeping, have been very stimulating and have exacerbated the child's anger and excitement, his own means of discharge prove inadequate and sleep is interfered with. Parents usually know this. They help the child avoid excess stimulation, make the bedtime routines calm, and allow him or her a transition period of quiet undisturbed privacy in his bed so he can do his own relaxing before he is ready to sleep. Chasing around, wrestling, tickling, or angry altercations before bedtime are as notorious sleep interruptors as are the sounds of parental parties or arguments during the child's sleep period.

The need for elimination is spontaneously accompanied by urges, most strongly so during the child's second year when his voluntary sphincter muscles develop and enable him to exercise conscious control over urine and bowel movements. At this time both pleasure-seeking and aggressive urges are connected with expulsion and retention and with the body products themselves. Toddlers show great interest and satisfaction in the touch, smell, size, consistency, and even taste of their bodily products, and as many mothers learn, they also use them to express anger, to defy, to control, to withhold in protest, or to mess with.

With the help of these urges the children get to know and appreciate as their own, parts of the body which they cannot see or easily reach. In time, these urges also help toward independent toilet mastery. But their main contribution lies in being channeled and diverted into areas of activity. Mothers help by allowing the child to be active in achieving control and mastery of his toileting, and by offering and supporting substitute gratifications for his pleasures and anger. They let him "mess" with water and toys in the tub or sink; they let him "hoard" little treasures of stones, acorns, and other things he likes to pick up and hold onto; they encourage him to express anger in words and provide opportunity for energetic bodily movement and activity.

But in this area of the urges, as with independence, the road of development is not necessarily a smooth one. Mothers may err in not allowing enough instinctual gratification or in overstimulating the child's urges, or in not helping him to redirect and to gratify them in different forms. The child, in turn, may not be willing to give up his direct urge satisfactions and accept substitutions. The resulting interferences and conflicts show themselves in many different ways, often distorting the role of needs and need fulfillment. For example, some youngsters who are toilet trained in their first year by being put on the potty and have no later opportunity to expel or withhold their bowel movements at will, make up for it in their eating habits. They may "hoard" their food in their cheeks instead of chewing and swallowing, and they may dawdle, smear, and mess excessively during meals. Or they may go to the opposite extreme and dread messiness so much that they don't want to feed themselves for fear of getting their hands dirty, and/or they may refuse all foods which vaguely remind them of stools in color or consistency, such as stews, puddings, boiled vegetables, or gravies.

But too much stimulation and gratification can also interfere: Tessa was not expected to become clean herself but her mother spent a lot of time cleaning her. For years she wiped and sponged Tessa's rectal and genital area, inspected it for rashes, powdered it and rubbed it with soothing ointments. Tessa liked these ministrations and invited them but could not cope with the excessive excitement they stimulated in her. She could not learn to master her toileting and kept on soiling, was always restless and irritable, with "ants in her pants" which prevented her from concentrating on play and activities in spite of good intelligence.

HELPING THE CHILD TO FIT NEED FULFILLMENT INTO DAILY LIVING

In the first few weeks, dealing with basic bodily needs makes up nearly all the business of the baby's daily life, but this soon changes. New needs arise, such as the need for company; urges manifest themselves more strongly and require their own gratifications, such as finger sucking; functions develop and have to be exercised, such as perception, motility, and speech. Increasingly, new activities, skills, and interests are learned and practiced. All this takes up time and energy, furnishes different satisfactions, and may conflict with the demands of the needs: "I am tired but I want to play longer"; "Running up and down the stairs is so much fun, I'll eat later." "Later" easily becomes "too late," when the overly hungry youngster greedily gulps down his food and gets a tummy ache, or when the overly tired one turns irritable and sleeps fitfully.

The fun of socializing with family members also starts to take up time and, increasingly, imposes conditions on the ways of meeting needs: "You can only sit at the dinner table with us if you eat nicely"; "You can't sit on Daddy's lap with dirty pants." In order to do all he wants to do and in order to be acceptable to all the people he wants to be with, the child has to learn to regulate his need fulfillments (e.g., eat at certain times) and to attain satisfactions in a manner that is customary and expected within his family and community (e.g., he needs to use a toilet for elimination).

It is no small achievement to keep our needs in proper perspective, to use "good manners" to satisfy them, and to live with them well. And it is, of course, the mother's job primarily to help her child achieve these difficult goals.

How does she go about it? And does the child work with her or against her? When it comes to regulating needs, the child works with her to a considerable extent. As his or her body grows bigger and stronger, needs become less frequent and urgent; for example, he eats more at one meal and gets hungry less often; he sleeps through the night and less during the day; and he can hold urine and stools for longer intervals and control elimination. The child's needs get used to daily rhythms and he can better tolerate and master their signals and postpone satisfactions. The mother watches for all these gradual changes and adjusts her expectations accordingly. She tries to keep to consistent meal and sleep times, gradually extends them to fit in with the family routines, and lets the child enjoy his new interests in between times. By and large this works out well for everyone. Sometimes it doesn't quite work out and there have to be makeshift arrangements; "The kids just can't wait when my husband gets home later, so I have to give them dinner earlier on those days"; "He didn't get his nap today because there was too much going on in the house, so he got crabby and I fed him early and let him go to bed early"; "When she's ill, she's off her schedule and nothing's right."

When families do not have routines, or when their routines are nowhere near the child's need rhythms (for example, very late dinners), the child cannot meet the expectations. He may get irritable and dissatisfied, may not be able to enjoy and enlarge his new interests and skills because his needs are never reliably at peace, and may, in the long run, have trouble regulating his needs and planning for and around them consistently. Many adults have trouble with this. Some don't get enough sleep, keep too busy, and endanger their health; some oversleep, get to work late, and endanger their jobs; some sleep at the wrong times, in the middle of a conversation, class, or at the movies. Likewise, some people never quite succeed in living well with their need for food, even when enough food is available to them. They may be unable ever to eat at a later hour or may forget about meals and then get terribly hungry; they may never remember to buy enough food and run out at inconvenient times or buy so much that it spoils before it can be used; they may regard eating as a necessary but unpleasant chore, or they may be so preoccupied with food that they have little time and energy to think of other things.

The younger the child, the better he thrives on "boring" routines, especially when it comes to need fulfillment. Variety only becomes the spice of life later, when the inner need signals are not so pressing and when need satisfaction is taken for granted and allows for some experimentation. Even as grown-ups, when we are ill, upset, or in a strange place, we often feel like a little child. We want our needs met at the right time and in the most familiar way because we worry a bit whether they will be met at all; for example, in the hospital nothing makes us more irritated than having to wait for our meal tray beyond the expected time, and there are few things we grumble about more than "How bad the food is." The dietitian just does not prepare our childhood favorites, and if she does, they don't quite taste the way we are used to, and, anyway, the nurse's aide may even forget to bring our food altogether! Similarly, on vacation trips, many people take no

pleasure in getting to know differently equipped bedrooms
and bathrooms and new tastes in foreign dishes, but distrust
them on principle and search out places which meet their
needs in familiar ways. That's one of the appeals of the
Holiday Inn, McDonald's, and Kentucky Fried Chicken in
such far-flung cities as Paris and Nairobi.

But when children who have experienced the reassuring
routines of early need fulfillment get older, they seek out and
enjoy the thrill of the new—new dishes, new ways of serving
them, new kinds of bedding, and new bathrooms with different fixtures or even no fixtures, like in some campgrounds.
Even at home they like to introduce changes: "Let's cook
something different"; "Let's party through the night and not
sleep at all"; or "Let's use sleeping bags in the living room or
camp out in the backyard." And then it is often the parents
who plump for the boring routines, half worried about their
youngsters' health, half being set in their ways and dreading
the extra work entailed.

When it comes to learning manners, the child also naturally meets the mother halfway in her attempts to teach him
to satisfy his needs in the ways the adults do in the family; for
example, sitting at the table, using implements for eating,
waiting to be served, eating neatly, or keeping clean pants
and using the toilet. Children who have a good enough relationship with their parents want to become like them and be
appreciated by them. For this reason, they are, much of the
time, eager to learn the parents' ways of satisfying needs, and
parents usually appeal to their children on these lines: "Now
you can use your fork like Daddy" (or "Use the toilet like the
grown-ups"); "You are getting so big. Isn't that nice. Aren't
you proud of yourself." And when the child is not quite willing
yet to make the extra effort, they encourage "*Soon* you'll want
to eat nicely (or, stay clean) and *then* you'll be such a big
boy/girl." They also point out the disadvantages of not having the right manners and therefore not being acceptable in
"society." "You can't go to the restaurant with dirty pants,
but when you get bigger and use the toilet and stay clean,
then we can take you out for dinner."

Obviously, manners can only be acquired when the child

becomes capable of developing the necessary inner controls and skills and when he wants to practice them with the help of his motivation: "I want to be big, I want to be like them." This implies that the adults set an example with their own manners, consistently. When manners are enforced before the child can manage them, they are so hard that they spoil the need satisfaction. Even grown-ups may say, "Using those chopsticks was so frustrating, I just couldn't enjoy the food and in the end gave up on it even though I was still hungry." Many of us also can only relish an orange, or watermelon, or piece of chicken, when we can hold it and bite into it, leaving aside all good manners.

When manners are required of the child but not of his loved adults, the child may perform well when watched but do without manners when he is not—in contrast to becoming a "gentleman" who, by one English definition, is "He who uses a butterknife when dining on his own." Toileting and sleeping also have to be performed with manners and there too the example of the adults in the family and the rules of the community matter. For example, the rule of privacy can only be learned when the adults in the family keep it. One little boy, reprimanded by his nursery school teacher for urinating in the playground, answered "My Daddy does his wee-wee in the yard." His mother was quite embarrassed when she was informed and perhaps realized that it is hard for children to learn very different manners for home and school.

It is easy to see how often things can go awry in this area of the child's need education, how easily mother may expect too much or too little regulation and manners (expect perfect table manners of her four-year-old or let him feed himself with his hands); or may expect it too soon or too late (expect toilet mastery too soon or too late), or may expect her child to perform differently from mom and dad or differently at home and in public. It is equally easy to recognize that the child may, at one time, become angry because his dinner is not ready at the right time and, at another time, may become just as angry because he is not ready to eat it at the right time. He may refuse to use his home toilet at one time, and at a later time, may refuse to use an unfamiliar toilet at the store. At best, the mother's correct gauging and the child's wish to become "big" will assure harmony most of the time, never all the time.

NEEDS AND THE MOTHER–CHILD RELATIONSHIP

Let us now turn to the mother–child relationship, the fulcrum through which the child's needs and their fulfillment are helped to take their rightful place in his or her life. Up until now we have looked at several aspects of the mothering person's task in regard to needs but we have hardly stressed that she does all she does as part of her close relationship with her child, and that this relationship is what makes it all work. Without this consistent, good enough relationship the mother could not feel with her child, could not sense what to do when, the child could not participate, respond, and make gains, and both of them could not feel good in the process.

The fortunate among us know that the crucial ingredient in a good meal is love (what else makes home cooking so special?), and that the snuggliest bed is made the way mom or dad used to tuck it in. Many of us also remember the joy of becoming independent, the pride in earning our first money and buying things with it. We may not recall the earliest steps along this road, the achievements of feeding and cleaning ourselves, and we rarely recognize that wanting to do for ourselves and enjoying it only happens to those of us who have had a full, loved, and loving share of being cared for and of having received support and admiration for wanting to be independent.

The mutually loving mother–child relationship adds a mutually satisfying element to need fulfillment, an important way of being together and doing together. It is no accident that "feeder" means both the one who provides the food and the one who eats it. During the first months the mother–child unit is so close that they almost perceive the two functions as one. Later, when they love each other as more separate people, eating together still makes up much of the fun of eating, and even adults usually prefer company at meals to eating alone. Eating alone does not taste so good.

That's why some of us can't be bothered to fix a meal for ourselves, and others overeat when alone, in the vain hope that more food can make up for the love of another. But in many areas of need fulfillment, doing for oneself does not mean missing out. With toileting, dressing, even sleeping, the first steps toward independence still include mother in a new social role, that of supporter and admirer. In time, children take all these forms of mother's love into themselves and, in caring for themselves, love themselves as she loved them.

The "it's fun doing it together" social aspect, which the mother–child relationship imparts to need fulfillment, is in part related to the urges. As we have said before, the pleasure-seeking urges are experienced in many body parts, most of which are also connected with needs and need fulfillment. To some extent they are gratified by the child's own activities, for example, mouthing, eating, chewing, and thumb sucking gratify the mouth. But this leaves out the most important aspect of the urges, the fact that, almost from the start they are focused on a loved person. They are stimulated and gratified through the bodily and social interaction with this loved person, as well as channeled and modified through the mutual bond. The mothering person is the young child's main loved one, and the child is one of the main loved ones to her. Her ministrations of suckling, feeding, holding, cleansing, and rocking stimulate and gratify primitive bodily sexual feelings and her ongoing relationship with the child helps to develop the subtler feelings of fondness and affection, of caring and sharing and being together. The child, in turn, stimulates and gratifies the mother. Mothers often experience nursing, fondling, kissing, and holding their baby as exciting and gratifying. At the same time, this fosters their fondness for the child and their enjoyment of his demonstrative love and closeness. This bodily and mental bond, forged in part with the help of the pleasure-seeking urges, makes the child as indispensable to the mother as she is to him. Through this relationship, the mother not only furthers the child's enjoyment of need fulfillment but, in Freud's words, teaches her child how to love. The need oriented pleasures of the early mother–child relationship lay the groundwork for the much

later, very sophisticated pattern of adult family life. Within
its framework the erstwhile youngster will, once again, combine all these trends: the bonds of consistent caring fondness
and affection with a sexual partner, the enjoyment of meeting his own and each other's needs, and the ability to include
children in this partnership and to do the same for them. But
all this is a long way off in the distant future and does not
preoccupy mother or child as they go about the business of
enjoying need fulfillment with each other.

One of the things that sometimes *is* on their minds is the
fact that there is not only love and fun in their relationship.
The mother is also the first main object of the child's aggressive urges, the target for his anger. He initially attacks her
directly, biting, pushing, hitting, and pinching, and learns
only gradually, through the relationship with her, how to
express and channel his anger so as not to harm her. The
mother's anger at the child is inevitable too, but it is, one
hopes, already mitigated by her love and well controlled and
modified in its expression. For this reason she does not harm
him and helps him to cope with his anger. When there is not
too much anger in the relationship, it can be accommodated,
partly expressed in words, partly channeled and modified.
Most of the time, even the mother's gradual attempts at regulating the child's needs and teaching of manners do not
arouse too much anger in the child, just as she does not
become too angry when he resists her lead, does not always
meet her expectations, or protests against them as an annoying interference. After all, this too is tempered by the helpful
aspects of the relationship, the wish to become like the loved
parents and to be appreciated by them.

When all goes well, the mother–child relationship works
for the best and manages to interweave all the various
strands into the solid fabric of personality growth for the
child along with pleasure and satisfaction for him and his
parents. Perhaps the most amazing thing is that, thanks to
their relationship with the child, mothers don't have to reason out all the steps in their difficult task but can rely on their
loving "feel" to get it right and to adjust it when it isn't quite
right. But to build this kind of relationship which can coordi-

nate and balance so many diverse forces within it, takes real, loving investment and a lot of devoted time and energy. Without that it cannot do its work and cannot bring sufficient pleasure to mother or child, to make up for the inevitable moments of mutual hardship and frustration.

Mother–child relationships are never ideal, only good enough at best. They are subject to many strains and stresses and when something goes awry, it often shows up as an interference in the mother–child interactions around need fulfillment and in the child's attitude to his needs. The numerous eating, sleeping, and toileting problems of young children indicate just how frequently such difficulties arise, and mothers' equally frequent puzzlement, annoyance, un-happiness, and guilt over them shows just how much they experience them as an obstacle in the relationship with the child and, often as not, as a failure on their part.

Some of the difficulties may indeed be due to the mother, others may be due to the child, and yet others may be due to extraneous events which impinge on their relationship, such as illness. Often enough, these factors combine and reinforce each other. Sometimes even the happiest family events, such as the birth of a new baby, may unbalance the mother–child relationship and affect their interactions around need fulfill-ment. For example, it is not uncommon for youngsters to react to the arrival of a sibling with sleep difficulties and loss of independence in self-feeding and toileting.

Sometimes difficulties with need fulfillment are not caused by disharmonies in the mother–child relationship but stem from the relationship itself. This happens when need fulfillment mainly serves to make the relationship gratify-ing, instead of the relationship serving to make need fulfill-ment gratifying: for example eating and feeding can become a main way of showing love, instead of love adding to the pleasure of eating. With young children this happens very readily because they connect their feelings about mother so intimately with their own needs that they often fail to distin-guish who really is gratified when their needs are met. They may eat when they like mother and want to please her, but grumble about her food or even refuse it when they are angry at her. Likewise, they may go to sleep nicely and produce their bowel movements in the toilet as though it were a loving gift for mother, rather than a satisfaction for themselves. Wise mothers sense this and do their utmost to set things straight for the child, in their attitude, behavior, and words. For example, when the child enjoys his dinner, they do not congratulate themselves and take it as a proof of the child's love but stress that *he* had himself a good time eating and they are glad for him; and when he is fussy, doesn't like what she cooked, and doesn't finish his meal, they don't feel rejected and hurt but say they're sorry he couldn't enjoy it and will perhaps feel more hungry tomorrow. The child's appetite, sleep, or stools are neither a reward nor an insult to *them*. If they have reason to suspect that the child's behavior is prompted by anger at them, they may even say, "It looks like you're angry at me. You could tell me what it is about. When you don't eat (or dirty your pants) you are mean to yourself, not to me. You can be mad at me and still enjoy your dinner (or be a big boy with clean pants)."

Even the wisest mothers, however, are not always wise. Their necessary closeness with their young child tends to make them feel and think as he does. As a result, they too may confuse who really benefits when the child eats well ("He won't eat *for me*") and who is disgraced when he is soiled ("*We* had three pairs of dirty pants today. I just don't know what to do!"). At such times it helps mothers to remind themselves that needs are ultimately every person's, even the youngest child's, own business.

WOULD IT NOT HELP IF OTHERS, LIKE THE FATHER, TOOK OVER SOME OF THE CHILD'S NEED FULFILLMENT?

The mother–child relationship, in our context, means the relationship with the mothering person, who usually but not always, is the mother. Her place in the primary one-to-one relationship may be taken by someone else, such as the father or grandmother. The primary relationship itself, however, is essential for the child's physical and mental survival during the first one to two years. Need fulfillment is inevitably a part of this relationship and the foundations of the child's attitudes to his or her needs are laid during this first period. By the time a child is two-and-a-half to three years old, he has usually taken over much of his bodily self-care (self-feeding with implements, toilet mastery, sleeping on his own, avoiding common dangers, the basic parts of washing and dressing himself). Beyond these early years, and with the basics accomplished, the child's need education continues and both parents contribute to it in varying measure, depending on the customs of the individual family. During the earlier period, there are usually times when mother-substitutes (father, grandmother, sitter) help out. Up to a point this works out well for all, and the child's growing relationships with the father and other family members help him to be interested in things other than need fulfillment which helps to put it in perspective.

However, when the mothering person shares with others too many of her need fulfilling interactions too often during the early period, it does not help. The shared need fulfilling times are important to the maintenance of the relationship, to the mother's ability to remain in tune with her infant, to the child's ability to love her and respond to her, and to the special pleasures each derives from them. When the primary relationship becomes too diluted, it becomes burdened with excessive anger or even indifference and can't do its essential beneficial work.

The one-to-one early relationship does have its drawbacks, but we can't cure them by throwing out the baby with the bath water. A more effective cure to the entanglements of the relationship are (1) for the mother to be aware of the pitfalls; (2) for the child to take over his own need fulfillment, which he usually wants to do sooner when he has had good one-to-one care; and (3) for needs to be met only when they have had a chance to assert themselves, such as offering food only when the child is really hungry, expecting him to sleep when he is really tired. This helps to foster the child's self-reliance and prevents need fulfillment from unnecessary and prolonged entanglement with the mother–child relationship.

WHEN SHOULD CHILDREN START TOILETING? SHOUILD CHILDREN HAVE TO TASTE EVERY DISH? SHOULD CHILDREN EVER BE ALLOWED TO STAY UP LATE?

It does not usually help to hand out specific "prescriptions" for these and other queries. What to do in a certain situation depends on the child, the parents, the family's current and past experiences. The "right" thing for one mother and child may be "wrong" for another. Advice therefore always requires a very good understanding of all the many factors at play. And it works best when the parents and child are able to listen and respond to each other, to gauge what fits, and to correct what doesn't. Even the "right" measure can turn out to be "wrong" in a relationship which lacks trust and mutual respect.

WHEN SHOULD PARENTS GET PROFESSIONAL HELP WITH THEIR CHILD'S DIFFICULTIES AROUND NEEDS?

In two situations: (1) When they are concerned. To an outsider the child's difficulty may appear negligible, but the parents' concern always implies that they sense something that deserves being looked into. (2) When the child's need fulfill-ment and need education is interfered with over a period of time: when he cannot enjoy need fulfillment, for example, loss of appetite, sleep troubles; when he cannot, age appropriately, take over responsibility for self-care, can't achieve toilet mastery, is persistently unwilling to learn to dress and wash himself; or when he cannot learn to regulate his needs age-appropriately; for example, falls asleep at school, always needs to go to the bathroom during class.

DO CHILDREN OUTGROW THEIR DIFFICULTIES WITH NEEDS?

It depends on the difficulty and on its causes. For example, a child's poor appetite may be due to the fact that he is expected to eat more than his hunger warrants. This may correct itself when he has a growth spurt, when he becomes bodily more active, or when he is allowed to help himself. However, a child's poor appetite may be due to not enjoying eating, perhaps because he is at a day care center and misses his mom (in which case his difficulty may subside when he is helped to overcome the stress or when he has a chance to eat more with mom during home meals). It may be due to an early difficulty in experiencing feeding as pleasurable (in which case his lack of appetite is not so likely to subside and, depending on the extent of the trouble, may endanger his health at a later time or may just mean that eating will never be important to him).

Development does tend to affect our attitudes to needs. During the elementary school years, the parent–child relationship is less intimate and need fulfillment naturally becomes more the child's own affair. In the process it usually sheds some of the earlier "for or against the parents" interferences. In adolescence, the newly powerful urges usually "invade" needs (eating binges and diets alternate, as do sleeping late and going without sleep, spending hours on bodily cleanliness and neglecting to wash his clothes or clean his room). During late adolescence and early adulthood, new identifications with the parents and others again help to reshape our attitudes to needs. But all these progressive changes rest on the early foundation and don't stray too far from it, for better or worse.

19

Pleasure in Living

When we enjoy many things in life very much, we feel good and living always seems worthwhile. We can even take in stride the inevitable hardships and make up for the loss of some pleasures because we have others left to choose from. When we enjoy only very few things very seldom, we feel unhappy and living does not seem so worthwhile. Every upset looms large and adds to our burden of misery, and when we are deprived of our few ways of having fun we have nothing to put in their place. For life to continue at all, there has to be some pleasure in living and that is the business of the pleasure-seeking urges. Fortunately, they are so flexible that, with the help of maturation and environment, they can come to be gratified in the most varied ways, in keeping with the kinds of pleasure particular societies and individuals permit and value.

Guiding the pleasure-seeking urges is largely the task of the parents during the child's years of emotional growth. It is an especially intricate task because the parents are not outsiders to the child's urges. As we have already seen they are also participants in their child's pleasures, they stimulate and gratify them, and they experience pleasure themselves in doing so. Yet without this kind of relationship they cannot help their child to feel good, to modify and divert his satisfactions, and to find new ways of gaining pleasure.

WHAT WE ALREADY KNOW ABOUT
THE PLEASURE-SEEKING URGES

By this time we are already familiar with a number of ways in which the pleasure-seeking urges work within the child's growing personality, and how the parents use and guide them through their relationship with the child. Let us remind ourselves by way of a summary. We have seen how these urges contribute to the enjoyment of need fulfillment, serving self-preservation (eating, eliminating, sleeping, liking his or her body and protecting it from harm).

In following the development of personality functions (tools of mastery), we have observed how, with the help of the parents' pleasure and appreciation, these urges are channeled into motility, speech, perception, and thinking. For example, in watching the toddler's ecstatic joy in running around, in crawling under and out of furniture, in pushing chairs and toys, and his thrill in babbling and forming words, we could feel with him his initial intense excitement in exercising his new abilities. We have also followed how, in the course of development, they cease to be an end in themselves and come to serve him as tools for achieving other goals. And we have seen how, in the process, the early excited delight is toned down to a more subtle sense of well-being, so much so that, as adults, we are hardly aware of it unless illness or unusual circumstances prevent us from using these functions. Then, and only then, do we realize what we have lost and can perhaps reexperience the infantile intense pleasure when we can resume walking or talking.

We have also observed how pleasure fuels the beginnings of the mother–child relationship in the first year. We have seen how much the pleasure-seeking urges are stimulated and gratified in the daily bodily interactions between mother and child around need fulfillment and affectionate interplays, how they are gradually toned down to mental feelings of loving, fondness, liking, and caring. And we have also seen how the pleasurable experiences of this first relationship prompt the child to seek out new relationships with the father and others in the family, and in the wider community, until ultimately they contribute to his or her adult relationships, sexual and nonsexual.

And we have noted that the pleasures derived from the early relationships with the parents are so great and so important that, for the sake of preserving them, the child is willing to take disappointments in stride and to learn to tolerate frustrations, to curb some of his satisfactions ("You have to eat with your spoon, not with your fingers") and to forego others ("No, you can't mess with your BMs"), and to take the parental love and demands into himself and make them a permanent part of his own personality in the form of self-esteem and conscience.

But we have also seen that, from early on, the child gratifies some of his bodily pleasure-seeking urges himself and that this helps him to be less dependent on the parents; for example, when the baby sucks his thumb or fingers, he provides pleasure and comfort for himself. We mentioned that the child's self-comforting activities tend to be focused on those parts of the body which, at successive stages in his development, are the main source of pleasurable feelings for him—the mouth in infancy, the rectal area during toddler-hood, and the genitals from the preschool years on—keeping in mind that there is also much overlap between these phases and that, all along, other body parts also provide pleasure. Among these are various body hollows (ears, nose, navel), the skin (providing pleasure in bathing, cleansing, caressing, holding), postural and muscle sensations stimulated through passive movement (rocking, swinging, being driven in a car), and through active movement (kicking, throwing, pushing, running, pedaling a tricycle, or using a swing). Many young children rub their cheeks, play with their fingers in their ears or noses, rock themselves as they go to sleep or on a rocking horse, jump up and down on beds, or seemingly never tire of swinging on a swing.

We have also already looked more closely at the role some of these infantile pleasure zones play in the child's later personality, and have followed the pathways by which they contribute to his growth and well-being. In regard to the early mouth pleasures we traced their later direct manifestations (enjoying eating, kissing as a way of showing affection, and as a part of adult sexual foreplay), their contribution in modified form (enjoyment of talking and singing), and their part in nonbodily mental activity (the enjoyment of "taking in" information, attitudes, and ideals and the important part this plays in learning and in acquiring personality traits and values).

Last but not least, we have touched on some of the conflicts the pleasure-seeking urges may cause, especially when they are gratified too little or too much; for example, the child may not want to give up mother's pleasurable care of his body, or may insist on pursuing his own pleasures independently of her.

THE CHANGING PATTERNS OF PLEASURES

As the child develops, some new pleasures emerge naturally on their own. Maturation itself transforms the needy greedy baby with his mouth-centered excitements and satisfactions into the assertive toddler who likes to be his own boss and do his own thing in his own way. He even wants to be boss of his mother, hugging, clinging, teasing, and tormenting her with his "yes–no" love, engaging her in tussles of tug-of-war, shrieking with delight as he runs away from her and invites her to chase after him, and clashing with her over their different ideas of what is fun. Depending on the mothers' attitude, and perhaps on just how pleased or exasperated they feel at the moment, they may describe their toddler as "He is so positive these days" or "She is so negative." Some of the child's new pleasures are readily shared by the mother, at least much of the time: the pleasures in motility, in talking, and in independent mastery, the pervasive "Me all by myself" when it comes to doing anything at all. In regard to other pleasures there is much divergence between them: The toddler likes to take apart, destroy, and throw away many of the things the mother treasures, but likes to hoard and collect many of the things she wants to get rid of. He "attacks" indiscriminately her pots, pans, and knick-knacks as well as his own new toys, and even when he asks her to make sand-pies or build block towers, his main fun comes in knocking them down gleefully. At the same time he fills his hands, pockets, and even mouth with stones, acorns, buttons, and beads and, to her dismay, hoards little caches of such "valuables." He likes to mess with things, while she prefers to keep them neat and clean and responds with disgust or annoyance when she finds him, once again, joyfully scattering the contents of drawers, smearing food on himself and his high chair, or splashing water from the faucet. Their clash over pleasures is especially pronounced when it comes to his favorite absorbing interest, the urine and bowel movements produced by himself and others. On a walk the toddler notices every dog turd. On the visit to the farm or zoo, his highlights are the defecating and urinating animals. Who did it, how big is it, how does it smell, and can one touch it and pick it up, are a never ending source of comments and questions. And this applies most especially to his own productions. We see it in the child's intensely preoccupied expression when he "makes" or holds back, squirming and wriggling, in his fascinated inspection of the contents of diapers and toilets, often accompanied by attempts to stir them around and examine them, in his delighted comparison of their size and consistency. Not only mothers, but fathers and baby-sitters are often called to admire "See, two big ones!" The child's pleasure even extends to the idea of tasting bodily products, as illustrated by one verbally precocious fourteen-month-old. During a contented family meal of hot dogs she suddenly pointed to the mustard jar and asked "Please pass the BM." Her parents sat stunned into silence and only her four-year-old sister remained unruffled and fulfilled the request with the simple comment "It's mustard. We don't eat BM."

In time the toddler pleasures subside and are, again spontaneously, overshadowed by the new pleasures of the nursery years. The parents welcome them with mixed feelings. On one hand they are glad that their child now maintains a more cooperative relationship with both of them, enjoys following the lead of their interests, and wants to do what they do, be it cooking, shopping, or working in the yard. They are flattered by his admiration of them and proud of his inquisitiveness, gladly demonstrate their skills, encourage his efforts to help and learn, and patiently answer his many questions of why and how. They also fulfill quite happily their other role in the "mutual admiration society" with their child, respond to his constant demands of "Look at me," "See what I can do" with duly complimentary interest, and share his great pleasure in achieving "superior status," be it a new skill in drawing a picture or looking impressively handsome in a new outfit, or looming extra tall from the top of the jungle gym. On the other hand, they often view with some misgivings the fact that their youngster's curiosity and pleasure in showing off tends to focus on bodily, especially sexual attributes. Not only has their interest in animals shifted to checking which are "Mommies" and "Daddies" and "Baby" dogs (cats, elephants, or horses), comparing the sizes, presence or absence of penises, and taking a keen interest in everything they do with them and with each other, but boys and girls show even greater fascination with exploring all this in people. They ask personal questions of family members, teachers, and sometimes strangers. They want to look at and know all about the different sexual organs and functions in men and women, boys and girls, and of course in their own bodies.

Being looked at is as much fun for them as looking. They often use any opportunity or pretext to prance around in the nude, like to run around naked at dressing and undressing times, and are apt to appear bare of an evening in the living room, just when neighbors have stopped over, with a righteous "Mommy, I can't find my nightie." One youngster even threw off his clothes, danced in the driveway and, when his surprised Mom came upon him, greeted her with "Spring has come!" More subtly, they tend to lift their dresses or don't quite finish pulling up their pants before leaving the bathroom. They also like to show off in words, sometimes in unexpected ways; for example, four-year-old Harry boasted to his nursery school class "My Daddy has the biggest penis in the whole town."

Doing and wanting to do, go with the pleasure in mutual looking. Youngsters may touch and handle their genitals, squeeze their thighs together, or hold back urine to experience and experiment with the many pleasurable sensations in this bodily area. They become easily stimulated and excited by bodily interactions with others: "Mommy, I want *you* to dry me. It tickles so nicely"; "Daddy, swing me around again and again." They may like to bump up and down on dad's knees or hang around his neck, touch the front of mommy's blouse or push into her. Shared toileting, bathing, and sleeping as well as playing "family" and "doctor" with siblings or peers, readily turn into mutual excited exploring and touching. The young child's own feelings also make him aware of the parents' adult intimate relationship and he wants to share in that too. Boys and girls often want to sleep in the parents' bed or have one parent sleep with them. They interrupt parents kissing, or even parents talking together. They imitate the parents' affectionate gestures with one another and try to treat the parent as their partner; for example, Paul would give his mother's behind a pat and put his arm round her as he had seen his father do. Valerie asked her Dad "Dance close with me, like you do with Mommy," and offers of "I'll marry you Mommy (or Daddy)" are frequent.

These infantile, pleasure-seeking urges wax and wane as they succeed each other and pave the way for the beginnings of adult sexuality in adolescence. Some of them become a part of personal well-being (e.g., feeling good about one's genitals), others contribute elements to later sexual enjoyment but will need to be directed to new loved ones outside the family (e.g., wishing for a sexual partner and including looking and being looked at in sexual foreplay). Some of these urges are unhelpful in their original form (e.g., the pleasure in messing, in destroying, tormenting, teasing, and being contrary). All of them, however, can contribute in an important way to the growth and enrichment of the child's personality if their energy is channeled into new pathways and gratified in new forms.

GETTING TO KNOW NEW PLEASURES

Children who have enjoyed life are usually eager to experience any new pleasure, especially when their trusted loved ones offer it, when they see them enjoy it, are drawn by the prospect of sharing it with them, and becoming like them. If mom or dad enjoy mixing the dough for cookies, washing the car, building sand castles, drawing, reading, tidying up, or whatever, surely it must be fun, and surely it must be fun to do it with them and like them: "Let me! I want to too!" But children often find that the new funs are not so easy to come by and involve some sacrifices. They usually entail skills that have to be learned, effort has to be put into the process, frustrating hurdles overcome, and restrictions observed; for example, "You can help me mix the dough, but—you have to put on an apron, you mustn't lick your fingers, it mustn't get on the floor, it has to be done this way and not that way, and no, you can't suddenly leave it and do something else without getting cleaned up." All this diminishes the fun of doing, delays the pleasure in the final accomplishment, and, even when one has mastered it all in the end, the new pleasure feels very different from the old one. Mixing dough well for real cookies is fun but not easy fun like "just messing" or making mudpies, and it is indeed far removed from it, in spite of some similarities. The old fun is all body pleasure, immediate and intense. The new fun is largely mental, subtler, toned down, slower to achieve. New pleasures, like all acquired tastes, take time and repeated experience before we can really enjoy them and appreciate their greatest advantage, the glow of the aftertaste. This part was altogether absent in the old pleasures whose fun stopped the moment we finished doing. The new pleasures last. They leave us feeling good and proud of ourselves long after the activity has ceased, and they earn appreciation from those whose opinions matter. These are powerful enticements to try again, to savor ever more new pleasures, to perfect mastery, and to add self-esteem combined with praise.

Learning new pleasures always entails some giving up of the old ones. They are mostly offered, not in addition, but instead; that is their other drawback. They come in parental terms of not this but that, not here but there, and sometimes of not now but later. "You can play with dough but not with mud (and certainly not with bowel movements)," "You can be naked in private but not in public," "You can't have a husband or wife now but only when you grow up" (which seems an eternity away). In some instances, new pleasures even involve a complete turn around: "You mustn't enjoy being messy, you need to enjoy being clean" or "You mustn't enjoy

being cruel, you have to enjoy showing pity and being kind."
This expectation of giving up the infantile body pleasures
becomes obvious from the way parents prohibit or discourage
them, and from the way they interfere with the new pleasures
as soon as the child shows signs of changing them back into
his old ones; for example, when mixing dough deteriorates
into real messing, mom or dad stop it; "That's not for messing. That's for making cookies. If you can't yet do that properly and go by the rules, we'll have to wait till you get bigger
but you'll have to stop for now." All this giving up and trying
is hard enough in the many situations where the child's
efforts are rewarded by joining the parents in their fun and
doing as they do. It is harder yet when he or she has to
renounce enjoyments they can pursue (such as when the child
is not allowed to gratify his wish for bodily intimacy with the
parents, but they can do so with each other). It is also hard
when the activities they enjoy are still beyond his capacities—
bodily ones, like making babies, and nonbodily ones, like
reading, writing, driving a car, cooking a meal. One young
woman recalled, during a class discussion of this topic, her
envious admiration of her mother writing checks, how desperately she scribbled on little pieces of paper to produce her
own "checks," and how relieved she was when her mother,
instead of laughing at her, said kindly "You'll learn. Your
time will come."

Obviously, channeling and transforming urges is not
quick and easy. It often goes back and forth. In nursery
school many children already use paints well, put the brushes
in the jars with the appropriate color, apply paint only to the
paper, and try to produce a picture with form and even content. But even an accomplished young painter who really
enjoys painting and is pleased and proud with his finished
product, is apt to have days when he, once again, indulges in
messing. Then the paints drip on the floor and make a gooey
scribble on the paper; his hands get painted or his clothes;
and, unless a watchful teacher intervenes, the whole enter-
prise can quickly turn into a gleeful orgy of splattering paints
on others and on the furniture. Nursery teachers have to be
very watchful, and are well aware that their pupils still travel
the rocky road toward new pleasures. Parents have known it

long before their children even enter nursery school. They know how to gauge when the child is ready to give up a pleasure (usually when he has developed enough skills to be somewhat successful at new pleasures); they know which new pleasure to offer and how to make the transition gradual (e.g., they start with water play and work up, step by step, toward paint with brushes); they know how to encourage and praise every move in the right direction and to help overcome failures and setbacks ("*Soon* you'll know how").

Above all, parents use words and support the child in using words to name and express his feelings, wishes, and thoughts. We already know how this helps. It provides a means of mastery and an avenue for limited discharge and gratification. We use words as a tool for thinking, for expressing and communicating *instead* of doing, and this makes it possible to have and enjoy the feelings, and yet control our behavior. In our society's laws this is recognized in the freedom of thought and speech. Privately, for the child, and later for the adult, it means that we can think what we want, that we can, more or less, say what we want, and that we can pretend; that is, fulfill our wishes in daydreams and, to some extent, in play. All these are satisfying outlets. They are not as satisfying as real doing but satisfying enough to bear the frustration of not doing. The child's emphatic "But I don't want to sleep in my bed. I want to sleep with you," helps him to conform to his parents' expectation of "I can understand that you want to and you can say it, but you can't really do it. I know it's hard, but you need to sleep in your bed and you'll be okay." Alone in his bed, many a child daydreams that he is sleeping with the parents after all, and when he plays "house" with his friends at nursery school he may take the pretend role of daddy and assign a place for his pretend bedroom with the pretend mommy. Without words all this limited and harmless fun would be denied to him. He would find it much harder to give up his infantile pleasures and to invest his energy in the new ones.

Words are especially helpful to the child and parents in coping with the early interests in and feelings about sexual organs and functions. In this area the parents cannot directly participate in the child's pleasures. Opportunities for looking further stimulate youngsters' urges and, at the same time, fail to convey accurate information. Going by what they can see, children can't help but arrive at the erroneous conclusion that boys are "haves" and girls "have-nots" because the crucial internal differences are not visible. And moreover adults of their own sex seem totally different because the secondary sexual characteristics obscure the similarities between the child's and adult's body. However, when parents respond to the child's interest by sharing truthful knowledge in simple, not technical words, they satisfy his curiosity sufficiently, without adding to his excitement and without fully excluding him. Knowing about sexual matters through words also helps children feel good about their sexual identity and future sexual role, and enables them to renounce their sexual demands on the parents in favor of nonsexual bonds of caring and affection. Not least, it assists in diverting their curiosity to learning about other things. As such it becomes an important part of self-motivated learning and finding out about the world.

WHAT ARE THE NEW PLEASURES AND HOW DO THEY ENRICH THE PERSONALITY?

Each infantile pleasure follows its own new channels. Some we have already discussed. For example, we saw that some of the child's love of messing is allowed substitute satisfaction with water, sand, clay, and can gradually lead to a new nonbodily pleasure in art and craft. Paint, a potentially messy medium, gets to be used to produce pictures or to paint houses, walls, and furniture. Liking to "get one's hands into it" becomes a part of gardening, cleaning, and cooking (how else can one make a meatloaf?). The young child's pleasure in possessing and hoarding can become more discriminate and lead to valuing and caring for his clothes, toys, money, artwork, and other skilled productions, as well as to enjoyable hobbies, or even professions, of collecting (trading cards, stamps, coins, books, art objects, antiques). The early pleasure in being the boss of his or her stools and urine, contributes not only to toilet mastery but to the pleasure in all masteries. It plays an important part in overcoming obstacles to achievement, in persevering with activities, and in enjoying accomplishments, a good job well done.

We have also already spoken of the way the child's infantile sexual curiosity finds new nonsexual gratifications in intellectual curiosity and in learning. The fun of being looked at, of showing off his or her body, is, with parental help, channeled into showing off clothes ("What a pretty dress!") and, more importantly, skills and achievements. Most preschoolers show off everything they do and make to their teacher, then keep it to show the parents and solicit their admiration, and like to put it up for display. Many refrigerators, bulletin boards, doors, shelves, and walls blossom with the children's productions, a constant source of pride to them and testimony to the parents' shared pleasure and efforts at supporting his or her development. Once showing off relinquishes its primitive exciting quality, it is used in feeling good about performing in front of others, be it reading aloud to the class, acting in a play, giving a talk, or just speaking up in discussions. Even the young child's wish to make a baby like the parents is partially diverted into the pleasure of creativity. It may be a humble little project, a special way of decorating the table or of arranging flowers, a newly invented game, a magic trick, a scientific theory, a work of art. It is always a special thrill to create something new. We acknowledge the early connection when we speak of "my brain child" or "the father of the idea."

But what about those early pleasures which are mostly unhelpful in later life and need to be turned around? How does the child who likes himself dirty come to like himself clean, and how does his enjoyment of hurting change to wanting to feel pity? Mothers often puzzle about that too. Some despair of ever getting their toddlers to be clean, much less wanting to be clean, while others say, "Why, I didn't do anything at all. He just trained himself." They overlook the fact that the child's wanting to be clean is not a question of training or not training, but of helping the child to be master of himself, and that a crucial element in this process is the child's changing attitude to dirt. That which was enjoyed turns into a source of disgust, and liking him or herself clean becomes the new pleasure. This is not accomplished by putting, or not putting, the child on the potty, by guessing when he needs to eliminate or by disregarding it. It happens gradually and inconspicuously through the mother–child relationship. In the beginning, especially when the baby is breast-fed and mother's milk makes up his main food intake, his stools are such that mothers, as a rule, do not mind taking care of them. But as new foods are added and increasingly outweigh or supplant nursing, the child's stools change and so does the mother's response. Thus, from the end of his or her first year on, when infants watch their mother's face as she changes their diapers, disposes of the contents, and cleanses their bodies, they invariably see an expression of involuntary disgust, at least a slightly wrinkled nose. They may also hear her comments to that effect, notice some fastidiousness in her movements when she, perhaps gingerly, handles the dirty items. And when she is done, or almost done, mother usually shows relief, may smile, hug her child, and say something about how nice he now smells and how good he looks to her when he is all clean. Most mothers are quite unaware of all this, but the child "drinks it in." Sometimes he imitates her: We often see very young toddlers with a disgusted face or repeating little phrases and exclamations of disgust ("Pooh, yucky!") while they happily stick their hands into the diaper pail or unflushed toilet. Their new disgust is wafer thin, no patch yet on the real pleasure in messing, but it may be a first sign of inner struggle between the two different attitudes. Later, teddy bears are sometimes told with disgust that they are dirty and smelly, although the child still does not object to this in himself. But in time this changes with the impact of the parents' attitude—their direct or indirect disgust at bodily products, their enjoyment of being clean themselves, their spontaneous closeness with the child when he is clean, their expectation and trust that he can become clean like them, and the child's admiration of them and wish to grow up. When children first repudiate dirtiness and make being clean their own thing, they often overshoot. They don't want to eat foods that remind them of bodily products, they may become fiends at cleaning up everything, or lining up everyone's shoes, they may not even want to go in the water, having just decided that it was "yucky" to be wet. All of this usually subsides in time and tones down to a reasonable pleasure in keeping themselves, their possessions, and surroundings neat and clean.

Likewise, the relationship with the parents and the example they set helps to reverse the child's enjoyment of hurting into becoming compassionate. The parents show their attitude in many ways: in their response to the child when he or she is hurt ("I am so sorry," "Poor thing," "There, there," "Let me help make it better"), in their compassion for other people and indeed for all living things, in their avoidance of inflicting pain on the child and others, and in their preventing or stopping the child from hurting anyone. How often children gleefully step on worms or ants, tease the dog or cat or their siblings, and how often parents swiftly interfere "Oh, no! That's not kind! Poor little thing. Come and be nice." Sometimes the pleasure in hurting is enjoyed vicariously, as in a morbid eagerness to hear of misfortunes, tragedies, and violence, or in watching, with fascination, movies and real incidents where people and animals are hurt, or in laughing when someone gets hurt. Young children's pleasure in hurting is unduly stimulated in such situations. They do not serve as a helpful outlet. Since in our Western societies cruelty is increasingly not permitted, a child's well-developed aversion to it and capacity for feeling pity will stand him or her in good stead in life. It will also help him to avoid developing a pleasure in being hurt, which is often the natural companion of hurting and which, if stimulated, may persist and interfere with his well-being. This, as we have said earlier, is also one of the reasons against the use of physical punishment.

TWO STEPS FORWARD AND ONE BACK

Development never proceeds in a smooth, direct line. The process of growing up, and changing urge satisfactions is a part of it, tends to grind to a temporary halt from time to time, and to go back and forth. Sometimes this is caused by the stress of an illness, of a change in routines, of family upheaval, or even of fatigue at the end of a long day. Sometimes the effort of coping with new maturational challenges is just too great to be sustained and progress takes a bit of "time out." As long as the child can recoup and resume the forward momentum, as long as he takes the proverbial two steps forward and one back in an ongoing way, he is doing all right. Parents and educators often have a hard time realizing this. They get so frustrated and worried, fearing that the child will get stuck and never make it, that they even forget that the child feels the same way, disappointed, hopeless, upset, and angry. The child is apt to feel even worse than the adults because he has not yet had the experience of being grown-up, of making it. For him the distance looms so great, the goals seem so unattainable. It helps a lot when the parents put the setbacks in perspective and convey their trust that things will go better again, and encourage the child along the way: "It's hard now but that happens to everyone. Soon things will go better. Just keep trying."

The parents' concern, however, is not always unfounded. Children can get "stuck" at a particular level and they can take steps back which are not followed by steps forward. How does one know when this has happened, and what causes it? Parents usually know that development is interfered with when the child reaches the next phase in age but not in appropriate functioning; for example, he or she may get to be a preschooler but continues to act like a toddler, or reverts to toddlerlike behavior for a long period, may mess instead of being pleased to keep clean, may enjoy teasing and being contrary instead of taking pleasure in showing up well. Similarly, a school-aged child may act like a preschooler or even like a toddler.

Many things may play a part in bringing about such developmental delays or arrests. Often they are related to the child experiencing too little urge satisfaction or too much urge stimulation. When children are expected to forego all satisfaction of an infantile urge before it even comes into its own in the course of their development, they may be unable to comply, or unable to channel and transform the pleasure appropriately, or they may comply but then need to go back to it when a later stress weakens their resources. For example,

Angela became toilet trained during her first year, before her pleasurable interest in bodily products emerged, but, in spite of mother's restrictions and prohibitions, she remained messy with food, untidy with her own and the family's belongings, and could not learn to use messy media in a creative way. The mother described her activity as being like a hurricane that leaves everything in a shambles in its wake. When Angela was four years old she was injured in an accident. She recovered her bodily health but reverted to wetting and soiling which continued until the mother sought professional help.

The opposite extreme, too much stimulation, may come about in several ways, but may interfere just as much with the child's ability to progress and to utilize his or her energy in new ways. Since infantile urges are usually so removed from what adults recognize as exciting, even parents may be unaware of how readily children are aroused and how easily they are overwhelmed by intense feelings which then preclude mastery. Thus, children may become overstimulated when left to enjoy their bodily pleasures for long periods (for example, to soil, wet, smear, or to play with their genitals) while their loved adults are absent or unavailable. More often people or experiences, unwittingly, overstimulate the child. This may apply to such things as parents' excessive and/or prolonged care of the child's body, especially of his or her rectal and genital areas (wiping, cleansing, applying ointments); frequent bodily fondling, kissing, and touching in affectionate interplays; wrestling and chasing games; bathing, toileting, dressing, and sleeping together which involve bodily contact and/or seeing each other naked; opportunity to witness adults' sexual intimacies or fights and arguments; repeated exposure to seeing or hearing incidents of a sexual nature or of hurting and being hurt through talk, TV movies, or books. It is of course impossible to protect children from everything that goes on in the world around them. It helps, however, to be aware of its impact on them. When youngsters have experienced things that may be hard for them to cope with, parents help by acknowledging their feelings (upset, confused, excited, scared), and by explaining matters calmly and simply to assist with mastery.

CAN ARRESTS IN THE DEVELOPMENT OF THE URGES PERSIST INTO ADULTHOOD? HOW DO THEY SHOW THEMSELVES AND CAN THEY BE HELPED?

Such arrests do not necessarily correct themselves, and, unless understood and helped, may in one form or another, continue to burden the child's and later adult's personality. For example, failure to shift the pleasure in curiosity and mastery from bodily to mental pursuits, may interfere with the motivation to learn and work; prevalent persistence of infantile sexual pleasures in hurting and being hurt, or in looking and being looked at, may lead to a preference for perverse practices in lieu of adult genital sexual enjoyment. Continued pleasure in being contrary, in arguing and mental sparring may spoil the chance for cooperative caring relationships. Some adult couples fight and even hurt each other constantly, not because they don't like each other, but because they do so in an infantile way. Their inability to let go of each other often shows in remaining together, or in repeated reunions interspersed with separations, or in continued mutual harassment even after a divorce.

Many factors may contribute to interruptions in personality development in childhood, and many more shape their ultimate outcome in the adult. When grown-ups suffer from difficulties of this nature, they can get help through treatment with a psychiatrist, psychoanalyst, or psychologist.

NUDITY IS NATURAL. I THINK CHILDREN SHOULD SEE THEIR PARENTS IN THE NUDE FROM THE START BECAUSE THEN THEY WILL NOT THINK OF IT AS SEXUAL

Societies, and individuals within them, have adopted different attitudes to the infantile, pleasure-seeking urge of looking and being looked at, both in regard to its early focus on bodies and in regard to its diverted and transformed outlets; that is, the enjoyment of curiosity in general and of showing off in a nonbodily way, such as clothes, skills, and achievements. However, as with all urges, this one too is always subject to restrictions in one or another area. In this country the law prohibits nudity in public, except in specified places and by consenting adults, and custom encourages enjoyment of showing and admiration of nonbodily attributes, especially skills and achievements. By implication, the pleasurable excitement which accompanies the urge satisfaction is taken for granted but restricted to the privacy of home, club, or secluded beach. Other societies, and some individuals in our society, deal with this urge by allowing looking and being looked at in its original bodily form but prohibiting the exciting feelings that accompany it. This holds true in nudist colonies as well as in families which practice nudity. Looking and being looked at without excitement is not a natural, but an acquired attitude, and children have to learn it, with the help of their parents. It involves dealing with the excited feelings by such measures as suppression, diversion, or dulling. It is particularly hard for children to accomplish during the preschool years, when this urge is at its most intense, becomes somewhat less difficult during the later school years when it subsides, only to intensify again in adolescence when it reemerges along with the newly strong urge of genital sexuality. The child's difficulty in learning to cope in this way is often exacerbated by the fact that the parents do not recognize just how hard the task is and demand immediate, rather than gradual success, while exposing him or her to a full measure of stimulation. Signs of the children's failure are commonly encountered; for example, continued enjoyment of looking and being looked at in secret, which may contribute to the later perversions of voyeurism and exhibitionism; "addiction" to watching TV; inability to ask about and understand sexual matters by means of words (not asking does not mean "knowing all about it" since the nature and functions of important internal organs cannot be deduced from visual observation); difficulty in diverting curiosity into self-motivated learning; inappropriate showing off, such as clowning or *showing off* in the bad sense of the term; and difficulty, even extreme shyness, in performing in front of others (as when called on to recite at school) or in taking pleasure in nonbodily showing off of skills and achievements.

It may seem ironic, but not surprising, that the same difficulties may result from educational methods which allow too much gratification as result from those which allow too little; prohibiting looking without giving verbal enlightenment may prove as unhelpful as giving the opportunity to see everything.

ISN'T CHILDREN'S CURIOSITY ABOUT BODIES, AS WELL AS THEIR TAKING THINGS APART, AN INTELLECTUAL INTEREST? THEY ARE NOT EXCITED, THEY ARE INQUISITIVE

Children are both excited and inquisitive. When the excited aspect of their curiosity is not recognized, when it is over-stimulated or harshly prohibited early on, the intellectual aspect may suffer. In normal development, the pleasure-seeking urges are a helpful companion for investing and furthering the intellectual functions. They make being inquisitive fun, just as they support need fulfillment and make eating fun. But they cannot play this part effectively, either when they are not allowed to participate at all during the initial development of a function or when they become so overstimulated that their energy cannot be transformed into nonbodily pleasure. In the former instance, learning and finding out may cease to provide satisfaction and will not be pursued, in the latter instance the curiosity may remain excitedly focused on bodily matters and will not extend to learning and finding out about other things.

SHOULD YOUNG CHILDREN BE TOLD ABOUT SEXUAL INTERCOURSE?

Children are helped when their questions are answered simply, truthfully, and to the extent that they can understand and integrate information at a given time. When parents are in tune with their child, they sense this correctly from what the child says, from what they know he has observed and experienced, and from the way he acts and plays. They know that sexual matters are often hard to grasp (not only because they are intellectually difficult but also because they are

linked with many intense feelings), that discussions therefore need to be follwed up to clear up misunderstandings, and
that it is important to find the right time and place for dealing
with the topic privately. Most children have questions about
how babies are made, can understand answers geared to their
level, and can in that context also understand better that
men's and women's bodies are different in order to fulfill this
function.

Unfortunately, many parents were not verbally informed
by their own parents and this makes it hard for them to be in
tune with their child and to find the right words. They may
feel tongue-tied and embarrassed, or they may become very
"scientific" and give microscopic details about ova and
sperms, or they may overwhelm their children with information they are not ready for. This is illustrated by the jocular
story of the mother who, in response to the child's question of
"Where did I come from?" launched into a lengthy account of
procreation, at the end of which the child said, "Well, all I
really wanted to know was whether I was born in Cleveland
or in Chicago." It always helps to ascertain first just exactly
what it is the child wants to know, how he or she came to
wonder about it, what his own ideas are, how he arrived at his
conclusions. If the child really wants to know "where I come
from," it often suffices at first to tell him or her that it takes a
mommy and a daddy, that they make a baby together when
they love each other in a special way.

Children usually forget much of the specific sexual
information the parents told them during the preschool
years, but they do remember the most important things: That
sexual matters are a private thing about which everyone has
feelings, that it is all right to want to know and ask about
them, and that the parents will answer inquiries in a helpful
way and leave the child with a comfortable feeling about it.

HOW MUCH MASTURBATION IS "TOO MUCH?"

Some people are altogether opposed to children masturbating,
others would place no restriction on it, and others yet are
uncertain as to what approach to follow and how to gauge

whether the child's masturbatory activities are within "normal" limits. Different customs and beliefs, as well as different attitudes and experiences in their individual lives, contribute to different ideas.

As we have noted earlier, children's self-comforting habits tend to follow the developmental phases of the pleasure-seeking urges, focusing first on the mouth, then successively on different bodily parts. For the preschooler and older child, his genitals are the main bodily pleasure zone and this manifests itself in masturbatory activities. Parents may occasionally notice their child masturbate in one form or another. However, after children are told, or deduce on their own, that this is a private matter, not appropriate in front of others, they usually limit themselves to times when they are alone. These are the times when self-comfort and discharge of minor tensions are helpful, for example before falling asleep. When masturbation serves the young child in this way, parents often do not even know about it.

However, when children are overstimulated, or worried about their bodies, or have missed their absent or unavailable parents too much, masturbation may intensify, as it becomes a way for the child to cope with these concerns. It may be an attempt to discharge excessive accumulated tensions, or to reassure him or herself of bodily intactness, or to compensate for the emotional loss of the parent. Since no amount of masturbation can effectively calm such concerns, it may then turn into an added worry for the child because he or she does not feel in control of it. Parents and educators usually notice this kind of masturbation because the child can no longer limit himself to privacy, and because it may interfere with the child's usual play and activities, through restlessness and diminished concentration. When the excited or worried feelings become so strong that they are master of the child, instead of the child being master of them, when they, so to speak, never leave him alone and overwhelm him, then masturbation is "too much." But this would not be an indication of too much fun and indulgence but of too much concern, and would warrant the parents' trying to understand and help, if need be with professional assistance.

ISN'T TV A BAD INFLUENCE ON CHILDREN, ESPECIALLY SINCE IT SHOWS SO MUCH VIOLENCE?

Television is not an unavoidable part of life. It does not impose itself on us willy-nilly. It is a controllable instrument that we use as and when we wish. A lot depends, therefore, on the parents' own TV watching habits and program preferences, and on their rules for the children's use of it.

With TV, as with all experiences, the parents are the child's natural shield against overwhelming and help in mastering stimuli. The parents judge which programs are suitable and, by sharing watching with the child or by knowing what is shown, assist him to understand it and to cope with the feelings it arouses. In this way, TV can serve as a means of entertainment and instruction (Hall, 1982a).

20

Putting Aggression to Use

In looking at aggression as an urge, an innate energy, we have already traced some of its developmental paths and seen how the growing personality uses it in helpful ways. We have touched on how it supports needs and need fulfillment; for example, by adding chewing and biting to satisfying independent eating, and by adding protest against hurt to self-protection. We have noted how, in the course of maturation, it links up with the phases of the pleasure-seeking urges. For example, during babyhood, when the mouth provides the most intense pleasurable satisfactions, the mouth is also used to discharge aggression through biting and screaming, and during the toddler period, when "being the boss," messing and withholding, and teasing and hurting, serve both to gain pleasure and to show anger—the very things that make the toddler so "positive" and "negative." In talking about frustrations we have seen, indirectly, how aggression assists in achieving satisfactions, how it helps us to clear obstacles and go after what we want, how in fact this is such an important role of aggression that some people view aggression only as a response to frustration. We have followed some of the ways in which aggression becomes channeled and transformed into activity, lends zest and initiative to what we do but, at the same time, loses its earlier destructive aspect, for example, in sports and bodily skills, in effective speech, and in grappling with problems through talking.

AGGRESSION IN THE SERVICE OF SELF-DEFENSE

In looking at aggression as a companion and ally to needs and pleasure-seeking urges, we have seen it linked to eating and to protesting bodily pain or discomfort, but have not yet stressed the prominent role aggression plays in every form of self-defense, one of our guardians of self-preservation. When our bodily or mental well-being is endangered, when our rights are disregarded, we normally get angry and stand up for ourselves, "I won't take that lying down. I'll do something about it." The baby is likely to scream, spit, and bite in self-defense. The toddler hits, kicks, pushes, and throws things. The older preschooler yells orders: "Stop it," "Get away," "No." Depending on the child and on the way he views the danger, he may do all those things.

In our society we very much go along with nature in this respect. We recognize a wide variety of individual rights, including the right to protect and defend oneself. But effective though it is, as well as legally permitted, self-defense does not consist of blind rage and does not allow indiscriminate means, nor is its goal necessarily to destroy the person or thing which endangers us. If we were to defend ourselves in such a manner, we could easily end up in greater danger than we were to start with. Good self-defense involves sizing up the situation realistically and using one's mobilized aggressive energy selectively, to achieve the best possible result. Sometimes this may indeed mean mustering full physical force to remove, incapacitate, even kill an attacker; sometimes it may mean a firm verbal command, or just a polite statement of protest. At other times, it may be best to run away or to get help; and there are also times when we have to keep our anger strictly in our thoughts and do nothing, lest we incur an even bigger injury. All this implies good control of aggression and being able to use it in a number of ways, through actions, words, or thoughts. It also implies other abilities, such as observing well and using good judgment. Endowment provides us with the necessary aggressive energy and, in the course of development, with several means of discharge; the inner control and know-how of using them appropriately is acquired primarily with the help of the parents, and other important adults, through the relationship with them.

It all starts with the parent's respect for the child, for the inviolate safety and integrity of his body, and dignity as a person. We have talked about how this situation of attitude affects the parents' handling of the child's needs and of discipline, and we can now add to it the parents' necessary respect for the child's urges and feelings. This includes accepting the child's right to angry protest in self-defense when he feels that the parents are encroaching on his "space." The toddler who struggles to be his own person in body, and the adolescent who struggles to be independent in mind and action, feel particularly vulnerable. They protest constantly and keenly against everything they experience as taking over, imposing, interfering, restricting, and prohibiting on the part of the parents. But preschoolers and school-aged children too are sensitive to not being considered and listened to, and not having their wishes, needs, and opinions taken into account. This does not mean that respectful parents don't say "no," that they allow their child to do what he or she wants, or that they let the child disregard *their* "space" in an inappropriate way. Realistic and necessary expectations have to be made and met in the interests of everyone's, including the child's, safety and well-being. Moreover, respect has to be mutual. The parents too have the right to protect themselves from the child's aggressive interference or abuse, while allowing him to speak up for himself or to use other age-appropriate means of self-defense.

When Alan was nine months old he was a healthy vigorous baby who screamed in loud protest when his mom kept him waiting, or when she tried to wash off his face while he was busy playing with something, or when his brother took away his toy. Mrs. B. certainly did not like Alan's screaming but she accepted it with equanimity, apologized for the various infringements, and tried to correct them. Brother had to return the toy to Alan and she herself, next time, did not surprise him with the washcloth on his face, but gave him a few words of preparation or waited for a more opportune moment. However, Mrs. B. did not let Alan bite. To the accompaniment of a firm "no," she would prevent or interrupt his biting by holding Alan at bay. In his second year, Alan sometimes hit out and kicked at his mom when he felt interfered with; for example, when she picked him up and carried him at a time when he wanted to walk, or when she took away the cookie box he had got off the shelf. Mrs. B. was glad that her little boy had progressed from screaming and biting to hitting out, but now that Alan had also begun to say a few words, she encouraged him to voice his protest verbally: "No hurting, Alan. You say 'no' to Mommy. When you're angry you can tell me like I tell you." She offered him the simple expressions "no" and "angry" because these were her ways of addressing him when he made her angry. Other mothers prefer other words: *bad, mean, stop it.* All these are effective for registering and expressing angry protest and are easily learned even by toddlers with limited speech. "Mommy" and "no" are usually among their first words. It is a big step from physical to verbal expression of anger but, if it is in keeping with the parents' behavior to the child, he can usually master it during the preschool years. Saying how angry he is also helps the child to preserve his dignity when he still has to *do* what is required. Little Alan oftentimes stomped up the stairs with angry shouts of "No, I won't go." His mother did not mind his protest as long as he was making his way upstairs. Earlier, Alan, like most toddlers, used to respond to requests with a little delay or with doing just one more time whatever he had been asked not to do. Mrs. B. allowed him these face-saving gestures, but she was delighted when he followed her suggestion of protesting in words, and she praised him for it. Later Alan became more competent and less helpless, gained more confidence in himself as a person in his own right, and felt himself less easily threatened, but sometimes he still grumbled protests under his breath or indulged in a few angry thoughts when he had to comply with things that were not to his liking. Most times, though, he no longer viewed obeying as a humiliating "giving in." Even his verbal anger became less loud and he could state his complaints more clearly and politely. Disagreements between him and his parents were tolerated. They could be angry at each other without scenes or fights, and could still respect each other. The B.'s had helped their older boy in the same way and saw to it that, all along, the rules for standing up for oneself were the same between the brothers as between child and parent.

When children are allowed and helped to defend themselves against their parents and siblings and are treated respectfully by them, they learn quickly how to stand up for their rights with outsiders and how to use means of self-defense which are appropriate to the situation. Without help within the family, children have a hard time learning to defend themselves in the community. They may not be able to stand up for themselves and become easy victims, or they may vent their stored up anger against others indiscriminately, either in retaliation for minor encroachments or as bullies of weaker and smaller peers. For example, they may angrily clobber another child for trying to take their toy instead of holding on to it with a firm, "No, it's mine," or they may lash out with full force on the pretext of, "He hit me first," or even of, "He was going to hit me," instead of a firm, "Stop it," or, if necessary, pushing the other child away or even getting help.

By the time children are in public school they have usually learned to just *think* how angry they are at, say, a teacher. On the one hand this is a mark of achievement in inner control, on the other hand, knowing that he is angry, and what he is angry about, is also the mark of being a person in his own right, and is a big help in figuring out what best to do about a situation.

USING AGGRESSION TO ATTAIN PLEASURES

Aggression not only serves us to defend ourselves against others but to attain pleasures for ourselves. The satisfactions we want are rarely readily at hand. Usually there are obstacles to overcome and, for the child especially, one of the obstacles often are the parents. Most parents appreciate their child as a "go-getter." They are glad when he enjoys lots of things and activities, goes out in a determined way to achieve them, and does not easily give up in the face of hardship from within or without. Parents are not always so glad to see their young child go after his pleasure with similar determination,

in part because they disapprove of some of his infantile pleasures, and in part because the child's determination is so
aggressive that he sometimes forges ahead without regard
for property, people, or even his own safety. The toddler who
is determined to get the cookie box, pulls up a chair, climbs the
shelves, throws the box down, and scatters the contents,
endangers himself, may ruin the box, and may deprive the
rest of the family of their share of cookies. And if the same
toddler still loves to tease and torment, he may go after his
pleasure with similar gusto till he has worn out his mother or
got himself scratched by the cat. When the parents interfere
and stop him before he is in big trouble, he is likely to get very
angry at them and show it, in typical toddler fashion, with
more angry responses. The preschooler too goes after his
wants in aggressive ways. In pursuit of being first and best,
he often pushes others aside ruthlessly to "get first in line,"
cheats to win a game, brags shamelessly, and "one-ups"
himself by belittling the others, often with humiliating sing-
song, "Nya, nya, you are the last," "I know how to skip. Look
at me! You don't even know how to. You are a baby!"

If the parents squash the child's aggression in attaining
pleasures too much and too harshly, he will not have it available in the form of proper determination. He may give up at
the first hurdle, whining "I can't do it" or crying "*You* do it,
it's too hard for me." By contrast, if they allow the child free
reign to pursue his infantile pleasures all along, by whatever
means he chooses, he may continue to do so in his ruthless
infantile way. Many parents, however, do find the difficult
middle road: They frustrate calmly and gradually, allow verbal anger, and point the way to more acceptable ways. They
also provide a model in their own behavior toward the child
and others. When the child cheats during a game, they don't
get angry, punish, or threaten never to play with him again,
but say something like, "Hey, I also don't like losing, but I
still stick by the rules. It's hard but you'll learn and then the
other kids will really want to play with you. They'll say 'He
plays fair, he's fun to play with.' So let's put back that card,
start over again, and this time you'll do it the fair way, like a
big guy." And when the child manages to survive a lost game,
fairly played, with a mere verbal, "Oh, shucks, I hate losing. I

never win," his father even praises him and lets him show off his big-boy achievement.

AGGRESSION FUELING ACTIVITIES

As some personality tools such as motility develop, it is easy to see how much aggression initially contributes to their exercise. A toddler on the go is a pleasure to behold, in that he is so determinedly active, but he is also a menace, in that he avoids nothing and stops at nothing. Less obviously, this happens with other tools too. Speech is used in anger, and we even encourage that, but young children's verbal anger is far from polite. They may be angrily loud, say mean things, threaten, hurl insults, and voice all kinds of evil wishes. Their ability to observe and think is likewise often aggressive. They insist on finding out and knowing things, won't take no for an answer, and often seem to observe and reason especially keenly in the areas where we would prefer them not to. Their ears and eyes are tuned not to miss out on the weaknesses and troubles of the adults, on shortcomings in their appearance and behavior, and they often startle and embarrass us with their frankness: "How come, Grandma, that your hands have spots all over them, and your neck is all hanging down? Is it because you're so old? Are you going to die soon?"; "My Daddy didn't want to go to the block party because they are all a bunch of busybodies. It's true, I heard him tell my Mom."

It is tempting to "jail" the toddler in a playpen, to punish a youngster for impolite and angry talk, to forbid him or her to listen and want to know, or to persuade them that their observations are incorrect or their feelings nonexistent: "You don't really hate the baby, you *like* him." Fortunately, most parents, though distressed by the aggressive onslaught of the child's new abilities, also enjoy his spunkiness a bit and sense that it will stand him in good stead and lose its initial abrasiveness, if they guide it rather than altogether suppress it. They help the toddler go from free-wheeling motility to learning motor skills (going up and down the stairs, tricycling, rolling a ball); they point out to the preschooler that bigger people are more polite when they are angry; they provide opportunities for the child to observe and learn other things

and explain about some matters being private within the
family and about hurting people's feelings. Even the best
parents are not always so patient and thoughtful. A sense of
humor helps to keep things in perspective.

At times, young children's aggression can be unprovoked and diffuse, discharged "all over" and against everyone and everything. This is especially evident with toddlers,
but also with older children at vulnerable times—when they
are tired at the end of the day, when they are getting over an
illness, when they have been "cooped up," when their opportunities for activity have been curtailed, or when their means
of control have been diminished by stress. It usually does not
help them to "blow off steam" and "get it out of their system."
Aggressive behavior does not exhaust itself, but tends to
stimulate more aggressive behavior. Channeling aggression
into activities at such times is more helpful. At first the activity may serve as an outlet for aggression, but in time the
activity can absorb the aggression and transform its energy
into helpful fuel, especially when a loved person supports and
encourages the child.

Three-year-old Henry often spent part of his nursery
school day hitting each child as he passed by. The teacher
forbade this and offered him a hammering toy. She showed
him how he could bang in its colored pegs. Henry liked his
teacher, watched her using the toy with interest, but at first
refused to participate. One day, however, Henry picked up on
her encouragement, really settled down to it, and left the
other children alone. As he hammered away, he called out the
children's names with each bang "Joseph," "Keith," "Bar-
bara." He had taken a small but significant step from aggression to activity. In time Henry came to like hammering for its
own sake. With the teacher's help, he branched out into car-
pentry. His goal was no longer to attack children but to
produce little wooden airplanes and other projects which he
cherished and which earned him much admiration.

AGGRESSION AS A PART OF THE PARENT-CHILD RELATIONSHIP

It is sometimes thought that parents and children don't or

shouldn't get angry at each other because they are so close, so intimately tied by bonds of mutual need, dependency, care, and love. Actually, the reverse is true: We don't get anywhere near as angry at people who don't matter to us as we do at those who mean a lot to us. The closer our ties and the more intimate our togetherness, the more we invest our relationships, not only with love but also with anger. There are many reasons for this, among which are the following: When we love someone very much, we want him or her to love us back just as much, and when it seems to us that the person does not fully reciprocate, we get very frustrated and hence angry ("If you loved me, you would do as I want you to"). Also, a close relationship always implies that we need the other person, depend on him or her. This carries with it a feeling of being at the partner's mercy, being helpless without him or her. Nothing makes us more angry than being helpless. Moreover, being lovingly close always demands a measure of surrendering, of sharing, and of giving up of oneself. This easily conflicts with our other need of being a separate independent individual. We get angry when we feel that the demands of loving and being loved interfere too much with our "space." Then we want to get away and "do our own thing." At other times we may measure ourselves competitively against the loved one, feel envious and angrily wish to take away his or her advantages, instead of giving more of ourselves.

No relationship, not even that of husband and wife, is closer in all these respects than the relationship between parent and child. They, who began their relationship as a part of one another's body, sense most keenly their helpless need for and dependence on each other, experience most readily rejection and frustration when the mutual demands of compliance and surrender go unmet, and, at the same time and because of their very closeness, feel so easily that the loved partner encroaches upon and usurps their "space" of individuality. It is not only the children who need and depend on the parents, demand their full loving absorption, and yet struggle for independence and resent parental interference. The same applies to the parents. They too need and depend on their child, feel hurt and frustrated when he or she asserts his self-sufficiency and independence, and at other times get angry at his or her "demandingness" when it threatens their individual integrity: "He doesn't leave me alone. He always wants something. I can't even be myself for a minute." And just as children get envious of their parents, so parents get envious of their children, envious of their youth, of their being taken care of, of their good fortune and comforts, often of the very advantages they, the parents, lovingly brought about. Perhaps the strange part is not that parents and children get angry at each other, but that their relationship engenders so much mutual pleasure and satisfaction that, for the most part, it manages to resolve and overcome these conflicts and subdue the anger it generates.

And this indeed is one of the most crucial tasks of the parent–child relationship: to "tame" aggression through love. Parents usually do get angry at the child, but the constancy and strength of their love for him helps them to be angry in such a way that they do not harm him and do not altogether stop loving him. In the process, they help their child to achieve the same mastery over his anger at them. It is not an easy task. Young children's anger easily overrides their love, knows little or no consideration, and at the least frustration, would prompt them to discard the loved one. However much they love their parents, when young children are angry they do not hesitate to lash out at them, and are often quite ready to exchange the "bad" mother or father of the moment for another one who may prove to be more gratifying. The bread and butter always seems better at the Jones's. In addition, toddlers tinge their love with aggression, so that even when they do love they make hurting and being hurt, bodily and mentally, part and parcel of it. Their hug is often hard to tell from an assault. Modifying the expression of anger so as not to hurt, forgiving, loving others in spite of their faults, and being capable of the kind of constant love which even tames anger, these are slow and difficult achievements. Not all of us reach these goals but, insofar as we do reach them it is with the help of our relationship with our parents.

When this relationship is consistent and good enough, and when the parents have, to a sufficient extent, mastered their own aggression vis-à-vis the child, the pleasures and satisfactions of mutual caring exercise a powerful pull. For its sake children want to modify their anger, want to master it like the admired parents, and ultimately, adopt their standards for themselves and make them a part of their conscience. The parents help by setting an example, by praising and disapproving, and by adapting their expectations to the child's capabilities. That is why they don't become too alarmed at their youngsters' furies, let their children be angry at them in words, though not in deeds, and act so as to assure them that their love will survive it all: "Well, you are real mad at me now but we also still like each other and that's why we don't hurt each other and stay together." Even when the parents are mature and can rely on good inner controls, it is not easy for them to master their anger at the child and to help him master his. The primitive intensity of the child's anger often threatens their adult controls and seduces them to respond to the child at his level: "I don't know what happened to me. I just lost my cool." This is one reason why adults are often less masters of their anger with their children than they are with adults, or even with other people's children. Fortunately, they do not have to be perfect, only good enough.

When children can learn to tame their anger toward the parents, the first and most important loved ones, it will stand them in good stead in their other and later relationships. Properly tamed aggression will also help them to develop a conscience that can effectively guide their behavior. The parents' values and prohibitions in regard to anger form a part of the child's conscience, but it is also shaped by the way the child feels about the parents and by how he views them. If the child is intensely angry himself, he is apt to think of them as "mean," to perceive them as very critical and punitive. Children sometimes feel that their parents are much stricter than the parents think they are, and this is often due to the fact that the children still judge the parents' anger at them by their own anger at the parents. When children struggle persistently with intense anger at the parents without being able to modify it, their conscience may come to resemble parents who are seen as terribly strict and unforgiving. Such an exaggeratedly harsh conscience, whose anger is untamed, is not a helpful guide. It may set unreasonably high standards and enforce them relentlessly. When its plagued owner inevitably fails to live up to them, it never forgives transgressions, is not satisfied with atonement and reparation, and never lets one feel good.

WHEN AGGRESSION GETS IN THE WAY

Aggressive urges do not always find their way into useful channels, do not always contribute appropriately to self-preservation, well-being, and acceptable social conduct, nor do they, in all people, fuel functions and activities in modified and transformed ways. In fact, the unhelpful, destructive manifestations of aggression are often the only ones noticed, and have earned aggression a thoroughly bad name.

We see unhelpful aggression when it is untamed by love and erupts in tempers and violent attacks on people and things, untempered by consideration and pity, or when, accompanied by pleasurable excitement, it seeks gratification in hurting and being hurt, in torturing, tormenting, and perverse sexual practices. When these behaviors, which are normally seen only in toddlers, are observed in older children and adults, they tell us that a part of the personality has remained a toddler while other parts have grown up. The more advanced parts may function separately and well at times, but they may also interact with the toddler part and render it much more troublesome. They lend it greater physical and mental strength and powerful means of expression which were not available to the toddler. A twenty-five-year-old "toddler" is much more dangerous than a two-year-old.

We see unhelpful aggression discharged through personality tools and activities instead of becoming modified and serving them as fuel and initiative; for example, some children misuse motility in sports as a license to barge into, attack, and ruthlessly subdue others, instead of using it as a means to exercise a skill (every sports coach knows and dreads such individuals). Likewise, observing and thinking can be used merely for destructive purposes instead of constructive and adaptive ones ("He is very smart and he thinks well, but all he uses it for is mischief and troublemaking"). Even speech, which is to serve as a tool for mastering aggression and expressing it appropriately, is often misused through "foul-mouthing," or by turning words into weapons to hurt, humiliate, and torment, to bite in sarcasm, or to strip others and lay bare their inadequacies in order to belittle them.

We see unhelpful aggression turned against the self, either physically, as in accident proneness and some forms of suicide, or mentally, as in unjustified and exaggerated self-criticism, torturing guilt, low self-esteem, and inability to enjoy successes. And we see its destructive impact on the personality when it interferes with need-fulfillment (e.g., when excessive mouth anger inhibits chewing and prevents enjoyable eating), and when it encroaches upon pleasurable comfort habits (e.g., when children pull out their hair, bang their heads hard, bite their nails to the quick, or scratch themselves until they bleed).

We are less often aware of the damaging effects of excessively inhibited aggression, of the ways in which it deprives children of zest and initiative, contributes to helplessness and hopelessness in the face of life's daily tasks and challenges, and interferes with feeling good and having fun.

Of course, aggression is not solely responsible for these and similar difficulties. The makeup of our personalities is so complex that we can never attribute a piece of behavior such as aggression to a single isolated factor, but it can and does play an important part.

How does aggression get to show itself in such unhelpful ways? Here again, many factors within and without the child interact to shape the individual outcome in a personality, but we can pinpoint a few things which make it difficult for aggression to be appropriately channeled and modified. We have already implicitly referred to a number of them. When we remind ourselves of parents' helpful measures, their opposites are obviously unhelpful. Among these would be the lack of a consistent parent–child relationship; that is, one interrupted too often by temporary separations or emotional withdrawals, by multiple caretakers, or by permanent changes in parenting persons. Even a consistent parent–

child relationship may not be good enough, in the sense of not
providing a sufficient loving investment and pleasurable
experiences in meeting the child's bodily and emotional
needs. Excessive aggression may be the outcome of diminished opportunities for love and pleasure. Some severely destructive delinquent children actually do suffer from a lack of
love and cannot be helped to modify their aggressive behavior until and unless they have an opportunity to form a consistent good enough relationship with parental figures (A.
Freud, 1949a). Such a relative lack of good enough experiences may however, not be due to deficits in parental handling or
to lack of a relationship. It may be caused by painful illnesses
and their treatments, or by congenital abnormalities which
make it impossible for the child to feel good. The parents' care
may not suffice to counteract the hurting and frustrating
experiences a child has to endure, through repeated surgeries
from early on, or as a result of major handicaps. Even limited
illnesses can interfere with important needs and functions,
such as when a baby's eating always hurts and hence cannot
bring pleasure or absorb aggression, or when a toddler cannot walk and therefore cannot channel aggression into motor
control. However, some difficulties may also arise within the
context of a consistent and good enough parental relationship with a healthy child, and may reflect unhelpful aspects
of parent–child interactions. For example, the parents' handling of their own aggression may set an unhelpful example
to emulate (they may be explosively angry); or the parents
may not allow the child enough age-appropriate expression
of anger and thus block the channels of discharge that could
lead to mastery ("You must never be angry at your parents");
or they may not provide opportunities for the child to invest
aggression in activity (perhaps by confining a toddler too
long in his bed, playpen, or pram); or they may insist on
"taking over" and deprive the child of active independence.
Most parents err in one or another direction at times. Usually
though, they also "read" the child's response and readjust
their handling accordingly. As long as the basic relationship
is a healthy one and parents correct their mistakes, children
forgive their parents and progress in their development after
a little setback.

IS IT HELPFUL FOR PARENTS TO LET THE CHILD "TAKE OUT" HIS ANGER ON SOMETHING ELSE, INSTEAD OF DIRECTING IT AGAINST THEM?

It is helpful for parents to provide opportunities for physical and other activities which can absorb aggressive energy but this proves helpful only in addition to, not instead of allowing and encouraging children to express anger in words directly to the parents. There are good reasons for this:

1. We can only come to terms with our anger when we are fully aware of whom it is aimed at and why. Misdirected anger, anger aimed at the wrong object for the wrong reason, remains active and can never stop or be modified. When parents encourage their child to hit the punching bag instead of them, they advise the child to misdirect his anger and do not help him to control and modify its form of expression. Unfortunately, parents and children often unwittingly collude in such misdirection of anger. Parents tend to prefer, consciously or unconsciously, that their children not be angry at them and blame them, and children are only too ready to redirect their anger from the loved, needed, and perhaps feared parents to less important "victims." For example, parents often like to think that the child is angry at their new baby rather than being angry at them for bringing it into the family, although even the tiniest child knows that a baby has not arrived of its own will and that the parents would not keep and love it unless they had wanted it. The child, for his part, may prefer to be angry at the baby instead of at the parents, lest he endanger his relationship with them which already appears threatened by the arrival of the new-comer. The misdirected anger at the baby may, however, remain active and will continue to burden the relationship between the siblings. Many ongoing sibling rivalries origi-nate from anger that really belongs to the parents. Some parents do not even accept their child's anger at the baby, but "let" him or her be aggressive to pets or to others outside the family. Such misdirected anger may protect the family rela-tionships but leads to trouble in other relationships as well as to possible difficulties with the community and its laws. In

these instances unexpressed anger at the authority of the parents turns into anger at society.

2. Anger against the parents has the best chance of being tamed by love, an important step in mastery. When parents divert the child's anger, even to a punching bag, the aggressive expression remains physical and does not become tamed, channeled into words, and tempered by consideration for the loved one. Children are then in danger of dividing up love and anger and, in order to keep some of their relationships "pure," have to keep "bad guys" forever at hand as targets for the other side of their mixed feelings. Such a solution is not helpful, can lead to intolerance and prejudice, and accounts to some extent for the fact that some kind and nice persons behave in a very ruthless, vindictive way to certain individuals or groups of people.

3. Aggression is most successfully channeled into activities when a portion of it is allowed direct expression. Activities can absorb and modify only a certain amount of aggressive energy. When all of a child's anger is to be invested and discharged through activities, the process may fail; either activities may not become invested enough and are not practiced because they do not feel satisfying, or they remain a form of aggressive discharge instead of using modified energy and serving as skills.

ARE TEMPER TANTRUMS ALWAYS A TODDLER FORM OF AGGRESSION?

The typical toddler temper is a short outburst of aggressive behavior which the child readily overcomes and in time masters as he learns to express anger in words. Temper tantrums, by contrast, represent, at any age, an overwhelming of the personality that leave the child exhausted, frightened, weepy, unhappy, and in need of comfort. Such temper tantrums may be due to a "volcanic" outburst of small amounts of anger which have gone unexpressed and have accumulated until their force sweeps aside all barriers, either unprovoked at the time, or in response to a minor frustration. These pathological accumulations and discharges can be prevented when children are helped to recognize all the events and situations that cause them to be angry and are encouraged to express their anger piecemeal at the time when it arises.

In young children especially, but sometimes also at a later age, temper tantrums of this nature can also represent anxiety attacks, rather than outbursts of aggression. Whereas the signs of adult anxiety attacks are usually vague fear, palpitations, and increased perspiration, children's anxiety attacks characteristically take the form of exhausting temper tantrums. Only close and knowledgeable observation can succeed in distinguishing an anxiety attack from a volcanic outburst of aggression. Both, however, require help and should not be treated as mere naughtiness.

DON'T CHILDREN OFTEN DO NAUGHTY THINGS, NOT OUT OF ANGER, BUT TO GET ATTENTION?

In some families children find that being "good" makes the parents turn away from them, whereas being "bad" attracts their concern. It is a pity when children feel they have to pay the price of parents' anger and punishment to gain an intense close interaction with them. Sometimes this happens with parents who are depressed or who, without realizing it, tend to withdraw emotionally; for example, a mother, while on the phone, may become completely absorbed in her conversation and literally forget her child. By contrast, most mothers, even while on the phone, keep an alert mental link with their child, aware all the time of what he is doing, nodding to him, listening to signs of his activity, knowing when the child really needs them, and at the right time, interrupting their phone call to help him. When children "act up" to get attention they often indicate that they feel the parent is not reliably available to help them with inner and outer dangers. Their naughtiness, though enjoyed in one way, is also an SOS signal, a sign that the parents leave him too much to his own devices and fail to meet his need for consistent caring investment (R. A. Furman and E. Furman, 1984).

DOES ONE FEEL ANGRY WHEN ONE TAKES
THE INITIATIVE OR IS VERY COMPETITIVE IN
SPORTS, IN SCHOOL, OR IN WORK?

When aggression is appropriately modified and absorbed in activities it is no longer "angry" and is not felt as such. It may be very active and forceful but stays within the limits of social rules and laws and is not devoid of consideration for others. However, aggression is not always so well absorbed and may contain a great deal more of the original destructive anger than a person is aware of. We can, and do, act aggressively without feeling angry at times. Children quite sincerely sometimes deny being angry even when engaged in very destructive behavior, and so do adults. Parents may be very humiliating, restrictive, punitive, and without knowing how aggressive they are, may actually think they are acting "for the good of the child" (see also chapter 21).

CHILDREN ARE SOMETIMES AGGRESSIVE
AND EVEN DELINQUENT THOUGH THEIR
PARENTS ARE KIND, LAW-ABIDING CITIZENS.
HOW DOES THIS HAPPEN?

Each of these situations needs to be explored and understood individually and would, no doubt, reveal different factors at work. In my therapeutic work with such families, I have learned about some of them. For example, sometimes children's unmodified anger at the parents manifested itself in opposition to everything the parents stood for and the children's troublesome behavior, like the toddler's, served as their weapon to hurt the parents; some parents acted very differently with their children than they did with people socially or in their work and, as a result, the children's aggressive behavior actually did reflect the parents' handling of them, although an outsider would not have seen that. In some cases, the parents had experienced, and resented, a lot of hardship in their growing up, and, wanting to spare their children, made no expectations, set no limits, and condoned inappropriate behavior in their youngsters. They usually did not realize either that they vicariously enjoyed the children's aggression or that they were indirectly very aggressive to them by not helping them to develop well. Some parents were very upright citizens but did not maintain a consistent and good enough relationship with the child. A wonderful parent who is never there cannot help his child to emulate him. In some instances, children's aggressive or delinquent difficulties were related to identifications with similar characteristics of earlier parent figures they had since lost (a nanny or other caretaker, or a previous parent lost through death, divorce, or adoption). Most often several of these and additional circumstances interacted to account for the unfortunate but nevertheless understandable results.

ISN'T AGGRESSIVE-DELINQUENT BEHAVIOR CAUSED BY POVERTY AND SOCIAL INEQUALITIES?

These factors add special and powerful frustrations that arouse a great deal of anger. A person who could cope with his anger under ordinary circumstances, may not be able to do so under conditions of such additional stress. However, even the most extreme socioeconomic hardships and personal misfortunes do not drive every sufferer to aggressive-delinquent behavior. We therefore should regard socioeconomic hardships as endangering stress factors but not as causes in themselves. This is likewise true of other stress factors, such as "bad company."

IS DELINQUENCY ALWAYS DUE TO LACK OF INNER CONTROL OF AGGRESSION?

Delinquency may actually be caused by a person's unrecognized guilt which demands punishment for him. We noted earlier that young school-aged children quite commonly commit minor delinquencies, such as theft of small articles, playing with matches, or damaging objects they are not supposed to handle. They usually leave clues and, unlike "real" delinquents, are easily detected by their caring adults. These children often struggle with the demands of a newly taken in, harsh, and ever critical conscience. Without being aware of their inner turmoil or motivations, they may temporarily stave off and satisfy the inner voice of self-criticism by inviting and receiving punishment from the outside. Usually these behaviors subside when the child's conscience becomes better integrated into his personality and serves more effectively as a guide to conduct. In some individuals such a guilt problem may persist, along with repeated attempts to appease it with the help of getting punished.

The police receive many unsolicited "confessions" and self-indictments for crimes that people only heard about but never committed—another instance of guilt driven behavior. Many of us can sympathize with such people because we sometimes feel like criminals even though we did not commit a real crime. For example, many people feel guilty when approached and questioned by police or other authorities even when they have ostensibly done nothing wrong. And there are few children who do not anticipate being accused of something when they are called to the principal's office, even though it may turn out that he gives them a commendation.

CAN TROUBLES WITH AGGRESSION BE OUTGROWN OR CORRECTED LATER ON? DO WE REALLY LEARN ALL ABOUT HANDLING AGGRESSION WHEN WE ARE LITTLE?

We do not learn all about aggression from and with our parents. They lay the important foundation. They help us take the crucial first steps. Building inner controls, finding appropriate pathways of expression, investing anger in ever new activities, adjusting our values and standards to the changing demands of living, and coping with the many situations of stressful frustration and hardship which fate inevitably imposes on everyone at times, including the special stress of learning how to deal with our anger at our children, these all are lifelong personality undertakings. They are influenced by many relationships and events and require ongoing effort and changes on our part.

Some difficulties with aggression in the course of development are temporary and are overcome. Others may become lasting or exacerbated. Individuals and their circumstances vary greatly, and it is therefore unwise to generalize. However, most often difficulties with aggression can be helped with psychological treatment if they have arisen in the context of a consistent and good enough early relationship. The most incorrigible problems with aggression are ultimately rooted in a lack of such a relationship during childhood.

21

Feelings

Feelings are what makes life rich. When we can experience them deeply, in all their variety and intensity, in all their many shades of happiness and misery, we truly live fully. This does not depend on how many adventures we encounter or how many blows fate metes out to us. Some people lead ostensibly very "exciting" lives, or very trying ones, but they remain emotionally poor and empty because their feelings are shallow or flat, or but briefly stirred. By contrast, other people's lives may seem very sheltered and uneventful, but may yet be filled to the brim with a wealth of deep and rich emotional experiences—the stuff that wisdom is made of. Nor do the riches of feelings depend on intelligence, intellect, and knowledge. True feelings do not require academic know-how or scientific proofs. As long as we have the ability to be aware of them and to bear them, they tell us correctly what goes on in our own bodies and minds, what other people's motivations and behaviors are about, how we relate with them and with the world around us. They enable us to experience and appreciate all the satisfactions and dissatisfactions, to know what we like and don't like, and they guide our thoughts and actions accordingly. Feelings constitute our emotional lives, some would say our souls. They keep us in touch with the workings of our vital energies, let us know about our needs and urges, enable us to enjoy meeting their demands, or feel angry and unhappy when we can't meet them.

We "know" of our need for sleep when we *feel* tired, which

prompts us to lie down. We enjoy sleeping well and are disgruntled when we can't sleep well, and we know when we are
slept out because we no longer feel tired. And it's the same
way with feeling hungry or feeling pain. When people gauge
their need for sleep, food, or any other need, "by the book,"
that is, by their learned knowledge about what their body
needs, then everything they do about their needs and need
fulfillment becomes a required chore, a duty imposed from
without, and ceases to be an enriching emotional experience.
How different it is when we go to bed because we feel tired and
pleasurably anticipate a good sleep, from when we tell ourselves (or are told) that we now have to lie down and sleep
because that's what our body needs. How different it is when
we feel hungry, prepare what tastes good, and then eat it with
relish, from when we eat, "at the right time," the prescribed
essential vitamins, proteins, and carbohydrates, regardless
of appetite. When needs are gauged and satisfied by knowledge alone, they preserve life but hardly make it worth living. Of course, feelings don't always add pleasure. When
needs can't be met or met well, when we can't go to sleep when
we are tired or can't sleep well, can't eat when we are hungry
or can't eat what we want, we feel angry, miserable, irritable,
desperate. But at least we are *we*, persons with a mind and
will of our own, even with an unhappiness of our own. Without these feelings life is lackluster, wishy-washy, and we are
less of a somebody. Even with a very young child, when he is
really enjoying his meal or is really angry or sad when he
can't have what he wants, we can't help but respect him, and
people often comment "He sure is all there, isn't he."

This goes for the urges too, both in their original and in
their modified forms. Feelings inform us of their promptings
and enable us to experience their satisfactions and frustrations. When sexual activities are performed with little or no
accompanying feelings, they become mere mechanical exercises. As such they are either rendered uninteresting and are
given up, or are endlessly sought out and repeated in the vain
hope for a more meaningful, satisfying experience next time.
In either case, sexuality without feelings adds little to living,
no rich pleasure and warm subtleties of loving, no pain of

frustration or pangs of longing or jealousy. Likewise, when we cannot feel angry, we may not be able to act angry to defend our legitimate interests, or we may be very aggressive without knowing it, but neither lets us feel alive. We may not like feeling angry, yet may even then realize that getting "good and mad" has something invigorating and satisfying to it, and is often preferable to the mere indifference of "I don't mind," "I don't care."

This also applies to the many subtler feelings, derived from excitement or aggression, which have infused our personality functions and activities and which make their exercise worth while for us. Talking, thinking, doing, working, and pursuing hobbies all make us feel, and that is an important reason why we seek them out and why we miss them when there is no chance to engage in them. Sometimes we love them or agonize over them, sometimes they quietly please or irritate us. Good feelings or bad, satisfying or frustrating, how empty and dull life would be without them.

As for relationships, feelings are the essence of them. They enrich us with their fondnesses, enjoyments, hatreds, sadnesses, loves, irritating tensions, envies and jealousies, delights and tendernesses, and a whole host of other feelings besides. Even when a relationship is broken, it leaves us with pleasurable and painful feeling memories to fill the void, and that's why having had something and lost it, is so much better than never to have had anything at all.

Moreover, true feelings, fully felt, give us a sense of certainty, a trust in ourselves and what we are about, and a "feel" about people and events. They help us to be masters of ourselves. Even when we feel helpless and know it, we are more in charge of ourselves than when we feel nothing.

And yet, our innate potential for having feelings and using them to enrich and serve us, is not realized at birth and does not mature of itself. Like most of personality functioning, it has to be nurtured in the soil of continuous and good enough relationships and gradually mastered in order to come to fruition. At best, its developmental process is surprisingly fragile, buffeted from within and without, and easily suffers stunting and distortion.

FEELINGS AND BODILY RESPONSES

Feelings arise from the body and, to an extent, always remain linked to it. Very young babies have bodily sensations and discharge them in a variety of bodily ways. The first primitive mental experiences of feeling good and feeling bad accompany bodily processes, and are, perhaps, the first indications of the emergence of a mental self. The baby's smile is initially a bodily response to digestive relaxation and comfort. Parents rightly herald it as a milestone when it begins to appear as an expression of mental feeling in interaction with the smiling mother and, later, in spontaneous recognition of her.

Everyone who has taken full care of a baby knows that he looks most like a person, not when he is very excited or very distressed, but when he simply feels good. This "feeling good" comes when he feels "on top of things," when his discomforts are at a minimum and his pleasures are not very intense. This state of mind usually does not last very long. Even an older baby, who can already sustain and show a much greater amount of enjoyment, becomes bodily distressed and soon overwhelmed when the pleasure reaches a certain intensity; for example, a baby may gurgle, laugh, and sparkle when bounced on his father's knees, but if dad continues the fun too long or goes about it too vigorously, the baby suddenly wrinkles up his face in distress, starts to writhe and cry, cannot be easily comforted into relaxation, and may even end up in an inconsolable paroxysm of screaming and thrashing. Mother then tends to scold dad, "You got him much too excited," to which dad defends himself with, "But he loved it," and she retorts "Not that much of it." She is annoyed because she knows that her overwhelmed baby will sleep fitfully, be unable to feed comfortably, and is likely to have gas pains. A baby's ability to feel bad mentally, (i.e., without marked bodily distress), develops even more slowly. A hungry baby may look unhappy and cry moderately for a very short while, but beyond that, if left to himself he becomes a screaming writhing bundle, and if mother tries to feed him in that state, he either won't take it in or will throw up and have a tummy ache. In short, feeling good and tolerating feeling good, encompassing it as a mental emotional experience, works at first only for small amounts of pleasurable sensations, and takes even longer to achieve in regard to unpleasurable ones. In time, however, the ability to feel increases and, in turn, becomes a means of coping with ever larger amounts of sensations and ever more intense ones. The feeling, as it were, gathers up and holds the sensations and gives them a mental pathway of discharge, with limited bodily involvement.

Overstimulated and distressed babies come to feel good, and bad, much later and, in extreme cases, not at all. They remain at the mercy of their sensations, showing labile extremes of excitement and distress but discharging them primarily through bodily processes. They tend to be tense, are hard to comfort, and respond to the least increase in inner and outer stimuli with troubles in sleeping, feeding, digesting, eliminating, with skin discomforts, and/or excessive random motility. Even under ordinary conditions, older babies, toddlers, and preschoolers still tend to show strong feelings with their bodies. This commonly manifests itself as lack of appetite, tummy pains, constipation or diarrhea, vomiting, feeling ill, being tired or restlessly hyperactive, and suffering from itching and skin discomforts. In response to a reprimand, three-year-old Wayne said to his mother angrily, "You, you, you make my tummy ache." He was not bodily ill but still felt his anger in a bodily way. The sooner children are helped to know their feelings and to express them effectively in words, the sooner are their bodily processes freed from the burden of discharging them.

Many adults have not achieved sufficiently effective mental pathways and experience bodily symptoms instead of or along with feelings. Common difficulties of this kind are "nervous" indigestion and "tension" headaches. In situations of extreme stress everyone is apt to notice their intensified bodily responses, and stress as such is known to trigger or aggravate many illnesses. The intimate link between feelings and the innermost workings of our bodies is also preserved through language. Feelings are "a matter of the heart"; we have "heartfelt sympathy" and "gut reactions"; we say "He makes me sick," "It's yucky," "That's disgusting,

it turns my stomach," "It gives me the chills," "It's a pain."
For the most part though, when we use such phrases we
describe our feelings and no longer experience them bodily.

NURTURING FEELINGS

By feeling with her baby, the mothering person plays an
important part in helping him to feel. She feels her infant's
capacity to tolerate pleasurable and distressing sensations
and tries to make sure that they don't exceed that level. At the
same time she contains his feelings for him and helps him to
tolerate them. When the baby feels good, she feels good, and
when he feels bad, she does too. But she feels it all mainly in
her mind (or should we say "heart"?), and although she
expresses her feeling through her facial features and perhaps
through words, she is calm enough to convey an attitude of,
"This is okay. This doesn't throw me. I can manage this." For
the infant who scans mother's face, is tuned to the emotional
variations of her voice, and senses her body tone, this is both
an assurance and a model. But mother often goes a step
further and literally helps her child to encompass and contain his sensations by gathering him up and enfolding him in
her arms, soothingly and comfortably. And then all the inner
turmoil which bewildered him, threatened to engulf him, or to
tear him to pieces, becomes, through mother, a manageable
feeling, sometimes a good one, sometimes a not good one, but
bearable all the same. As the parents accompany their
empathy and support with words, they give their child names
for their own and his feelings—happy, angry, sad, hurt.
These names help the child to form a mental symbol, an idea,
of the sensations he experiences. The word gives them shape
within himself, holds them together, perhaps not unlike the
way the parents' arms around him held them together, and in
time, when he can say these words, they also serve him as
mental channels of discharge which facilitate mastery (Katan, 1961). In this way feelings increasingly become a mental
function. They remain in tune with the body and inform us
about it, but provide a mental way of experiencing, mastering, and discharging. This protects our bodily processes from
stress and enables us to control our actions.

A child's ability to feel, and to tolerate his feelings, depends for a long time on being felt with by mother, and also by father, and on their help in containing his feelings. When a toddler, and even a preschooler, has a strong feeling, he first looks to the parents, checking whether they mirror his feeling, whether they feel with him, how they contain it, and if need be, he gets their help with it: through a nod, facial expression, through their words, or a hug. Young children often cannot feel at all unless the parent feels with them and unless they can rely on him or her to help contain the feeling.

Twenty-two-month-old Pat, well developed and lively, attended a day care center. He had formed a trusting relationship with Ms. G., his caretaker, whom he shared with a few other youngsters. One day Ms. G. noticed that Pat was a little quiet and occasionally flapped one ear with his hand. She surmised that something was wrong but, although he had often come for help to her with minor complaints, he did not respond to her sympathetic questions and showed no affect. She phoned his mother to come and get him and was glad that Pat willingly curled up on her lap while they waited. As soon as Pat saw his Mom in the door, he ran into her open arms and sobbed bitterly as she held and comforted him. It turned out that Pat was suffering from an ear infection and had obviously been in considerable pain. In spite of his close relationship with his caretaker, however, he could not fully feel his pain or communicate it until he was with his mother (E. Furman, 1984a).

Susan and Joel, both twenty-four-months-old, attended a different day care center, where a large group of children and staff working in irregular shifts made a close relationship between child and caretaker very difficult to establish. Although Susan had been in the center for many months, she was distant and aloof, though conforming. Joel was a quiet newcomer. One day, Joel and Susan were sitting near each other when, out of the blue, Joel bit Susan's arm several times before the alarmed caretaker could separate them. It was striking that neither the attacker nor the victim showed or expressed any feeling before, during, or after the incident. There were no signs of anger, pain, or fear. Both looked blank and did not respond to the adult's concern, comfort, or repri-

mand. When the respective parents were informed at pick-up
time, they did not address their children's feelings and the
children still showed none. Susan's mother, always harried,
responded with "She'll get over it. Serves her right anyway
because she used to bite," and Joel's father merely rebuked
him. When the day care staff discussed the incident and their
own upset with their consultant, they recalled that Susan had
never shown feelings at the center or when observed with her
mother, and that Joel had not expressed the expectable upset
and anger during his recent separation–adjustment period.
The children's inability to feel seemed not only related to their
insufficiently close relationships with the staff but to their
parents' inability to feel with them. Susan's mother could not
feel with her daughter's pain or possible anger and could not
comfort her. Joel's father could not feel that his son must
have been angry to bite, much less inquire what he might
have been angry about. Their experience with other youngsters led the staff to suspect that Joel was angry at the adults,
at his parents and at them, for being left at the center. They
embarked on an ultimately rather successful program of
helping these children to feel and of helping their parents to
feel with them. Susan learned to use her feelings to protect
herself, and Joel, once able to feel his anger and express it in
words, could better control his aggressive actions.

Even grown-ups need someone to share and contain their
feelings when the stress is unusual. Mr. Z., a twenty-one-year-
old student, recalled a recent car accident from which he
barely escaped unhurt. He called the police, the tow truck,
took care of everything, and then phoned his parents. As soon
as he heard his father's concerned, "I am so sorry," he
realized just how scared and upset he was, burst into tears
and shared his feelings, relieved because he knew his father
understood.

Often though, even with much less powerful feelings, we
continue to need an empathic sharer and container, "This
makes me so happy, I can't wait to get home and tell my
family," or "This is just so maddening, I'll have to tell them
all about it at home." To feel and be felt with is not only part of
the parent–child relationship. Later on, it becomes a vital

part of every friendship. A true friend is one who can feel with us, listen sympathetically, and not be "thrown" by our feelings but help us to bear, contain, and master them so that we gain a measure of relief.

As the child's capacity to feel increases, his feelings become less closely tied to the body. Now even intense pleasure can be felt and contained before it becomes overwhelming and unbearably "bad." This does not always hold, as parents of schoolchildren well know when they call out to them, "Stop all that excited laughing and running around! Now it's still fun, but soon you'll be crying and complaining." Unpleasurable feelings can also be endured better, though even schoolchildren may still need to be reminded, "Now come on, this is a little hurt. You don't need to carry on quite that much about it!" At the same time, both good and bad feelings become more varied and finely shaded, and acquire specific and different meanings. There is annoyed, angry, furious; there is disappointed, sad, lonely, helpless, envious, and jealous. There is a wide range of pleasant feelings—comfortable, happy, delighted, excited, pleased. All along, the parents help by feeling with their child and by giving him or her the words to name and express what is felt. When talking about feelings with each other is part of the parent–child relationship, young children often invent their own terms to describe their or the parent's feelings. One two-and-a-half-year-old accurately told his pleased-feeling mother, "You have a smile inside today"; another youngster watched her brother dashing about irritably to collect his things and she commented, "Tommy has the angry jumpies." When children are able to feel, they can also feel with others. Their observations of themselves and of others are often stunningly penetrating, disarmingly frank, thoughtful and wise. Some adults may be taken aback by such comments and laugh with embarrassment which humiliates children, but parents who respect their children's feelings take them seriously and respond to them in kind. They even find their children helpful and value them as friends, because they can share and understand so much so deeply—sometimes more so than other adults.

SOME WAYS IN WHICH PARENTS ARE NOT
HELPFUL WITH FEELINGS

When parents really help their children with feelings, they help them to experience feelings, to contain and tolerate them, and to discharge them mainly through thought and speech. They do not ignore their children's feelings, nor do they confuse them or take them away. But parents themselves may not have been helped with feelings when they were little and their attitudes may get in the way of helping their children.

Sometimes parents are not in tune and cannot feel with their baby or young child. Then they cannot mirror correctly what he or she feels and, as a result, cannot help him to contain what he experiences and give it mental shape and content. The infant finds no echo in their faces, voices or movements, no pattern for structuring and mastering what goes on within him. He may then not learn to build a meaningful link between sensations and feelings. His feelings may remain primitively labile and overwhelming, or they may become blank, dull, and flat, or they may take the form of vague chronic moods, irritable, anxious, or excitable. In either case, they will fail truly to reflect and crystallize his inner experience, while his discharges continue to be channeled through bodily processes and behavioral manifestations.

Sometimes parents do feel with their child but are unable to contain the feelings and to give them controlled mental expression. Instead, they become as frantic or excited as the child and so overwhelmed by what they feel that they too may resort to mainly bodily discharges: shrieking and waving arms, or tensing up and turning rigid, or fussing and bustling aimlessly. Children may come to do likewise with their feelings, or they may shy away from having feelings altogether because their overwhelmed and overwhelming parents scare them.

Some parents are quite content to assist their children with good feelings, comfortable and happy ones, but find it hard to help them with "bad" feelings, pain, sadness, or anger. They may wish to spare their children discomfort, may wish to avoid feeling guilty at having caused it, contributed to it, or failed to prevent it, and they may also wish to avoid reciprocating their youngsters' feelings; for example, getting angry at the child who is angry at them. They may also feel that, on moral grounds, nobody should entertain "bad" feelings. Whatever the reason it affects their tolerance and support of the child's unpleasant feelings.

Parents may ignore the child's feeling and try to suppress its behavioral manifestations, like Susan's and Joel's mother and father in our earlier illustration. As we later learned through working with these parents, they could not recognize, or help their children recognize pain and anger because they could not bear their own discomfort at having left them, exposed them to unhappiness, and caused them to be sad and angry. As long as the children did not feel anything, the parents did not need to feel bad. These parents therefore did not connect the children's behavior with feelings and actually ordered the children not to express feelings through their behavior: no biting, no crying. As soon as the parents could be helped to feel their own uncomfortable feelings, guilt, they could also help their children feel theirs, loneliness and anger.

Some parents sense that the child would show his feelings if he were with them and they stay away from him in the hope that the feelings will disappear if there is no opportunity to show them. For example, mothers may leave without saying goodbye to their children ("sneaking away"), they may arrange for father or another adult to transport their child to and from nursery school or day care center. They may not accompany their child to the doctor, and they may not visit him in the hospital, all in order to avoid tears or anger. In these instances, the parents, and other adults, often mistake the cart for the horse. They assume that the parent's presence causes the child's feelings, rather than that the feelings are there but cannot be felt and contained except in the presence of the parent. It looks to them as if the child felt fine until the parent upset him: "He stopped crying the moment mother left and was okay from then on." "It's not good for him to get so upset, so it would be better if you didn't visit him." The child who does not show and verbalize unhappy feelings because

there is no one there to feel with him, is not okay. He is merely
deprived of becoming aware of his feelings and of gradually
mastering them through words with the help of the loved
parent.

Some parents so much want their child to have only good
feelings that they superimpose a happy feeling on his
unhappy one. When the infant cries or looks distressed and
angry, they laugh and bounce and tickle him to get him to
laugh too; when their toddler or preschooler is angry and
complains about his parents' going out, they persuade him
how much fun he'll have with the baby-sitter or how exciting
it will be to stay up late and watch more TV. When his pet fish
dies they quickly buy a new and bigger one so that, instead of
being sad, he will be thrilled with owning something better.
When there is a scary story or program, they pretend it's
really funny and merits hilarity. Such children's "happy"
feelings are shrill, brittle, and false. False feelings cut us off
from what goes on within us, instead of helping us to cope
with it. False feelings may also cut us off from others because
we cannot feel with others without being in good touch with
our own feelings, and because others regard false feelings as
inappropriate; for example, some children, and even adults,
giggle when they see a handicapped person, smile when
reprimanded, or tell funny jokes on sad occasions.

But even when parents feel with their child and comfort
him, their comfort is not helpful if intended to smooth over
and stop his feelings: "Hush, hush, it's all better now,"
"You're not sad any more, are you?" Comfort works best
when it alleviates distress enough to make it manageable and
when it offers ways of appropriate expressions, mainly verbal expression, accompanied by the limited bodily discharge
associated with feelings—frowning, smiling, laughing, crying, posture, movements. This constitutes mastery.

WHEN FEELINGS SEEM DANGEROUS
TO CHILDREN

Children's difficulties with tolerating and mastering feelings
are by no means simply due to parental handling. Consider-

able obstacles within the child work against his or her ability to live with feelings. *We* may know of the many ways in which feelings are useful and enriching to the personality, but to the child, and the young child especially, they are often a menace.

In infancy and during the toddler years, when tolerance is still limited, feelings easily become "too big." Then they overwhelm, or threaten to overwhelm, an experience most babies have endured at times. Older persons sometimes describe it: "It came rushing up like a tidal wave"; "It made me feel like I was about to explode." The very young child is always close to the danger that his feelings will have him instead of he having them. And so he, though notoriously oblivious to dangers from the outside (the ones grown-ups call the "real" dangers), keenly senses this inner danger which is so real to him. The mothering person who is in tune with her child, senses his vulnerability. This enables her to protect him, and to calm and contain his feelings for him. In doing so she helps the child to develop his own stamina for feelings, but, in the meantime and until he can really trust his own ability to keep his feelings within manageable limits (and that's a long time!), the child depends on her availability. This is a very important reason why very young children need their mothers always to be there and why it is so difficult for them to accept a substitute. They are not worried that their needs will not be met, or that they will fall ill, or that the house will burn down. They worry that they will be at the mercy of their sensations and feelings, stemming from whatever cause, which only mother can empathize with and "tame." The mere idea of being without mother makes the feelings seem potentially more dangerous. It is a bit like when we start to swim in deep water before we are really sure of our swimming skills. If someone we trust is nearby and watches out for us, it's not half as scary as when we are all on our own, or when we are not sure that whoever is there really knows that we may need help and could really rescue us in case of need. But even this is not a very good simile. It leaves out the very little child's limited ability to communicate and understand which makes him much more helpless, and it leaves out the fact that when mother is not available, the child's longing, sadness, and anger at missing her as a loved one already greatly tax his feeling capacity.

When mother is not there, or is there but does not help them with their feelings, some children indeed become overwhelmed with dread and distress, while others, toddlers especially, often "act up" or bother mother "to get attention," letting her know in this way that they feel the inner danger rising. From the second half of the first year on, however, youngsters also avoid the danger of too big feelings by not having feelings at all. This is not their deliberate decision. It is a protective device, perhaps like an anesthetic which frees us from experiencing what is happening to us. When a child copes in this manner, mother is not likely to notice that the child is bothered by her unavailability, and, if she was actually absent, she is apt to hear "He was fine. Didn't even notice you were gone." This may be helpful to the child for a while, may keep him going and enable him to postpone feeling until it is safe, until mother returns and is there to help. However, when feelings are banished from awareness most of the time because they seem too dangerous, the child cannot develop his ability to tolerate and master them and they cannot come to serve him.

Usually, parents try to protect their child from being left alone with "too big" feelings. That is why they try to adjust the time spans of their absences or unavailability to the child's tolerance for feelings and, all along, help him with them to increase his mastery; for example, mother may encourage the child to share his feelings before she leaves, and make this a part of preparing him for her absence. She may likewise encourage and accept his feelings on her return, "Well, how did it go? Was it hard?" She may let him know, as best as possible, just how long she will be gone, may leave "a bit of Mom" with him to keep (her old purse, scarf, key case), and if she thinks her absence may exceed his limit, she may periodically check in to talk with him by phone. Moreover, she tries to use sitters who have the kind of relationship with the child which will enable them to help him with his feelings, who will empathize with and support his feelings, including those related to the missing mother. But parents help a lot even just by understanding how scary big feelings can be, and by letting the child know they understand, as well as by assuring him that it will get easier to handle as he gets older.

Children are not only afraid that feelings may get too big. They also do not like the discomfort of unpleasant feelings, are not eager to feel them, and are apt to shy away from them even when the parents are there and would help: "It doesn't bother me," "I am not scared," "I don't miss my Mom," "I don't care, I'm not mad." Sometimes not feeling extends to not noticing the situation which may engender feelings; for example, a toddler may avoid noticing mother's preparations for leaving, may not seem to hear her good-bye, give no indication of thinking about her after she is gone, and pay no attention to her return, as if she had never left at all. It is always tempting for the caring adults to leave sleeping lions alone, and be glad there was no fuss, but many mothers are aware that their child will be better off in the long run if they remind him of the reality and of his feelings about it, and they help him to make them, if not pleasant, at least bearable. Thus, when parents notice that the child avoids difficult feelings in situations which warrant them, they encourage him or her to let himself feel them, and to learn that they can be mastered. "You didn't like to hear that I'll be going out, did you? It's all right not to like it. It's even all right not to like Mom." Or, "It's hard when I'm busy with the baby. I am sorry. You can tell me." Or "I know it feels bad when I scold you. It's okay to feel bad. Mom and Dad also sometimes feel bad."

In time feelings threaten in yet another way when the wishes and fantasies that accompany them seem to endanger the loved ones who are the child's protector, or seem to threaten the relationships with them, or are thought to provoke possible retaliation from them. When older toddlers or preschoolers get very angry at mom and, in their anger, want to hurt her, send her away, no longer love her or have anything to do with her because she is "so mean," they worry that this may really happen, or that she will get so angry back that she will no longer care for them, or that she might even do to them the very things they want to do to her. When mom then gets angry at them for some reason, or happens to fall ill, or has to leave, they easily see it as the consequence of their own anger. Similarly, when their loving feelings for dad, grandma, or sitter get very strong, they often fear that their disloyalty will leave too little love for mom, that they may wish to have the other person for their new mom and reject the old mom altogether, and that mom may do likewise unto them. She may love her job or her new baby better than them and abandon them. Some children cling to mother and dare not like nursery school lest they get to like it too much. Some, for the same reason, test their mother's response by letting her know that they like someone else better and want to stay with him or her. Envy can be felt as threatening when the child wants to take away the parents' desirable attributes and possessions and fears their anger and retaliation; and so can jealousy, when the child cannot bear to be left out of the parents' partnership and when his intense love for one parent makes him want to take the place of the other one. (Supposing that other parent, who is so much bigger and stronger gets wind of it and pays him back?)

Again, parents help. They reassure the child that the wishes and thoughts that go with feelings don't come true and that they would not let the child act on them: "You can feel angry and wish mean things but they won't really happen." (Children don't always like that reassurance; some say, "But *my* wishes do come true because I can wish so hard!") Parents explain that coincidental events are related to causes other than the child's feelings. "I am not going to work because you were mad at me or because I am mad at you, but because I need to earn money to buy food and clothes and toys." And they also reassure that they do not harbor similar feelings and/or that they will not retaliate: "It's okay to like nursery school. You'll still like me and I'll still like you and you'll always be my little girl. And when I'm at work—or with the baby—I still think of you and I don't like work—or the baby—better than you." Or "I know you'd like to have my things, but I won't really let you take them and when I get angry at you I won't hurt you or take away your things."

WHAT HAPPENS TO UNRECOGNIZED FEELINGS

How do children themselves deal with feelings which seem dangerous? After all, they do not always become over-whelmed, they do not always want mother right there so she can help in case their feelings get out of hand, nor do they always tell us, "I'm afraid I'm going to be too angry," or "I'll get to love Grandmother too much when she takes care of me," or "I'll get too envious and want to steal your things." We know already that very young children who cannot expe-rience feelings consciously tend to continue to discharge sen-sations through bodily processes, or revert to that. Indeed, young children's frequent troubles with eating, sleeping, toi-leting, and other interferences with their bodily needs and well-being are often a sign that they cannot cope with their feelings. We also know already that children often bypass being aware of their feelings and, instead, discharge them through actions. They may bite, hit, or destroy things without feeling angry; they may take others' possessions without being aware of feeling envious, or insist on sleeping in the parents' bed without recognizing that they feel jealous and left out.

But these are not their only ways of coping. Often chil-dren do become very scared but of something outside of them-selves. Instead of an inside danger which is so hard to pinpoint, to contain, and to get away from, their fears focus on an outside danger which is relatively safer—you can locate and control it better and you can hide from it more effectively. Dangerous feelings thus turn into irrational fears.

Toddlers, who often struggle with big angry feelings, tend to be afraid of things that sound very loud and hence angry: thunder, big machines, garbage trucks, vacuum clean-ers. Some parents try to reassure their youngsters that these things are safe; some try to explain intellectually how they work. The most helpful approach is to tell the child what they are not, that these things are not angry and don't act out of anger. Two-year-old Marilyn was terrified of the siren noise made by ambulance and police cars. Her parents' patient

explanations about them hurrying to help people proved of no
avail. One day Marilyn's mother disappointed her and the
little girl responded by imitating a siren noise herself, right
near her mother's face. "I think you are very angry," said her
mother, "I wish you'd tell me instead of making this terrible
noise." After a moment's thought though, she added "Now I
understand why you are so scared of sirens! I guess you think
they are as angry as you are! But they are not angry at all,
they just make a big noise so all the cars can hear them and
will stop to let them go ahead." Marilyn looked a bit sheepish
and buried her head in Mom's lap. It was the end of her fear of
sirens. Of course, some of the things the children fear, such as
a thunderstorm, may be dangerous and the children may
have heard that, but this reality accounts only for part of
their fear. The anger they attribute to it makes it seem much
more dangerous. As the young child is helped to tolerate,
master, and express his feelings more appropriately, these
early fears usually subside.

The preschoolers' irrational fears are more elaborate and
sophisticated and may include several worrisome ideas, but
basically they too represent the child's unconscious mental
attempt to substitute a "safer" fear for one less safe, an outside danger for one which stems from his feelings and wishes.
Ronny, aged four, was quite scared of robbers and insisted on
closing his windows and locking all doors at night: "A robber
might come and take all our things." His mother noticed that
Ronny often greeted Dad lately in a disgruntled mood and
borrowed Dad's hat and briefcase to impersonate him after
dinner. This gave her the idea that perhaps Ronny himself
had some "take away" envious feelings. She shared her idea
with her son and asked him just exactly what the robber
would take if he came into their home. "All of Daddy's
money," replied Ronny, adding, "Don't you know he puts all
his silver coins on the dresser at night?" Dad did indeed put
his change on the dresser. When mother wondered whether
perhaps Ronny had "robber wishes" for Dad's money, the
boy blurted out, "And I did, I took two of his silver." It turned
out that Ronny had hidden away two of Dad's dimes, was
plagued by guilt and fear of what dad would do to him in
retaliation. The dimes were returned to dad. Dad told Ronny

that he could well understand his wanting to take Dad's things to be big because he used to feel that way about his Dad when he was still little. But whereas wanting to take away was all right, really doing it was not, and Ronny would need to do his own growing to get big and that would take time. Ronny felt relieved and was no longer afraid of robbers. When Ronny, like many other youngsters, could not acknowledge and cope with his infantile envy, his feelings were in part expressed in actions and in part "given" to an imaginary robber who at least could be controlled with the help of locks.

Real events, experienced or heard of, play their part. They may trigger the child's fear, they may confirm his imagined dangers, they may provide a plausible content, or they may contribute elements of "outside" fear to "inside" fear. Real events also arouse feelings on their own account and inevitably add to the amount of feelings a child has to cope with. Parents help by limiting their children's exposure to experiences which are likely to intensify their feelings beyond bearable limits. But when their child develops an exaggerated or irrational fear they usually sense that something is troubling him and that their best chance of helping is to figure out with him what causes it, perhaps by asking the child to tell them more about it: What will the monster do? Why would it do just that? How does it look? Sometimes parents hear surprising but ultimately enlightening answers.

Three-and-a-half-year-old Sheila had become very scared of the weekly garbage collection. She was already anxious when mother prepared the bags of rubbish the night before; she often could not sleep lest the truck come early; when she heard it she quickly hid away and then peeked furtively through the window to make sure it had left. In response to mother's inquiries, Sheila voiced her awe at how big it was and how much could be put into it. "It really takes away everything," she marveled "and it never brings anything back, does it?" "Well, it only takes what people put out. That's its job." "But sometimes people make mistakes. Remember when you threw away Dad's letter and he never found it and he was mad." Yes, mother remembered that, and she suddenly also remembered that, many months ago, when Sheila's little brother was born, Sheila had offered to bring him downstairs to be put out with the garbage "because it was time to send him away again." Mother had assured her that he would stay with them and that there was enough love for both of them. In time, Sheila had seemed to have got to like him and played with him. As if guessing mother's thought, Sheila said "Mommy, they don't take children by mistake, do they?" This clarified matters and mother could now assure Sheila that parents don't get rid of children, even when they are very angry and want to be mean, like sending away their little brothers or anyone else. Sheila gave Mommy a hug. Mother realized that Sheila had not coped with her anger as well as it had looked. She helped Sheila recognize and master it better, piecemeal, as suitable situations turned up. Sheila responded and that made her harder to live with for quite some time, but her fear subsided, and eventually she was master in her own house of many feelings.

Sheila's, like all children's, irrational or exaggerated fear did make sense once it could be understood. Oftentimes parents can and do enlist their child's help in the process.

Although fears can protect children to some extent from the danger of their feelings, their minds use also other protective devices which enable them to feel even more comfortable. Again, they are not measures they choose to employ, but measures that operate unconsciously when an inner danger becomes too threatening. There are as many such mechanisms as there are individuals, but some are widely used and we have already come across a few of them. One we illustrated in connection with the child not noticing when mother prepared to leave. Like the proverbial ostrich, these children may be "blind" to situations that are likely to cause them dangerous feelings. We have also talked about children who substitute a happy feeling for an unhappy one, such as smiling when reprimanded or cracking jokes when there is reason to be sad. They may also "love" injections and scary movies. Similarly, instead of feeling painfully helpless, toddlers may turn into powerful little dictators, and little boys who feel inferior may, perhaps with the help of cowboy boots and toy guns, impress themselves and others with their "machismo." We have also mentioned children who, with or without parental encouragement, misdirect their feelings and vent them on "safer" targets, such as being angry at the baby, or at other little children, instead of at their parents. Children may also exchange one cause for another; for example, it may feel safer to be unhappy because "they canceled my favorite TV program" than to be unhappy because grandma is ill or because dad is out of town.

Often children attribute their unwanted feelings to others, as happened with Ronny; we also talked about such children seeing their own anger in the parents and experiencing the parents as much "meaner" and more punitive than they really are. Sadness, and other feelings too, may be seen only in others but go unrecognized in the child himself. "My sister cries and cries because we had to give away our dog, but I don't mind."

These and other inner protections against feelings may be helpful to an extent, but if they are used persistently and widely, even in situations that could be mastered, and if they interfere considerably with recognizing and tolerating feelings, then they become a real danger. They cause troubles of their own. They cut the child off from his feelings and make it impossible for him to master and use them. They may get him into difficulties. (Supposing he doesn't notice an oncoming car because he would get too scared if he saw it!) Worst of all, perhaps, they may interfere with his development: Every phase in personality development requires that we come to terms with its special emotional tasks. We can only accomplish that by experiencing and mastering the feelings connected with them: be it accepting himself as a boy or herself as a girl, or having to come to terms with having to grow up slowly and bearing frustrations in the meantime, or coming to terms with being grown-up and having to renounce some of our attachments to our parents. In addition, life may bring unexpected trials and hardships whose attendant feelings also have to be endured and mastered. When children do not have their feelings available, they cannot master these tasks and are in danger of "getting stuck." Their personality development may be interfered with because their energies may continue to be tied up in battling old conflicts instead of being free to deal with the problems of the present.

Parents are usually not aware of these dangers but they

sense when their child is not in touch with his feelings and cannot share them. They often have a feel for when, defensively, he is "putting it on too thick." They may well recognize the underlying unwanted feelings and try to make them more acceptable for him; for example, when "only sister" cries for the family dog, dad may say "Well, I am sad for him too. We all loved him and it would be strange if we did not miss him." Many parents interfere when the child's way of warding off feelings gets in the way of daily behavior; for example, when their little boy insists on wearing his cowboy boots and toy gun to nursery school all the time, the parents may ask him to dispense with them sometimes and say something like: "Most boys want to look big and strong, especially when they are still new at nursery school and aren't so sure what the other kids will think of them. It's always hard at first to be in a new place but the boots and gun won't really make it all right. In time you'll feel better when you learn to do well all the things they do at school, and then the others will also think well of you."

WHAT HAPPENS WHEN CHILDREN KEEP THEIR FEARS? DO THEY EVENTUALLY OUTGROW THEM?

Some fears do subside as the child learns to tolerate his feelings better, resolves developmental conflicts of one phase, and progresses to the next. Sometimes, however, the outcome is not so constructive. One fear may pass, only to be replaced by another one, or the fear may pass but another, apparently unrelated difficulty may arise instead. For example, a child may then need to ward off all feelings; or his bodily needs may suffer interference with sleep, eating, or toileting problems; or a restriction in functioning, such as a learning trouble, may replace the fear; or a difficulty in relationships may intensify, such as getting into squabbles and arguments or feeling disliked; or the child may remain emotionally "immature," may fail to face and cope with the developmental tasks of growing up. These maladaptive solutions indicate that the child could not come to terms with the "dangerous" feelings that caused his earlier fear and that they continue to burden him unduly.

It is sometimes difficult to know at the time whether the child will or will not be able to master the "dangerous" feelings that his fear signals. When the fear is intense, goes on for some time, and interferes with the child's daily life, chances are he has trouble coping. Parents help best by seeking professional advice. A stitch in time saves nine—understanding and resolving children's fears during their preschool years is much easier and more effective, and prevents further interferences in personality growth. Symptoms related to these emotional difficulties can also be treated later, but it is inevitably harder and takes longer.

WHEN PEOPLE DISCHARGE THEIR FEELINGS THROUGH BODILY PROCESSES, DO THEY HAVE PSYCHOSOMATIC ILLNESSES?

The early closeness between body and feelings is normal and even if it persists it causes various forms of bodily distress but not *psychosomatic illness*. The latter term is usually reserved for cases where a bodily anomaly or weakness exists that either causes bodily symptoms or is so vulnerable that it starts to give rise to symptoms when subjected to additional stress from any source. The psychological factor in true psychosomatic illness is always secondary and may operate in two ways: (1) The affected bodily organ may provide a readily available channel for bodily discharge of sensations and feelings. This may make it harder for feelings to become a mainly mental function, just as it would be harder to divert a stream of water along a new pathway when there is a leak en route which drains it off. At the same time, as the sensations and feelings continue to be "sidetracked" and discharged through the affected organ (skin, breathing apparatus, intestines, etc.), they aggravate its condition and worsen the symptoms. (2) Feelings, especially "dangerous" feelings, may constitute one of the stresses which overtax the vulnerable affected organ so that its malfunction causes manifest symptoms (R. A. Furman, 1969).

Psychological treatment of psychosomatic illnesses does not cure the somatic anomaly or weakness. It can help to reduce the stress, if the stress is of a psychological nature, and/or to divert feelings from the area of bodily discharge into a mental pathway, where the person can then be aware of them and discharge them primarily through thought and speech.

WHY IS IT SO BAD NOT TO HAVE "BAD" FEELINGS?

We need all our feelings to serve us. Even the "bad" ones are of help; for example, sadness helps us to keep in mind our loved ones when they are absent, anger helps us to stand up for ourselves, helplessness may help us to resign ourselves, if need be. Recognizing our own "bad" feelings also helps us to feel with others when they have them, and enables us to deepen our relationships with them—a good-times-only friend is not a real friend.

Last, but not least, unpleasant feelings also help us by contrast to enjoy and appreciate the pleasant ones. It happens not infrequently that when people "do away" with their "bad" feelings, their "good" ones become blunted or lost as well.

USING INNER RESOURCES TO ENRICH LIFE: NEEDS, URGES AND FEELINGS

Basic Concepts

• The innate vital energy of every personality manifests itself in needs, urges, and feelings.

• When appropriately mastered, they contribute to health, growth, and richness in all areas of functioning.

• Needs, urges, and feelings undergo many changes in the course of development, as do the child's means of controlling and gratifying them.

• Parents and other adults facilitate this development.

22

Death and Bereavement

**WHAT DOES "DEAD" MEAN? HOW DO
CHILDREN LEARN ABOUT IT?**

Most children encounter death earlier and more frequently
than birth. As toddlers, when they are usually able to distinguish animate from inanimate objects in their familiar surroundings, when they know that the teddy, doll, or table will
not do things on their own whereas another child or animal
will, they also observe that living functions can cease irrevocably, that what is alive can become dead. They note that
the fly, swatted on the table, no longer buzzes, that the wasp
sprayed with insecticide on the windowpane, no longer flies
around, that the ant or worm stepped on on the ground, no
longer crawls, that the squashed mosquito no longer stings.
They do not expect them to resume their activities. They may
pick up a dead insect or worm, finger it thoughtfully or
squash it with glee, without concern that it may get away or
that it may hurt them. They also know that these corpses are
disposed of in certain ways, put into the garbage, flushed
away, or thrown into the bushes. The occasional dead animal
seen by the roadside and TV cartoons (often the first program
toddlers watch) add to their experiences with death and
emphasize deliberate or accidental killing as its cause. Death
from natural causes, through old age or sickness, is most
often encountered in relation to flowers and plants—the
wilted bouquet, the leafless dead bush.

When parents allow themselves to be aware of their
youngsters' observations, can listen to their spoken and

implied questions, and answer them realistically and calmly, they help them to form a competent basic concept of the concrete aspects of death. They then know that "dead" means the cessation of the living functions they can observe in themselves and in others: it does not move, eat, sleep, it does not make sounds, does not see, hear, or feel, not even pain. (Heartbeat, breathing, and brain activity are unfamiliar ideas for children and do not help them to understand death, but older toddlers sometimes add another function that is vital in their minds to the parent's list, "And it doesn't do BM.") They also know that "dead" means permanence, that a living thing can die but a dead one cannot regain life. They get to know some of the causes of death—purposeful and accidental hurt, sickness, and old age—and they learn quite a bit about the disposal of the dead, sometimes including burial, if a dead animal is buried in the backyard. They may even be familiar with some aspects of decomposition, for example, the way it shows with plants.

During the preschool years, experiences with death multiply and afford many opportunities for the child to extend and deepen his concept of death. It may also become confused through new misunderstandings which need to be clarified, and through newly added feelings, some appropriate and some inappropriate, which have to be sorted out and coped with. Preschoolers inevitably see, hear, or overhear news items about deaths from TV, radio, newspaper pictures, and conversation. They watch television more often and are, at least peripherally, included in programs intended for older family members. In the city, they come across funeral processions and ambulances which hold up traffic, they drive by cemeteries and funeral homes; in rural areas, they are closer to experiences with hunting and fishing, with animals killing other animals, and with slaughter for food. Young children often contribute unwelcome inquiries to family meals: "Where did this meat come from?"; "Did they kill the cow?"; "Is the chicken dead now?"; "What part of the pig is this?"; "Did they hurt the pig and did it scream?" They also tend to comment freely on other reminders of death in daily life: "Is your fur coat made of killed animals? Which ones? How many? Who killed them? What did they do with the rest of the animal?" "Was this stuffed bear alive? Who killed it? Did it have babies?"

Three-and-a-half-year-old Elizabeth found a dead bird outside the door. From prior experience she concluded correctly that it had flown into the picture window and killed itself. She picked it up, said, "Poor birdie" and then, on her way with it to the wooded area at the end of the backyard, added "It's dead. I'll put it in the woods under the leaves and it'll turn to earth."

Elizabeth was fortunate on many counts. She had obviously been helped by her parents to understand what "dead" means and how we deal with its concrete aspects. They had not burdened and confused her with religious or philosophical explanations, knowing that her young mind could not yet grasp and integrate abstract ideas. She had a chance to learn about death through the common daily experiences with insects, small animals, and plants to which she related matter-of-factly, and which did not touch her personally and arouse painful feelings. She had been fortunate in other ways too. She had not been overstimulated by real or "pretend" experiences in which death involved angry violence or excited hurting and being hurt, and she had been helped to cope with her own early excited–angry hurting impulses by turning them into pity, so that her main feeling response was "Poor birdie." She also had not suffered bereavement or fear for her own life, was spared the very intense feelings that attend such experiences, and could therefore develop a sensible understanding of death that would stand her in good stead later in dealing with more difficult aspects.

In our contemporary Western societies, many young children's experiences with death approximate those of Elizabeth, yet not many children develop as clear and coherent a concept of death. This is mainly due to the fact that so many parents find it so difficult to be in tune with their youngsters' observations and thinking in this area and to talk with them about it at their level of interest and understanding. As with sexual matters, or even more so, parents may not have received help with it from their own parents. They may also have suffered early encounters with death that were too painful to master; or they may fear that any consideration of death will arouse their own and their child's concerns about his and their deaths. For all of us, the fact that death is an inevitable aspect of life remains a fearful and difficult thing to contemplate, one we shy away from, think about only when we have to, and find hard to come to terms with. Parents with young children, in the midst of a period that brims with life, often feel that death has no right to encroach upon them, that they can afford to keep it out of their own minds, and can spare their children. This wishful attitude blinds them to the actual frequency of their children's observations of death, to its interesting novelty for them, that they have not yet learned to screen out the way adults often do. However, most parents want to assist their children with all aspects of life and are even willing to include death, when they realize how helpful it is for children to learn about it step by step, starting with ordinary daily experiences, and focusing on the concrete understanding of what "dead" means. Their wish to do well by the child often enables them to overcome their own inner qualms sufficiently to work on the basic concept with him, which will serve as a base for coping with the harder aspects yet to come.

During the later preschool years, children begin to include people they know, as well as themselves, among those who may die, and they struggle to extend their concept of death to "Everyone has to die eventually." In the neighborhood and at nursery school, they hear of the deaths of grandparents, relatives, and pets. In their own families a distant relative may die, or someone daddy knows at work, or the parents may need to attend a funeral and the children note their sad and upset expressions. All these experiences provide opportunities for further questions and answers, help the child solidify his grasp of death, of its causes, and how it applies to people: what causes people's deaths, what is a full or an interrupted life span, how we dispose of human dead bodies, and which rites we observe in this connection. These experiences also bring death closer. They touch on the realization that this could happen to my loved ones and even to me. This often causes concern and anguish: "Mommy, how old are people when they die?"; "Mommy, how old are you?";

"Is that very old?"; "Ginny's Grandma died. Will our Grandma die too?" At times, however, the knowledge of death also provides a content for angry wishes, for "drop dead" thoughts. Mostly these are but dimly imagined or appear in disguised concerns or worries that something will happen to a loved one, but occasionally we hear them verbalized outright: "I hate you. I want you to go away and never come back. I wish you would die!"

No parent enjoys dealing with the children's death-related worries and angers, but many parents manage even this quite well. They do not panic at the child's questions and statements and, without denying mortality, stress that they expect the full life cycle to continue and that premature deaths in others are very unusual: "I am sorry that Mr. X. died. He was very old. He was a grandpa for a long time, and that's when people die." Or, "I am sorry that your friend's Dad is dead. It is very unusual for a Mommy or Daddy to die. Your Dad and I expect to live a long time. We will take care of you all along, and when you grow up and have children, we'll enjoy being their grandparents. Or, "Your Grandma is old but she is not very old, and I expect her to live for a long time. Usually people don't die until they get very, very old." And when they are faced with the child's angry wishes, or with the concerns that arise from them, they may counter with, "Well, people never die because someone wanted it. You and I will go on being alive and well." Likewise, the child's own worry that he may die is put in its proper perspective: "You are very safe and we keep you safe. We expect you to grow up and be a mommy (or daddy) and then a grandma (or grandpa), and perhaps even a great grandma (or grandpa). I know you heard about the little girl who died, but she had a very special, unusual illness, and that's scary and sad, but it's not like the illnesses you get. Most illnesses doctors can help with and people get well again."

The idea that all life eventually ends is best assimilated when it does not present an immediate threat to the child or his loved ones, when real causes are distinguished from imaginary ones, and when it is clear that neither angry feelings nor lack of love as such bring death about.

During the subsequent years of elementary schooling,

these concepts become more fully integrated. As occasions arise, children learn more about the rites we follow when a death happens: the services, the choice between burial and cremation, the ways we express support and sympathy. During this phase in their development, children also begin to think in abstract terms and can add religious or philosophical beliefs to their earlier concrete understanding of death, such as beliefs in the survival of the soul or spirit.

A child's grasp of the basic concrete aspects of death is a prerequisite for coping with a bereavement; that is, with the loss through death of a person with whom he maintained a relationship. When fate confronts young children with such losses before they know at least what "dead" means, it is much harder for them both to learn this concept and to cope with the bereavement.

COPING WITH A BEREAVEMENT

In the course of life we inevitably encounter many losses. We lose money and precious possessions; we may lose parts of our bodies, such as a limb, or parts of our mental self, such as self-esteem; we lose relationships, through temporary or permanent separation, or through emotional withdrawal, or through maturation, such as the loss of the nursing mother at weaning or of the childhood parents during the adolescent transition into adulthood. In spite of some similarities, however, the loss of a loved one through death is unique. It is a truly total and final loss and it carries a special threat to the bereaved by reminding them that they and their other loved ones may die too. When we suffer a bereavement, our minds have to undertake a special mental task in order to master it.

The bereavement task consists essentially of three phases (E. Furman, 1974). The first phase includes understanding and accepting the fact that the loved one is dead, knowing what "dead" means, what the cause of this particular death was, and how and where the bodily remains are disposed of. It also includes coping with the concerns of "Can this happen to me" and assuring oneself that one's own needs will be met, so that life will continue and will be worth living. When these aspects are sufficiently mastered, the next phase unfolds of itself. We call it mourning. It helps us to adjust ourselves to the reality that the deceased is no longer available in the external world. Gradually, as the inner work of mourning proceeds, we enter the last phase in which we resume living without the deceased, in the manner appropriate to our age.

UNDERSTANDING AND ACCEPTING THE DEATH, ITS CAUSES, AND CIRCUMSTANCES

Each bereavement is an individual experience. It happens to individuals whose personalities differ, catches them at different moments in their lives, concerns the loss of very different relationships, and is surrounded by unique circumstances. All this inevitably affects the way in which a person copes with the bereavement task and the extent to which he or she can successfully master it. Children, from their late toddler or early preschool years on, use the same means and can master this difficult task too, if, and only if, their parents can help them with it, as they help them with everything else. The younger the child, the more he needs parental assistance. But adolescents too, and even adults, find it difficult, if not impossible, to mourn alone, without at least the opportunity to share their feelings and to experience the satisfaction of being understood, which makes their remaining relationships and continuing life itself worthwhile. Let us then look more closely at what the bereavement task entails, and how inner and outer factors may help or hinder it.

Children may lose grandparents through death, or older aunts, uncles, and family friends with whom they were close, or pets with whom they shared their daily lives. More often than we realize, they may also experience the death of a friend or schoolmate, a sitter or teacher, or even a sibling. Some of these deaths may have approached slowly and could be anticipated as the children had opportunities to observe the increasing signs of debility caused by sickness and/or old age. Others are sudden, untimely, caused by circumstances which are terrifying in themselves, such as an accident, violence, heart failure, or sudden infant death syndrome. It is helpful when the parents themselves can share the news as soon as possible, let the child know that they will help him

with it, and that he will be included in what the family feels
and does about it. "I have a very sad thing to tell you. I just
found out that Grandma died. That's very hard for all of us.
We'll talk about it many times. I want you to understand all
about it. We'll stay together and help each other." It is fortunate when the child already knows what "dead" means, or
when the parents need only to help him to extend the concept
to people ("Do you remember the dead birdie we found? Well,
Grandma is dead like that birdie.") It is very hard for parents
to have to explain concrete death at such a time and for
children to begin to learn about it, but it is the first necessary
step. At best, all children will review their ideas about death
and, over a period of time, at least the younger ones will
comment or ask questions as they struggle to get it straight.
The days immediately following a death are usually harrying
for the whole family as they go through the funeral and
observe the rites that accompany it. It is easy to forget about
the children at this time or to exclude them in order to spare
them hardship, but it is just then that they most need to be
kept informed, need to be helped to begin to understand what
is happening and why, to share feelings with the family, and
to have their support and continuing care and love. Preschoolers are not usually helped by attending all the services,
or by viewing the body, although they may manage even that
when they do so with a parent who is truly available to them
emotionally and able to attend to their needs and questions
throughout. They often benefit most from being told what
their elders are doing and what is happening to the bodily
remains of the deceased, while the child himself perhaps
stays at home with a familiar sitter who can also talk with
him about it. At a later time, visits to the grave afford another
opportunity for the child to see for himself and to integrate his
understanding. Older children may prefer to participate
directly in all or most of the proceedings with the parents.

Understanding the cause of death is also a part of the
initial work. It is often as hard, or harder, than coping with
the death itself or with the disposal of the body. It may be a
very scary cause, where parents' explanations have to be
geared not to further upset the child with gory details, or it
may be one that is difficult for youngsters to grasp. For

example, children who still think very concretely have interpreted the term *heart attack* as a vicious bodily assault on the patient; they have understood much more readily such wordings as "He had a special sickness inside his body, in a part called the heart. The sickness made his heart not work." However, misunderstandings of the cause of death, as well as of other aspects related to it, arise very often. They can be clarified when the parents appreciate that they not only need to tell their child but also need to listen for his responses, and when they take it for granted that these difficult matters have to be talked over many times before they can be sufficiently mastered.

Adults as well as children need to be clear on all the concrete and particular aspects of the death. Usually adults have access to all the information as a matter of course and are not aware how important this is for them. We come to appreciate it only in the relatively rare instances where we do not know what happened, or cannot understand or accept the cause of death, or where we are uncertain as to what happened to the bodily remains of the deceased; for example, when soldiers are reported missing in action whose deaths cannot be confirmed or bodies returned, or when dead newborns are disposed of by the hospital without the parents' participation in the arrangements and rites. Such circumstances often make it impossible for the family to come to terms and to proceed with the bereavement task. Children, in most instances, do not have access to the necessary information and cannot understand and accept it without parental help. This handicaps many children in coping with their bereavement. One little boy asked over and over "Where is Grandma?" His family thought for a long time that he did not understand, or could not accept, the fact that she was dead, until it became clear that he was quite literally inquiring about where her dead body was, an aspect he had not been told.

Intertwined with the understanding of the facts is the implied threat to the survivor and his need to assure himself of the satisfactory continuity of his own life. Adults as well as children focus on this, and even the special meals and gifts of food that are so often a part of funeral observances, are

intended to help the survivors partake of the pleasures of
meeting their needs and to remind them of the continuing
care and love of others. Children approach these concerns in
their own ways. Oftentimes they ask, "Can this happen to
me, or to you?" They are helped by a reassuring answer: "No,
I expect you and us to live a full long life." But they may also
put their questions indirectly, through sudden trivial demands,
through insistence on following the usual routines, and
through resenting the disruptions caused by the caring
adults' involvement with funeral arrangements or by their
emotional preoccupation with the death. It may seem selfish,
even annoying, but actually contains a very important and
necessary question: "Will life still be worthwhile for me and
will you still help make it so?" Instead of complying with each
demand for the sake of reassurance, or rejecting all of them
out of lack of empathy, it helps to do one's best and to address
the real issue in words: "I love you as much as ever, I'll take
care of you as always, and we'll go on doing all the things
together that are fun and that we need to do, even though
Grandma died. It's only hard just now. Wait a little longer
and then I'll get your new sneakers (or, take you to the park
again, or play Lotto with you)."

MOURNING

It may take days or weeks before these initial difficult steps
are sufficiently mastered, and misunderstandings and doubts
cleared up, but whenever it is achieved, mourning gets under
way. It is not necessarily marked by an outward show
of feelings, by crying or sobbing. Like all internal workings,
it may proceed silently, perceptible perhaps only to the keen,
empathic observer and sharer. Mourning consists of two
apparently opposite processes, detachment and identification.

Detachment is the better known process. It entails the
repeated remembering of life with the deceased, and as each
shared experience is vividly recalled and emotionally relived,
it serves to loosen our bonds with the lost partner in the
relationship and gradually to accept reality without him or
her. Memories may come spontaneously or may be triggered

by circumstances and events: "Sunday afternoon makes me especially think of Grandma, that's when she always used to visit." "Last time we were here, Grandma was with us." Children often remember in actions, rather than words, doing what they used to do with the deceased. They also rely on using concrete mementos of the deceased to reexperience life with him or her, and parents help children by allowing them to keep belongings as well as pictures of the lost loved one. Detachment is known for the intensity and variety of feelings it engenders—longing, pain, anguish, sadness, guilt, anger, helplessness, dejection. Sometimes the feelings are so hard to bear that children feel overwhelmed and need parental comfort; or children may, for the same reason, shy away from their feelings and avoid even thinking about the deceased. This is when, as with all seemingly dangerous feelings, they need the parents' reminders by talking about the dead, by pointing out that everyone has many feelings at such times, and by supporting the child in allowing himself to feel his or her feelings too. Earlier help in tolerating strong and unpleasant feelings comes in most useful. The greatest obstacle to a child's mourning may come from his parents' difficulty in experiencing their own feelings, because that makes it so hard for them to recognize and support the child's.

The second process, identification, consists of taking into oneself some part of the deceased and making it one's own. In this way we are helped to keep him or her with us always. Adults often take over a dead loved one's interests and activities, or values and attitudes, and enrich their own personalities. Eight-year-old Hal was especially keen on word puzzles and had become very proficient at them over a number of years. It was a hobby that gave him much pleasure, although no other member of his family shared his interest. During his treatment for emotional difficulties, this interest was traced to his relationship with his grandfather who had often played word games with the boy. The grandfather had died when Hal was barely four years old, but his legacy had become an important part of the grandson's mental makeup.

Sometimes, however, we may also keep within ourselves unhelpful aspects. Some children adopt idiosyncrasies of the deceased or signs of illness they had observed in them, such as, in one case, a stooped gait. When the parents recognized this maladaptive legacy in their four-year-old son Aron, they helped by pointing it out and offering him a better way of coping: "I see you walk like Grandpa used to walk. That's really not the way he wanted to walk. It was only part of his being old and ill. It's nice to be like Grandpa but I think he'd like you to do some of the things he really enjoyed. Remember how he always fed the birds with you. Perhaps that is something you would like to do too. I'll help you put out a feeder and we can always fill it together, like he did." Aron enjoyed feeding the birds and soon resumed his upright energetic gait.

RESUMING LIVING WITHOUT THE LOST LOVED ONE

Mourning may take a very long time, may never end altogether, but the acute phase passes, and it becomes more intermittent. Once again energy is freed for taking up life's usual routines and activities, and perhaps forming new relationships that will take their place along the memories of the old ones, although they will never actually replace them. This process marks the last phase and mastery of the bereavement task.

Coping with a bereavement is always a long and difficult task, one we wish we could spare ourselves and our children. Sometimes we try to hide the sad news of a death from them, or sidetrack their thoughts about it instead of helping them to understand, or tacitly encourage them to avoid their painful feelings about it, or quickly offer them a substitute relationship in the hope they then won't miss the lost one. Unfortunately it never really works out well. There is no avoiding the hardship. Shortcuts may seem easier at the time, but an unworked through and unmastered bereavement, like undigested food which remains in the stomach, is bound to cause difficulty in the long run.

WHEN A CHILD'S PARENT DIES

After all we have said about the crucial role of the parent–child relationship, it goes without saying that the death of a parent is the most tragic and traumatic event in a child's life. The child invests so much in the relationship with the parents, and his or her other relationships are so much less intense, that no relationship between adults can be compared to it. Of course, the younger the child, the more is all of his loving and being loved focused on them, but even for the adolescents the tie with the parents is still their mainstay, and the death of a parent is still the biggest loss.

To the child the parent is not only a loved person, a partner in a relationship. The parent is also a part of the child's own personality. When the parent dies, the child loses a part of himself, the part or parts of his functioning which were still performed by the parent and would have become his own, through their relationship, only in the course of further maturation. The parent would also still have been the one to help his child to cope with the bereavement, and now is not available even to do that.

All the aspects of the bereavement task that we have already discussed, apply also to the loss of a parent through death, only more so. Parents of growing children inevitably die untimely deaths and the circumstances surrounding them are always especially frightening and hence difficult to understand and accept. The death of a parent is also a much greater threat to the child's own survival, intensifies the fear of "me next," and immeasurably increases the concerns whether one will be able to go on living and if so, whether life will still be worthwhile. Likewise, the mourning process is made much more painful and difficult and the deceased parent's support with it is sorely missed. The ultimate resumption of normal living is severely handicapped because, for the developing child, the relationship with the parent is so essential for further growth.

Children, at all ages, therefore, frequently run into difficulties in coping with one or more aspects of the bereavement task. Symptoms and maladjustments of every variety may surface as signs of the unresolved inner struggle, even when their manifest appearance bears no relation to the bereavement. In bereaved children who have undergone psychoanalytic treatment, it was possible to trace the unconscious links between their difficulty in coping with the bereavement and such diverse troubles as eating and sleeping problems, troubles with learning and peer relations, delinquency, fears, and many more. Quite often, however, a child's inability to deal with the loss of a parent becomes evident only years later when he or she faces the developmental tasks of the next maturational phase and is unable to cope with them; unable, for example, to progress in adolescence following an earlier bereavement during the school years.

Yet many children do master even this most difficult bereavement task when their surviving parent, or familiar parent substitute, is able to shoulder the almost equally difficult task of assisting them with it. It is sometimes thought that a widow or widower, bereaved and stressed themselves, cannot take on such a burden, cannot cope with their own suffering, and help their child with his. But many do, because of the special rewards it entails. Parenting well, doing their best by their child, brings them a great deal of gratification, raises their self-esteem at a time of depletion, and provides solace in sharing feelings. They find that, in bad times as in good ones, the child gives as much to the parent as the parent gives to the child, when they can feel with one another.

WOULD NOT RELIGIOUS BELIEFS HELP TO COMFORT YOUNG CHILDREN AS THEY OFTEN COMFORT ADULTS?

Unfortunately young children's concrete thinking distorts religious beliefs and tends to make them confusing and frightening rather than comforting. For example, Charlie interpreted the idea of "God took him to live in heaven" so literally that he did not dare venture into the street lest "God" reach down, grab him, and take him away from his parents. Cynthia was scared to go on an airplane because she feared she would remain up in the sky, in "heaven," and never return home. Sean plagued his parents with puzzled questions as to the details of heavenly life: "Are there birthday parties in heaven? Do they have the same candles on cakes? Do they serve spinach?" In several instances children later turned away from religion because it had scared them so when they were little.

The parents' own attitudes also play an important part. Sometimes parents who are not believers themselves, offer their young children religious ideas about death in lieu of concrete ones, because they hope this will spare them their own doubts and concerns. The children inevitably sense that the parents' feelings are at odds with their words. By contrast, some very religious parents thoughtfully delay religious teachings until their children are of school age, and focus on concrete understanding of death before then, because they want to be sure that religion will not be misconceived and misused, but allowed its rightful place at the right time. Many parents are just uncertain as to how to help their children, uncertain even about their own attitudes to death. When religious concepts are used because "I didn't know what else to say," they are unhelpful. In such instances it is usually more honest and reassuring to deal with the concrete aspects of "dead" first and to answer later questions of belief with "I don't know. Different people believe different things. I have thought about it a lot but I haven't decided yet for myself. It's a hard thing. As you get older and think about it more, maybe you will decide what you want to believe."

WHAT SHOULD PARENTS DO WHEN THEY ARE SO "HUNG UP" ABOUT DEATH THAT THEY JUST CAN'T TALK ABOUT IT OR CAN'T TALK ABOUT IT WITHOUT GETTING ALL UPSET?

Perhaps no parent is always ready to answer questions right away, about this or other difficult topics, needs time to collect himself, and tells the child that he will think about his good question and get back to him later. Children wait patiently when they can trust that the parent really will take up the topic with them in time. When parents find that these subjects always upset them very much, it helps them and their child to say, "Look, I find that awfully hard to talk about and I always get upset about it. But that's my trouble and I hope it won't be yours. There are many people who don't get as upset and worried as I do. I am sorry." They may opt for "In the meantime, I'll do my best, but sometimes I'll have to stop and come back to it later, so be patient." Alternatively they may refer the child to the other parent or to another familiar person to talk things over: "It's best you talk to Dad (or so-and-so) about this because they don't get so upset and will be able to help you better."

It is not shameful for a parent to have trouble with something. It is only unfortunate when he can't acknowledge it and voice the hope that the child will not have to be like him in this respect.

WHAT HAPPENS WHEN INFANTS AND YOUNG TODDLERS ARE BEREAVED, BEFORE THEY CAN UNDERSTAND DEATH?

Insofar as the infant has already had a beginning relationship with the deceased person (perhaps a sibling or grandparent), he will be aware of the loss. Even if he cannot talk yet himself, it will help to tell him that the dead person will not return, to support his feelings and memories, and to assure him that his parents will always return, even when they go away for short periods. Infants are also secondarily affected by the parents' change of mood, preoccupation, and increased absences that are often a part of their response to the bereavement. This can be mitigated when parents keep it in mind and make a special effort not to "forget" their infant and not to overstress his tolerance. In time, as the child gets a little older and learns what "dead" means, he will learn also to apply it to the person he lost but still remembers. It is a difficult task because in these instances "dead" refers to people from the start and is therefore much more threatening.

When infants lose their mothering person through death, it is of utmost importance that she be replaced at once by a preferably already familiar, full-time substitute, who takes over all aspects of parenting, softens the blow of the disrupted relationship, and continues to provide the bodily and emotional care so vital to the distressed baby's survival and development. The understanding of what happened and why, will come gradually, with help, as opportunities arise; for example, in connection with pictures of the deceased mother, family conversations about her, or anniversaries that sadden the surviving adults and puzzle the child. Often too the child is confronted with the comments of outsiders. For example, eighteen-months-old Molly was raised by her devoted grandmother and father since her mother died shortly after her birth. When grandmother and Molly strolled in the park, other youngsters invariably came up to talk and play with them and commented, "Are you her Grandma? Where is her Mommy? Why doesn't her Mommy take her for a walk?"

It would be a mistake to think that infants are spared hardship. Theirs is often greater, even under optimal circumstances, because they cannot understand and cope at the time, and because, as they get older, they are inevitably prematurely exposed to the fact that people too die. It is not an unmasterable burden but it is a burden. To bear it and to cope with it requires much ongoing help from the surviving parenting figures.

An Afterthought

Have you asked yourself, as so many have, this question: Why have we talked so much about children's early life and so little about when they are older? Don't many people other than their parents influence their development in those later years, and isn't that part of their development just as important?

When we look at a building we see all its parts above the ground, but not its foundation. We rarely even think about its foundation, and when we do occasionally see it during construction, it appears dull, uninteresting, and unimportant. We can't wait for the "real" building, the upper visible structure, to take shape, so that we will know what it is all about. We forget that the foundation is the most crucial part, that it determines what can be built up and whether what is built on it will hold up.

The child's early years are his foundation, buried and out of view, forgotten by himself and often disregarded by others, along with the raw materials he or she contributed and the parents' work which helped to mold them together into a coherent whole. The later years, the years of building the visible structure of the personality, are more readily open to view, as are those who participate in giving it its final shape.

We have been looking at what goes on when the foundation is laid.

References

Aichhorn, A. (1925), *Wayward Youth*. New York: Viking Press, 1945.

Andersen, H. C. (1837), The emperor's new clothes. In: *Fairy tales*. New York: World Publishing Company, pp. 66–71, 1946.

Anthony, E. J. (1970), The influence of maternal psychosis on children - Folie à deux. In: *Parenthood—Its Psychology and Psychopathology*, ed. E. J. Anthony & T. Benedek. Boston: Little, Brown.

———— Koupernik, C. Eds. (1973), *The Child In His Family: The Impact of Disease and Death*. Yearbook of the International Association for Child Psychiatry and Allied Professions, Vol. 2. New York: John Wiley & Sons.

Barnes, M. J. (1964), Reactions to the death of a mother. *The Psychoanalytic Study of the Child* 19: 334–357. New York: International Universities Press.

Blum, H. P. (1983), Adoptive parents: generative conflict and generational continuity. *The Psychoanalytic Study of the Child* 38: 141–163. New Haven: Yale Univ. Press.

Bowlby, J. (1944), 44 juvenile thieves. Their characters and home-life. *Internat. J. Psycho-Anal.* 25: 19–53.

———— (1951), Maternal care and mental health. *Bull. WHO*, 3: 355–533.

Burlingham, D. (1952), *Twins: A Study of Three Pairs of Identical Twins*. New York: International Universities Press.

———— Barron, A. T. (1963), A study of identical twins: their analytic material compared with existing observation data of their early childhood. *The Psychoanalytic Study of the Child* 18: 367–423. New York: International Universities Press.

———— (1973). The preoedipal infant-father relationship. *The Psychoanalytic Study of the Child*, 28: 23–47. New Haven, CT: Yale University Press.

Capote, T. (1965), *In Cold Blood*. New York: New American Library.

Fleming, E. (1974), Lucy. In: *A Child's Parent Dies*, ed. E. Furman, pp. 219–232. New Haven: Yale University Press.

Freud, A. (1946), Freedom from want in early education. In: *The Writings of Anna Freud*, 4: 425–441. New York: International Universities Press, 1968.

———— (1947), The establishment of feeding habits. In: *The Writings of Anna Freud*, 4: 442–457. New York: International Universities Press, 1968.

———— (1949a), Aggression in relation to emotional development. *The Psychoanalytic Study of the Child*, 3/4: 37–42. New York: International Universities Press.

———— (1949b), Notes on aggression. In: *The Writings of Anna Freud*, 4: 60–74. New York: International Universities Press, 1968.

———— (1952), The role of bodily illness in the mental life of children. *The Psychoanalytic Study of the Child*, 7: 69–81. New York: International Universities Press.

———— (1953), Some remarks on infant observation. *The Psychoanalytic Study of the Child*, 8: 9–19. New York: International Universities Press.

———— (1956), Psychoanalytic knowledge applied to the rearing of children. In: *The Writings of Anna Freud*, 5: 265–280. New York: International Universities Press, 1969.

———— (1958), Adolescence. *The Psychoanalytic Study of the Child*, 13: 255–278. New York: International Universities Press.

———— (1963), The concept of developmental lines. *The Psychoanalytic Study of the Child*, 18: 245–265. New York: International Universities Press.

———— Burlingham, D. (1943), *War and Children*. New York: International Universities Press.

———— ———— (1944), *Infants Without Families*. New York: International Universities Press.

Freud, S. (1916), Criminals from a sense of guilt. *Standard Edition*, 14: 332–333. London: Hogarth Press, 1957.

Friedlander, K. (1947), *The Psycho-Analytical Approach to Juvenile Delinquency*. New York: International Universities Press.

Furman, E. (1969a), Some thoughts on the pleasure in working. *Bull. Phila. Assn. Psychoanal.* 19: 4:197–212.

———— (1969b). Observations on entry to nursery school. *Bull. Phila. Assn. Psychoanal.* 19:133–152

———— (1974), *A Child's Parent Dies*. New Haven, CT: Yale University Press.

_____ (1977a), The roles of parents and teachers in the life of the young child. In: *What Nursery School Teachers Ask Us About: Psychoanalytic Consultations in Preschools*, ed. E. Furman. Madison, CT: International Universities Press, 1986, pp. 3–19.

_____ (1977b), Readiness for kindergarten. In: *What Nursery School Teachers Ask Us About: Psychoanalytic Consultations in Preschools*, ed. E. Furman. Madison, CT: International Universities Press, 1986, pp. 207–233.

_____ (1980), Early latency—Normal and pathological aspects. In: *The Course of Life. Psychoanalytic Contributions Toward Understanding Personality Development*, Vol. 2, ed. S. I. Greenspan & G. H. Pollock. Washington, DC: NIMH. pp. 1–32.

_____ (1981a), Children with toddler-like behavior in the nursery school. In: *What Nursery School Teachers Ask Us About: Psychoanalytic Consultations in Preschools*, ed. E. Furman. Madison, CT: International Universities Press, 1986, pp. 149–164. Also Pamphlet Series of the Cleveland Center for Research in Child Development. 2084 Cornell Road, Cleveland, Ohio 44106.

_____ (1981b), Treatment-via-the-parent: a case of bereavement. *J. Child Psychother*. 7: 89–101.

_____ (1982a), On discipline in the Nursery School. In: *What Nursery School Teachers Ask Us About: Psychoanalytic Consultations in Preschools*, ed. E. Furman. Madison, CT: International Universities Press, 1986, pp. 69–87. Also Pamphlet Series of the Cleveland Center for Research in Child Development. 2084 Cornell Road, Cleveland, Ohio 44106.

_____ (1982b), Mothers have to be there to be left. *The Psychoanalytic Study of the Child*, 37: 15–28. New Haven, CT: Yale University Press.

_____ (1983), Something is better than nothing. *Hampstead Bull.*, 6: 168–171.

_____ (1984a), Mothers, toddlers and care. In: *ERIC, ED 256 479*. Urbana, IL: University of Illinois at Urbana-Champaign, 1985. Also Pamphlet Series of the Cleveland Center for Research in Child Development, 2084 Cornell Road, Cleveland, Ohio 44106.

_____ (1984b), Some difficulties in assessing depression and suicide in childhood and adolescence. In: *Suicide in the Young*, ed. H. S. Sudak, A. B. Ford, & N. B. Rushforth. Littleton, MA: Wright P.S.G. Inc., pp. 245–258.

_____ (1985a), Learning to feel good about sexual differences. In: *What Nursery School Teachers Ask Us About: Psychoanalytic Consultations in Preschools*. Madison, CT: International Universities Press, 1986. pp. 101–122. Also Pamphlet Series of the Cleveland Center for Research in Child Development, 2084 Cornell Road, Cleveland, Ohio 44106.

———— (1985b), *Play and Work in Early Childhood.* Cleveland: Pamphlet Series of the Cleveland Center for Research in Child Development, 2084 Cornell Road, Cleveland, Ohio 44106.

———— Furman, R. A. (in press), Some effects of the one-parent family on personality development. In: *The Problem of Loss and Mourning: Psychoanalytic Perspectives,* ed. D. R. Dietrich. Madison, CT: International Universities Press.

Furman, R. A. (1969), Psychosomatic disorders. In: *The Therapeutic Nursery School,* ed. R. A. Furman & A. Katan. New York: International Universities Press, pp. 231–273.

———— Katan, A. (1969), *The Therapeutic Nursery School.* New York: International Universities Press.

———— (1980), Some vicissitudes of the transition into latency. In: *The Course of Life: Psychoanalytic Contributions Toward Understanding Personality Development,* Vol. 2. ed. S. I. Greenspan & G. H. Pollock. Washington, DC: NIMH, pp. 33–43.

———— (1983), The father-child relationship. In: *What Nursery School Teachers Ask Us About: Psychoanalytic Consultations in Preschools,* ed. E. Furman. Madison, CT: International Universities Press, 1986. pp. 21–34. Also Pamphlet Series of the Cleveland Center for Research in Child Development. 2084 Cornell Road, Cleveland, Ohio 44106.

———— Furman, E. (1984), Intermittent decathexis—A type of parental dysfunction. *Internat. J. Psycho-Anal.,* 65: 423–433.

Goldstein, S. & Solnit, A. J. (1984), *Divorce and Your Child.* New Haven, CT: Yale University Press.

Hall, R. (1982a), Living with Spiderman et al.—Mastering aggression and excitement. In: *What Nursery School Teachers Ask Us About: Psychoanalytic Consultations in Preschools,* ed. E. Furman. Madison, CT: International Universities Press, 1986, pp. 89–99.

———— (1982b), Helping children with speech. In: *What Nursery School Teachers Ask Us About: Psychoanalytic Consultations in Preschools,* ed. E. Furman. Madison, CT: International Universities Press, 1986, pp. 125–126. Also Pamphlet Series of the Cleveland Center for Research in Child Development, 2084 Cornell Road, Cleveland, Ohio 44106.

Ionesco, E. (1950), The bald soprano. In: *Four Plays, Eugene Ionesco,* trans. D. M. Allen. New York: Grove Press, 1958, pp. 8–42.

Katan, A. (1961), Some thoughts about the role of verbalization in early childhood. *The Psychoanalytic Study of the Child*, 16: 184-188. New York: International Universities Press.

Klima, E., & Bellugi, U. (1979), *The Signs of Language*. Cambridge, MA & London: Harvard University Press.

Krementz, J. (1982), *How It Feels to Be Adopted*. New York: Alfred Knopf.

Menning, B. (1977), *Infertility*. Englewood, NJ: Prentice-Hall.

Provence, S. & Lipton, R. C. (1962), *Infants in Institutions. A Comparison of Their Development During the First Year of Life with Family-Reared Infants*. New York: International Universities Press.

Pruett, K. D. (1983), Infants of primary nurturing fathers. *The Psychoanalytic Study of the Child*, 38: 257-277. New Haven, CT: Yale University Press.

Schechter, M. (1970), About adoptive parents. In: *Parenthood*, ed. E. J. Anthony & T. Benedek, pp. 353-371. Boston: Little, Brown.

Spitz, R. A. (1945), Hospitalism. An inquiry into the genesis of psychiatric conditions in early childhood. *The Psychoanalytic Study of the Child*, 1: 53-74. New York: International Universities Press.

———— (1946), Hospitalism. A follow-up report. *The Psychoanalytic Study of the Child*, 2: 113-117. New York: International Universities Press.

Stevenson, O. (1954), The first treasured possession. A study of the part played by specially loved objects and toys in the lives of certain children. With a Preface by D. W. Winnicott. *The Psychoanalytic Study of the Child*, 9: 199-217. New York: International Universities Press.

Terhune, C. B. (1979), The role of hearing in early ego organization. *The Psychoanalytic Study of the Child*, 34: 371-383. New Haven, CT: Yale University Press.

Wallerstein, J., & Kelly, J. (1980) *Surviving the Breakup: How Children and Parents Cope With Divorce*. New York: Basic Books.

Wieder, H. (1977), The family romance fantasies of adopted children. *Psychoanal. Quart.* 46: 185-200.

Winnicott, D. W. (1940), Communication at the Scientific Meeting of the British Psychoanalytical Society. Quoted in: The beginnings and fruition of the self—An essay on D. W. Winnicott by M. Khan, J. A. Davis, & M. E. V. Davis. In: *Scientific Foundations of Pediatrics*, ed. J. A. Davis & J. Dobbing. London: W. B. Saunders Co., 1974, pp. 625-641.

———— (1953), Transitional objects and transitional phenomena. *Internat. J. Psycho-Anal.*, 24: 89-97.

Related Reading

A number of publications were referred to in the text and listed in the Reference Section, and a few more are offered for further reading, to amplify or illustrate some of the topics. Some may strike a familiar chord and fit in with your thinking and feeling; others may seem cumbersome or go against the grain. As with all that has been written in this book, you, the reader, will know best which items seem helpful and which to set aside.

Relationships—Infants

Brazelton, T. Berry (1981), *On Becoming a Family.* New York: Delacort Publishers.

Fraiberg, S. (1977), *Every Child's Birthright: In Defense of Mothering.* New York: Basic Books.

Robertson, J., & Robertson, J. (1982), *A Baby in the Family. Loving and Being Loved.* London: Rutledge & Kegan Paul.

Tolstoy, L. (1876) *Anna Karenina.* New York: Bantam Books, 1981.

Winnicott, D. W. (1957), *Mother and Child.* New York: Basic Books.

———— (1978), *The Child, the Family, and the Outside World.* New York: Penguin Books.

Relationships—Preschoolers

Buxbaum, E. (1949), *Your Child Makes Sense.* New York: International Universities Press.

Freud, A. (1949), Nursery school education: its uses and dangers. In: *The Writings of Anna Freud*, 4:545–559. New York: International Universities Press, 1968.

———— (1962), The emotional and social development of young children. In: *The Writings of Anna Freud*, 5:336–351. New York: International Universities Press, 1969.

McDonald, M. (1970), *Not by the Color of Their Skin: The Impact of*

Racial Differences on the Child's Development. New York: International Universities Press.

Miles, B. (1959), *Having A Friend.* New York: Alfred A. Knopf (a children's book).

Minarik, E. H. (1961), *Little Bear's Visit.* New York: Harper & Brothers (a children's book).

O'Connor, F. (1952), My Oedipus complex. In: *Collected Stories.* New York: Vintage Books, Random House, pp. 282–291, 1982.

Relationships—Schoolchildren

Blos, J. W. (1979), *A Gathering of Days.* New York: Charles Scribner's SMS (a children's book).

Eckert, A. W. (1971), *Incident at Hawk's Hill.* Boston: Little, Brown (a children's book).

Freud, A. (1930), The latency period. In: *The Writings of Anna Freud,* 1:105–120. New York: International Universities Press, 1968.

———— (1952), Answering teachers' questions. In: *The Writings of Anna Freud,* 4: 560–568. New York: International Universities Press, 1968.

Simmons, E. (1963), *Mary Changes Her Clothes.* New York: D. McKay Co. (a children's book).

Smith, R. P., (1957) *Where Did You Go? Out. What Did You Do? Nothing.* New York: W. W. Norton.

Controls and Masteries

Furman, E. (1986), Stress in the nursery school. In: *What Nursery School Teachers Ask Us About: Psychoanalytic Consultations in Preschools.* Madison, CT: International Universities Press, pp. 53–68.

O'Connor, Frank (1944), First confession. In: *Collected Stories.* New York: Vintage Books, Random House, 1982, pp. 175–182.

Zolotow, Charlotte (1957), *Over and Over.* New York: Harper & Row (a children's book).

———— (1961), *The Three Funny Friends.* New York: Harper & Row (a children's book).

Needs, Urges, and Feelings

Freud, A. (1946), Freedom from want in early education. In: *The*

Writings of Anna Freud, 4: 425–441. New York: International Universities Press, 1968.

———— (1947), The establishment of feeding habits. In: *The Writings of Anna Freud* 4:442–457. New York: International Universities Press, 1968.

———— (1956), Psychoanalytic knowledge applied to the rearing of children. In: *The Writings of Anna Freud*, 5: 265–280. New York: International Universities Press, 1969.

Furman, E. (1985), Learning to feel good about sexual differences. Cleveland: Pamphlet Series of the Cleveland Center for Research in Child Development, 2084 Cornell Road, Cleveland, Ohio 44106. In: *What Nursery School Teachers Ask Us About—Psychoanalytic Consultations in Preschools*. Madison, CT: International Universities Press, 1986, pp. 101–122.

Payne, E. (1944), *Katy No-Pocket*. Boston: Houghton Mifflin Co. (a children's book).

Index